Writings of Larisa Reisner

Historical Materialism Book Series

The Historical Materialism Book Series is a major publishing initiative of the radical left. The capitalist crisis of the twenty-first century has been met by a resurgence of interest in critical Marxist theory. At the same time, the publishing institutions committed to Marxism have contracted markedly since the high point of the 1970s. The Historical Materialism Book Series is dedicated to addressing this situation by making available important works of Marxist theory. The aim of the series is to publish important theoretical contributions as the basis for vigorous intellectual debate and exchange on the left.

The peer-reviewed series publishes original monographs, translated texts, and reprints of classics across the bounds of academic disciplinary agendas and across the divisions of the left. The series is particularly concerned to encourage the internationalization of Marxist debate and aims to translate significant studies from beyond the English-speaking world.

For a full list of titles in the Historical Materialism Book Series available in paperback from Haymarket Books, visit: www.haymarketbooks.org/series_collections/1-historical-materialism.

Writings of Larisa Reisner

Edited and translated by
Cathy Porter
Richard Chappell

Haymarket Books
Chicago, IL

First published in 2023 by Brill Academic Publishers, The Netherlands
© 2023 Koninklijke Brill NV, Leiden, The Netherlands

Published in paperback in 2024 by
Haymarket Books
P.O. Box 180165
Chicago, IL 60618
773-583-7884
www.haymarketbooks.org

ISBN: 979-8-88890-336-0

Distributed to the trade in the US through Consortium Book Sales and
Distribution (www.cbsd.com) and internationally through Ingram
Publisher Services International (www.ingramcontent.com).

This book was published with the generous support of Lannan
Foundation, Wallace Action Fund, and the Marguerite Casey Foundation.

Special discounts are available for bulk purchases by organizations and
institutions. Please call 773-583-7884 or email info@haymarketbooks.org
for more information.

Cover art and design by David Mabb. Cover art is a detail from *Painting
31, Rhythm 69, (William Morris Block Printed Pattern Book, with Hans Richter
Storyboard, developed from Richter's Rhythmus 25 and Kazimir Malevich's
film script Artistic and Scientific Film – Painting and Architectural Concerns –
Approaching the New Plastic Architectural System)*. Paint and wallpaper on
canvas (2007).

Printed in the United States.

Library of Congress Cataloging-in-Publication data is available.

Contents

Larisa Reisner (1895–1926)

Acknowledgements

The translations and the accompanying volume, *Larisa Reisner. A Biography*, were made possible thanks to a Nina Fishman Award from the Barry Amiel and Norman Melburn Trust, whose objectives are to advance public education, learning and knowledge about all aspects of the philosophy of Marxism, the study of socialism and the working-class movement. Nina Fishman was a long-term trustee. She was also an important political thinker, activist and historian. The Award commemorates her legacy by promoting the publication of works that would have interested her.

Warm thanks to Sebastian Budgen and Danny Hayward at Historical Materialism, to Manon Vrolijk at Brill, for her professionalism and attention to detail with the typesetting, and all her help and encouragement, and to Sezgin Boynik, of Rab-Rab Press, for appreciating her genius, and for his commitment to keeping her memory alive through her writings.

Timeline

1894   Tsar Nicholas II comes to throne.

1895   2 May: Larisa Reisner born in Lublin in tsarist Poland.

1896   Disastrous harvests and famines. Strikes in St Petersburg spread across Russia.

1898   Founding of the Marxist Social Democratic Workers' Party, headed by Lenin, affiliated to Socialist International. Larisa's father exiled to Siberia for his political activities. For the next five years the Reisners live in the city of Tomsk, where he lectures at the university.

1901–2   Terrorists in the new Socialist Revolutionary Party assassinate government officials. Workers strike, peasants loot and expropriate estates, students riot and occupy for reforms. Reisner supports their cause.

1903–7   The Reisners live in exile in Berlin.

1904   The Tsar's war with Japan triggers more strikes, riots and student demonstrations across Russia. Reisner joins the Bolsheviks, and successfully defends German socialists arrested for 'crimes against the Tsar'.

1905   9 January: 'Bloody Sunday' sets off Russia's first revolution.

1907   The revolution is defeated. Terrorists carry out over 2,000 assassinations. The Tsar capitulates with an amnesty for political exiles. The Reisners return to Russia.

1908   The reaction is triumphant. Reisner is falsely accused of being a government spy.

1911   The Tsar's peasant 'holy man' Rasputin encourages him to embark on two disastrous wars in the Balkans. Unrest in the factories and universities gains new momentum, with more assassinations and peasant riots.

1912   Larisa leaves school with a gold medal and enters the university, writes poetry, and throws herself into St Petersburg's bohemian nightlife.

1913   Publishes her play 'Atlantis'.

1914   2 August: Russia declares war on Germany. St Petersburg renamed Petrograd.

1915   The tsarist army collapses, living costs soar, wages slump, and there is open talk of revolution. Larisa and her father publish their satirical anti-war literary magazine *Rudin*. That winter she embarks on a love affair with the poet Nikolai Gumilyov.

1916   *Rudin* closed by the censors. She writes for Maxim Gorky's socialist anti-war magazine *Chronicle*.

1917 March revolution topples the Tsar. She writes for Gorky's new socialist daily newspaper *New Life*, which publishes some of Russia's greatest writers, and joins the education programme of the Petrograd Soviet of Workers' and Soldiers' Deputies, teaching literacy and literature in the factories. Her teaching takes her to the Kronstadt naval base, where she starts an affair with the Bolshevik sailor Fyodor Raskolnikov, Chair of the Kronstadt Soviet. 25 October: Bolsheviks take power at the 2nd All-Russian Congress of Soviets, and declare Russia's withdrawal from the war. She works for the new Commissariat of Education, preparing cheap editions of the Russian classics for mass publication, and cataloguing the tsars' art treasures in the Hermitage Gallery.

1918 April: moves to Moscow with her family when the capital is evacuated from Petrograd, in anticipation of the German invasion.

Summer: Joins the Bolshevik Party and marries Raskolnikov, now Commander of the new Volga Naval Flotilla. Leaves with him for the Volga front to defend the Revolution, writing her 'Letters from the Front' for *Izvestiya*, the official paper of the Soviet.

December: Elected first woman Political Commissar of Naval General Staff.

1919 Fights in the battles for the Volga city of Tsaritsyn. When it falls to the Whites, she leaves with the Flotilla for the port of Astrakhan, capital of Kazakhstan, to secure Bolsheviks' access to the Caspian Sea, patrolled by British ships.

1920 May: Joins campaign to drive British forces from the Persian port of Badar-e Anzali, Britain's main base on the Caspian.

June: Returns to Petrograd. Speaks at writers' meetings, writes articles, teaches at Kronstadt and at the new workers' colleges, the *rabfaks*.

1921 April: Raskolnikov appointed Russia's first Ambassador to Afghanistan. She works for the Soviet diplomatic mission in Kabul, persuading women in the Emir's harem to support the Bolsheviks, writing articles for the Soviet press and reporting back to the Communist International in Moscow, the Comintern.

1923 June: Returns to Moscow without Raskolnikov and divorces him.

September–January: Works illegally in Berlin and Hamburg as a Comintern agent, writing articles and essays about the defeated Hamburg uprising. Embarks on an affair with the Comintern Secretary, Karl Radek.

1924 January and May: Publication of her books *Hamburg at the Barricades, Berlin, October 1923*, and *The Front*.

1924   May–October: Travels to the Urals and Eastern Ukraine, reporting
        for *Izvestiya.* on workers' lives in the mines and factories. Adopts
        fourteen-year-old Alyosha Makarov. December: Publication of her
        book about her travels, *Coal Iron and Living People.*

1925   May: Returns to Germany for medical treatment, then travels
        around mines and factories of the Ruhr Valley, writing the articles for
        Izvestiya that became her book *In Hindenburg's Country.*
        August: Publication of her book *Afghanistan.* Works on her essays
        on Russia's Decembrist uprising.

1926   Early January: Publication of her first Decembrist essay and *In
        Hindenburg's Country.* 9 February: She dies of typhoid fever in the
        Kremlin Hospital.

Introduction

'She flashed across the revolutionary sky like a blazing meteor, dazzling all in her path', Trotsky wrote. 'She had the soul of a great warrior, joined to the soul of a great poet', wrote her lover Karl Radek. Fighter, commissar, diplomat, writer, usually all at the same time, Larisa Reisner was a legend of the Russian Revolution, widely seen as its greatest journalist, whose writings from Russia and Ukraine, Germany, Persia and Afghanistan, were published in the new mass-circulation Soviet press, and were read by millions, workers, intellectuals, and the newly literate.

Centuries of tsarism had left over two-thirds of the Russian population illiterate, and journalism was part of the new government's campaign to spread literacy and culture in the midst of poverty, foreign invasion and economic blockade. She wrote as a Marxist, guiding readers to socialism, encouraging confidence, collectivism and Party spirit. And she wrote as a poet, of workers' epic struggles to make a new Russia to inspire the world. A figure of great stature in the Bolshevik Party, special correspondent for *Izvestiya*, daily paper of the Supreme Soviet, her voice in all her writings was always uniquely her own, bursting with energy, colour and imagination, endlessly funny and clever and satirical, with a sharp eye for the absurd, the fraudulent and bogus. She believed journalists should stay as close as possible to the lives of those making the new society, and report what they saw 'without varnish or adornment', and she derided the 'soul-daubers, who dip their critical brushes in the buckets of cheap idealism', 'Workers' labours and sacrifices give them the right to make the sharpest criticisms', she wrote, 'and the sharper these criticisms are, the more clearly we will see the face of the new post-revolutionary Russia'.

She is a powerful presence in all her writings, and yet she virtually writes herself out of them. A 'new woman' of the Revolution, a charismatic leader of women, who blazed a trail for them in the Revolution, and took for granted the new freedoms opening up for them after October, the progressive new laws on their economic and sexual equality, she was never involved in the politics of the women's liberation movement, and her closest friendships were with men. An aristocrat and intellectual, she fought shoulder to shoulder with workers in the collective struggle for class justice and equality, and for women's place in the reorganisation of power.

The six books of her journalism – *The Front, Afghanistan, Berlin October 1923, Hamburg at the Barricades, Coal Iron and Living People* and *In Hindenburg's Country* – published together here for the first time in English translation, were all written in the nine years before her death, in 1926, at the age of thirty-one. Her final masterpieces, written in the last year of her life, political and psychological portraits of Russia's first doomed revolutionaries, the Decembrists, will soon be out in my translations with Rab-Rab Press in Helsinki. Readers of these translations of her books wanting to learn more about her can refer to their companion volume, published by Historical Materialism/Brill, the new edition of my *Larisa Reisner. A Biography*, with its index and copious footnotes, and its bibliography of works studied in writing about her, published in Russia and abroad. A mass of different versions of Reisner emerge from the memoirs of those close to her, all of them fascinating, and her short life in the Revolution was an extraordinary one, even in those extraordinary times.

She was born in 1895 in Lublin, a regional capital of Tsarist Poland, fifty miles from Rosa Luxemburg's birthplace, Zamość. Both towns were in the Pale of Settlement, the tsars' 'Residential Provinces' for Jews, which by the nineteenth century covered almost a million square kilometres of the Russian Empire. Her mother was from the noblest of Lublin's aristocratic Russian families, impoverished landowners, descended from generations of writers and artists close to the court. Her father, a law lecturer at Lublin University, was from an equally cultured and impoverished aristocratic family of Baltic German barons and landowners. As a student in St Petersburg he had read Marx, and had been involved in underground political circles, and he arrived in Lublin as a Marxist and atheist, with a police record.

Eight months before her birth, Tsar Nicholas II came to the throne, like his father Alexander III a convinced autocrat and rabid anti-Semite, who forbade peasants to leave the villages, expelled Jews from the cities, and personally sponsored the Black Hundreds gangs, prototypes for Hitler's Brownshirts, to organise brutal pogroms against Jews in areas of the Pale. The early years of his reign saw an explosion of factory strikes across Russia, which increasingly turned into political strikes against the autocracy itself. Students rioted and occupied the universities, and Reisner spoke at student meetings in Lublin. 'There is no Law in Russia. Laws are dictated by the criminal political interests of the tsarist state', he told them.

When Larisa was three, he was ordered out of Lublin and banished into semi-exile in Siberia, to teach Law at the University of Tomsk, where the family lived for the next five years. A popular supporter of student causes, he worked with a local strike support group raising funds for sacked workers, and attended underground meetings of the Siberian branch of the Marxist Russian Social Democratic Labour Party, led by the exiled Lenin. In 1903, the Ministry of Education ordered 'this arrogant liberal' to be sacked, for 'abusing his Chair to promote enmity and disrespect for law and order in Russia', and the family fled to Germany.

For four years they lived as political exiles in Berlin, often in dire poverty, where he supported them as best he could with teaching and writing jobs. Berlin was at the centre of Russia's revolutionary diaspora in Europe, home of Germany's mighty Social Democrat Party, the largest socialist party in the world, leader of the Socialist International. He joined the party, and allied himself to its left revolutionary wing, led by Rosa Luxemburg and Reichstag deputy Karl Liebknecht, fierce critics of the leadership's growing conservatism, chauvinism and bureaucracy, and Liebknecht and his Russian wife became the Reisners' closest friends in Berlin.

Larisa and her younger brother Igor, born in Siberia, were both bilingual from birth in Russian and German, but German became her first language. Those years in exile were formative for her, and exile would be the central theme of her unfinished autobiographical novel *Requiem* she began writing in 1919, about her life before the Revolution.

The family sheltered Russians on the run from the German police, and Reisner kept in touch with underground circles in Russia, widening his legal expertise to construct defences for those arrested, and in 1904 he joined the Bolshevik Party, travelling to Switzerland and Finland to meet Lenin in exile, writing articles and pamphlets for the Bolshevik press.

He left the Bolsheviks two years later, sickened by the chaos and violence of the 1905 revolution, and was drawn to the non-violent philosophy of the 'Seeking Marxists', who were discovering revolutionary new insights into human behaviour and social relations in the works of Freud.

Under the Tsar's amnesty of 1907, he was one of over a hundred political exiles considered safe to be allowed back to Russia, and was appointed Professor of Constitutional Law at St Petersburg University, where he remained under close police surveillance. Larisa and Igor were enrolled in elite St Petersburg private schools, and both excelled academically. They were also allowed an extraordinary amount of freedom as children, and she later told a friend she had picked up her revolutionary fighting skills on the rough streets of the capital – 'in the wonderful fights in which I was seen as an unparalleled expert when I was twelve, even by the boys'.

She left school at seventeen, with the gold medal awarded to Russia's top students. Women, like Jews, were allowed only to audit university courses, and she enrolled as an external student at St Petersburg University in courses in Law, Literature and Philosophy. She also won a place as a full student at St Petersburg's prestigious independent Psychoneurology Institute, with its policy of 'unrestricted admission to women and Jewish students'.

She became part of a circle of student socialists and poets, and poured out a mass of poems set in an atmosphere of revolutionary heroism and struggle. Vadim Andreev, son of the Reisners' friend the writer Leonid Andreev, who lived with the family for two years as a child, remembered her in 1913 as 'a young girl writing poetry and dreaming of revolution, because in the Reisner family it was impossible not to, and enjoying even more the radiance of her youth and her unusual beauty. Few men escaped the fate of falling desperately in love with her. But any who dared to speak of their feelings would be banished, like a heretic from church'.

When Russia mobilised for war in 1914, thousands in newly renamed Petrograd enlisted, and the Reisners parted company with many of their old socialist friends who became patriots. In 1916, she abandoned her student poetry for journalism, and was the moving spirit behind the sharply satirical anti-war magazine *Rudin* she brought out with her father, managing its finances, commissioning articles, poems and cartoons, cajoling and battling with the military censors to get them published. *Rudin* was closed by the police after the eighth issue, and she started writing for Maxim Gorky's anti-war journal *Chronicle*, which published the early stories of Isaac Babel, articles by the exiled revolutionaries Anatoly Lunacharsky and Alexandra Kollontai, and the poems of Alexander Blok and the Futurist Vladimir Mayakovsky.

She joined the crowds who gathered for Mayakovsky's performances in Petrograd's clubs and cafes, striding the stage in his face paint, hurling abuse, mocking 'beautiful' poetry – 'storming the future, with his rage, his love, his hunger for life and revolution', she wrote in *Chronicle*. But the Futurists never had any detectable influence on her writing, and she was inspired all her life by the Symbolist poetry of Blok, and the 'Acmeists' Anna Akhmatova and Nikolai Gumilyov. As a student, she embarked on a wild love affair with the charismatic and unfaithful Gumilyov, an ardent patriot who volunteered for the front, and their brief meetings on his leaves in the capital were sustained by long ecstatic letters, published in a 1980 edition of his previously unpublished works.

The March 1917 revolution that toppled the Tsar sent them on their different ways. All university courses were suspended, and from then on she got her education in the revolutionary movement, joining the education programme of the Petrograd Soviet of Workers' and Soldiers' Deputies, giving literacy and literature classes in workers' clubs in Petrograd's poor suburbs and the surrounding towns, writing articles about the new workers' culture of the revolution, the street theatre, songs and poetry – 'the creative pulse of the revolution, which is making culture the property of the people, the true inheritors of the treasures of the past'.

Her teaching work took her to the Bolshevik stronghold of 'Red Kronstadt', the largest naval base of the Imperial Fleet, twenty miles from the capital. In March, sailors had led a mass armed mutiny against their officers, declaring the new 'Kronstadt Republic', electing a Revolutionary Committee to prepare the garrison for Soviet power. In charge of the Committee's education programme was the Bolshevik commander Fyodor Ilin, Chair of the Kronstadt Soviet and Party, better known by his underground name Fyodor Raskolnikov, who recruited her to give classes on the battleships, and that spring was the start of their tempestuous six-year love affair.

There were several accounts of her activities on the night of 25 October, when the Bolsheviks took power. According to Vadim Andreev, she sailed from Kronstadt to Petrograd with Raskolnikov and the sailors on the Battleship *Aurora*, and it was she who gave the orders for the blank cannon to be fired at the Winter Palace where the Provisional Government was in session, signalling the birth of the new Russia.

Immediately after the Revolution, she worked for the new Commissar of Education, Anatoly Lunacharsky, who appointed her to the editorial board of the new State Publishing House, *Gosizdat*, preparing cheap paperback editions of the Russian and foreign classics for mass publication. He also appointed her to the Commissariat's Commission for the Preservation of Artistic and Historic Monuments, and she was the first journalist to enter the Winter Palace after October, as head of the Commission's team cataloguing the tsars' art treasures in the Hermitage Gallery, now the property of the people.

Her father rejoined the Party, and as Russia's leading authority on constitutional law, he was appointed by Lenin to write the first Soviet Constitution, the Declaration of the Rights of Working People, which enshrined in law the dictatorship of the proletariat, making Russia the first workers' state in the world. He worked at the Commissariats of Labour, Health, Education and Justice on their first decrees, raising wages, introducing equal pay for women, free healthcare and education, abolishing tsarist ranks and titles, and the Jewish Pale. And he prepared the groundwork for one of the Revolution's most difficult and contentious pieces of legislation, disestablishing the Orthodox Church.

The British and French governments had quickly formed a military alliance to defeat Soviet power in the most economically profitable parts of Russia, and were funding and arming the tsarist officers and generals of the new counter-revolutionary White Guards. In May 1918, British-backed forces of the White Czech army began their advance along the River Volga, the vital transport route connecting European Russia to the Caspian Sea and the oilfields of Central Asia. Soviets in Bolshevik-held towns were overthrown, and replaced with

Constituent Assembly Committees, embryos of Russia's future national government. Nationalised enterprises were returned to their old owners, and workers and Bolsheviks were killed in their thousands.

As the Allied intervention struck into the heart of the country, the war became a people's war of total social mobilisation. Trotsky, now Commissar of War, travelled thousands of miles to thousands of fronts on the armoured train in which he lived for virtually the entire Civil War, mobilising the Bolsheviks' straggling bands of fighters into the new Red Army. Raskolnikov was elected Vice Commissar of the Red Navy, and Reisner resigned from her work with Lunacharsky to work with him at the Naval Commissariat, as a commissar of the General Staff.

In June, they registered their marriage in one of the Bolsheviks' new state 'red wedding' ceremonies, then left with a battalion of sailors for the Bolshevik-held city of Kazan, the Whites' main target on the Volga, where Raskolnikov was appointed Commander of the new Volga Naval Flotilla.

For the next two years, she sailed on the great warships of the Flotilla from Kazan to the Caspian, as cavalry instructor, flag-secretary and reconnaissance officer, fighting with the sailors under Raskolnikov's and Trotsky's command in the battles for Svyazhsk, Kazan and Tsaritsyn, driving the Whites from Astrakhan and Azerbaijan, and British naval forces from their base in Persia. As commissar, she had to instil confidence and confidence and fight with the men to the end. A major part of commissars' work was also spreading culture and education at the front, and in breaks in the fighting, she gave literacy and literature classes on board the ships, and worked on her diaries of the campaign, her 'Letters from the Front'.

As the Red Navy's only high-ranking woman commander, she had to fight to be listened to and respected by the sailors, fighting them off with her fists when necessary. Trotsky wrote of her great courage in battle, and those who fought with her recalled the endless trials and 'tests' they subjected her to. There is virtually nothing in her 'Letters' about her personal life at the front, and Raskolnikov is simply *Flotkom*, Flotilla Commander. After the first and most personal of them, from Kazan, they are no longer her story, they are the collective story of the Revolution, and each page is filled with unforgettable characters, and has hundreds more behind them.

Published between 1918 and 1921 in *Izvestiya* and the popular Marxist literary journal *Red Virgin Soil*, they were then reworked and reshaped for her book *The Front*, published by *Red Virgin Soil* in 1924.

The writing hurtles along, conveying the energy and rhythm of events in dizzying torrents of words, passages of lyrical poetry punctuated by brief staccato cut to the bone reports of battles, defeats and victories. She wrote with the telegraphic immediacy and editing techniques of the early Soviet cinema, cutting from the beauty of the Volga landscape to some of the most tragic episodes of the Civil War, and the mass graves of the White Terror, from big battle scenes to close-up portraits of individuals, and she brought them all unforgettably to life.

The Front pioneered a new kind of literary political journalism, in which journalists were creators of life, involved directly in events and reporting back. Her writing also had its vocal critics. Her unusual and beautiful way with words was seen by many as too refined and poetic to convey the reality of workers' lives in the Revolution, and hardline defenders of proletarian purity claimed her class disqualified her from writing of events from the correct political perspective. The journalist Vladimir Polyansky, of the Proletarian Cultural Organisation *Proletkult*, writing 'in the name of worker peasant Russia', found 'the author's purely intellectual psychology dull and incomprehensible', and accused her of 'emasculating the Russian language'.

Trotsky is known to have considered *The Front*, with Isaac Babel's *Red Cavalry Stories*, to be the most outstanding works of the Civil War, and reviews in *Izvestiya, Pravda* and the magazines *The Bookseller* and *Red Fleet* called the work a masterpiece. 'Anyone who wants to understand this exceptional epoch, and how people made the Revolution and how the Revolution made them, must read this captivating book', the poet Nikolai Smirnov wrote in *Izvestiya*. 'The Front* is exceptional for its psychological insight into those who fought for two years from the Baltic to Persia, and for its analysis of the ideas for which they went through the fire', wrote the journalist Igor Ilinsky in *Pravda*.

Her glowing praise for Trotsky's organisational genius in the battles for Svyazhsk, and his role in victory, made her chapter on the 'glorious epic of Svyazhsk' unpublishable in subsequent Soviet editions of her works, and her dedication to him was removed from the chapter 'July 1919'. A facsimile of the 1924 original of 'Svyazshk' was published online in Russia in 2017, to celebrate the centenary of the Revolution, followed a year later by the publication of the complete uncensored *Front*, and the translation here is from that. I took the liberty in the interests of clarity and chronology of changing the order of 'Tsaritsyn' and 'July 1919', as well as the order of three of the pieces in her last work, *In Hindenburg's Country* (Pieces in this work and *Berlin, October 1923* are sketches and essays, so aren't marked in the works' contents as chapters).

Two years after the Revolution, the Bolsheviks had been fighting the armies of fourteen foreign states and their White Guard allies. But by the end of 1920, against unimaginable odds, the invaders had been thrown out and the Whites defeated. Over fourteen million had died in battle, or from starvation or disease.

Millions of women were widowed, millions of orphans lived on the streets, and the economy was in ruins. Yet despite the shortage of paper and ink and the predicted death of literature, the end of the Civil War saw an extraordinary flowering of new writing. Many of Russia's established writers who had fled abroad after the Revolution were returning to work with the Bolsheviks, and a mass of new writers' groups, led by the Futurists and *Proletkult*, were issuing their journals and manifestos on the purpose and meaning of literature in the new Russia.

On her return from the front in 1920, she attended meetings of the different groups in Petrograd's cafes, workers' clubs and factories, and wrote for their publications. But she was never a follower of programmes or platforms. She was closest in spirit to the journal *Red Virgin Soil*, publisher of *The Front*, launched by Gorky and Lenin to bring the best literature of the Revolution, communist and non-communist, to the new workers' intelligentsia in the factories, the army, and the new colleges preparing them to enter the universities, the *rabfaks*. The only qualifications required at the *rabfaks* were to be proletarian and literate, and she ran literature classes there, and dedicated *The Front* to her students – 'our future statesmen and judges, scientists and professors, hungry for knowledge, working by day and studying by night, selling their last pair of shoes to buy the works of Lenin and Marx, who in a few short years must not only assimilate the old culture, but shape its most valuable features into new ideological forms'.

In the spring of 1921, Raskolnikov was appointed Soviet ambassador to Afghanistan, the Bolsheviks' first venture in foreign diplomacy, at the centre of their complicated relations with British imperial power in Asia. They were briefed together at the Commissariat of Foreign Affairs on the politics and history of Afghanistan, as the Commissariat's first 'red ambassadors', and were instructed to 'avoid at all costs the fatal mistake of trying to implant communism artificially into the country, and provoking Britain into another war'. They were to establish friendly relations with the reforming King Amanullah and his family, and assure them of the Bolsheviks' support for Afghanistan's neutrality and independence from Britain, while using their espionage skills to gather information about British activities in Kabul, reporting back to the Comintern in Moscow. She was assigned the delicate task of gaining access to Amanullah's harem, and convincing the two queens, his all-powerful wife and mother, of the Russians' friendly intentions in Kabul.

She rode on horseback at the head of the Soviet diplomatic caravan on the two-month journey from the Russian border, across the perilous rocky passes of the Hindu Kush to Kabul, and her first sketches from Afghanistan, published in *Pravda* and *Red Virgin Soil*, were drawn from her diaries of the journey, a riotous lyrical mosaic of wild mountain landscapes, glimpses of history, portraits of their Afghan guards, and of the nomads' caravans and herdsmen's families they met on the way.

For the next two years she lived with the eighty members of the Soviet mission in Kabul, joining Raskolnikov in all his official engagements, sending articles and essays back to Russia on Afghanistan's first hospital, factory and military school, filled with sharp observations about Amanullah's reforms and Afghan life.

She was savagely funny about the Bolsheviks' British counterparts in Kabul – 'with their white helmets and their smiles cutting their faces like the notches on their bullets, and their staggering contempt for these people of an inferior race'. She paid tribute to Afghanistan's national heroes and heroines, the mountain tribespeople living on the borders with India, who for a century had been fighting the most powerful army in the world, defending their settlements against British bombing raids and the poisoning of their flocks and pastures. And in her essay *Fascists In Asia*, published in *Red Virgin Soil* in November 1922, a month after Mussolini's march on Rome, she identified the origins of the new doctrine of fascism in Britain's gangster colonialism in India and its eastern 'protectorates'.

She wrote of Kabul's bazaars and festivals, its mullahs and veiled women, of grand audiences at the Palace with Amanullah and his family, and the life of his harem. She became an honoured guest of the two queens and their entourages, attending examination day at the girls' school in the harem, the first in Afghanistan, and banquets at which women danced and threw off their veils and passed the hashish pipe round.

She sent the relevant information back to the Comintern in Moscow, and worked on her book *Afghanistan*. 'I can imagine the Comintern's joy when they read about the sunrises and sunsets and the flowers and humming-birds in the Palace gardens, without which an old communist like me can't describe the Revolution or the reaction to it', she wrote home. 'You know my weakness for aestheticism, and I want the pages of *Afghanistan* to smell not just of big grey politics, but of the scent of the flowering almond trees, and the bright aromas of the bazaar'.

Published in the autumn of 1925 by the State Publishing House, with the rousing final chapter 'Fascists In Asia' also published as a pamphlet, *Afghanistan* was savaged in the *Proletkult* press for its exoticism. 'Larisa's prose becomes ever more lush and self-indulgent. Like an aging woman looking in the glass and seeing more wrinkles on her face, she looks into her soul and sees new cavities there', wrote an anonymous reviewer in the *Proletkult* magazine *Communist*.

Pravda praised her as the first Soviet journalist to show the human face of fascism, and for 'exposing the true state of Soviet-British relations in Afghanistan, and the tireless ineradicable hatred between the two worlds that lies beneath the ceremonies of diplomatic etiquette'. Nikolai Smirnov in *Izvestiya* saw the work as a model of political journalism: 'Afghanistan belongs with those great works that smell more of gunpowder than roses'.

She left Afghanistan in the summer of 1923 without Raskolnikov and divorced him, and returned to the Russia of the New Economic Policy, the NEP.

In a desperate bid to rebuild Russia's shattered economy after the Civil War, and induce the West to lift its economic blockade, a series of major concessions had been made to capitalism, with the restoration of a significant amount of private enterprise. The all-out collectivisation of farms was relaxed, allowing peasants to sell grain surplus to state requirements on the open market, and managers trained under the old regime, the 'specialists', were being brought back to run the factories, along with the old capitalist system of workers' bonuses, fines and layoffs.

'Larisa understood, as we all did, that scope had to be given to the business initiative of the peasants to obtain the raw material for industry, if only not to die of hunger', Radek wrote. 'But in the summer of 1923, she was uneasy. In her heart, she longed for a heroic breakthrough to the new social order, with arms in hand, and to breathe the air of revolution again'.

As Secretary of the Comintern, it was Radek who dealt with her application that autumn for a post in Germany, where mass strikes seemed to be taking the country close to revolution.

In January, the armies of France and Belgium had marched into the industrial Ruhr Valley, the centre of Germany's coal and steel industries, to seize the country's unpaid war reparations ordered by Versailles. Firms went bankrupt, and the Mark collapsed. Striking workers were laid off in their thousands by managers desperate to save their businesses from ruin and Germany from revolution, and there was a surge of support for the Nazis, who blamed Jews, foreigners and communists for bringing the country to its knees.

As the fate of the Weimar Republic hung in the balance, the Comintern had to give guidance in the crisis to Germany's small new Communist Party. As the Comintern's leading authority on Germany, Radek urged caution. He had lived in Berlin through the near suicide of the party in the defeated 1918 revolution, and he had been deeply affected by the murders of its leaders Rosa Luxemburg and Karl Liebknecht. A majority on the Comintern Executive believed a communist-led mass uprising in Germany could be the start of a nationwide showdown between workers and state, which would then spread to the rest of the world. Hugely outvoted, he was forced to back a rising in early November in Dresden, capital of 'Red Saxony', where socialists and communists held the balance of power in the state parliament. This would be the base from which to arm Dresden's sixty thousand workers reported to be ready to fight.

Since she was bilingual in the language, she was the obvious choice for him to send to Germany, and he appointed her to work illegally in Berlin, as a liaison officer between its Comintern agents and Dresden's communists. He provided her with a false German passport, and gave her a crash course in the techniques of illegal underground work. But he saw her main asset as her pen, and he arranged for her report back to *Pravda, Izvestiya* and *Red Paper* on events as they unfolded. 'I knew that Larisa, better than anyone else, could make the link between our two proletarian armies', he wrote, 'for she wasn't simply a contemplative artist, she was a fighting artist, who could see the struggle from inside, and could convey its dynamics'.

As he had predicted, Dresden's communists lacked the power or numbers to rally a mass rising, and the insurrection had to be aborted. Three days later, in a desperate last show of resistance, fourteen hundred workers led by the Communist Party occupied twenty-six police stations in Hamburg, Germany's second largest city, the largest port in Europe, and seized their weapons. Within twenty-four hours, the rising had been crushed, and Radek had no option but to approve the party's decision to retreat. The following day, he joined her in Berlin, and what had started as a working relationship quickly developed into a romantic one.

She attended sessions of the Reichstag, and reported back to the Comintern on the army of Berlin's starving unemployed in the dole queues, and the abject failure of the Social Democrat Party to provide any leadership against the rise of Hitler's Nazis. She drew on her reports for her book of essays *Berlin, October 1923*, which ends with a party meeting she attended the day after Hitler's 'beer-hall *putsch*' in Munich. 'Possibly the last encounter between the party's ruling bureaucratic elite and the workers whose support they rely on, whose interests they're pledged to defend, against whom the fascists promised to unleash their thugs within twenty-four hours', she wrote. 'Not one word to them from the leaders of this so-called "socialist workers' party" about how to defend themselves and avoid a bloodbath, no fighting slogans, no worked out plan of defence'.

In November Radek sent her to Hamburg, where she stayed with workers' families, studied trial records and attended court hearings, writing the articles and essays from the ruins of the uprising that became her book *Hamburg at the Barricades*.

She captured the speed and energy of modern Hamburg in her joyful pile-up of images – 'lying on the shores of the North Sea, waterproof as a pilot's oilskin, stinking like a sailor's pipe', its language 'soaked in the sea, like some rare creature of the deep, salty as cod, ripe and juicy as Dutch cheese, rude, smelly and cheerful as English vodka'. She evoked the drama and romanticism of the rising, the 'smell' of revolution, and she brought it to life through the stories of its fighters – 'the hope of the new Germany'. Several chapters of the book were first published in Germany, with much of the dialogue at the most dramatic moments of the struggle kept in German in the complete Russian edition, heightening the sense of eye-witness immediacy.

The insurgents fought with unbelievable courage, she wrote. 'But what was the point of continuing the struggle in isolation, flaring up in the midst of the general collapse?' And she blamed their lack of support elsewhere in Germany on the 'Social Democrat traitors' – the party's 'pseudo socialists, Mensheviks and bureaucrats, whose avoidance of decisive action has entered the bloodstream of the workers' movement'. She wrote of the leadership's collusion with the *Reichswehr* in suppressing the rising, and in the savage reprisals that followed, when thousands were arrested or went underground, and for security reasons most of the names are given as initials.

Hamburg at the Barricades and *Berlin, October 1923* are unforgettable portraits of workers' lives in Germany ten years before the Nazis took power. They were published together in Russia in January 1924, by the Comintern's International Aid Organisation for Revolutionary Fighters, MOPR, to rapturous reviews. 'We want to write like that or not at all!' the novelist Yury Libedinsky said at the books' launch party at Moscow's House of the Press. The poet Vera Inber saw *Hamburg* as a turning point in her work: 'She writes with incredible accessibility for those untrained in scientific truths, yet without mindless popularisation. For the first time she abandons aestheticism for its own sake, and describes the subterranean depths she can no longer deny, and they no longer frighten her'. According to the journalist Lev Sosnovsky, who had set her 'tests' as a writer after the Revolution, 'it was impossible now to ignore her, because there was simply no better writer among us'.

In May 1924, she left Moscow on her next writing assignment, reporting on workers' lives in the new conditions of the NEP in the industrial heartlands of the Soviet Union, in the Urals and the Donbas region of Eastern Ukraine. 'Being a person with an immediate grasp of history, she needed more than merely reading and discussions', Radek wrote. 'She had to find out what was happening in the depths of the masses, who in the final count dictate the course of history'.

She spent the next three months travelling around the ancient factory and mining settlements of the Northern Urals, with their primitive pits, mills and foundries, staying with workers' families as she had in Germany, joining them on their shifts, writing the essays for *Izvestiya* that later became her book *Coal Iron and Living People*. Within two decades, the mines and factories she visited would be modernised and mechanised in the mass industrialisation of the Five Year Plans, but they had been barely functioning when workers took them over at the end of the Civil War. She wrote of the broken machinery, the failure and suffering, and of 'workers' superhuman endurance, labouring to drag Russia out of poverty, on the rations of 1920, which will one day be displayed in museums – a pound and three-quarters of flour per family a day, a pound of sugar a month, a quarter of a pound of meat, a twentieth of fat and vegetables, and four cigarettes'. Yet within four years productivity had reached its pre-war levels, she wrote, and had often outstripped them.

She went down the iron mine at Bilimbay, and the coalmines at Kyzyl, the largest working mines in the Northern Urals. She explored the mighty Nadezhdinsky Metallurgy Plant, 'pride of the Urals', and she rode on horseback to the platinum mines in the swamplands high in the Urals Mountains, containing ninety percent of the earth's deposits of the metal. She then left the Urals for Ukraine, and stayed in the Donbas coalmining town of Gorlovka (now Horlivka), joining miners on their shifts in some of the deepest and most dangerous pits in the world.

Her journalist's notebooks were meticulous records of new factories and machines, with columns of data and statistics. But the Revolution's greatest resource was its people, and her notebooks 'Living Portraits' were filled with sketches of the workers who became the heroes and heroines of *Coal Iron and Living People*. Like *Hamburg* and *The Front*, the book has a cast of thousands, and cuts from big set pieces and crowd scenes to close-ups of individuals, telling their stories and bringing them to life.

She was the first Soviet journalist to report on this epoch of workers' lives in Russia. Thousands had come straight from fighting in the Civil War to defend the Revolution on the new industrial front, and she saw 'the same brotherhood and class solidarity, which nothing the capitalist world throws at them can shake'. The Revolution had lifted millions out of extreme poverty, and she wrote of the shorter working day, the increased wages and better food, the free education, housing and healthcare. She met those who had found their way to books and politics and the Party, and she joined the recruitment drive for the 'Lenin Enrolment', which doubled the Party's membership between 1923 and 1925 to over a million. She was also writing of the new capitalist management techniques of the NEP, which prioritised hitting industrial targets over workers' health and happiness.

Russia's heavy industry, nationalised after the Revolution, remained under state control. Smaller enterprises were grouped together on a commercial

profit-making basis, as semi-autonomous industrial Trusts, and economic competition was leading to layoffs, pay cuts and deteriorating working conditions.
The Bolsheviks' first decree, issued a few weeks after the Revolution, had cut
the working day to eight hours. These had then been reduced to six, and the
Trusts now wanted to bring back the eight-hour day for the same pay.

She wrote of the dangerous working conditions in the factories, particularly
in those employing mainly women. She wrote of the housing crisis, the per-
ennial curse of the Soviet system, and she stayed with workers in their fetid
slums and barracks. She described the bread queues and the empty shelves in
the shops, and the painful reality of the new Soviet health system, stretched
to breaking point by the Civil War, strangled by red tape. And she reported on
factory and Party meetings at which workers cried out against the new highly
paid managers' scandalous neglect of their needs.

She had written *The Front* for workers at the *rabfaks*. *Coal Iron and Living
People* was written for those in the factories and mines, a resolutely warm-
hearted denunciation of NEP corruption and Party incompetence and bureaucracy, filled with an inexhaustible faith in workers' creativity and class solidarity, enduring unspeakable hardships to build the new socialist economy that
could compete with the West.

On the journey back to Moscow, she stayed for a month in the industrial
Ukrainian city of Dnepropetrovsk (now Dnipro). And there she fostered a small
twelve-year-old boy, Alyosha Makarov, who had been begging on the streets,
one of seven children of a Bolshevik factory worker killed fighting the Whites,
whose mother was unable to feed them all on her wages as a cleaner. She
returned to Moscow with him in October, fed him up, took him to a clinic for
his ringworm and rickets, found him a good school and helped him with his
homework, arranged piano lessons for him, taught him to ice-skate, and somehow organised her writing around him.

Coal Iron and Living People was published in December 1924 by the State
Publishing House, a montage of scenes from her travels, interweaving stories
of workers' lives with episodes from the past, from the era of serfdom to the
birth of capitalism, and the revolutionary struggles of her lifetime.

The book shone a light on a world that was unfamiliar to many of her readers,
and Vera Inber found it a depressing read – 'as if her shoulders were weighed
down by her heavy miner's cape, and she was robbed of her strength by the
harsh sunless underground ugliness of the mines'.

The literary critic Zhores Elsberg wrote of her 'enormous genuine optim-
ism', and her 'poetry of everyday life'. *Pravda* and *Izvestiya* praised *Coal Iron
and Living People* as a brilliant account of workers' lives seven years after the
Revolution, gripping and atmospheric, filled with pathos and poetry. The poet

Maria Shkapskaya saw her as a consummate stylist, who could make even statistics poetic, while insisting on the importance of facts and figures and scrupulous research – 'You have to be able to count not only the stars in the sky, but the kopecks in the government's pockets'. 'Nothing in our literature now is more truthful, accurate or direct', wrote the *Proletkult* journalist Vladimir Polyansky, who eight months earlier had called *The Front* 'dull and incomprehensible'.

The *Izvestiya* journalist Nikolai Smirnov recalled crowds of worker and peasant journalists from the factories and villages visiting her at the paper's offices to show her their stories, and that after talking to them she always took her writing away for further work – 'for she was very demanding of the written word, particularly her own'.

She was also ill and exhausted. She had contracted malaria in Persia, and would ignore the warning symptoms, and she had barely rested from her punishing five-month travels. And in the spring of 1925, after a series of increasingly severe attacks, she booked herself into a specialist tropical diseases clinic in Hamburg.

In the two years since she was last in Germany, the powerful militarist bloc in the Reichstag had moved the government drastically to the right. A week before she arrived in April, Field Marshal von Hindenburg, former Head of the Kaiser's General Staff, was elected second President of the Weimar Republic, who eight years later would appoint Hitler Chancellor of the Third Reich. It was Hindenburg's brutal regimes in large parts of occupied Eastern Europe during the First World War that inspired the Nazi pathology of *Lebensraum*, and the first ss units were already on the streets, providing Hitler with armed protection at his rallies, attacking communists, 'non-Aryans' and Jews.

She discharged herself from her clinic to march in a large anti-Nazi demonstration, organised by the Hamburg Communist Party, then left Hamburg for the industrial Ruhr Valley, and spent the next month travelling around the 'Arsenal of the World', still under French occupation, writing the sketches and essays for *Pravda, Izvestiya* and *Red Paper* that became her book *In Hindenburg's Country*.

Her portraits of workers' lives in the wake of Germany's two failed revolutions are all set against Hindenburg's drive for a new war. *In Hindenburg's Country* opens in the city of Essen, home of the Krupp steel empire, capitalism's largest business monopoly and weapons manufacturers, which had armed the victorious Prussian army in the Franco-Prussian War and the Imperial German Army in the First World War, and would serve the Nazi war machine throughout the entire Second World War. Forbidden by the Versailles Treaty to produce weapons, Krupp had had to close his armaments factories, including his vast

Hindenburg plant, and was turning out cash-registers and false teeth. But it was only a matter of time before normal business resumed, she wrote, preparing the world for new wars 'whose horrors are still unknown to humanity, a new mode of death, and a new strategy, unlike any before'.

She interviewed managers in their oak-panelled boardrooms, 'with their own General Staff and diplomatic corps, and portraits of their kings on the walls'. And not satisfied with their answers to her questions, she visited the abandoned army barracks in Essen's outskirts housing its starving unemployed, 'surviving on too little to live on, too much to die on', and recorded their stories of poverty and shattered hopes. She then joined a milkman on his rounds of the city's poor tenements, and in her sketch 'Milk' she wrote of 'the illusion of food, the stink of workers' boots drying by the fire. That smell is sweeter than incense, for it means they're working, and won't die'.

From Essen she travelled east to Dessau in Saxony, birthplace of the German aviation industry and the Junkers aircraft factory, where 'kindly Junkers' invited her into his special laboratory to watch him working with his dedicated team of scientists on their latest state of the art all-aluminium three-engine passenger plane. She wrote of the 'noble madness' of the first flying experiments, when 'humanity cleared its path to the sky on blood-spattered paper wings', of 'Count Zeppelin's stupid sausages', and of Junkers' three new aircraft now waiting in the hangar to be rolled into the field, 'seeing the patch of sky in the doorway and realising what it's for'.

'Ullstein' is a dazzling satire on Berlin's Ullstein media empire, publishers of Germany's major newspapers, with its stockmarket reports and celebrity gossip and fake news, its 'novels you read on the lavatory' turned into popular films, its women's magazines and endless adverts – all thrown onto the streets every day at lightning speed, captured in the speed and energy of the writing. And now profits were under threat from Germany's new post-war press barons, who were 'turning the "non-party" papers to which the average German philistine has become accustomed into mouthpieces for the most rabid reaction, condemning new generations of workers to be slaughtered in new wars'. And if Ullstein is to survive he must join them, 'propping up the great wooden statue of Hindenburg opposite the Victory Column outside the Reichstag'.

Her travels around the Ruhr ended in the coalmining area of Westphalia, where she went down the mines and learnt about miners' lives after the defeated revolution, about the pay cuts and layoffs and maintenance economies following Germany's 1918 coal crisis and the French occupation, about the treachery of their union bosses, siding with management in sabotaging their recent strike. And again and again in all the despair and confusion she was hearing their hopes for Russia, 'like exiles talking of their distant homeland. And linked to these hopes is another, at present just a pale shoot growing without sunlight in the weak light of their lamps – the idea of working-class unity'.

In Hindenburg's Country was published in January 1926 by the *Pravda* publishing house, in a huge print-run of half a million. Vera Inber saw the book as a *tour de force* of Soviet journalism, and her most accomplished work, by turns epic and intimate, full of poetry and big ideas and the everyday details of workers' lives. 'People and places are described by a writer who has achieved new brilliance. The characteristic beauty and refinement of her prose are transformed by a mature pen, unafraid to write well today, knowing it will be even better tomorrow'. '*In Hindenburg's Country*, like *Hamburg at the Barricades*, is written not by an observer, but by a fighter in the world revolution', wrote Nikolai Smirnov in *Izvestiya*. 'She is always drawn to broad epic themes, and the sparkling well of her talent has grown strong in the Revolution. But she is also a genius of the miniature. She has the ability to bring distance near with one apt image, and she writes with a sharpened stiletto. Nothing is too small or too commonplace. She sees all the heroism, sacrifice and poetry in the day-to-day work of building socialism'.

A week after *In Hindenburg's Country* was published, *Izvestiya* brought out the first of her four essays on the Decembrists, which the literary critic Victor Shklovsky considered the best things she ever wrote, filled with empathy and imagination and living breathing characters, deeply researched, from material newly released from the archives after the Revolution. She returned to the archives to research her next two books, works of historical fiction. But they were never written. The limitless demands she made of herself took an intolerable toll on her health, already ravaged by malaria, and eight and a half years after the Revolution, her prodigious energy finally gave out.

In late January 1926, she was overcome with headaches and a high fever, and her family rushed her to the Kremlin Hospital, where doctors diagnosed typhoid fever. She died on 9 February, three months before her thirty-first birthday.

Her body lay in state for two days at the House of the Press with her grieving family and friends, and five thousand mourners followed her coffin through the streets of Moscow to the Vagankovo Cemetery, the cemetery of writers and artists, where she was laid to rest on the Square of the Communards, and the poet Boris Pasternak read his eulogy 'Memories of Reisner' at her grave. Years later, Pasternak told a friend, 'I named the heroine of my novel *Doctor Zhivago* Lara in memory of Larisa Mikhailovna Reisner'.

She was remembered in hundreds of obituaries by those who had known her at different times of her life, in Russia, Germany and Afghanistan, her comrades in struggle and her fellow writers, and in Radek's long love letter to her memory, the source of all the quotations here, which was reprinted as the Preface to her two-volume *Collected Works*, published two years after her death.

Missing were all references to Trotsky, and to dozens of others she was close to who were later shot or disappeared into the icy wastes of the gulag. She was too nuanced and critical a writer and too close to Trotsky to have survived Stalin's purges and the stifling of literary dissent, and for the next thirty years her works disappeared from print. She began to be published again in the new post-Stalin Russia, with two heavily edited and annotated editions of her *Selected Works*, in 1958 and 1965, with warmly appreciative introductions. More of her writings and letters appeared in various Soviet literary publications, and in 1969 her surviving friends and comrades brought out their anthology *Larisa Reisner Remembered by her Contemporaries*.

Richard Chappell first introduced readers in this country to her writings with his 1977 translations of her works from Germany, used in this collection, and in 1985 Eleonora Solovei brought out her brief but touching and insightful *Larisa Reisner. A Sketch of her Life and Work*. The first edition of my biography was published in 1988, three years before the end of the Soviet Union, and since then more of her works have been republished in Russia, with new material released from her archives. Galina Przhiborovskaya has drawn on these new sources in her impressively researched first full-length Russian biography, published in 2008, and she was an invaluable guide when I was working on the second edition of mine.

There are also plenty of those in Putin's Russia for whom she is a hate figure. She has always been a favourite target of the Revolution's enemies, with their hatred and pornographisation of the women who fought for it, and her writings have been mocked as Party hackwork and something of a joke. I hope our translations of these masterpieces of the Revolution give some idea of their power and beauty.

As protests explode across the globe against the crimes of capitalism, and journalists are silenced and tortured for publishing the truth, her message of hope and solidarity reminds us that a world without capitalism is possible, and the fight for this new world was the story of her life and writings. 'The one theme of her works is the October Revolution', Radek wrote, 'and as long as people struggle, think and feel, and are drawn to find out "what it was like", they will read her books, and won't put them down until they reach the last page, for they have the smell of revolution on their breath'.

Cathy Porter

The Front

∵

The Front

Published in the journal *Krasnaya Nov* (Red Virgin Soil), Moscow, 1924.

Author's Preface

There are buildings in Moscow and Petrograd where young people from workers and peasants' families are studying to enter the universities. They live in cramped communal flats, and unlike students in the past, striding along the spacious sunny corridors to their lectures, they study in the damp shabby classrooms of our new workers' colleges, the *rabfaks*.

These students, our future statesmen and judges, scientists, writers and professors, keeping 'Left, Left, Left' all the time, must in a few short years not only assimilate the old culture, but shape all its most positive and valuable features into new ideological forms.

The Revolution has devoured its professional revolutionaries. Before long there will be almost no one left from the assault columns of Great October, who fought to defend Petrograd and Kazan, Siberia and the Far East, Perekop and the Caspian desert. Our new proletarian culture, our glorious future, will be made not by these fighters for the Revolution, but by the new generation in the *rabfaks*, hungry for knowledge, working by day and studying at night, selling their last pair of shoes to buy the works of Lenin and Marx.

You children of the proletariat are brave principled people, who have fearlessly rejected the mystical consolations of bourgeois aesthetics. Say the word 'Beauty' at the *rabfaks*, and they'll jeer. 'Creativity' and 'Feelings', and they'll bang the desks and leave. That's natural. If we see such things now as mere 'bourgeois sentimentality', it's because they were beaten out of us in the hungry typhus-ridden years of the Civil War.

But beware you don't deny the truth of those years, and fall into the old bourgeois trap that has survived them so successfully. Our refined *Apollo* aesthetes and literature-lovers, repelled by the Revolution in its naked glory, hold their noses at such vulgar words as 'heroism', 'sacrifice' and 'brotherhood'. But what if we have experienced these cruel beautiful things, and can find a way to write about them – how much others can sip from the spoon!

For two years, twenty thousand Kronstadt and Baltic Sea sailors and their flotilla of warships, tugs and armoured barges sailed thousands of miles, from the Baltic Sea to the Persian border. In those years they went through the fire, ate bread with straw, rotted with fever on dirty beds in lice-ridden hospitals, fought with old artillery and aeroplanes that fell to bits from bad fuel. And yet they finally defeated the enemy, three times stronger than they were. Don't we need to find new words for this? A new language to defeat the native cowardice of our soft human flesh, so easily torn by any rusty nail? To see beyond the blood and filth, beyond the terrible social welfare offices, where the wife of the flag-officer on the battleship the *Karl Liebknecht* weeps with fear that he will be blown up tomorrow, and even the rubber boots he is given were pulled off a dead man.

The blood runs out quickly and is gone. Without the soothing lies of God and religion, does dying mean simply saying 'my boots are yours', and passing on? Isn't there beauty too, when the commander of a battleship, fired at from a White ambush, shouts to his panicking sailors on the bridge, 'In the name of the Workers' Republic, quick fire from the stern!', and they unglue their stomachs from the sides and run to their guns?

There was creativity too, not the bourgeoisie's, but ours. Our Flotilla had to blow up some enemy warships supplied by the British, who magnificently armed the White Fleet, and a communist engineer named Brzezinsky discovered that you could pack a row of explosives under the keel of an ordinary fishing-boat, and arm a whole squadron of them. Needless to say, people volunteered for the desperately dangerous task of laying them, and they failed only because they were betrayed by a fisherman working for the enemy. The old communist Comrade Popov was shot. Sailors no longer saw him on board the battleship the *Intrepid*, in his long frock-coat and white puttees, accompanied to his meetings with the commanders by his cheerful little Pomeranian dog. And he died a hero, refusing to talk under torture. Is there a revolutionary psychology or not?

This book is dedicated to the *rabfaks*. Let them curse it. Let heretical words like 'they loved' and 'they died beautifully' stick in their throats. But let them read how it was from Kazan to Anzali, about the victories and defeats on the Volga, the Kama and the Caspian Sea, in the years of the Great Russian Revolution.

Kazan

The town has already fallen. There's nothing worse than retreat. At our staff headquarters in the Siberian Guesthouse, doors slam on empty rooms littered with abandoned papers and possessions, and people who haven't been seen for months appear in the corridors, furtively wearing their tsarist medals and cockades, not daring yet to shout their rabid 'Kill them!'

Women say goodbye to loved ones in doorways hung with their now useless signs saying 'Operations' and 'Secretariat', while behind them the servants sweep out the revolutionary filth. All the bitterness of our defeat is there, as the dust flies up from the doormats and they bang their brooms, throwing our still warm traces from the rooms.

The lines of the Whites' artillery are visible in the distance, the porch is packed with tense dusty faces. Shouts go up as our cavalry clatter along the road, and trucks full of soldiers roar past, shaking the windows. Our final resistance has begun, but their flight kills our last hope. And when the first shells hit the muddy paddock beside the Kremlin, then the guesthouse, containing the *Flotkom* and those who will be the last to go, by which time there will be nowhere for them to go, we know all is lost.

As the shells shatter the crumbling cornices of the building, we leave without looking back, trying not to think of the sweeping servants, or the terrible washed-out road our armoured car must pass, or won't pass.

Under my coat I'm carrying some top-secret documents and a small mobile printing-press, which I have to deliver to the first Red patrols we meet. It's a strange feeling, passing houses with their locked doors and windows, knowing that our comrades in the cursed Siberian Guesthouse will fight to the last drop of their blood. Some will be captured and killed, some will survive. All words are forgotten, all the formulae that help us keep our presence of mind, leaving only a sharp cutting grief, and a vague 'in the name of' something, which makes us leave or stay. Fighting back the tears, the head repeats that we must retreat calmly, without humiliating haste or panic.

Escaping with us are families and children. A woman ahead of us has a baby dangling from her arms, and a frightened goat on a string. Pouring across the golden summer fields is a flood of poverty – soldiers and families, carts laden with pots and pans and winter coats. I remember it felt safer with this living mass. Who were they? Communists? Hardly. I doubt the woman with the baby and goat had a Party card. At each clap of gunfire, each gust of fear in the crowd, she crossed herself to all the belfries. She was simply the people, escaping from the Czech liberators.

Outside the town, the wave of refugees thinned. The carts and women and children continued straight ahead, as if driven by some mass instinct. Single people turned down the side roads and cut across the ploughed fields, walking without coats or hats under showers of rain, falling in the slippery mud and picking themselves up again.

The showers became a downpour, and the fields turned to black clay. A heavy blue cloud hung over Kazan, already captured. The sounds of gunshots stopped, and there were distant flashes of lightning. A flock of crows stretched to the horizon.

I don't remember now how many we were, stumbling through the mud that stopped our every step, only that we were heading for what we hoped was the little railway town of Svyazhsk. All senses were sharpened, especially in those first hours. Everything relied on some animal sense that made us choose the right road, the right village, rather than two others. A barking dog, the glance of a passer-by, the silhouette of a tree – everything took on the colour of danger, or a calm 'it's safe'.

Walking at the front, clutching his briefcase, was our Party official, bare-headed, in his soaked ridiculously smart jacket. After the last desperate nights in the town, he longed only to lie down and sleep, and he saw and understood few of the secret signs of our shared journey. Our guide was a small one-eyed sailor named Mishka, who strode firmly across the mud on his bow legs, and the rain didn't stop him seeing with his one cheerful blue eye, and we felt safe with him.

After an argument with Comrade Briefcase, who was for keeping straight ahead, driven on by exhaustion and the rain, he took us sharp left, on a five-mile detour around a village to the highway, glinting in the darkness, then confidently led us to the next village, where he knocked at the door of a dark farmhouse, and told us to 'make fast'. We happily pulled off our wet boots and fell asleep on the floor. The hay, the human warmth, the icon lamp in the corner, and like a dream, soothing away all painful thoughts, a small piece of warm black bread.

When we woke next morning, the room was crowded with refugees from Kazan. The Whites' arrests and executions had already started, and people were escaping as best they could. Comrade Briefcase, with the naivety of a true intellectual, had decided to improve his already impenetrable incognito by putting on a worker's cloth cap, which made him look like an escaped criminal.

Our host was the village schoolmaster. He badly wanted to take the conqueror's tone with us, but there were so many of the conquered, with such a dejected appearance, he merely confined himself to a few mild admonitions. And he was a good man, who fed us all for free, then showed us the path to Svyazhsk, angrily waving his arms as he argued with us about the Constituent Assembly. And that path saved our life. There were ambushes on the main road, which most of the rest of the crowd had taken.

Why Svyazhsk? The name of this little station on the shores of the Volga, which would later play such a vital role in the recapture of Kazan, is remembered now as something elemental, the furnace in which the nucleus of the Red Army was forged in the heat of the retreat. I don't know if our commanders had identified it as the base from which the army would consolidate its power, or its name had simply been thrown into the escaping crowds, but it was there that the flood of refugees was heading.

Civil war rules on the main roads. Turn onto the cart tracks, through the sweet-smelling meadows marking the boundaries between the villages, and there is peace, the transparent silence of late summer. We walked barefoot, carrying our bread and boots on sticks on our shoulders. Mishka found a long shepherd's crook, and kept flicking it behind Briefcase's back, making him jump with fear. No, it must be said Comrade Briefcase wasn't much of a hero. We avoided the villages, apart from those occupied by the Old Believers,[1] where the milk was as thick as in the heavenly kingdom, and the women were as sweet as honey. Not once did the Old Believers betray us or leave us hungry. But on the third day we were almost caught. Briefcase was exhausted and had hurt his leg, and our sailor comrades were so sick of choking on dust like landlubbers that Mishka finally gave in to their grumbling.

After a brief reconnaissance, he led us to the nearest village, and at first all went well. A cool porch, hot tea, cucumbers and hard-boiled eggs, and a grey indifferent host. We were just thanking our good luck, when we had a visitor, wearing a tight high-waisted blue caftan tied with a red sash, with a bushy black beard 'a la russe' – a fighting landowner, or the village constable.

Our host became even greyer, and cast sidelong glances at him as he peered inquisitively at Mishka and Briefcase, and the sailors politely drinking tea. Then he said, 'So they chased you out of Kazan then?'

Mishka quickly answered for us. 'Oh no, we're holiday-makers looking for a nice dacha with a view of the river and all conveniences. Can you recommend one?' Our guide had the wild unshaven appearance of a true Southerner, dark, cheerful and desperate.

---

1 Old Believers, anathemised in the seventeenth century as 'schismatics' for continuing the old liturgical practices of the Orthodox Church after the reforms of the Patriarch Nikon, forced to settle in remote rural areas of Russia to escape arrest and persecution.

'You can't fool me!' the man guffawed. 'I bet this one had to grab his briefcase in a hurry! You're one of us, aren't you?' he winked at Comrade B. with an eye like a ball of fat.

Mishka decided to call his bluff, and rattled off a list of orders to the Red Army – 'and for God's sake send more 12-inch rifles and high-velocity shrapnel from Kronstadt without delay!'

Having thoroughly confused the man, he stared intently at us, tilted his head slightly in the direction of the open steppe, where the shadows of riders were visible in the far distance, their lances like dark needles against the sky, then headed briskly for the door, and all of us, with Briefcase in the lead, dashed off at speed into the garden and across the fields.

We spent the rest of the day dozing under the golden haystacks not far from the road. Groups of Cossacks rode past, and the other Misha, Comrade Ipodi, kept having to nudge Briefcase awake to stop him snoring and giving us away.

A dark village on a stormy night. Lightning streaked across the sky, carts rumbled past, horses whinnied with fear. Lights flashed in the darkness, and a convoy heading for Svyazhsk stopped and inspected us with torches, and we recognised the surviving members of one of our unit's Political Department. I handed over the printing-press and papers, and we continued on our way with them.

All night the convoy dragged along the washed-out track under the endless rain. A horse became trapped in the mud, and the order passed down the line for the carts to stop. The flickering torches, the squelching footsteps, the heavy breathing of the trapped horse, then we were moving again. The rain whipped our faces, the forest creaked in the wind, and flashes of lightning revealed glimpses of white exhausted faces, and the shuddering sides of the horses, wet from the storm. Then darkness again.

Next morning was like all mornings of retreat. Blistered feet, some snatched sleep under a wet haystack, the sailors' jokes at the back of our field kitchen, where everyone took turns to smoke and relax. Comrade Sheimann's wife floated silently across the dead fields, her face wrapped in a white shawl, hearing and seeing nothing. She had had no news of her husband, and her fears were overwhelming her, and her silent certainty was unbearable to us.

Late that night, we reached a railway-station on the Volga, where we immediately fell asleep on the cold floor of a goods train. Two days lost on the wet empty tracks. Then the screech of wheels and the longed-for jolt, and we were in Svyazhsk.

Crowds of people packed the offices of the Revolutionary War Council, shouting, jostling, demanding information. Sheimann's bloodless face floated past. She had learnt that her husband had been killed in Kazan. With no news of our other comrades, Misha Ipodi and I volunteered to return there and reconnoitre behind enemy lines.

Comrade Bakinsky wrote passes for us on cigarette papers to get us past our patrols, and told us to go to the commanders of the Latvian Rifles for horses. 'You can ride to the outskirts of Kazan and walk the rest of the way', he said. And the Latvians did help us. They found us army greatcoats, boots and trousers, and brought us two horses. But heavens, how was I to ride this enormous animal? What was I to do with my boots, to which someone had thoughtfully screwed enormous spurs? We set off at a walk. Then we began to trot, and it was agony, and we had twenty more miles to go.

But my first meeting with the chestnut stallion Beauty was the start of a tender friendship between us that would last for the next three years. We had left the Volga far behind, and had reached the railway-line at the edge of the forest, when suddenly he shied. I cracked the whip, but he looked back at me with burning eyes and trembling ears, and refused to move. The cavalrymen escorting us rode up and laughed. Then in front of our noses three bolts shot past, one after the other, three dusty red explosions, three deaths.

We rode back into the forest, past wounded trees standing stiff and silent as if condemned, and came across a group of our soldiers in a clearing, eating around a damped-down fire. Their soup cans steamed in the damp grass, and the smell of boiled cabbage mingled with the fresh forest smells of resin and wild strawberries. After questioning us in a whisper and checking our papers, they invited us to share their soup with them. It tasted ridiculously good.

A few miles away in the next village, an artilleryman was plotting our position, with the aid of the numbers on his map and his wise animal instinct. The trees rooted themselves in the ground and gathered their strength. A forest bird warbled timidly, then stopped. The soldiers put down their soup and listened. One caught an ant in his spoon and watched it scuttle off in the silence. A minute later a shell howled over our heads into the depths of the forest, smashing chips of bark from a nearby tree. It hadn't hit us and we relaxed, and the spoons were back in the soup again.

Shells thundered in the distance as we rode on through the dying enchanted forest, and arrived at a small railway station. A sickening empty place. Dead horses lay on the tracks, with a few carriages arranged in twos and threes at a distance from each other, like a game of grandmother's footsteps.

Next to the station was a row of abandoned dachas, and in the largest of these was the staff headquarters of the Red Latvian Rifles. A few hours later, it would be blown up by the Whites' artillery, killing one of our finest command-ers, Comrade Yudin. But Yudin was still alive then, and we spent the last hours of his life with him, pulsing like a bursting vein.

After checking our papers and putting them on the table, he gave orders for us to be fed and given beds in the next room. And as we rested and drank tea, we could hear him on the phone to the Revolutionary War Council in Svyazhsk: 'You know a Leizner? Yes, Leizner ... You gave her a pass? Good, we just wondered ...'.

Someone visiting the bank on business always feels like a thief. The barred windows, the immaculate account books and gleaming safes – all this polite-ness behind clicking locks instantly induces a sense of guilt. And when Com-rade Yudin called Svyazhsk, I realised how suspicious I must seem. And my god, my accent! 'I'm going to Kazan on secret business', I'd said loudly. I must obvi-ously be a spy.

It was dusk when Yudin returned to our room. His face was invisible in the darkness, but his whole figure in his baggy riding britches, his hands calmly in his pockets, radiated friendliness, and after questioning us about our route, he encouraged us to continue, since we were clearly set on this insane jour-ney.

I was gloomily inspecting my enormous boots and trousers, when I saw that the Ukrainian soldier who had brought us our tea was interested in them too. 'Madame Comrade, why don't we swap?' he said. 'You give me your uniform, and I'll give you a proper lady's outfit with frills and feathers'. He then went up to the attic and brought down some gold-braided courtier's trousers, a chic pink Parisian corset, a suit for Misha, and to my joy, a nice dark dress. A soldier put on the corset, the courtier's trousers were soon on the proud backside of the messenger-boy, and Misha and I left this fancy dress party as a respectable bourgeois couple. 'Good luck, till we meet again', Yudin said, shaking our hands, secretly convinced we wouldn't come out of the forest alive, while death stood behind his back, mocking him in the darkness.

Thanks to our convincing disguises, we were arrested at the first Red patrol we came to, despite knowing all the passwords and having the correct papers, and a furious Misha was escorted back to our headquarters. It was midnight before he returned, and the sentry gave us some good advice as we set off. 'Stay in the trees, away from the railway tracks. They shine at night, you'll be spotted immediately'.

We walked along the silent forest paths in the pitch blackness. After a few hours, two riders approached. At first we were wary of them, but they turned out to be our cavalry scouts, and we exchanged greetings. Warmed by this human contact, we walked on. The forest washed tiredness over us like a black lake. I remember the stars, the fears of having no home, no bed, no tomorrow – all the usual fears of city people far from the main roads.

We were approaching the first settlement when we heard piercing screams from the bath house. We knocked on the door and were invited in, where a young Kirghiz woman was in labour on the floor. She had been there for three days, but new faces and the touch of unknown hands soothed her nerves and encouraged her will to live, and an hour later, with a terrible shudder, the baby was born. She immediately grew calm, murmuring some words in her language through her wet hair, then fell asleep, still gripping my hand with her dry bird-like fingers.

Next morning, the baby was christened in church, wrapped in my silk petti-coat, blessed by various heathen gods assembled for the occasion. The christen-ing held us up for a day, and the priest clearly sensed a dangerous devilish power in the newly arrived godparents. But the happy father gratefully insisted on driving us in his cart to Kazan. 'I wasn't born yesterday, I can see you're good people, thank god!' he said.

'And what will you say if we're stopped?' we asked him.

'I'll say I'm taking the master and his wife home from holiday. Everyone knows me around here, they'll believe me'.

We set off through the forest. The wheels of the cart sank into the wet grass, and the air was sweet with resin and damp with dew. Only the tapping of the woodpeckers and the distant rumble of gunfire broke the silence. Ahead lay Kazan.

Russia's provincial towns are torn and ugly, identical as stale spicecakes, and White Kazan shines with special ugliness, with its watermelons and dusty wooden fences and its terrible churned-up roads, pitted by shells. But not one patrol stopped us, and we drove into the Admiralty Quarter unable to believe our luck, although the town's undeniable ugliness forced us to accept that this wasn't a dream, but the insanity of new White Guard Kazan.

'Where are you taking us?' we asked our driver.

Flicking the horse's plump back with his reins, he turned round with a crafty smile. 'To the District Superintendent's house. He's an old pal of mine, he runs things around here. You need somewhere safe, and you'll be safe with him!'

Misha and I exchanged looks. The District Superintendent! We had no idea what our friend had in mind for us.

The cart turned into a wide dusty street lined with rows of wooden houses, with chickens in the yards and creaking gates, and closed sleeping green and white shutters. Wispy clouds drifted over the pale blue sky, like the steam from an after-dinner samovar. A little piece of merchant heaven, like Gorky's Okurov Town, depicted in the bright folk colours of the painter Kustodiev.

Our enterprising driver stopped his cart outside the largest of the houses, kissed us goodbye, and patriotically delivered us into the hands of the Superintendent, who had appeared on the porch to greet us.

Misha and I then fell into our roles as an officer and his wife in this private theatre of the absurd. The main part of the Superintendent's house was the setting for a comedy of merchant manners, with its geraniums at the windows, its freshly waxed floors and icons in the corners, and its framed photographs of members of the local court on the writing desk. Amongst the stiff collars and old-fashioned frock-coats, it wasn't hard to spot our host, with his bulging eyes and flat forehead covered in flies.

Appropriately for a fair-minded, even-handed prosecutor of people, he had a spiteful screeching wife, with her hair scraped back over her smooth skull. Their plump pink daughter, Pasha, spent her days resting her large bosom on the low windowsill, looking out at the street, spitting sunflower seeds at the rare passers-by. The happy heiress didn't bother her head with politics, just wrinkled her button nose when her mother had one of her ugly hysterical scenes with the tenants in the basement, saying 'Please Mama, not so loud, how coarse you are!'

Huddled beneath the Superintendent's waxed floors and geraniums lived seventeen workers' families. The Revolution had temporarily disturbed relations between those on the upper and lower storeys, and the Superintendent's roots, patriarchally drawing their nourishment from the basement, had suffered several nips and blows that had even threatened Pasha's dowry. The last straw was when one of the lodgers expropriated her fluffy white goat for his children to play with.

Then in July, God intervened in these sordid human affairs. Order and justice jumped out of their frames and shook the dead pages of the law, and Pashenka at her post at the window wasn't shocked or distressed to see the unruly lodger being led away, never to be seen again. After that, everything returned to normal. The new authorities threw cartloads of workers' bodies in the Volga, and the Superintendent's family happily licked their lips and sucked up the grief of the basement, where people dared not weep or make a sound.

It was as God and the Bolsheviks were going at it tooth and nail that we moved in with the Superintendent. At first he bristled, like a hedgehog caught snacking on a live frog in broad daylight, starting his tasty treat from long habit with its shuddering hind legs. But after drinking tea with us and cursing the Jews and Bolsheviks, he seemed satisfied with our politics, and accepted us as his lodgers. Then he went off to town to celebrate at the Whites' headquarters by reporting another worker from the basement.

Everyone was drinking tea that evening when the police came for him. Mama listened happily to the commotion below, and Papa delivered a long speech about how regrettable it was, but that as an officer and Christian he couldn't have criminals in his house. If only he could have seen the poison he was spreading over our souls.

Pasha in her pink muslin dress, her soul fluttering in a cloudless sky full of paper doves and forget-me-nots, poured a sixth cup of tea for their neighbour the schoolmaster, known by all in the basement as 'the fiancé', a title filled with unutterable contempt for his scrawny beard and spectacles and intellectual demeanour. As sobs rose from the basement, Mama laughed like butter in a frying pan, Papa peered regally over the pages of the *New Times* for 1911, and the schoolmaster tenderly explained to Pasha about the Constituent Assembly.

Early next morning, Misha went off to reconnoitre in town, taking all our money and papers with him. The Superintendent left on patrol, searching workers for weapons. Mama went down to the basement to feast on the dregs of its grief, like curdling milk in the darkness. Pasha curled up with her novel about the handsome Raoul. I scanned the newspaper for the names of our comrades who had been killed, but saw none I recognised. Fat black flies buzzed at the windows, and the room sank into a stupor. Thus in their different ways the residents passed the time.

Then suddenly, at about two in the afternoon, the calm was broken by a series of muffled explosions, significantly closer than before, ripping the merchants' satin sky with the mourning bands of shrapnel smoke. A heavy silence followed. The street emptied, and people in the basement stopped weeping and whispering and waited. The Superintendent came home flustered, and was describing at length over dinner the results of his search, when the first iron nuts exploded over the roof. Pasha and Mama jumped up in fright, but he calmed them with another interminable speech, and the thistles sat up straight again and raised their bristling heads.

As an 'officer's wife', I had to reassure my hosts of the Reds' weakness. 'What sort of men are they? They're cowards, common rabble, they'll run off at the first shot!'

'You're so right, Madame', the Superintendent said.

Boom! Another shell crashed over our heads, and my heart did a mad happy dance for our red devils. Leaving his lofty strategic considerations for another time, the Superintendent put on an extra pair of trousers, and disappeared with his family and the goat into the bath house.

It was then that I first met the residents of the basement. They were standing at the top of the stairs, men, children, women with babies, resting their heads against the low doorpost, gazing at the barrage in the sky and at the door of the bath house, from which came the frightened bleating of the goat. We understood each other without words. The wife of the worker arrested last night asked me my name in a whisper. 'Your husband escaped, it said in the paper, you mustn't stay here!' She moved her baby, struggling to reach the brown nipple on her thin breast, and listened to the bombardment outside. 'Do you think they've shot mine already? What if the Reds don't come and free him ...?' Then not waiting for an answer, for she already knew it, as dark and hopeless as the basement, she became lost to everything but the symphony of explosions shaking the house.

They came closer, in long volleys, confidently covering the quieter bursts of the Whites' rapid answering fire. Then from somewhere across the river came new gulps of metal, at first intermittently, then with an ominous regularity. Were they ours or theirs? Alas, there was no mistaking the sound. They weren't firing at Kazan, but at our troops. The storm raged in the sunny sky for another hour, then moved away. The shells exploded less frequently, and finally fell silent. And from far in the distance, neither receding nor advancing, like the echo of ocean breakers, came the sounds of gunfire.

For two or three hours, maybe longer, my friend rested her head on the doorpost, without moving or saying a word. Then finally she lifted her face, smeared with dust and tears and defeat, picked her sleeping baby from the step, and returned to the basement.

A word in the Superintendent's ear might have saved some of these families from the White Terror. But needless to say, none of them would have considered such a thing.

Misha didn't return that night or the next morning, and I had no money or papers. The Superintendent questioned me closely about my 'husband', and I convinced him that as an officer he must have been mobilised, and he advised me to visit the Whites' headquarters in town for information.

The streets were the same, but it was hard to recognise them. It was only a week since our retreat, but it was as if ten years had passed. Everything was different – the officers, the ladies from educated families in nurses' uniforms, the open shops, the rollicking hysterical gaiety of the cafes – the whole tawdry transient rash on the body of the defeated Revolution.

In the suburbs, the tram stopped to let a cart through, loaded with the naked bodies of dead workers, their arms and legs dangling over the sides like branches. The cart clattered slowly past a fence plastered with placards saying 'All Power to the Constituent Assembly'. Little did those who put this constitutional lie there know that such images would soon be appearing on our revolutionary posters.

It wasn't hard to get a pass to the Whites' headquarters on Gruzinskaya Street. The doors to the offices were patrolled by *gimnazium* schoolboys of fifteen or sixteen, and scurrying round were officers who a week ago had been working for the Revolutionary War Council. The whole provincial intelligentsia was stirring, kitted out in smart cavalry britches and spurs, throwing itself into this sea of amateur government business, with its amateur Red Cross, amateur espionage, and amateur sacrifice at the altar of the Fatherland.

How good the White regime is on the third day of its creation! What sweet intelligent faces the typists have, tapping away cheerfully on their Remingtons. Two smartly uniformed officers stand stiffly to attention at the entrance to the main office, like those who used to guard the Imperial bedchamber. Through these doors appear if not generals, then at least captains or majors, with their unbuttoned service jackets, luxurious whiskers and dazzling white shirts. And modestly blending in with all this military business, gilding the spurs and epaulettes with their brilliance, the occasional teacher or academic. How flirtatiously they flash their university badges! On my second visit I saw a well-known professor, with the thick grey hair and soft-brimmed hat fashionable among learned lovers of the 'sensitive radical young', gabbling in a low voice to a disdainful Junker about 'unreliable elements' in his neighbourhood.

I made two more visits to Gruzinskaya Street over the next two days, and a sympathetic secretary gave me the names of some of our comrades who had escaped. But having to live this lie, listening to my host's views on the Jews and the triumph of Holy Orthodoxy, was becoming unbearable, and he was growing increasingly suspicious. My friends in the basement warned me I must escape before it was too late, and on the third morning I prepared to leave, never to return.

Hiding my pass in a crust of bread in my pocket, I headed for the front door, where a woman from the basement pushed a three-rouble note into my hand. But at the gate I was stopped by the Superintendent.

'May I ask where you're off to at this time of day, dear lady?' he said.

'To our headquarters, they promised me definite information this morning', I said.

'You must let me accompany you then. I can offer you protection, as it were'.

'Please don't bother, I can manage on my own', I said.

But the harder I tried to shake him off, the more he clung to me, like a fly to fly-paper. 'I wouldn't dream of abandoning you. Surely you won't deprive an old man of the pleasure of escorting you?'

Immediately we arrived, an efficient secretary appeared out of nowhere and led us upstairs, past crowds of petitioners and staring typists, followed by the flashing steel of a soldier's bayonet. My gallant escort left me in the waiting-room, crowded with prisoners, relatives and guards, then hurried next door to report me to Lieutenant Ivanov – the 'Mademoiselle Fifi' of White Kazan, famous for beating railway workers on the soles of their feet 'for the Revolution'.

Looking round, I saw a group of our sailors. Like all sailors, they embodied all the drama and heroism of Great October, with their strong bare necks and sunburnt faces, and their caps saying *Comrade Andrei, Sevastopol,* or simply the *Red Fleet.* Their boatswain turned and looked deep into my eyes, revealing his naked soul and his powerful chest, which in a few moments would be turned to the wall – with a cross hanging from a bootlace, not for God, but for good luck.

The pulse beat for two, three, I don't know how many seconds. But his eyes no longer appealed for help, and were covered in something grey, like the tarpaulin on guns in bad weather. Rifle butts clicked, and the sailors were led away. At the door he stopped and turned back. Goodbye, said his eyes. The room spun, and I heard a splash of water, and the surging rush of the sea on a windy day, sharp, silvery and angry.

Then it was my turn. Sitting at a green baize table in his white tunic was Ivanov, with his clean white hands and pale eyebrowless eyes and shaved head, white as a boiled egg. Next to him sat a French officer. I don't remember his name, just something cold and sneering about him, not missing a thing, so he could turn it all into a good story later for his fellow officers. Opposite them sat the stenographer, with his straight parting and fountain pen, fixing a flourishing tail to my name at the top of the page.

'Age? Social class? Occupation?'

Ivanov smiled a broad genial smile at my answers. Then suddenly this man with his carefully timed pauses, like a well-fed cat playing with a superfluous mouse, exchanging winks with the French officer at my underwear, removed from me during my preliminary interrogation and folded neatly beside his inkwell – suddenly this urbane witty interrogator smashed his fist on the table, and roared, 'You piece of sh*t, I'll make you sing, bitch!' Then turning to the Frenchman, who had been discreetly sitting in on this fatherly interview, he said rudely 'Go downstairs, I'll call you if I need you'. The man hurried to the door, lashing me and his colleague and ally with a look of contempt, and Ivanov continued in his soft voice with his soft lying smile. Then he said, 'Just a moment, we'll need a prosecutor before we continue'.

The room had three doors. The one he went through with the stenographer was on the left. The one on the right, guarded by a sentry, led into the waiting-room. The middle one was the winter door, tacked with felt and bolted firmly shut.

There are moments of mad magical happiness in life, and on that grey morning, glimpsed through the hopeless bars of the window, I experienced a miracle. As soon as Ivanov left, the sentry, exhausted by his habit of switching from mocking courtesy to animal shrieks, opened his door to calm his nerves outside with a smoke. Only the butt of his rifle and the hem of his coat were in the room. How many seconds would it take him to finish his cigarette?

I dashed to the locked middle door, ripped the tacks off the felt and pushed the bolt with all my strength, and finally it swung open, and I found myself on a back staircase. Quietly bolting the door behind me, I ran down to the street. At the window of Ivanov's office, I could see the sentry standing with his back to the street, smoking and swatting flies.

A cab drove up at a brisk trot, and I climbed in. 'Where to?' said the bearded driver. I tried to speak, but couldn't get the words out. He looked back at my bloody face and torn clothes, and at the Whites' headquarters. Then rising to his full height on his seat, he whipped his grey mare into a gallop, and we thundered along Kazan's terrible roads, past dusty alleyways and courtyards and back streets, to the gates of his building.

His son was fighting with the Bolsheviks, and his wife was the wonderful Avdotya Markovna, red and white and three girths wide, warm as an oven, kind as the sun on her village shawl. Taking it off to cover my bare shoulders, she took me in her arms, and I howled like a piglet on her boundless motherly breast, and she howled too, and said some special tender words to me, comforting as warm buns fresh from the oven. 'Come dear, let's drink tea', she said, then she listened to my story from beginning to end, and cursed Ivanov so roundly that the roosters scratching the sun-warmed dung in the yard crowed with joy.

Two hours later, wrapped in her shawl, with the three rubles and a pound of bread in my pocket, I left the gates of Kazan. I had no trouble getting through the first White patrol, which was busy inspecting a cart, and avoided the next one by slipping through some bushes. The peasant who stopped to drive me to the next village also saved me that day, the happiest day of my life. After we had trotted along in silence for a few miles, he said in the same voice as that of the cab driver and Avdotya Markovna and all the poor in Russia who were unquestionably on our side in those first days of the Revolution, with its retreats and defeats, who helped thousands of comrades scattered on its wide roads to survive: 'Time to get out now, girl. Enough pretending, I know what you are. Go to the village on the left, your people are there. That black cloud on the right is the Czech cavalry'.

After running a mile across the fields, I finally caught up with our front line, and was greeted by an officer from Comrade Yudin's staff. Tactfully pretending not to notice my distress, he sat beside me on the ploughed earth and rolled a cigarette. 'So what happened to that "husband" of yours?' he said.

Svyazhsk

Whenever two comrades get together who fought the Czechs in 1918 outside Kazan, and went on to fight in Tsaritsyn, Samara and the Urals, one of them is bound to say 'Remember Svyazhsk?', and they'll clasp each other's hands again especially warmly.

Why Svyazhsk? It's one of our revolutionary legends, still unchronicled, but told again and again, from one end of vast Russia to the other. Every old Bolshevik and soldier from the first units of the Workers' and Peasants' Army, returning home after the three years of the Civil War, will recall the glorious epic of Svyazhsk, the key to central Russia, the crossroads from which the tide of the revolutionary offensive began to roll in all directions – in the east, towards the Urals, in the north, towards Arkhangelsk and Poland, in the south, towards the Caucasus, the shores of the Caspian and the Persian border. Not all at once, of course. But it was only after Svyazhsk and Kazan that the Red Army was fused into the political fighting force whose methods, with various modifications, are now studied in every military academy of the Socialist Republic.

On 6 August, when the Red units hastily thrown together to fight the Whites fled from Kazan, the best and most class-conscious of them were drawn to Svyazhsk, the nearest railway station on the Volga. And there they decided to take a stand and fight. By the time the deserters from Kazan were almost at Nizhny Novgorod, the dam erected at Svyazhsk had already stopped the advancing Czechs, and their commander, Major Blagotic, who tried to take the railway-bridge over the Volga in a night attack, was ambushed and killed. Thus in this very first clash between the Whites, who had just taken Kazan, and were consequently stronger in weapons and morale, and the nucleus of the new Red Army, fighting to defend the bridgehead over the river, the head of the Czechs' offensive was chopped off, and in Blagotic the Czechs lost their most popular and gifted commander.

Neither the Whites, flushed from their victory in Kazan, nor the Reds, rallying around Svyazhsk, had any idea of the historic importance these first skirmishes would have.

It's hard now to convey the military importance of Svyazhsk without a map, or the testimonies of comrades who fought in the ranks of the Fifth Army. Much has already been forgotten, names and faces flash past in a fog. But what no one will ever forget was our feeling of supreme responsibility for holding Svyazhsk. This was what united all of its defenders, from members of the Revolutionary

War Council to the last Red soldier, desperately searching for his lost regiment, who turned back to fight to the last, with his worn-out rifle in his hands, and an iron determination in his soul. Everyone knew that a step back would have opened the Volga down to Nizhny Novgorod, allowing the enemy an unobstructed path to Moscow. Retreat would have meant the beginning of the end, the death sentence on the Republic of the Soviets.

How correct this was strategically, I don't know. Maybe if our army had been pushed back even further, it might have joined up at another of the innumerable black dots on the map, from which to carry its banners to victory. But it was unquestionably correct from the viewpoint of morale. Retreat wasn't an option. We had to hold out with our backs to the bridge, and knowing that the fate of the Revolution was being decided there filled us with an extraordinary sense of hope. The complexities of the situation could be summarised thus: no retreat from the Volga, no surrender of Svyazhsk or the bridge, which the Red Army had to hold if it was to recapture Kazan.

The Arrival of Trotsky's Train

Four days after the fall of Kazan, Trotsky arrived in Svyazhsk with fifty young Party activists. His train came to a stop at the station, the engine puffed a little, was uncoupled, left to drink water, and didn't return. The carriages remained on the tracks, as immovable as the peasants' thatched huts along the line, making clear that they were there to stay and wouldn't be leaving. And little by little, the fantastic faith that this godforsaken station could be the starting point for a new offensive against the Whites began to take the shape of reality.

Every day Svyazhsk held out, against an enemy vastly superior in numbers and weapons, increased its strength and confidence. Reinforcements began to arrive from villages along the Volga, at first one by one, then in small detachments, and before long new armed communist combat units were being sent to the Kazan front, in a far better state of repair.

I can see it now, this Svyazhsk where not a single soldier fought under compulsion, where everything that was alive was fighting to defend the Revolution, bound together by voluntary ties of discipline in a struggle that had seemed so hopeless at the outset. Those who slept on the station floor, in straw littered with broken glass, were afraid of nothing, and were almost past any hope of victory. No one asked when it would end. Tomorrow didn't exist. There was only a brief, hot, smoky today, and we lived for it as we live at harvest time. Morning, noon, night – each minute had to be lived through and used up to the last second. Each hour had to be reaped finely, like ripe wheat cut down to the roots. The days seemed so rich, so utterly unlike previous life. No sooner did one pass than it seemed like a miracle. And it was a miracle. Planes came and went, dropping bombs on the station. But our machine-gunners on the roofs of the carriages fired back, and the bombs failed to damage them. The sickening steady beat of the artillery comes closer then withdraws, and a soldier in a ragged army cape, civilian hat and worn out shoes, one of the defenders of Svyazhsk, takes his watch from his pocket and grins, 'At 0300 hours, or 0400, or 0620, I'm still alive. Svyazhsk is holding out. Trotsky's train is still here, with a light in the window of the Political Department. Good. Another day over'.

There were almost no medical supplies. God knows how the doctors dressed the wounds. The desperateness of our situation banished all fear and shame. Soldiers going to the field kitchen with their soup cans passed the injured and dying, lying in the open on stretchers. But death held no terrors. To lie on the ground in a wet army coat caked in mud and blood, with a face that was no longer human – it was expected every minute and was taken for granted.

True brotherhood exists in moments of dire need and danger, sacred and unrepeatable in a single lifetime. Anyone who hasn't lain on the floor at night in lice-covered rags, thinking how wonderful life is, how infinitely wonderful, has never lived! The old life was overthrown, and Russia was fighting with its bare hands for something greater than the patch of starlight visible through the broken window – for the future of humanity, and the white swans of rebirth.

Once in a century people discover a new truth, which they defend to the last drop of their blood. And mixed with these beautiful words, terrible in their beauty, is the smell of sweat, the living breath of those sleeping next to each other on the floor. No nightmares, no sentimentality. And tomorrow will be another day, and the Czech Bolshevik Comrade G. will fry eggs for the 'gang', and our *Flotkom* will put on his clean shirt, washed last night and stiff with frost. Tomorrow someone will die, knowing in their last moments that death is only one of many possibilities, not the main one at all, and that Svyazhsk still hasn't been taken, and that the message scribbled in chalk on the dirty wall of the station, 'Workers of the World Unite!', is still there.

Against the Tide

The rainy days of August came, but our thin, poorly equipped lines held out, and an enormous spider's web of telephone and telegraph wires began to operate at Svyazhsk's tiny station – this barely discernible dot on the map of Russia which the Revolution was clinging to in its hour of despair.

All Trotsky's organisational genius now became apparent. Across openly sabotaged railway-lines, he managed to get new regiments and artillery through, and everything the army needed for the resistance. This was in 1918, it should be remembered, when demobilisation from the Imperialist War was at its height, and the sight of a detachment of Red soldiers marching through the streets of Moscow would cause a sensation. It meant swimming against the tide, beating back the exhaustion of four years of war and the stormy waters of the Revolution, which was sweeping away the hated tsarist command structure like so much flotsam.

Yet against all odds, supplies arrived before our eyes – newspapers, overcoats and boots. Wherever boots are handed out for keeps, you'll find an army standing strong on its feet, with no thought of deserting. Boots are no laughing matter!

The most perilous front line of the Republic now hung on the thin thread of the railway line, blazing and setting off a conflagration that would last for the next three years of the Civil War. I remember by a miracle some letters from Moscow got through, describing the bourgeoisie's glee as they waited for Svyazhsk to fall, like the Paris Commune. Yet each of Svyazhsk's defenders without exception, even those who wavered and were afraid, performed unbelievable, heroic deeds. If the Order of the Red Banner had existed then, it would have been awarded to thousands; they outdid themselves, like spring streams overflowing their banks.

The Leaders of the Defence

In Svyazhsk, Trotsky gave his new Red Army a backbone of steel, refusing to yield an inch, inspiring its fighters with his ruthless authority and icy calm. But he wasn't alone. Gathered around him were several old Party activists from the Revolutionary War Council of the Eastern Front and the Military Councils of various armies, who future historians will describe as the Marshals of the Civil War. Comrade Lepetenko, Chief of Staff of the Red Fleet, one of the most courageous and self-sacrificing soldiers of the Revolution, whose biography could well provide this book with its best chapter. Rosengoltz and Gusev, Ivan Nikitich Smirnov, Kobozev, Mezhlauk and Raskolnikov, and the sailor Nikolai Markin, founder of the Red Fleet and one of its most outstanding heroes, and many, many other comrades whose names I no longer recall.

From the very first day, Rosengoltz set about building a communications network of the utmost simplicity and precision, with clearly defined functions. The Revolutionary War Council had its office in his carriage, with maps and telephones springing up around him, and his cables from Svyazhsk fed the propaganda throughout the country. Whenever work faltered, he would be brought in a like a queen bee to a disturbed hive, and his telegraph wires would soon be buzzing with new cells. Softly spoken, with his pale gentle face, there was something totally unmilitary about his appearance, despite his army greatcoat and the enormous pistol at his belt. The great strength he conveyed came from his quick natural ability to invigorate the sluggish bloodstream to a feverish pace. At Trotsky's side he was a dynamo, working his powerful levers day and night to forge his unbreakable apparatus.

Then there was Comrade Smirnov of the Revolutionary War Council, head of the Political Department of the Fifth Army. I don't remember now exactly what all his jobs were. But whatever his rank or title, no one commanded as much respect as Ivan Nikitich, the incarnation of the revolutionary ethic at Svyazhsk, and the highest example of its communist conscience. Even non-Party soldiers who hadn't known him before responded immediately to the exceptional warmth and purity of his personality. He probably had no idea how much he was feared, how soldiers were afraid to be seen as weak or wanting before this man who never raised his voice, and was always simply himself, calm, cheerful, modest and courageous.

Everyone knew that in the worst moments he would be the strongest, the most fearless. With Trotsky, it was the sacred demagogy of battle, to die with our last bullet gone, oblivious to our wounds, his words and gestures evoking the most heroic episodes of the great French Revolution. But with Comrade Smirnov at our side, we knew we could be calm when we were against the wall, facing interrogation by the Whites in some hell of a prison. That was how we spoke of him on the cold nights, whispering to each other as we huddled close together on the floor.

Boris Danilovich Mikhailov came a little later, straight from Moscow, as I recall. He arrived in a civilian coat, with the bright, slightly feverish expression of someone who has spent many years in a tsarist jail, and within a few hours he was intoxicated by Svyazhsk. Changing into an army uniform, he went out on patrol in the vicinity of Kazan, and came back three days later, exhausted, burnt by the wind and crawling with lice, but still in one piece. It's fascinating to see the changes people go through when they first arrive at the revolutionary front: they blaze up like a straw roof lit on all sides, and when the fire cools they have turned to steel, fireproof and indestructible.

The youngest member of Trotsky's staff was Valerian Ivanovich Mezhlauk, Secretary of the Kazan Soviet. His wife had been tortured and had suffered indescribably, and his younger brother had been shot. But there was an unspoken agreement at Svyazhsk not to discuss our personal sorrows, and

Mezhlauk kept an honourable silence, did his job, and strode through the mud in his long cavalry coat, his burning eyes fixed on the distant target of Kazan.

It was already becoming clear to the Whites that a fighting force was being assembled at Svyazhsk that would prove formidable. Intermittent skirmishes around the town soon came to an end, and a regular siege began, with large organised forces on both sides. But the enemy kept letting the moment slip. Comrade Slavin, one of our colonels, not a particularly distinguished one, but who knew his business and did it efficiently, worked out with Trotsky the key objectives of our defence, and carried them through with Latvian precision. Svyazhsk planted its feet on the ground and stood firm, lowering its broad forehead at Kazan, tossing its sharp horns like bayonets.

One of the last to leave Kazan was General Vatzetis, Commander in Chief of the Eastern Front. Two weeks before the final assault, he arrived in Svyazhsk to go over the details with Trotsky. We knew little of what was discussed, but one thing was a matter of common knowledge, and was greeted with unanimous approval: the 'Old Man', as the sailors called Trotsky, opposed Vatzetis's proposal to take Kazan from the left, eastern shore, which was flat and exposed, and convinced him that our main forces should advance from the docks in the west, closer to the centre.

The Whites Attack

Against daily counter-attacks from the Fifth Army, and heavy twenty-four-hour fighting, three leading lights of White Guard Russia, Kappel, Fortunatov and Savinkov, drew up plans to end the protracted siege of Svyazhsk. The start of the operation was a brilliant success. After an extended circling manoeuvre, Kappel's large army descended on the nearby station of Shikhrana, killing the guards, setting fire to a munitions train in a siding and blowing up the tracks, cutting the connection to Svyazhsk. Then they slaughtered everyone in the village.

A group of us visited a few hours later, and saw the ruins of what had once been a human habitation, like a Goyaesque vision of hell – the dead bodies, the blood on the roads, the trees bending under the weight of the corpses. The brutal murders of Shikhrana's small defending force and station employees almost paled into insignificance against the carnage. And that wasn't all. With the mindless pogrom savagery typical of these gentlemen who have never felt themselves to be the future citizens of Russia or its true masters, the cottages and wells and little vegetable plots had been smashed to rubble. In one courtyard, all the chickens in the chicken coop were riddled with bullets, and the mangled corpse of a cow lay with its intestines ripped out, butchered like the dead 'yids' and communists.

From Shikhrana, Savinkov's forces had then advanced along the railway track towards Svyazhsk and the Volga, and our armoured train the *Free Russia*, mounted with long-range naval guns, had been sent to intercept them. But its commander failed to rise to the task. Fearing that he was surrounded on all sides, he abandoned the train to 'report back' to the Revolutionary War Council, and the *Free Russia* was blown up while he was gone.

Its derailed hulk lay for a long time under the embankment outside Svyazhsk, and its loss left the river wide open. The Whites were now just a mile from our headquarters, and panic ensued. A few members of the Political Department rushed to the piers and boarded steamboats. The regiment holding one of the fronts further upstream deserted *en masse*, led by their commissars and commanders, and by morning the panicking crowd was invading the staff ships of the Volga Flotilla.

By then virtually the entire Fifth Army had left Svyazhsk for the offensive against Kazan. Only Trotsky and a few commanders and the staff on his train remained.

How Svyazhsk Was Saved

Lev Davydovich mobilised everyone on his train who could hold a rifle – wireless operators, office boys and medical staff, plus the sailors under Lepetenko's command. There were about five hundred in all; the enemy numbered twice that. The army's offices were deserted, the rear no longer existed. Everything was thrown into this battle with the Whites, as they advanced on Svyazhsk.

The closer they came, the greater the carnage. The entire road from Shikhrana to the first houses was ripped up by their artillery, littered with dead horses, empty shell cases and abandoned weapons. They rolled to the edge of the town, and were slowed down by the charred skeleton of our armoured train on the tracks, still smoking and smelling of molten metal. Exhausted after their forced forty-eight-hour march, they surged back like a receding wave, and found themselves facing the reservists from Svyazhsk. The battle lasted several hours, leaving scores of dead on both sides. The Whites, thinking they were up against a crack new unit their scouts had failed to spot, overestimated their strength. Little did they realise the Reds were just a handful of hastily improvised fighters, with no one but Trotsky and Slavin in command, sitting over their maps in their smoke-filled carriage with the bullets whistling past.

Throughout that night, as on all previous nights, Lev Davydovich's train stayed on the tracks. Not a single unit of the Fifth Army advancing on Kazan left to cover virtually defenceless Svyazhsk, and the Red Army and the Fleet learned of the battle only after it was over, when the Whites had retreated from what they assumed to be an entire regiment.

The following day, Trotsky ordered the deserters who had fled to the ships at the crucial moment to be arrested, and twenty-seven were shot. There was much talk of the executions afterwards, particularly far from the front, where people often had little idea how precarious was our hold on the road to Moscow, or of our desperate offensive against Kazan, undertaken with our last strength and resources.

Among those who were shot were several communists, good comrades, who had endured years of prison and exile before the Revolution, and had served the Republic honourably. And of course, it was a tragedy. But many in the army had seen communists as exempt from the law, who could desert and get away with it, while an ordinary rank and filer would be shot like a dog. For soldiers who had suffered every possible privation for six weeks, fighting practically with their bare hands, no fine speeches could justify 'extenuating circumstances' for cowardice, and if it hadn't been for Trotsky's exceptional courage, the prestige of the Party in the army and the Revolutionary War Council would have been finished for good.

All who lived the life of the Red Army then, and grew strong with it in the battles for Svyazhsk and Kazan, knew that its solidarity and iron spirit would never have been forged, the fusion between the Party and the masses, the commanders and the rank and file, would never have been achieved, if on the eve of storming Kazan, where hundreds would lose their lives, the Party failed to demonstrate clearly, before the eyes of the whole army, that it was prepared to make this great and terrible sacrifice for the Revolution: that the laws of comradely discipline were binding for communists too, and the Party had the courage to apply these laws ruthlessly to its own members.

The twenty-seven were shot, and it helped to repair the damage to the army's unity and morale. When soldiers saw communists being punished for cowardice, not just former tsarist officers and ordinary privates, it made the least class-conscious and most likely to desert pull themselves together and join those who went without compulsion into battle, knowing it wasn't only the fate of Kazan that was being decided, but the fate of the entire Revolution.

In those weeks of attack and defence, the Red Army found a new strength and confidence, and in the face of unimaginable hardships, it worked out its new laws and duties. For the first time, panic in the face of the enemy's military superiority disappeared, and from the elemental instinct of self–preservation, new methods of warfare were born.

Trotsky's Role

It's clear now that the creator of the Red Army, the future chair of the Revolutionary War Council of the Republic, would have had to have been in Svyazhsk, to have lived through all its experiences in those weeks, summoning up all his organisational genius and his inexorable will in the battles to defend it.

But there is another force in revolutionary war, without which victory is impossible, and that is the romanticism of the Revolution, which inspired people to throw themselves straight from the barricades of 1917 into the harsh discipline of the army, without losing the light step learnt from street battles and political demonstrations, or the quick thinking gained from decades of underground work.

To be victorious, all the incandescent passion of 1917 had to be harnessed to the hated patterns of the old army. Previously, commanders had tackled problems of indiscipline with moth-eaten conjuring tricks. A general on a white horse would be called to the stage to cut the blood and marrow of the revolution into republics, banners and slogans. But in military matters, as in others, the Bolsheviks came up with their own rules. War and insurrection fused into one, and the army became inseparably linked to the Party, whose banners proclaimed the unity of their goals with the sharpest slogans of the class struggle.

All this was still unformulated at Svyazhsk, still hanging in the air. No one then could see clearly what form this new army would take. The Workers' and Peasants' Army was still searching for its identity, its own slogans. There was no programme laying down how this titanic organism would evolve, just a creative premonition of this unique military revolutionary organisation, to which each new battle suggested some fresh new initiative.

Trotsky's great strength as a commander was his ability to catch in flight the slightest gesture of the masses, which contained the germ of these longed-for new formulae. He identified and set in motion hundreds of little practices that allowed besieged Svyazhsk to simplify its work in battle. And not only in narrow technical matters. Each successful new combination of the military 'specialists' and their commissars – the tsarist officers who had come over to the Revolution, and those appointed to supervise them and take responsibility for their commands – had to be tested in practice before being turned into an order, a circular or decree. And in this way, the living revolutionary experience was preserved and enshrined. It wasn't the mediocrity of compromise that was required, but the best, most creative ideas produced by the soldiers themselves in the heat of battle. In great things and small – in such complex matters as the division of labour between members of the Revolutionary War Council, or in the snappy friendly gestures of greeting between soldier and commanders, all of them busy and in a hurry – everything had to be drawn from life, and assimilated as the norm. And whenever things weren't working, and there was bungling or dawdling, it was necessary to identify what was wrong, and pull out some creative new solution, like a midwife pulling out a baby in a difficult birth.

Of course, it would have been possible to articulate the problems correctly and mould the army into a form that was ideologically flawless, yet kill its spirit by drowning it in paperwork and bureaucratic formulae. To avoid this, it was necessary to be a great revolutionary, with the intuition of a poet and the internal telegraph of the leader of a great power. Ultimately it was the revolutionary instinct that was the supreme judge, purging all lurking counterrevolutionary backsliding in the name of this higher proletarian justice, without allowing itself to atrophy or become divorced from life, or burdening soldiers with the cruel rules and regulations of the old Imperial army.

Trotsky possessed this intuitive sense. The revolutionary in him was never pushed aside by the soldier, the leader, the commander. And when a deserter was confronted with his terrible voice, he stood in fear of him, as of one of us, a great rebel who would punish anyone guilty of cowardice or treason – treason not only to the army, but to the World Proletarian Revolution. If Trotsky had been a coward, he would have been crushed by this extraordinary army, and it would never have forgiven him for the fraternal blood of the twenty-seven that anointed its first victory.

We Take Kazan

One sunny autumn morning, ten swift agile torpedo boats from the Baltic Fleet sailed down the Volga to Svyazhsk, and their arrival created a sensation. We now had the river covered. A series of battles with the White Flotilla ensued, three or four a day, covered by our floating batteries concealed along the shore, and our ships began to venture further towards Kazan.

On the night of 28 August, Trotsky and the *Flotkom* sailed for Kazan on the destroyer the *Endurance*, at the head of a squadron of gunboats in battle formation with their lights out. Slipping through the narrow entrance to the harbour, they fired at a caravan of the enemy's oil barges, which went up in flames. The Whites fired back, grazing the bows of the *Endurance* and breaking its rudder chain, and it rammed one of its own gunboats. But engineers managed to repair the damage as they sailed back to join the rest of the ships, which were pounding the Whites' forces on both sides of the river, and the squadron returned unharmed.

Two days after this, news reached Svyazhsk that Lenin had been shot as he left a factory meeting, and Lev Davydovich had to return to Moscow. But he was back a week later, having assured Lenin of the success of the Volga campaign.

Neither the Whites' attempt on Vladimir Ilich's life nor their raid on Svyazhsk could stop the Red Army and Navy now. Our forays against Kazan were crowned on 9 September, when sailors under Comrade Markin sailed to the city, docked at the western beachhead, then went ashore and disabled the Whites' artillery with their machine guns, removing the locks from the barrels.

Next day the Red Army took Kazan.

The main forces of our Flotilla had left late that night. Our bulky assortment of vessels, escorted by destroyers, sailed silently with their lights out along the cold black Volga, the waves splashing the foam from their wake in the moonlight, as they passed the Whites' artillery, hidden behind the green roof of the half-demolished mill, and the burnt hulk of their oil barge the *Dolphin*, beached on the deserted bank.

How strange it felt, following the river's familiar bends and inlets which death had stalked for so many weeks, from dawn to night. Night birds skimmed noiselessly over the water, steaming with a light mist in the cold air. Yesterday its shores were being pounded by tornadoes of shells. Destroyers had slipped through the smoke in golden sheaves of flames, their two-gun batteries firing once a minute like steel hiccups, and the sailors ducked and mopped the blood from the decks, shuddering from the impact. Now the Volga was silent, flowing on to the Caspian as it had for thousands of years, remembering nothing.

By 5.30 in the morning we had reached Kazan's harbour, and anchored without firing a shot. The first flickers of dawn appeared in the sky, and the humped shapes of shattered cranes and charred telegraph poles loomed like phantoms in the greyish pink light. The cannon on the waterfront were deserted, propping their faces in their wet hands, frozen in mute despair. Death's kingdom washed by the icy roses of the northern dawn.

Fog. We shiver from the cold and tension. The air smells of tarred ropes and machine oil, and a gunner in his blue collar gazes in wonder at the silent city. This is victory.

CHAPTER 3

From Kazan to Sarapul

The bells ringing the night watches on our staff ship the *Summer Tide* sound strangely like the bells of Petersburg's Peter and Paul Fortress. But instead of the majestically flowing Neva, they ring out over the cold choppy waters of the River Kama, with its deserted shores and islands of drowned trees.

It's dark on the bridge. The raised prows of our destroyers cut across the land-scape like wild war horses of the sea. Sparks fly from the funnels, and silent figures appear in brief flashes of light, as distinctive as in daylight, in equally distinctive poses. The signaller with his red flags, dancing their laconic cere-monial dance in the night wind. The gunner's epic movements, graceful and effortless from years of practice, sweeping the tarpaulin off the artillery in one stroke, like a dancer tearing off the sorcerer's veil. And above all our fears of the battles ahead, above the heat and smoke of the furnace blazing in the depths of the hold, above the levers on the mast that work the telegraph, rises the green morning star.

Our first ships are far ahead, beyond the bend in the river, and we sail close to the shore. A light flickers in the darkness, then disappears – the Whites, or one of Kozhevnikov's partisan detachments, stumbling through the dense river undergrowth deep in the rear.

Captain Ovchinnikov, of Commmander Azin's legendary 28th Cavalry Divi-sion, who later fought all across Russia, from the cold Kama to the deserts of Baku and Astrakhan, is calm and undemonstrative, a man of few words, all of them to the point. The burly pilot at the helm, who looks like a woodsprite, with his peasant sheepskin jerkin and long tousled grey hair, steers our ship past the river's perilous snarls and bends. 'It'll snow soon, the air smells of it', he says.

The Kama is at its most beautiful in the first light of dawn. The water outside Sarapul is deep and wide, flowing through steep yellow clay ravines, dividing between dozens of little islands, reflecting the silver outlines of the pine trees on its silky surface. Our noiseless battleships don't break the enchanted silence. A clump of ducks skim across the shallows, and a flock of swans spread their wings, pierced by the late autumn sun. Far in the distance, an eagle circles over a white church.

The leeward shore is swarming with Whites. But they aren't expecting us, and there are no shots from the bank. The main engine hatch opens, and the mechanic peers out, wiping the soot from his face, happily breathing in the sharp morning air, which has turned northern and autumnal overnight.

We have covered over fifty miles in the night, and Sarapul's lacy railway bridge appears in the distance. The crew rest and wash at the tap, and play with the two little black puppies we rescued in our last battle.

'Men on the left shore!' shouts our lookout, and there's more tense waiting on deck. But they are our infantrymen, who have recognised us and are waving red flags in the air.

The little figures in their grey army coats run along the bank, shouting friendly greetings at our advancing Flotilla, and the bridge and docks are a forest of red banners. We proceed under the bridge and turn left, and hear the Whites firing at our soldiers who have run out to welcome us. Through our field-glasses we have a clear view of the town, surrounded on all sides by the Whites, but now occupied by units of Azin's Cavalry Division, who our arrival has united with our forces downriver.

Sailing closer we see a mass of Red Army caps, peasant coats and kerchiefs, people clinging to railings, perched on barges, filling the roads and the square, and it's all so joyfully ours and so welcoming. On a slope above the harbour, a brass band strikes up the *Marseillaise*. The drummer, his eyes fixed on our ships, keeps breaking the rhythm, and the trumpeter happily skips bars ahead of the disgruntled conductor, like a bolting horse. But finally all the loose ends are tied up, and we sail smoothly to the pier.

As our sailors scatter on shore, the questions start: 'How did you get through, comrades? Did you smash them?'

'We did, mate! We gave them a good thrashing and chased them up the Belaya!'

Then a young woman pushes through the crowd, sobbing, 'The Whites took mine away when they left, they put them all on a barge! He was a sailor, just like you!'

His handkerchief, her last memory of him, wet with her tears, is passed from sailor to sailor, smoothing the rough sleeves of their jackets.

How much bestial cruelty the Whites inflicted when they retreated. Yes, war is cruel, but civil war is unspeakable. Sarapul, Chistopol, Elabuga, Chelny – the names of hundreds of little towns and villages along the Kama are written in the history of the Revolution with blood. In one village, they threw the wives and children of Red soldiers in the river, not sparing their newborn infants. In another, the only surviving witnesses to the slaughter are the blazing red maples of autumn, and the dried lakes of blood on the road.

The wives and children of the dead don't run abroad to write their memoirs about the cruelty of the *Cheka*,[1] and the burning of their ancestral estates

---

1   *Cheka*, the Bolsheviks' political police force, the Extraordinary Commission for the Struggle

with their Rembrandts and libraries. No one trumpets to sensitive Europe about the thousands shot by the Whites along the Kama, their bodies carried by the current to the mud flats, washed up on its uninhabited shores. Can any who sailed on our lumbering iron turtles, the *Speedy*, the *Intrepid* and *Vanya the Communist*, remember a day when a soldier in his army greatcoat didn't float silently past, his head shaved against typhus, his hand bobbing in the water, before finally sinking to the bottom? Was there a single village where we weren't greeted with sobs of grief? Where among the distraught people who clumsily helped us with our moorings (for they were shore-dwellers, not sailors), there weren't dozens of widows and sick starving orphans? The shriek of the anchor chains couldn't drown their weeping, nor the fiercely beating heart, nor the commander's voice, hoarse with strain, shouting from a mile away that Samara is ours.

The woman in the crowd is joined by another, old and bent, her face scarred by suffering. 'Don't cry, tell us what happened', the sailors say, but her words are lost in tears.

We learn that when the Whites retreated, they loaded six hundred of our people onto their giant battery barge the *Stenka Razin*, armed with long-range guns, and sailed them off no one knew where, probably to Ufa or Votkinsk. An hour later, the sirens call the sailors back to the ships, and they are given their orders, to sail upstream after the barge and rescue the prisoners. 'Six hundred men, comrades, six hundred', the *Flotkom* keeps saying.

We were flying white flags, planning to trick the enemy into thinking we were part of Admiral Stark's long awaited White Volga Flotilla. They weren't expecting us, and their dugouts and barbed-wire entanglements were clearly visible from the river, as if offered to us on a plate. Our ships moved slowly along the shore, picking the best spots to anchor. The hatches to the powder magazines were opened, the ammunition was moved on deck, the gunners lined up their targets, then the order was given to fire. Shots thundered from the barrels, raking the ground with a dry metallic roar, and ten or fifteen seconds later the enemy had vanished in fountains of black smoke.

Then the targets were changed: 'Two big ones to the right, and one to the left!' The artillery from the *Endurance* hit the church, and the *Intrepid* opened fire, and we slipped off in the mayhem, hoping to cover the twenty miles to the village of Galyany before nightfall.

Against Sabotage and Counterrevolution, set up in December 1917. Later the GPU, the NKVD, and in 1954 the KGB. After the end of the Soviet Union, the FSB.

Three hours later, on a hill beyond a bend in the river, Galyany came in sight. The *Stenka Razin*, guarded by sentries, was anchored by an island near the left shore. Our ships approached the pier, then stopped, and started turning round – an extraordinarily difficult manoeuvre in this shallow narrow stretch of water. 'Don't fire until you receive orders'. The signallers relayed the *Flotkom*'s message from the *Speedy* down the line of ships.

The situation was as follows: the Whites' heavy artillery had been placed next to the church, some sixty yards from the river, with more in the belfry. Standing on the hill above the church were groups of curious peasants and armed soldiers. Through the bushes we glimpsed the white tents of their encampment, and the smoke from their kitchen. The officers lay relaxing on the bank, following our ships' manoeuvres with interest. The floating grave waited silent and motionless.

Without giving itself away, the *Intrepid* approached to check that its precious cargo was still on board. Then the *Speedy* signalled the order of operations from ship to ship. The sailors took aim, ready to shoot if the enemy moved, while keeping an eye out for their infantry. How to move the barge, moored between the narrow banks of the river by the island and the shallows, was another matter.

But as luck would have it, just then the Whites' tugboat *Dawn* came steaming towards the pier. The *Flotkom*, in his White naval officer's cap, addressed its captain imperiously through his loud-hailer: 'In the name of Admiral Stark, Commander of this Flotilla, I order you to approach the barge with the prisoners and attach it to the tug, then follow us along the river towards Ufa!'

The captain, trained by the Whites not to question orders, turned the *Dawn* towards the barge. Endless minutes passed as it shuffled noisily through the water, smoking and puffing steam and slapping its gill-like paddles. The crew winched out the capstan and began securing the cable to the barge, and we held our breath, unable to believe this fairytale, asking each other in a whisper if it could be moved, so close, but still so impossibly distant. Probably not … But spurred on by its captain's shouts, the *Dawn* performed magnificently. The sentries on the *Stenka Razin* put down their guns and weighed anchor, and the barge moved a little, slowly shifting its weight to the tug. The cables slackened then grew taut as the heavy giant inched forward, and the *Flotkom* calmed the confused crew through his loud-hailer: 'In the Commander's name, I order you to proceed! We'll sail ahead and cover you!'

'But we haven't enough fuel!' they protested.

'Never mind, we'll load up on the way', he replied, then unhurriedly, to avoid raising the suspicion of the officers on shore, we started back to Sarapul.

In the hold of the barge, the prisoners had no idea where they were being taken. A sailor later described digging a hole with his penknife in the planks of the stern, which let in their only light. And as he peered out at the chink of sky and water, with its mysterious vessels and their silent crews, the faces surrounding him were like one face, silent and motionless, not knowing whether to read a ray of hope in his eyes or new danger.

'Can't tell if they're ours or theirs, they all look the same', he said. 'No dammit, they're ours, they look human – they're our sailors!' But after three weeks in the hold, covered in nothing but strips of sacking, lying in their own excrement, the starving prisoners dared not believe him.

In Sarapul, people gathered on the pier to welcome them back. But even after our sailors had boarded the barge and arrested the sentries, they couldn't go down to them, cursing and weeping as they called them up. Four hundred and thirty of the six hundred had survived, and none had thought they would be saved. Only yesterday, they had exchanged their last shirt with the guards for a crust of bread, and the torn bodies of the three Krasnoperov brothers and thirty others had been thrown from their cell on bayonets. For days, their quarter-pound bread rations hadn't been dropped through the hole in the ceiling. For what was the point of wasting leftovers on this doomed crowd, whose end would come soon, on some grey bloodless morning, or at night, an unknown end, but infinitely cruel. And suddenly our sailors were opening the hatch to the silvery dawn sky, calling them up with that longed for long-forbidden word 'Comrade'.

Still fearing a new trap, they stumbled back from the dead. What miracles we saw on the barge! There were even some Chinese prisoners, although none of us had heard of Chinese people living in these cold parts, and they fell at the sailors' feet, crying out to them in their language, thanking them for risking their lives to bring them back.

The whole town turned out to greet them. The gangway was lowered, and one by one the four hundred and thirty came ashore, past an honour guard of sailors. But the shaken crowds still managed a wonderful gallows humour at the sight of this procession back from the dead, covered in sacks and straw.

'Hey brothers, who dressed you up so smart?'

'Let's make it the uniform of the Constituent Assembly, with a rope round their necks!'

'Look out, don't tread on my toes!' a prisoner shouted back, pointing to his dirty bare bandaged feet.

Then as they moved from the shore, in voices rusty from their stinking pit, the prisoners began singing the *Marseillaise*, and they went on singing until they reached the town square. Impossible to describe the tears of joy, as families were reunited with a son, a father or brother, sitting with them on the grass as they described their sufferings, then going off to thank their comrades again for saving them.

Among the sailors who had shared the whole of our three-month journey with us from Kazan to Sarapul were several former tsarist officers, in their gold-braided caps. Never before had they been welcomed with such brotherly love and respect. Never before had they seen that wonderful spirit of class unity, as when the prisoners' mothers thanked them for saving their children from death.

CHAPTER 4

Markin

Each morning our pilot on the *Summer Tide* informs us of the falling temperatures. Chunks of ice float past, and the murky surface of the water is covered in mist, a sure sign of winter.

In a few days, the Flotilla is to leave the Kama until the spring, and the sailors are celebrating the end of our dangerous campaign from Kazan to Sarapul. As our departure approaches, these shores feel especially dear to us – every bend in the river cleared of the enemy, every moss-covered pine tree on its steep banks. We remember the battles, the hours of anxious waiting, the hopes and fears – not for ourselves, but for great 1918, whose fate depends on the sailors' courage and the accuracy of their fire. The fierce waters of the Kama, churned by our high prows, pounded by shells, will soon be covered with ice, hiding its treacherous depths that have claimed our best comrades and our cruellest enemies. Who knows in what waters we will fight next year, which comrades will stand on the bridges of our battleships, so familiar and precious to us?

Beating its paddles, its signal-lamp swinging in the darkness, our supply ship sets off for Nizhny Novgorod for provisions, accompanied by three long blasts from its siren. Each of the ships' sirens is as distinctive as the voice of a friend – the sharp cry of the *Roshal*, the piercing whistle of the *Volodarsky*, the deep bass howl of the *Vanya the Communist*. These farewell greetings are also used by the sailors to call for help when they are in desperate danger, and are associated with the most painful memories.

For hours the siren of the *Vanya the Communist* howled as it blazed on the freezing river, hit by enemy shells. Columns of water shot up, and the charred remains of some buckets and stools bobbed in the current, with the black specks of bodies struggling desperately to swim ashore. And still the siren didn't stop, wreathed in flames, the hopeless siren of death.

It had all happened quite unexpectedly. A day earlier, we had been celebrating a major victory against the White Flotilla. Our ships had broken into their rear on both banks, and after a two-day battle at the village of Bitka, we drove them upriver. The chase lasted another two days, and on the third morning, we anchored in a delightful stretch of the Kama, pale blue and amber and turquoise in the bright November sun. The ships were low on ammunition, with only eighteen to twenty rounds left, and our scouts had brought news that the enemy were in the nearby village of Drunken Forest. We were unable to capture it without our infantry, which was invariably late, and while we waited, our three motorised cutters were sent off to reconnoitre. The sailors watched cheerfully as they shot off out of range of the Whites' artillery in clouds of spray, rising and falling in fluffy snow-white rainbows above the shallows.

A flock of swans flew up, scattered by the hoots of our hydroplane, filling the air with the sound of their flapping wings. The sailors took aim at the shore, and Comrade Markin, commander of the *Vanya the Communist*, who loved danger and was drawn to it like a boy, couldn't watch these games from the sidelines, and was enticed by the mysterious forests and rocky cliffs of Drunken Forest, where the Whites' artillery lay silently in wait for him.

No one remembers now how the *Communist* slipped from its moorings along the forbidden shore. But suddenly, just a few yards away, Markin saw the motionless muzzles of the Whites' machine guns pointing at him through the trees. One ship can't fight a shore detachment alone, but drunk from yesterday's victory, the *Communist* approached with guns blazing. We sing hymns to the madness of the brave, but there are times when even the greatest courage is futile, and Markin's death was foreordained.

The *Flotkom* left on the *Intrepid* to order him back. What a turmoil of emotions gripped those on the bridge – not fear, no one succumbed to that cowardly emotion, just the sharp gnawing uncertainty of waiting, which every sailor knows so well.

The brief exchange between the two ships would be Markin's last.

'What are you firing at, Markin?' the *Flotkom* shouted through his loudhailer.

'At their artillery!'

'Where?'

'There, look, behind the trees!'

'Turn round immediately! Sail back!'

But it was too late. As soon as the *Communist* turned to follow the *Intrepid*, the Whites, fearing their trophy was slipping away from them, opened fire from the shore. A hail of shells hit the *Communist*, tearing the air with a sucking sound, ripping the bows, the stern and the bridge. A few minutes later, golden tongues of flames were licking the engine and it was billowing smoke. Then its siren called for help.

Despite the bombardment, we still hoped to tow the stricken ship to safety, as we had outside Kazan with the *Tashkent*. But the *Communist*'s rudder had been shattered in the first blast, and it was being tossed from shore to shore. The *Intrepid*, approaching at great risk through the firing, was unable to pull it back, and was forced to retreat. How the enemy missed the ship is a mystery. It was saved by its amazing speed and the accuracy of its fire, and was escorted back by two large gulls flying around the prow, unafraid of the shells, disappearing only when they hit the water.

We waited for Markin all night, but he didn't return. He had gone down with the *Communist*, with his fierce curses and his blue eyes, his animal instinct for the enemy's presence, his generosity and unselfishness, his iron will, his pride, his goodness and his heroism. And the artillerists mourned him, and the silent pilot at his wheel, and the lookouts in their towers, their windows streaming with tears.

One of the few who survived was his second-in-command, Comrade Poplevin, a quiet, exceptionally brave and modest man, one of the best of our Flotilla, whose pale face for a long time bore the traces of death. When the sun gleamed in the cloudless autumn sky, and the water lapped peacefully under the golden banks, and late at night, when the exhausted sailors were asleep, he would stand alone on the bridge, watching and listening for the slightest sound, vowing to avenge the loss of his beloved friend and their ship.

We were down to our last ammunition, and our infantry still hadn't arrived. Then just before first light, the tarpaulin was lifted from the prow of one of our cutters to reveal a row of four dark cylindrical trip-wired 'Fish' mines, like whiskered buckets. The *Flotkom* conferred over his maps with our mine-layers and senior commanders and the navigator of our flagship. Then he called four sailors and officers on deck, shook their hands especially warmly, and ordered them to board the cutter.

A few minutes later, it had disappeared behind an island. It was light when it returned with its empty prow. Now all we had to do was wait.

The Whites had celebrated the sinking of the *Communist* with two days of drinking. But on the third day they continued their advance. Their ships sailed grandly in a column in each other's wake, as if on parade. Admiral Stark himself, Commander of the White Flotilla, was taking part in his first Volga campaign, and his flag flew over the *Eagle*. Then suddenly, as the procession drew level with the island, a massive explosion ripped the hull from their flagship the *Endeavour*.

The mines had done their work, and now the charred hulks of the two ships lay on the icy shores of the Kama, the Whites' *Endeavour* and our *Vanya the Communist*. And deep under the water, perhaps the current was washing Markin's body against the bodies of those whose guns had finished him off with his drowning men.

The sailors prepare sadly to leave the Kama, possibly for the last time. Nothing brings people closer than shared dangers – the sleepless nights on the bridge, the agonising efforts of will, invisible to outsiders, which prepare them for battle.

History will never be able to do justice to the daily acts of heroism by the sailors of our Flotilla. The names of those whose courage, modesty and discipline, all given of their free will, helped to create the new Red Fleet, are still barely known. Of course individuals don't make history. But there were so few in tsarist Russia who cut through the old orthodoxies and threw themselves into real working struggles. And now there were hundreds of thousands of them, and I had the good fortune to meet many of them on our ships, who at critical moments stepped out from the crowd and showed true leadership and authority – those who knew their heroic role, and encouraged others to rise to their level.

There was Comrade Eliseev, an outstanding gun-layer, with eleven years' service, his eyes always fixed on the far distance, his eyebrows singed off after he sank one of the enemy's ships from six miles away. There was Comrade Babkin, who helped lay the mines that sank the *Endeavour*, feverish and desperate from the illness that would soon kill him, regally squandering his precious talents and his indomitable carefree spirit. And there was Nikolai Nikolaevich Struisky, our flagship's navigator in the second half of our Kama campaign, a former tsarist officer who served Soviet power irreproachably throughout the rest of the Civil War.

One of the most capable and highly qualified of our sailors, Struisky had been mobilised virtually by force, and was escorted to the front in a convoy of his fellow officers, arriving on the *Summer Tide* believing everything he read in the *Stock Exchange Gazette*, hating the Bolsheviks, convinced they were all German spies. Next morning, as he prepared to fight his first battle with us, he treated us with the sullen contempt of one forced to defend a hated criminal cause. But after the first shots, all that changed. You can't do things by halves when hundreds of sailors' lives and their ships, their glorious fighting machines, rely on one word from their commanders. A steel thread connects each of them to the captain on the bridge, whose voice directs its speed and commands the pilot, turning the wheel with his shaking hands. Forgetting politics, a good officer bravely carries out his professional duties, answering shot with shot. And afterwards he is joined to the sailors, the commissars and the red flag on the mast by the pride of victory, and the satisfaction of knowing that his authority as an officer and intellectual is valued and respected.

The following week brought Struisky even closer to us. And after our triumphant welcome at a little town liberated from the Whites, as the workers crowded round the sailors and pressed the aristocratic hand of our new 'red officer' arriving in this foreign land, he looked shyly at them, not daring to believe he was a comrade now too, part of the 'great struggle uniting the human race' in the town band's rough provincial rendition of the *Internationale*. Someone made a speech, angry and ungrammatical, and a week ago he would have sneered. But now his hands were shaking, and his heart missed a beat, and he realised to his horror that he was in tears, and that these people weren't a gang of German spies, but the whole of Russia, whose survival depended on his skill and experience and years of study. And he knew that this Russia – the Russia of the workers and soviets, the deserters, peasant women and young boys, and the Jewish agitator Comrade Abram – was the one he would fight for to the end, braving the danger and hunger and the lice, not knowing how things would turn out, just that this was his country's only hope for justice and a future.

A few days later, Comrade Struisky washed the gunpowder and coaldust from his face, put on a clean collar and buttoned his tunic, with the fading traces of its torn-off tsarist chevrons and epaulettes, and went to the cabin of the Bolshevik commanders to talk things over with them. He spoke firmly, gripping the arms of his chair with both hands, as if being pitched in a storm.

'First, I don't believe Lenin and the others returning to Russia in 1917 in their sealed train were in the pay of the Germans'. He paused, remembering his naval corps, the banquets on the Tsar's yacht the *Standard*, and their golden weapons of war, with its endless wrecks and defeats, and finally long overdue October. 'Second, Russia is with you, and I'm with you too', he went on. 'I'll say this to any younger comrades interested in my views. Third, we were an hour late taking Elabuga yesterday. We saw the hats of the hundred peasants on the shore splashed with their brains. Nothing like that must ever happen again. From now on we'll sail at night. They may ambush us, but …' He pulled a copy of *War Manoeuvres of River Flotillas in the Northern and Southern States* from his pocket, and thumbed through it.

To the Caspian

Our advance to the Caspian has begun, and evenings are spent poring over our naval maps. They're not like normal river maps. The Volga's winding shores are speckled with stars and stark black lines, indicating its treacherous shallows and headlong currents, before the sea opens its arms wider in the salty waters of the Delta, and it divides into thousands of sleeves, whose shoulders are lost in the mist. Fishing boats sail past on their swallows' wings, and if the sleepy fishermen don't guard their catches, our rifles get tangled in their nets, dragging them along like seaweed.

The ships sail in close formation throughout the campaign, in constant radio contact with each other. Daily battles pass in a dream, and the sailors live a tense secret life. In the pale light of the lamp, the commanders bend over their chessboard, playing against invisible opponents hundreds of miles across their cunning difficult maps, in Baku, Embe, and Petrovsk Port.[1] Sometimes their eyes are veiled in mist, as they anticipate the dangers ahead. There are innumerable theoretical knots to untangle. Among thousands of possibilities is victory, then gnawing doubts between two routes – the longer safer one to the Persian Gulf, or the more enticing shorter one. Then the impossible becomes possible, the mist clears, the Red Knight checkmates the White King, and the Flying Dutchman sails on through the waves.

As the sailors wait for the next battles, the older ones smoke quietly and write long letters home, and the young ones experience a special joy at the fullness of life. There will be long weeks without shore leave, without a woman. But never has summer been so spectacular, waist deep in vines, buried to the neck in ripening barley. Never have the nights been so full of stars, or the steppe whiter under its carpet of wild flowers. The blood surges to the rhythm of the galloping horses, their wild manes flowing in the wind, and the steppe is like the sea. To the sea, the blue sea!

Hundreds of poems, louder than glory, wider than hexameters, have been written about the Caspian, with its tranquil surfaces and immeasurable depths.

---

1   Petrovsk Port, now Makhachkala, capital of Daghestan, on the western shores of the Caspian.

Only a narrow strip of the sea belongs to us. But even this strip makes us drunk with joy, and we're too excited to sleep.

The full moon is wreathed in dazzling white clouds, flooding the figures on deck with light. The shaven-headed flag-officer, the handsome cabin-boy squatting on his heels, the tall bearded machine gunner, the pilot with his broad phlegmatic face – all are seized with longing for the sea.

Our floating battery, black as a rock, is escorted by a family of winged schooners. Behind them rises the smoke from the rest of the Flotilla. At the prows of our ships are ancient carved wooden figures – naiads, eagles and virgin saints – protecting us from misfortune, their eyes fixed in expressions of iron will on the far distance.

Our scouts report that the Whites will attack in two hours, and the sailors use the time to doze, smoke, and hang their washing on the line. But they know with every nerve in their body the purpose of this journey to the sea, and their faces are tense but calm, like a smile breaking through a bad dream.

After our tour of inspection of the ships, we return from the pitching cutter to the calm of our staff-ship. Tea steams in iron mugs, and the men drink quietly, almost shily. The rocking water softens the outlines of the shores, dissolving the tiredness of the night.

Finally the alarm sounds, and the silhouettes of the enemy are visible ahead. As we sail past the charred remains of their battleship the *Arag*, blown up by our mines, we feel strangely light-headed. The Whites boldly carry out their manoeuvres on all sides. Two moving shadows circle our battery without opening fire, luring it on. Then suddenly seven bursts of smoke – seven of their ships firing at four of ours. We stop, and an artillery battle begins.

The battery's gun-position officer, Sobolev, a modest fair-haired man in spectacles, with the face of an intellectual, has focused all the love and creativity of his youth, swallowed up by poverty and study, on the speed and accuracy and special peculiarities of its firepower. But the Whites are well prepared. It seems the great stranger is armed with six heavy rifles, and three shells hit the battery's bows in rapid succession. Shards of metal glow in the water like giant fish, and its siren shatters the air.

A week after Sobolev was killed, Commander Eliseev's battery made contact with the Whites' *Hadji-Hadji*, which holed it in thirty-nine places and disabled one of its cannon. The commissar, with a bullet in his side, didn't leave the bridge, and the captain was carried off with the rest of the dead.

We sail on through the fog, and when it clears in the morning, we are in a warm happy land.

The Raven flies through the poet's window in his night of despair, and perches on his bust of Pallas Athena, his guardian and judge, mocking him with its raucous 'Nevermore!' Then morning comes, and it flies off and is gone.

Outside the town the Raven stops at a field, steaming with the ashy threads of a cold mist, and struts across the earth like a lord. 'Nevermore!' it croaks, making the morning air even colder, but the village birds are too stupid to understand. Then flapping its great wings, it flies off to rest its weary body in the warmth of the South, where the river flows into the sea.

With its ebbs and flows, its reeds and fishing nets, this is the kingdom of the gulls. Their eyes are like pearls in oyster shells, their wings are like sickle moons, skimming the water, scattering beads of spray. Swooping down, as if to the crossbeam of a scaffold or the cross of a grave, the Raven straightens its claws, which have trampled the books of magicians, and beats its chest at the rippling water, recoiling in horror at its reflection. The gulls weep and laugh, piercing the air with their cries. Then searching the sky with its hooded eyes, the Raven flies heavily on, like a bad conscience, to the desert.

And there the exiled king makes its new home, where the crimson sun sets over the burning sands, and rare poisonous moths come out at night. Where battles rage all day in the heat and dust of the shuddering shores, and riderless horses throw off their saddles and hurl themselves into the river to swim to the other side. Hearing death in its voice, a hideous army of birds flies across the empty steppe, seeking their prey, chasing the invisible path of the bullets. The river carries the sailors' leaking vessels along the shores, with the bodies of the dead falling from the prows. The water washes away the blood, and the good ferryman of Eternity carries them across the black Styx, and drops them on the shingle. Its wings bless those who have abandoned their weapons and fled, lighting fires on the muddy banks in the hope of being rescued. And when people find them next morning, and lift their eyelids and check their pulses, it mocks them from the sky with its 'Nevermore!'

'I am Zhelikovsky's wife', she says.

The ice melts with the soothing relief of tears. Her face, her enflamed eyelids, her hair under her white headscarf, her whole being, is still warm with the breath of her beloved husband, killed in battle. Her wide eyes can still see him going off before daybreak, full of foreboding, leaving his simple sailor's breakfast uneaten, and her voice becomes angry, scolding him in the sharp tone she uses to hide her love for him.

Now Zhelikovsky's wife has become Zhelikovsky himself. They are his hands, reaching out for help, his eyes, blinded by the fire, his precious beaten head, sinking to the bottom of the river. She has survived seeing his terrible body washed slowly past the paddles of our ship, and there is nothing we can say to console her. She is the wife of a hero, one of the best, and she is calm, knowing that despite his suffering he will be carried to the sea, which he loved. From the narrow river to eternity, she says. And we want to ask the pitiless moment to give those we love a proud pure death, and save them from betrayal and torture. Let them die in battle with their comrades, with their rifles in their hands, like Zhelikovsky, who died fighting for the Soviet Republic.

CHAPTER 6

Tsaritsyn

There are tubs of red oleanders in the yard of our staff headquarters. Our commanders who are leading the raid on Tsaritsyn tomorrow are resting in this comfortable little white cottage on the banks of the river, with its clean sheets, curtains at the windows, and cotton canopies over the beds. The potted house plants are miraculously green against the snow-white ovens, and on the wall is an oil painting of a chubby Adam and Eve in Paradise. Our landlady, an angry rich widow, jingles the golden windowpanes of the veranda with her heavy tread as she brings us glasses of tea.

No one knows what tomorrow will bring, but everyone is in inexplicably high spirits – the *Flotkom*, Misha Kalinin,[1] with his face like a burst balloon, his tousled hair sticking up like thistles, Cavalry Commander Azin, his boyish face filled with a wild joy and the weight of his new responsibilities.

Memories of the cottage on the moonlit shore, the fast horses of the Asian *troikas* galloping to the river, the last hand-to-hand fighting, have lost their vividness with time. The sharpest memory is of the old musical box our hostess kept playing in the next room to distract us from our meeting. The cylinder had rusted and the key was lost, and long after the battles were over, it went on singing its sweet sentimental song in the empty cottage about the sorrows and betrayals of love.

For hours the terrible music of war raged on the river. Our flagship was the *Karl Marx*. The Whites' ships passed like phantoms in the night, pounding the shore with their shells, lighting the steep forested cliffs with flashes of gold. Fountains of water shot up from the depths of the river, and columns of red streaked the blackness. It seemed they would never end, and slam shut the door of the baking oven.

The firing soon turned into a steady coordinated thunder, and the battle began in earnest. The air was thick with gunpowder, and each ship fought separately, one to one with the invisible enemy. A flock of our destroyers appeared over the headland, followed by black minesweepers with lowered visors – knights of the sea and night, sad fishermen of their dead catch. Then

---

1 Mikhail Kalinin (1875–1946). President of Executive of the Party Central Committee from 1919 until his death.

shortly before dawn the firing stopped, and our scouts were sent ashore to meet up with our first frontline units.

We saw them from the ships, advancing along the top of the cliffs towards Tsaritsyn. It's hard to write about them now, to remember the little figures marching to their deaths, however the battle turned out. Suddenly a cry rings out – what? Nothing, one has been shot. 'Stay tight, bastards!' the sergeant roars, his lips trembling, because they're the front line, and have no choice but to advance.

At first light, British planes appear overhead. Constant bombing until late at night, first at the town, then at the river. But after the desperate fighting and the sleepless nights, when our heads are spinning and everyone calls each other 'ty', they're hardly frightening at all.

Two hoots of our sirens mean 'enemy plane', and one after another, they repeat this piercing message. It's a lottery of misfortunes. One of our destroyers is pierced in the heart by four shells. We watch it sink with a hideous shriek, scattering debris over the next ship. The hull of the *Intrepid* is hit. The commander and three of his men are wounded, and the crew struggle to defend themselves and repair the damage as the bombardment intensifies.

One by one our ships disappear in a cloud of smoke and wreckage – the batteries moving calmly and slowly, knowing the impossibility of escape, the cutters with their whiskers of grey foam, the spluttering engines of the destroyers hotly defending themselves, etching clouds of fire in the sky.

Towards evening, the outlines of figures appeared high on the headland. An hour later, there were hundreds of them. Our army was retreating, and the roads from Tsaritsyn were packed with people escaping. But our soldiers organised the evacuation calmly and efficiently, with a line of gentle camels assembled to carry the women and children and ammunition across the steppe.

People and places flash past in a dream. But sometimes among a sea of faces, we see one we remember forever, however brief the meeting.

Lying on the sofa in the cashier's office was a wounded nurse, rescued by our soldiers. She was ridiculously young, with the high sweet voice of a child, and she had barely survived her injuries. Her left eye, her cheek and her chin were covered in bandages, and her small freckled nose was bloody with shrapnel. And the most adult worrying thing about her was her harsh persistent cough.

She had set off with her regiment from a remote corner of Ukraine, on the long dangerous journey east. After the purgatory of the main roads, the hell of the trains, the burning fear of being separated from her comrades, losing the names and faces of those she had been joined to by the Revolution, she finally reached the Volga, and the dirty human sea opened up before the simple purity of her soul.

After the battle she crawled to the Whites' first-aid post, but they refused to bandage her wounds, and threw her out in the rain. Sitting all night on the porch, without the strength to move, she lifted something cold covering her eye, and it was her cheek. Fortunately next morning the Whites' 'infirmary' fled, and the crushed little figure was saved by our troops.

In her papers were innumerable citations from her regiment, all vying to praise her courage, and she glanced at them with her one good eye, a blueish grey, flecked with dark specks like the trembling leaves of wild poplars in autumn. No one has been granted to see the true face of the Revolution yet, but in those terrible days it was the face of that girl, covered in bandages, her full soft peasant lips stained with a pink foam of blood.

On the ship that evening, the sailors wipe the mud from their boots, tidy the ward-room, put jars of red mountain-ash berries on the table, light the lamp, and drink tea.

Sitting on the left in his general's epaulettes is sharp-eyed old Commander Shorin, with his deep bass voice and iron will. Beside him is staff-officer Ivanov, a gentle courteous man, incapable of offending anyone, with his military map slung neatly over his shoulders. Across from them, in his tall lambskin Cossack cap, his order of the Red Banner pinned to his black shirt, is Kazhanov, legendary commander of the Flotilla's landing parties, with his rough pale profile curved like a sabre, his narrow slanting eyes, his swift silent movements, and the scent of his perfume, which he loves like a girl.

The Dutch painters, masters of the group portrait, liked to contrast their cast of gentlemen, in their starched white collars and black robes, with the figure of a sceptic and atheist, a distinguished young doctor perhaps, holding a scalpel, standing half-turned to the spectator with an amused smile. In our group this is Comrade Mikhailov, commissar of the Revolutionary War Council, with a copy of *Izvestiya* poking from the pocket of his leather jacket. Sitting next to him is Comrade Trifonov. Trifonov sees the world through a splinter of the devil's mirror. Long years in tsarist jails and the underground have taught him to barricade himself behind a wall of anonymity, and this brave clever man, this great Bolshevik and soldier, has a morbid fear of showing his emotions. The winds of 1919 have torn the grey spectacles from his eyes, and fresh green grass pokes through the holes in his barricade, but still he fights to the death to guard the precious underground of his soul.

Then there is Azin. How to describe Azin? He's the little town of Ogryz, cut off from the Kama. He's the third-class railway carriage lit with candles from the ballroom of a ransacked estate. He's the cable of his field telegraph in the bushes, wet with night dew, guarded by sentries numb with cold and exhaustion. He's the tattered army maps smeared with ink and tea in his divisional headquarters, thick with cigarette smoke, where the commander of some lost unit arrives one night after coming within twelve miles of the Whites' outpost, and collapses on the floor in a blessed sleep.

Azin created his division from nothing, licking his rough partisans, river pirates, anarchists and steppe Cossacks into shape. He cursed and protected his men, and caught deserters and flogged them with his bare hands. He lost and captured Sarapul and scores of other difficult little towns, and he had dozens of White officers shot, and released or mobilised thousands more. He rode his tall proud horses into battle at the head of his units, and he led the mad face-to-face cavalry charge at Tsaritsyn, forgetting he had no right to risk his life as their commander, and he didn't drink a drop until the fighting was over.

It was Azin who organised the welcoming parties on shore, turning the ships back if the band wasn't ready, so he could take the honours ten minutes later wrapped in his magnificent Circassian felt cloak, which he wore even in the heat of summer. A band played the *Internationale*, and comrades who had finally had time to shave and sew the buttons on their one pair of trousers made long speeches. He knew this was what the men needed, a break from their twenty-four-hour battle duties, with music and speeches, so they could sail off rested in the morning for more weeks of fighting.

Maps and charts left Azin cold. He would listen like a dead man to the cables issuing like hammer blows from Shorin's machine, as he directed with his iron operational reins who was to fight and who was to stay behind, cheerfully lacing his commands with the choice curses he used with those he liked best. And when he ordered Azin to stand down because he had a broken arm, he wept with rage like a woman.

Azin thrashed his cheeky orderlies for stealing a peasant's piglet, and he caroused like an animal for nights on end, blacker than soot, with vodka, music and women. But only after he had made sure his men were safe, putting up barricades with them and digging trenches, sending off scouts to check they were properly defended.

Was there anyone like Azin? He loved his units passionately, he loved and understood every raw recruit, every boy away from his mother for the first time, with his coat five sizes too big for him, and his ears sticking out from his huge army cap, who longed only to drop his heavy gun. He fought with them, and won victories with them, and he crossed from one end of Russia to the other with them, from the Volga and the Kama to Tsaritsyn and Saratov, only to fall into the enemy's hands on the lower Volga outside Perekop, the day before we arrived. Then after torturing him to death, the Whites slandered his memory, spreading lies that he had betrayed the Red Army.

Soldier, marksman, hero, Azin educated his soldiers and commissars and achieved miracles, and after he died his division kept his name, sitting proudly in their rags and generals' trouser-stripes on their sturdy hill ponies, brought from the Urals to Astrakhan, riding at their old brisk pace from the sandy shores of Baku to the Persian border.

That night in the ward-room, the discussion is about heroism – a strange topic, since most present have won numerous medals for their bravery.

Mikhailov, our sceptic and intellectual in the leather jacket, calmly stirs his tea, and says he has finally grown up at the front. Making the revolution isn't about heroism or romantic dreams, it's a job to be done, and he has happily submitted to the mighty engine of history, without doubts or regrets. For the intellectual who becomes a soldier of the Revolution, brotherly solidarity and sacrifice soon become a habit. Until then, if he is not to lose his still fragile equilibrium, he must keep his feet firmly on the ground, and remind himself constantly that two and two makes four.

Shorin craftily slips an extra sugar lump in his tea while the brainy commissar speaks. There's been too much of this talk lately, messing up his charts and cables, and he's sick of it. He's proud of the red medal he wears on his chest, and the frontline communiqués he reads are filled with the same longing for victory he longs for. Not for Shorin the grey victory of the everyday, the hankering for the mediocre. Yet this man seems to mock all his lofty aspirations and everything he's fighting for.

Misha Kalinin, exhausted by the often fruitless bravery he considers his duty as a communist, doesn't join the discussion. Nor does Azin, his face still red from his last ticking-off from Shorin. But the commissar is getting on his nerves. He can't understand why life is such a grey empty thing for him, and has to be skewered and examined under a microscope. Azin's legs still ache from the saddle, and his whole body is filled with the melancholy of early autumn, its sharp sweet smells, the long shadows of the trees already tinged with gold, the green of the meadows flourishing in their last brightness. He was almost killed out on patrol today, and each new danger makes life more precious to him. He doesn't know where this sudden tenderness he feels comes from – from the wounded sailors he met on the shore, from the kind-eyed camels pulling their little wicker gun carriages across the steppe, or from his first letter from home after so many months. And now this man tells him there's no such thing as heroism, and no point to life, with its wonders and miracles and mighty acts of will.

'Oh, for ...!' A warning look from the commissar makes him bite his tongue, and he wants to show him the map with the red circle of the Republic, the only one in the world, heroically defended by the exhausted people, and ask him if life could ever be sweeter than in these great years. If people didn't see anything now, if they didn't experience the anger, the pity and the glory that filled even the wretchedest days, what was there to live for?

CHAPTER 7

July 1919. To Lev Davydovich Trotsky

'Comrade Commander! Permission for our Executive Committee to sail in front!'

'Out of the question! You must sail with us and show us the villages occupied by the enemy!'

The first speaker is the chair of the local soviet, a wiry sunburnt little man, who escaped from his steppe village before the Whites arrived. He reports that two Cossack regiments have occupied the next village twenty miles upriver, and placed four cannon on the church square, and they are to advance on our headquarters in R. at dawn.

'Where are they now?' we ask him.

'They're swimming. The men and horses are relaxing in the river before the battle'.

It's a burning hot day. Upstream the wild horde are splashing in the river like Michelangelo's bathing soldiers, their broad backs gleaming in the sun. Tonight they'll attack.

The river weaves between the golden banks. Fish slip through the shallows. If it wasn't for the battle ahead, how good it would be, sailing through the warm sleepy waters. A low pink moon comes up. A magical evening, sharp with the smell of wormwood, soft as the flourishing vines. Our warships sail silently against the current. Time disappears. The telegraph mast crackles in the sky, catching falling stars in its net.

We reach the village where hundreds of the enemy are sleeping, dreaming of tomorrow's battle. Our ships anchor in the darkness, and our heavy guns line up their targets. Fire rips from their great bodies, and men are already dying on shore.

Gun-position officer Ivan Ivanovich stands on the bridge in his felt peasant boots, lit up by the magical brightness of the shells. And with each explosion he covers his ears with his hands, and a smile appears on his face, and he has an almost childlike sense of his power. On the armoured deck of this great warship stands Ivan Ivanovich, a peasant from the village of Solodniki, and this vast silent giant, with its complex machinery and its circling telegraph levers on the masts, must submit to his will. Never before has a peasant in felt boots stood on this high proud bridge, above the ten-inch rifles and the shells, above the whole of Russia, the whole of humanity, being smashed to pieces and starting again with the Revolution.

Beside him in the darkness, deafened by the noise, is Commander Vekman, star of Moscow's Naval Academy. He removes the cotton-wool from his ears and turns to him, mutely curled in a ball of joy. 'Above or below the belfry, Comrade Ivan Ivanovich? Are we hitting our targets?' Ivan Ivanovich doesn't reply, but Vekman sees from his shining eyes that they are.

It grows light. The thunder on the shore continues, and a house burns to the ground.

'That's Mikita's house', Ivan Ivanovich says. 'He's a rich peasant with ten cows, he had the White commanders staying with him'.

There's no response from the enemy, and we hear them rushing to escape in the darkness, half dressed, galloping across the steppe on their unbroken horses, pursued by the resurrected spectre of the Golden Horde.

Our guns fall silent, and we sail on.

The *Flotkom* has received a cable from N., and tonight he is in the hold, preparing for tomorrow's meeting there. We're sorry to be leaving V. at the height of the Whites' attack, which is now in its second day. Artillery thunders night and day on the river, and the sailors sleep in snatches, with their bread and guns under their heads.

All the lights are off. The secretary's wavering pen records our latest cables by the light of a candle. Black moths flutter to the flame, flickering in the breeze. The stars sway in the water, and the commanders' voices merge with the steady clatter of the telegraph. In the pauses between messages, the mast sends inaudible tender greetings to the sky, which answers with flashes of lightning behind a heavy blue cloud.

The old men of the Revolution are wonderful. For years they lived respectable lives, then at an age when most want to draw the curtains and rest, an irresistible impulse draws them back to the wild spirit of their youth.

Men like Alexander Vasilevich Saburov. His eldest son was killed in the Imperialist War, and his wife aged and slipped into an ashy twilight of fears and superstitions. Saburov himself lived through everything, from fighting at the front as a tsarist naval lieutenant, to emigration in Paris. Like thousands of exiles, he struggled to survive, but he worked his way up from a humble carpenter in a factory to its manager. He was fifty-eight when the Revolution broke out, and he immediately dropped everything and returned to Russia.

Soon afterwards, he left for the Baltic as a Red naval commander. And as he sailed the grey sea, sitting high on the spar-deck, listening to the sailors below, and to the waves pounding the prows of his ship, he thought of his misspent youth, and of this insanely youthful future opening up before him.

Outside Kazan, at the height of the Czechs' attack, Saburov was commander of our slow heavy battery barge the *Seryozha*, and he was an outstanding artillerist. Small, with his slanting Tartar eyes, his French turns of phrase, and his shaggy beard, from which invariably poked the stem of his old pipe, he sat whistling over his guns, squinting at Kazan's Sumbeki Tower, as noble and ancient as himself. Then he gave orders to fire. After the third round the Whites fired back, and our small tugboat puffed over to pull the *Seryozha* to safety.

Oh the contrasts! The hulking giant, and its faultlessly accurate fire. The huge guns, directed by small lively endlessly good-humoured Alexander Vasilevich, who normally wouldn't hurt a fly, but becomes cold as a stone when death passes by on its dripping wings, fearing to break the spell of his royal old age.

We've met Admiral Behrens again, Commander of the Naval Forces of the Republic. When Behrens first arrived at the front, his goodness and intelligence were constantly affronted by the boorishness of the Revolution, which he treats like an elderly grandee managing a badly behaved prince. But as rationalist and intellectual, he was convinced from the start by the irrefutable logic of October, and was prepared to draw the necessary conclusions from its great barbaric truths, which lit up all the palaces and chapels of his aristocratic soul. He couldn't be silent when his heart cried out for pity, and he rejoiced when the storm shook the waxed floors of the Admiralty and occupied his ancestral home. When asked to swear his oath of allegiance to the Revolution, he did so with all the courtesy of a philosopher and poet. And suddenly this lover of Voltaire, who thought life had nothing more to offer him, discovered the last most tender love of his life – for youth and creativity, and for the cruel beautiful angel splashed with the people's blood and tears which had come to judge the whole world.

The Revolution made Behrens roll up his lacy cuffs and dig with his own hands the grave of his defeated class. He is responsible for arming our ships against the counterrevolution, and he has no doubts that our little Flotilla, crammed to the bows with heroism, must and will win. After the fall of Tsaritsyn he sat for a long time alone in his cabin, like a father who had lost his son.

There are times when the slightest thing seems full of ominous significance, and tests us to our limits. When the rising sun prophesies a long terrible day, and the nights are endless and crimson like a bad dream. At such times it's easy to understand people's ancient superstitions about the cry of a bird, the sound of a falling stone, the rustle and rattle of inanimate things. Where does it come from, this nameless terror of the unknown, this sudden inescapable exhaustion of the spirit, descending like a mountain mist on a valley? It's not the battles that are frightening, that age the young and strong and wither their hearts and nerves and make them fight badly, it's this secret disease of the soul. Call it what you like – hysteria, mass hypnosis – it's the hidden incurable sickness of war.

Even the healthiest units can wake one morning overwhelmed with mind-numbing fear. And then all the forces of reason are needed to stop them abandoning their posts, all its icy concentrated strength to banish these spectres that are more dangerous than the visible enemy.

Such a day came for us too. How and why, no one will ever know. A horse and wagon shot across the steppe in a cloud of dust. That's all. Horse and driver flew between our dugouts and the enemy's, with no thought or purpose but to get away. The flecks of foam on the horse's flanks, the tilt of its head, the creak of its harness, all merged into one uncontrollable impulse – escape, escape, escape.

Nothing had changed. The river flowed on, reflecting the outlines of our ships on its silky surface, and the wagon was merely taking an invalid to hospital, lying on a bundle of fresh hay. But our lookouts in the tower were frozen with fear.

The ashen-faced officer gripped the mouthpiece of his telephone with all his strength, and put it to his ear. Dozens of eyes scanned the empty steppe, and soon spotted figures on the horizon, moving from left and right, coming closer, a fantastic cloud of the invincible enemy, approaching from all directions. Messages flew across ten wires from our ships to our communications trenches. A machine gun took a pot-shot at the shore. The lookouts, their hands fluttering like frightened wings, could barely raise their field-glasses to their eyes. Two White planes circled overhead, like birds of prey, scenting carrion from many miles away. The panic spread, then reached its limit. For the next five days, those in the tower didn't take their eyes off the approaching armies, calculating the speed of their advance, guiding the direction of the ships' fire. Even after the first wave of riders poured into the town, and we heard the first shots of street fighting, the lookouts' faces were as calm as a full sail in a still sea.

For five days, our little garrison in the town didn't sleep, answering fire with fire, turning their faces from death, taking the weapons from the fallen and not speaking of them. And although Black Cliff was virtually cut off on all sides, with only a narrow strip of land connecting it to the river and our Flotilla, none of our infantry would have considered retreating.

Then someone in the tower spotted horses, and the fear was back. The signaller's flags summoned our senior artillery officer to the tower, Comrade Kuzminsky, and everyone gazed at his face, which they knew and loved, as he scanned the horizon with his field-glasses. At first he was tight-lipped. Taking a deep breath, he wiped his precious lenses, and his eyes became ghostly again as they focused on the far distance. More silent watching and waiting Then he put down his glasses, and his eyes became crafty and human, his black beard twitched, and his gold teeth flashed in a big smile. 'They aren't horses, comrades, they're cows!'

People in the tower calmed down for a while. But an hour later the fear struck again, more uncontrollably than ever. The peaceful sky was a smoky pinkish grey in the sunset, and for some reason, without a word said, everyone had turned from the distant outline of the monastery, from which trouble had been expected that morning, to the open sea of the steppe, where nothing was visible for hundreds of miles but the soaring eagles.

Then with a preoccupied far-away look, like someone listening to distant underground music, Kuzminsky ordered a single shell to be fired at a totally unexpected spot on the shore. A second later, a deafening shot rang out, flattening the feather-grass and turning it silver. Two more shells pounded the same spot, with exactly the same result. More tense waiting in the tower, where all our commanders had gathered. Surely for all Kuzminsky's brilliant skills as a mathematician and soldier, he was mistaken, and his shots fired into the unknown had merely disturbed the wild flowers. Then suddenly he gave the command 'White Fire!'

They seemed to come from nowhere, rising from the ground in thick green columns, three thousand Cossacks, Circassians and Kalmyks, driven by the shells from Black Cliff. By lining up the map's coordinates with what he saw around him, Kuzminsky had deduced everything – the little gully overflowing its banks after the summer downpour, flooding the cliff where the enemy had assembled for the attack.

They scrambled up its slippery slopes with their horses, striking matches under their wet capes in the darkness, losing men at every step, cursing us for staying in the river for six days and avoiding them. How well our men in the garrison slept that night after cleaning their weapons. And how happily they set off at daybreak for their next battle.

CHAPTER 8

Astrakhan

Blue nights. The endless steppe. Tartars lie dozing by the railway embankment under a thin Polovtsian moon, swarthy and crested in their tall lambskin caps like birds of prey, hugging their native rocks as they did in the days of Prince Igor. And now Rus is marching past them again to fight in the South.[1]

Military trains rumble past in the darkness. But people are calmer at these remote steppe stations than at the terrible stations in the cities, part army camps, part hospitals, part bivouacs for the homeless. A pure wind blows the dust from them across the boundless expanse, and even the smoke from the engines smells of sagebrush.

The Civil War has already come into its own here. It entered people's lives when the first trains brought the dead and wounded back from the front, and won't leave until the fighting is over.

One of those who returned is a man of about forty, with close-cropped hair and narrow Tartar eyes, reflecting the calm golden depths of his soul. The left sleeve of his grey army shirt is knotted at the elbow and clotted with blood, where his arm was torn off by a Cossack sabre. But there is no trace of bitterness on his broad face, burnt by the fierce southern sun.

With him is his thirteen-year-old son, tall and beautiful and utterly unconscious of his beauty, half-child, half-soldier, with the profile of a fighting Byzantine angel. I remembered that boy's face for a long time. It was always turned slightly to one side, as if facing a high wind, glowing in the reflection of the Revolution that had touched his childhood with its burning wings. He probably won't live to be a man, read books, or sleep with a woman. These rushing times will carry him far across the steppe, where he will be ambushed by the Whites, and after fighting shoulder to shoulder with his brothers, he will be broken, and birds of prey will circle over his body.

Premonitions of death, like plates of congealed fat on the faces of the weak, left their best features on this brave smiling child. This is how the children of the Revolution die.

---

1   Prince Igor, Orthodox Christian ruler of Rus, the first Russian state in Kiev, fought two wars between 912 and 945 to capture Constantinople, and was defeated in battle with the Polovtsians, nomadic people of the Eurasian steppes.

Astrakhan lies like a burning yellow rock on the overflowing banks of the Volga, sultry and oppressive. The golden thread of the railway track running into the town glints above a murky sea of salty water. The sun beats down on a waste-land of dust and rocks and low faceless buildings, and the reek of sewage makes it hard to breathe.

But at night Astrakhan comes to life. Faces exhausted by fever and the heat of the day are eerily pale under the electric lights of the park. And at the centre of the park, in a grove of thin maples, is a huge glass coffin, overflowing with a wild profusion of flowers, lilies, roses, poppies and scented stocks, reflecting the radiance within, the most beautiful revolutionaries' grave I have ever seen.

In the brackish desert outside Astrakhan are the oases where the Tatars tend their ancient orchards, vineyards and beehives, ruled by Eastern gods smiling their golden smiles at the sun. An ox circles slowly round a creaking mill, drawing water from a muddy well. Roses spill their heady perfume in the air, mingling with the scent of mint and honey. Peaches drop silently onto the silky grass, plums ooze hot wine from their dry amber skins. The fiery tomatoes on their withered stalks look overdressed, as if wearing their Sunday best to work.

From high above the sleepy gardens comes a distant buzzing sound, like the bees in the vineyards, a good omen for summer. It grows louder, but paradise bubbles on. Then suddenly the gardeners scatter, abandoning their beds and trellises, as three enemy birds swoop down in a triangle from a fluffy white cloud, and roar off towards the town – British fighter planes, fuelled by good British petrol, their silver wings flashing in the sun.

From behind the trees, our one little aircraft prepares to meet the low-flying predators. The pilot tries to ignite his rusty engine, corroded by the cheap mixture of fuels in its veins. It chokes and cuts out, it's a hopeless flight. But finally he gets airborne, shooting straight up noisily into the air without circling before take-off, like a warrior in full armour rushing to the top of an invisible mountain.

Who is this unknown pilot? Whose deaths have inspired his insane heroic flight? Below him lies defenceless Astrakhan, with its dirty streets and its hated guests, who want to kill the Revolution and the red flight of life. And as he flies up, our one machine gun on the shore turns its Cyclopean eye on its targets, and throws death into the sky. Plumes of smoke curl over the planes, and they turn back. And as their scaly bodies snake off into the distance, our airman flies in a wide joyful arc, his face pale under its mask, his shining eyes fixed on the vanishing fighting birds.

Where wasps, flowers and dragons are embroidered in gold ...
NIKOLAI GUMILYOV[2]

The sky is a fiery pink. Far from the orchards and the battle above, an ox-cart rumbles into Astrakhan. The dirty suburbs slink up to the Kremlin on the hill, like stray dogs. In the Kalmyk quarter, old men in white stockings and silk robes sit dreaming in doorways, their faces glowing in the sun like their ancient Buddhist deities.

Before me is a Buddhist figurine, rescued by our scouts from a burning Kalmyk steppe settlement. Gleaming against a dark green background, sensuous as the southern spring, is the pink canopy of dawn. Beneath, its slender limbs gracefully crossed, sits the god of morning. The face is the same dark green, and the mouth smiles a sharp, semicircular smile. One hand holds a ceremonial bell, the other a sand clock. But this is nothing like the sand clock in Dürer's *Melencolia*, whose grains measure despair, it is the clock of eternal renewal and awakening. To right and left, dividing the emerald sky above, are the sun and moon, both heavenly bodies edged with pink clouds, blending with the crimson of the Buddha's halo. Beyond lies infinity.

The eyes of this oriental Aurora are extraordinary, slightly slanting, with agate brows, and between them is the Morning Star. They're like the eyes in the most mysterious portraits of the Renaissance, but without their artistic ambiguity – cold, wise, focused in on themselves. The arms are those of a woman, covered in red bracelets. But the chest is flat. This most beautiful of the ancient gods is immaculate, with the torso of a youth. It is the laughing Dawn, whose eyes express all the joy and wonder of the approaching day, and at its feet lie the earth and a dark forest, and a bright waking clearing, lit by the sun.

Aux armes citoyens,
Le jour de gloire est arrivé.

The colours of our banners are red or black. Black is for funerals. A naval band marches towards the sweltering town. Boots thunder over the dead highway, trumpets gleam, the banners are dark and heavy as rocks, their folds trembling slightly, dreaming of the deep cool skies of a northern spring, and the first gulls over Kronstadt.

---

2 Nikolai Gumilyov (1886–1921), one of Russia's most celebrated poets before the Revolution, Reisner's former lover.

Astrakhan lies with closed eyes, dripping with sweat, finding no relief in the canals, which steam with malaria. It's slightly easier to breathe on the river, with its light-masted fishing-boats bobbing on the water. The sailors march on, and above the rocks and the dust soars the *Marseillaise*. After passing through all the emotions of grief for the dead, the song rises to its climax, and an eagle on the horizon looks down at the wide blue river, flowing through the salty sands to the sea, and sees the whole of life stretching ahead to the end of time.

The drum and the clashing trumpet honour the coffin as it sails forward on the men's shoulders. Shrouded in the mourning veil of the music, the little procession follows the river to the outskirts of town. Passers-by stop and stare, and the funeral theme flies on the wings of memory, fluttering the sailors' banners, brushed by the dust from the *Speedy*'s funnels. The men look down as they remember that night, and the mighty throat of the trumpet rattles with tears. Then it recovers, and the revolutionary battle hymn soars again into the sky.

The *Speedy* was out on patrol, far from the rest of the Flotilla, when it was ambushed from the shore. It opened fire from both its cannon, and the enemy shot back point-blank. Then in the chaos of the defence, as the gunners changed their targets, and the navigator ducked to dodge the shells whistling past his head, the little signaller, Erikov, stood on a box and saw them hit the prow and stern of his ship, which relied on the slightest vibration of his voice and will, and he was wounded and silently died.

The *Marseillaise* finishes its story, and the dead man rocks gently on his brothers' shoulders. He wants to know who will have his bunk now, who will stand on the bridge in the mornings, signalling from ship to ship with his graceful alphabet of flags. But death does not remove its hands from his cold lips, and his coffin is laid in the ground, followed by two waves of grief, like the pure salty foam against the bows of his ship.

Astrakhan's pilot is Polozenko, a giant of a man, heavy and slow, with a dark face and black hair. His huge hands are scarred and calloused, but extraordinarily quick and supple, always moving things to some hidden point of equilibrium. Everything Polozenko touches with his hands falls into two equal and symmetrical parts, which support and make sense of each other in the void.

Burnt with a Japanese needle into his sunburnt arm, from the wrist to the elbow, is a dragon, and when he flies up in his broken-down plane, pursued by flying shrapnel, tossed by the storm, driven by the madness of the brave, he flexes his arm and the monster comes to life. Smoke billows from its jaws, and its tail lifts like the blade of a dagger, and Polozenko laughs, and the wind rips the laughter from him as he throws his metal tears to the ground.

His six-month-old son died in Astrakhan last week, and since then he has gone up three or four times a day, despite all warnings. And there's something new in Polozenko's great soul now, which people turn their eyes from and don't want to see – the impotence of the Farnese Hercules.

In Astrakhan's naval hospital is the remains of a family, the Kryuchkovs. Two weeks ago, they were eating their small meal at home, when a British plane dropped a bomb through their leaking roof. The mother survived, with two of her children, little boys of eight and two. The rest of the family were blown to pieces, buried under splinters of wood and clods of earth.

The two-year-old's leg had to be amputated, and in the twelve days and nights since the operation, the mother has sat with her sleepless baby in the hospital. She has auburn hair and a broad high-cheekboned face, and terrified unseeing eyes. Her tiny son in her arms is naked, covered in a white blanket, with a huge bundle of gauze and bandages on his little sunburnt leg.

His hands twitch, but his pale face is thoughtful, like the face of a dying god. His eyes close with exhaustion, but his brow shines with such wisdom that the young doctor, who has seen everything in this hospital, lifts his hand from his cheek, and the frightened mother stops weeping.

Perhaps when children die, they see in a dream the life they haven't lived. Perhaps at the end of their suffering, in one night of fever, they experience the whole of their future, then give it up, like a magnificent robe worn only once for a special occasion and taken off forever. His eyelids tremble and half open. His body is smeared with dirt, and the blood from his wound seeps through his bandage. His mother gazes at him dazed with grief, and the sailor in the next bed with the bandaged chest tries to comfort her. 'There there, he can manage with one leg. The little chap's clever, he can study to be a telegraphist'.

Why a telegraphist? The sailor worries he has said the wrong thing. But he has to say something to out-talk the tears and the blood.

Little Fedya watches calmly as his bandage is changed. He has a great soul.

CHAPTER 9

From Astrakhan to Baku

Astrakhan comes slowly back to life after the long hard winter. Pale blades of grass poke through the sands, and the peach and apple orchards are flooded with warmth, their blossoms indescribably vibrant against the bare shores of the Caspian.

The town timidly warms its leaking roofs in the April sun, without heat or light, cold and naked as towns are only in the East. But how precious every stone of Astrakhan is to the Revolution, every bend in its roads, crooked as frost-bitten fingers. How many unbelievable sacrifices for Soviet Russia were made here, at the rusty gates to Asia.

In defending Petrograd, people were fighting for the power of Russia's ancient capital, for its squares and monuments sanctified by the Revolution. Everything inspired their resistance – Red Kronstadt, the run-down factories braving cold and hunger to produce weapons for the Red Army, Peter's Admiralty, the Winter Palace, containing nothing now but the tsars' paintings. Every step of the proletarian forces marching off to fight for Petrograd evoked an iron response from the rest of Russia, and will never be forgotten. But how much heroism was needed to defend Astrakhan. People here were inspired neither by love for the town nor by revolutionary tradition, but by a sense of duty. And not just some cold abstract duty. It was the collective will not to abandon it to the British, and cut off our access to the Caspian.

One last picture sums up the heroism of Astrakhan's resistance. Workers at the Nobel shipyard, who had gone without food and heat all winter, had hoisted onto the docks the enormous upturned body of one of our battery barges, holed by a British mine, and were working through the night to repair it. Below them flowed the cold dark river, and the electric lights blazed all night on the barge's innumerable props and struts, as they welded and patched over the cracks, joining metal to metal with their healing hammers, covering the ragged seams with smooth young steel.

Our ships left Astrakhan's harbour, and anchored in the pale turbulent waters of the channel. The cables creaked, and the swaying masts made arcs in the air. Migrating birds rested on the decks, and at night people lit beacons of reeds on the shores.

Our guard-ship guided us past the minefields, and we finally reached the open sea. After three years of river war, it was like a rush to the head. For hours the sailors didn't leave the decks, resting like the birds and remembering their travels, written in the waves in ribbons of foam. Oil-towers rose from the water like miracles, and like miracles, our tankers passed with the first cargoes of fuel for Astrakhan. We happily coordinated our speed and slowed down for them, and the masts danced as if drunk, and we were too excited to sleep or eat.

Above the railway line running along the seashore from Petrovsk Port, thousands of our soldiers are crossing the foothills of the Caucasus, with their artillery, carts and horses. The purple crags of the mountains are wreathed in morning mist, and the eagerly advancing troops raise clouds of dust. The riders, with their distinctive loose-reined seat, have covered thousands of miles on their skinny hawk-nosed ponies, which steam as if poured with boiling water. All these soldiers and riders, who have crossed Russia from Arkhangelsk to Astrakhan, from the Urals to the Caspian, are on their way to Baku, to march through its streets before thousands of spectators in a victorious May Day parade.

At the front are the local regiments who have come over to us from the British, with their smart British boots, uniforms and weapons. These national guardsmen look completely European, straight-backed, marching strictly in step, spaced as neatly as if with a ruler. Their horses too look nothing like ours, as plump and sleek as Tsar Nicholas's horse in the statue outside the railway station. 'It's all thunder and lightning with them, wave a handkerchief at them and they're off. Where's ours?' laughs a woman from the Balakhani suburbs, her blue eyes flashing.

Then our regiments appear, in their ragged uniforms, blackened by the sun, but marching easily and naturally with the correct marching step. They have crossed the whole of the Republic to the Caucasus at this pace, without swaggering or dawdling or any special drill, and the earth thunders to their iron rhythm. Where did they learn this classic step, loved by Caesar, which Europe's prison barracks try in vain to drum into their troops? Every oil worker from Balakhani and Black City, every bourgeois from Baku, knows their path won't stop here, and this human flood rolling through the city will go further, beyond the borders of Azerbaijan.

The sailors' and soldiers' spirit wasn't swallowed up by Baku's wealth and glamour. They strolled through its streets with a relaxed, interested air, which frightened the bourgeoisie more than the Bolsheviks' expropriations. And when they went off to defend the town against the advancing Mensheviks, they fought with their usual courage and discipline. Baku's bourgeoisie surrendered to the conquerors, and our troops barely noticed them.

It's true that there hadn't been a proper revolution in Baku. The stark poverty we had become unused to in Soviet Russia still oozed from every crevice, flowing through the streets like oil. For three nights the city didn't sleep for fear of a bourgeois counterrevolution, and our searchlight from the sea scanned the silent folds of the hills with its pitiless glare, evoking images of Turkey's slaughter of the Armenians.[1] If only our glorious game could begin! Workers were suffocating in Baku's February-style revolution, which offered them nothing.

But October was already stirring in the dark suburbs, and the Musavatists[2] angrily awaited the coming storm. Oil workers from Balakhani and Black City began to appear in the town, their oily clothes and pale faces reflected in the windows of the shops, piled with foreign goods, and the earth came to life. The rocks were rolled from the oil wells, and swollen currents of the precious life-giving liquid poured along the wide pipelines from their black entrails, like a mother with too much milk.

---

1   An estimated two million Armenians were massacred or deported from Turkey by the Ottoman and Turkish governments between 1915 and the early 1920s, with thousands of those fleeing persecution escaping to Baku and Astrakhan.

2   Members of Azerbaijan's nationalist Muslim Musavat party, in power in Baku under the British occupation from September 1918 until April 1920, when they were ousted by the Red Army.

CHAPTER 10

From Baku to Persia

In Baku the Fleet drank oil for two weeks, replenished its supplies, and was pampered in Baku's luxurious shipyards, like wounded soldiers finally arriving at a good hospital in the rear.

Our ships were a mass of barely healed injuries, stuck with rough temporary patches. After Astrakhan's impoverished shipyards, they could now be repaired properly, down to the last screw, without having to worry about every drop of oil, before they set sail for Persia.

The crowds who came to see us off that morning were surprised not to see our slow narrow shooter-destroyers in the harbour. They had sailed off the night before with their lights out, fanning out in a spectral procession around barren Nargin Island, waiting to be joined by the rest of the Flotilla.

Next day, 18 May, the entire White Fleet at the Persian port of Badar-e Anzali was captured, and the occupying British forces were in headlong retreat. The Caspian was now a free Soviet sea, surrounded by friendly republics.

In Anzali, the power of Imperial Britain clashed with the power of the workers' state, and lost. On 18 May 1920, for the first time in the East, regular British troops were defeated in open battle, and barely escaped humiliating capture. This wasn't just anywhere, it was Persia, weakened by its forced alliance with the British, duped by them into signing all sorts of extortionate treaties. And now the British were slinking off in shame.

For the local population, their departure was the source of much amusement. The whole town dropped its normal business for the day, and people sat on the piers, smoking and eating oranges and throwing the peel in the water, watching as their old lords and masters meekly obeyed the *Flotkom*'s orders to board a cutter for our flagship the *Karl Liebknecht*, where they hoped to wangle an honourable surrender.

At the rear of their departing convoy were various luxuries, including a grand piano and a special bath, the private property of Brigadier Bateman-Champain, none of which escaped people's mocking eyes, and the smoke from their cigarettes was filled with laughter and gossip. The bazaar buzzed with stories of how the English officers were so seasick on the Russian ship they had to keep stopping the negotiations to throw up over the sides, and when our commanders asked how officers of the greatest naval power in the world could be seasick, they could only grunt and heave.

Oh, people in Persia see things, and having seen the weakness of the occupying forces, they'll never forget it. The poor of Persia, bent like a ram's horn, can now look the British in the face and not give an inch. And another thing increased their respect for Soviet Russia. The Bolsheviks in Anzali spared the Turks and Indians who had fought with the British. Not one European foreign ministry would have bothered to send us a note if these 'coloureds' had disappeared from the face of the earth, and they shook with fear when they fell into the hands of the 'terrible Bolsheviks'. Tall and graceful as gods, with their bronze profiles and frightened souls, they wept for mercy. But they weren't only given their freedom, they were treated with a warmth and brotherly respect they had never known from their masters in India. Many had fought in the Whites' bayonet attacks on our Flotilla's landing-parties, but they left us as our friends, returning to their ruby lands with news of a new brotherly solidarity, and a new transformed world.

The fat governor of Anzali, polite and slippery as sin, quickly assessed the situation and paid 'les bolscheviks' a visit on our flagship the *Sinitsyn*, to enquire if his dear guests planned to leave Persian waters soon, or would be blessing his country with a longer visit. The interpreter bowed. The governor sucked on a lemon, smiled sweetly and bowed. The *Sinitsyn*'s commanding officer, who had faultlessly directed its fire for three years, bowed. The mechanic Chirikov in his oily tunic, with the calm face of an old sea dog who has seen everything, bowed. The cannon on deck bowed, and the mocking tips of the masts.

'Don't worry Governor, we've had such a warm welcome from your people we couldn't possibly consider a swift departure', our *Flotkom* said. 'We don't want to offend them, so we'll stay'.

More bows, and the governor scuttled ashore, green with seasickness and his excess of hospitality. 'And by the way, we're expecting a visit from your national hero, Mirza Kuchek-Khan!'[1] the *Flotkom* shouted down to him from the deck.

Thousands had already gathered on the shore to hear the great Persian orator speak. Seated at his feet were his *Jangali* followers, with their long dusty hair tied back with beaded headbands, and their fiery hennaed beards, like those of the ancient Persian kings. Before them the crowds sat rapt and motionless, as if cast from bronze, not missing a word of Kuchek's message, which spread in their bright language from neighbour to neighbour, from one leafy orchard and watering-hole to the next, across the barren hills to the borders with India and Mesopotamia. Without radio or telegraph, the people of Persia knew of Britain's fruitless bloody imperialist war in Egypt, and of the secret

---

1 Kuchek-Khan (1880–21). In June 1920 appointed President of the new Autonomous Soviet Republic of Iran, the first such republic outside Soviet territory, based in the capital of Gilan Province, Rasht.

packed meetings on the Afghan border the British were powerless to stop, and they were beginning to throw off their slave's shackles and think for themselves.

Revolution came to Persia like a veiled woman, covered from head to foot in oppressive laws and prejudices. But the hardest thing had been achieved: people had lost their faith in Britain's invincibility, and had turned their backs on its gold, its weapons, and its monstrous arrogance and cruelty. For so long Anzali had simmered in silence, its anger maturing like wine in the darkness. But miracles were needed to wake the poor from their apathy and exhaustion. And the first of these miracles to wake Northern Iran was the defeat of the British in Anzali. The second was Kuchek-Khan's arrival in the town, and his meeting with us on board our ship.

For three years, Kuchek's name had been the talk of Anzali. And now suddenly everything had been turned upside-down, and old men fell before him to kiss his incorruptible hands, and fanatics abandoned their prayer mats and merchants their stalls, and the bootblack boy climbed on his box on his bare brown feet to get a better view, and crowds of the poor and dispossessed poured from all corners to hear the words of the tall figure distantly visible above the crowds. For three years, he and his followers had hidden in the forests and mountains of Gilan and Qazvin, and the English had offered a bag of gold for his head. And now here was his precious head, black against the sky with its halo of dark curls, like the hero on an old Persian coin.

For hours he prayed to his god before he came to our ship to join his name to the Persian revolution. And when he finally arrived, escorted by his faithful Kurdish guards in their wolfskin hats, his eyes were clear and serious, with the living shades of water and metal, and his voice was as soft as a woman's. As his interpreter finished translating, and he celebrated his friendship with us with a tentative smile, it was hard to believe he had been speaking of the transfer of weapons, and Persia's glorious rebirth.

The liberation of Anzali was the end of our three-year campaign, which had started at Kazan and Svyazhsk, and had covered thousands of miles, from the cold Kama to the burning saltmarshes of the South, from the wide Volga to the treacherous mines of the Astrakhan channel, and finally to the Caspian. And having completed its final mission, the Flotilla began to demobilise its warships.

For three years the old fighters had suffered heart attacks from the shells shaking their mighty engines. But by the time they left the Baku channel, they had already achieved the apparently impossible, and pushed open the locked doors of the East with their armoured fists. The artillery disappeared from their iron-clad decks, and the powder-boxes were filled with rice or oil, and they sailed back to Astrakhan not as fearsome dreadnoughts, but as powerful working vessels, slow caravans pushing into the hungry factory heart of Russia.

How close this magical country and its people feel to us. Leave Anzali's harbour, with its canopied Japanese fishing vessels and Russian warships, leave the shallow waters of the enamel lagoon, like a smooth blue brow between its sandy hills of foam, and the Persian countryside breathes and opens up to us.

Our car passes herds of sleek black hump-backed buffaloes, with little wide-apart horns, like eyebrows. Dense mysterious smells waft from the pomegranate and acacia trees lining the road, and muddy streams of water trickle across like liquid clay, irrigating the hungry roots of the trees, the thick reed hedges, the emerald chessboards of the rice fields. As the light fades and the tropical heat leaves the fields, they're alive with sinister hunched figures, like shadows of some unknown species. But by day, the sun over the distant mountains blesses them with its smile. Rice shoots poke through the glassy water, and little girls wade timidly around on their thin legs, knee-deep in mud, bent double over the stalks, not lifting their veiled faces and their muddy hands from their work, breathing in the sweet air shot with the barely noticeable shivering sweats of malaria.

Around a bend in the road we pass a cluster of straw-thatched mud shacks on airy wooden stilts. A line of men walks home in single file, with bundles of hay, fishing nets, clay pots, oars and damp sails slung from poles on their shoulders. Their golden faces are framed by their long black hair, cut in a square line above their eyes and falling over their temples, and their light barefoot walk is unlike ours, and their language is foreign. But as they turn back to stare at us, they look so familiar. They are fishermen and peasants, slender from poverty and endless toil, supple as the stalks of their beloved rice.

We pass caravans of camels, with their small heads and long bare necks and saddles of carpets, bright tassels dangling from their chins. Mules trot along, struggling to lift their strong hooves under the weight of their panniers. Rose gardens, rice fields, a soft breeze, and finally we reach the former governor's residence in Rasht.

The great leaves of a plantain tree fall through the office windows from the garden, which faces north, breathing in the shadows of early morning. The bright clear air is filled with a chorus of birdsong and the sweet smell of roses, steaming in the southern sun.

The room is quiet and spacious, with carpets on the walls and varnished wooden floors. Kuchek-Khan sits at the desk, wearing a plain brown shirt with a white collar, which sets off the beauty of his dark face. And as he says goodbye to us, he turns to the light and watches us with his extraordinary eyes, with the innate caution of an Eastern prince. The interpreter translates his last words to us, and he looks sad but calm, Persia's lone revolutionary, doomed to die at the hands of the corrupt warlords or the British, whose weapons he must rely on.

Then suddenly the tragic faces in the room break into smiles of childlike joy, as the Fleet's old friend the 'air sausage' appears outside the window. How often we have seen its plump body over Tsaritsyn and Astrakhan, on the shores of the Volga, searching for enemy aircraft, directing our ships' fire. The sailors have grown to love it and feel safe under it. And now our sweet monster has risen in Persia's enamel sky, scanning the tropical undergrowth, the emerald fields, the roads whiter than milk.

The bazaar panics. The mullahs and little boys scatter, and a herd of frightened camels, abandoned by their drivers, stampede along the road. The balloon makes a stunning impression – all the authority of the Revolution moving calmly through the clouds, swaying in the breeze, connected to earth by its fine iron rods, taking over the world, cheerfully sticking its tongue out at the enemy. For centuries, the West has used its technological superiority to crush its colonies, and now this technology is in the hands of the Persian revolution, which has driven the British from the Caspian in disgrace.

Kuchek gazes happily through the window at our sailors in the bazaar, their cap ribbons fluttering among the turbans and wolfskin hats. Then the telephone rings. There's fighting eight miles from Rasht, and he must leave immediately with his staff – his clever commanding officer, the bravest of his followers, and his spectacled commissar of finances, with his rifle slung over his shoulder, worrying about how he'll feed and pay the thousands of hungry peasants joining them.

'To Tabriz!' shouts the last departing Red sailor in his frayed blue collar. Two Indian cavalrymen escaping from the British gallop up on their wild horses to greet him, beaming with joy. 'For Soviet power!' they shout as they gallop off. Then our cars speed back towards Anzali, and Kuchek is gone. Will we ever see him again?

The road passes through a forest, and one of our sailors stops at a tall beech tree, pushes his cap to the back of his head, dips his hand in a bucket of paste, and smears the trunk of this patriarch of the woods. Silence. The heavy fragrant air, the rustling insects, the deserted road, and the first Soviet poster bringing news to Persia of the World Revolution.

CHAPTER 11

In Petersburg

After three years of revolutionary war, it was almost frightening to return to Petersburg. What had happened to the city of the Revolution, capital of Russia's unique new spiritual culture?

Terrible stories of cold and hunger had reached distant parts of the Republic, that it was a dying city, and was staying alive only to fight the Whites, who were advancing from all directions – from Poland and the Gulf of Finland, from Narva and Reval on the Baltic. But what did we find? Not only was it not dying, but a thousand signs bore witness to its regeneration. The noble symmetry of its squares and avenues had a new spartan simplicity, resting under soft carpets of weeds from the weight of the hurrying crowds. The suburbs rested from clouds of car exhaust and the stink of the rotting wooden pavements, most chopped up for firewood. The abandoned parks and gardens rested and flourished wildly in the warmth of the northern summer, making up for the years of crippled summers. The islands of the Neva had become green havens of rest for thousands of sick children and exhausted slaves of labour.

Was this the sleep of death? Was Petersburg doomed to become just another charming lifeless eighteenth-century city, like a Russian Brusges? No, this was the dizzying exhaustion of convalescence, the peace of a hospital ward in the first warmth of summer, the silence of the Field of Mars, where people come to honour their brothers killed in battle.

Petersburg hasn't died, it has saved its history and its monuments to the Revolution, and every Red soldier on each of our ten fronts played their part in defending it. Paralysed Siberia, the Volga cut off at its joints, Ukraine, falling away from Russia in rotting chunks – nowhere inspired such desperate hope and love as proletarian Petersburg. On the Volga, on the shores of the Caspian, in the malaria swamps of Astrakhan, people cried out to it in the emptiness and despair, praying to it in the face of death, for the most precious thing in the world – the birthplace of the Revolution, empty and wild, slowly recovering its strength after the death agony of the old epoch and the birth of the new one, blessed by eternity.

Afghanistan

∵

Afghanistan

Published by the State Publishing House (*Gosizdat*), Moscow, 1925

Our Asia and the Asia Across the Border

First Days. Uzbekistan

Hundreds of miles of peace. The valley warms itself in the sun. Ploughmen move slowly across the fields to the edge of the horizon, raising clouds of dust. The harrows hop behind them, breaking the earth with their iron teeth. A Red cavalry soldier rides home on his peasant pony. The Civil War feels insanely distant here. It's impossible to imagine shells falling on the soft winter crops and the ancient ditches, flooded by the spring rains. Boundless peace.

The Railway Halt

Crowds of Asians, peasants and Red soldiers, jostling and haggling. A forest of faces, and where the bark is soft and pink are their rustling voices. Clustered round a woman selling a towel are mighty oaks, graceful willows, gnarled stumps blasted by the storm. 'How much? Ten? I'll give you five!' laughs a peasant in a shaggy fur cap, clutching his money, the whites of his eyes flashing like silver coins thrown into a mountain stream.

An Asian bootblack with a bushy black beard sits on the ground, gripping his box between his knees like a jewel-case. Inscrutable as Pushkin's Chernomor,[1] indifferent to his fate, he guards his shining polishes and his red velvet cloth, torn from Ludmilla's cloak, and calmly watches the dirty bare feet of the passers-by. His face is dark, and his trade is ephemeral.

Turkestan

Smoke drifts across the flat earth to the sky. The moon casts its light over hundreds of miles of silence, roads laid waste by Tamerlane, wildernesses that never sleep. It's impossible to read here. Heine's hot tears sink into the earth. Even the bawdy tales of the Empress Elizabeth and her diplomats and lovers –

---

1 Chernomor, the evil sorcerer who abducts the heroine of Pushkin's fairytale poem 'Ruslan and Ludmilla'. To rescue Ludmilla, Ruslan must pass through the valley of the dead, an ancient battlefield littered with the bones of Chernomor's victims.

Shuvalov with his lace, cold Bestuzhev, Lomonosov with his odes – pale in the frozen emptiness. There can be no history here, the study of the dead, just a handful of sand mixed with sunlight and salt.

The Steppe

The air smells of aromatic herbs and spices and Asian life. A Kirghiz woman in an embroidered headdress puts a clay pot under a ewe and slowly milks her. The lamb hops around on its weak legs, nuzzling its mother's udders and the woman's skirt. Hundreds of skylarks fill the golden sky with their song. The wind sings its endless seraphic music in the dunes, rolling the sun-warmed sand into new hills and valleys, filled with the hot honey of the day, from which camels unhurriedly graze the green fluff.

The Past

How far we have come – thousands of miles, and thousands of years back in time. The rocks remember Tamerlane as if it was yesterday, and the tracks of the new railway line still echo with the wild clatter of his carts.

How much sun and healing warmth the desert spreads – Tashkent, shimmering like a dark emerald, and finally medieval Bukhara.

Its cool covered bazaars stretch for miles. Pigeons warble in the roofs, dripping rain from a golden midday shower, and old men with the beards of prophets, in their snow-white turbans and bright robes, sit at the doorways to their stalls, smelling the damp roses and counting their money. Tiny donkeys run around laden with reeds, fresh clover and veiled women. One of our officers rides through the crowd in his tall cavalry helmet, like a conqueror of Jerusalem, a Paladin of the Red Star.

Best of all are the gardens of the harem, a paradise of vines, roses, peacocks, pools, swans, tents and buzzing bees. Women sit on carpets laid out under the trees, drinking tea and eating spicy sweets in a silence that mutes the streams and makes the trees stop growing. The smells are so powerful you long to close your eyes, lie on the burning flagstones of the courtyard, and become lighter than the swallows flying round the carved wooden balustrades of the buildings.

Doors lead off the yard to a row of small white rooms decorated with peacock feathers, with little alcoves containing pairs of teapots, a big and a small one, like courting pigeons. And in each of these rooms lives a child-woman of thirteen or fourteen, bewitching and corrupted, slender as the grapevine. Their long hair is braided into hundreds of little plaits, and their toenails are painted bright crimson, and they run barefoot across the carpet in their red and yellow *shalwars*, lowering their eyes and covering their smiles with their hands. Full of curiosity, the little imps come closer, laughing and twittering like birds, touching me with their cool fingers and stroking my hands. I think we liked each other a lot.

Kushka[2]

In the old fortress town of Kushka on the border with Afghanistan, we're joined by eighty Afghan and Russian interpreters and guards, and over a hundred and fifty horses, pack ponies, camels, mules and donkeys, assembled to carry all of us and our luggage the six hundred miles across the Hindu Kush to Kabul.

Hot winds whip the dust from the slopes, like the ashes from a vanished world. But the streets are cool and shady, lined with rustling streams and mulberry trees, which drop their ripe fruits onto the roofs of the whitewashed huts where our soldiers are quartered. It's a real Russian garrison town, with its patrol posts and vigilant commanders. Men who haven't seen an unveiled woman for years peacefully wash their underwear in the river, and wage a constant battle with the peasants who slip across the frontier every night to steal each other's fat-tailed sheep – the famous 'Jamshid Problem', the main stumbling-block to our policies in the East.

A post hammered by tsarist forces into the bare slope of the hill marks the start of Asia proper, enclosed by the blue line of the mountains and the golden belt of the desert. Kushka's cavalry squadron escorts our caravan to Childukheran, our first stopping point in Afghanistan, and all day we hear Russian spoken, and see Red Army helmets flashing among the white turbans. As darkness falls, there are tears in the commander's eyes as he bends tenderly over his horse in the lamplight, his whole magnificent figure reminiscent of Captain Mironov in Pushkin's *Captain's Daughter*. Then he clasps our hands and the Russians leave, and we're on our own.

---

2 Now known by its Turkmen name Serhetabad, or the 'Junction' in frontier slang, the main route for the trafficking of heroin from Afghanistan into Europe.

From Kushka to Herat

After riding all day in the baking sun, which rises slowly from dawn to the white heat of midday, then spills like a river into evening, night is a joy, our reward for all the heat and exhaustion. The path winds across sandy hills and valleys to a broad rocky plateau, like a tilting tombstone from which eternity has erased the inscriptions. Over its edges, the smooth spurs of the Hindu Kush rise to the pale sun. Along the way we pass the skeletons of horses fallen on the passes, torn and terrible, their hooves still attached to their bloody legs. As soon as our horses' droppings touch the ground they're eaten by insects, which hungrily devour any remains of life from our exhausted caravan. Life isn't totally consumed by the heat, it has turned its face to the ground and is holding its breath. Hundreds of creatures stir in the dust. Beetles roll their dung balls, lizards leave their ashy trails, locusts rustle in the scrub, and the horses' hooves raise showers of crickets, filling the air with their dry music.

An hour passes, two hours, three – time is a long red ribbon, and the path is the pumping of the heart. The sun floods the brain with blinding bursts of heat, and visions of Asia, naked on a blazing sword.

Tamerlaine's Citadel

We pass fertile oases, where people and animals stop to drink the pure water bubbling from the rocks. After a brief rest the bugle sounds, and the ceremonial litter bearing our twenty women typists and interpreters sways past between two carts, escorted by wild Afghan horsemen.

The path climbs steeply up from the valley. A temperamental stallion in the line of pack-horses rears up, trying to throw off his heavy load, and our first riders soon approach the next mountain pass. A wild magnificent picture.

Then the path plunges down to another plateau. The curtain of the sun moves slowly westwards across the boundless depths of a shady gorge, overhung with jagged crags of lava and brown marble. Vast columns tower over the emptiness, like palaces rising to the sky, defying dizziness from their eagle heights. Their indescribable splendour and disarray haven't changed since the beginning of time, waiting in this workshop at the edge of the universe for the creative act to be completed. But it's as if at the moment of the most burning desire to live, when the clashing rocks were giving birth to a new world, cooling death passed through the seething metals and scarred them with torment.

The horses slowly pick their way on their strong hooves down to the mountain river at the bottom of the next valley. Breathing deeply, their ears trembling, they drink from its pure cold water and rest in the silence.

Carved into the cliffs above, in a gleaming enamel band inlaid with lapis lazuli, which artists have long forgotten the art of making, is a conical Timurid watchtower. And a little way off, at the edge of the sands, abandoned to the sun and the jackals, stands a palace.

Its ramparts and high square outer walls have collapsed into piles of bricks, but its cool interior hall is still intact, with wide alcoves and comfortable seats where food used to be eaten. In the delicate shell-like tracery of the ceilings are narrow openings for the fires, now open to the sky and the wild pigeons. Once the spicy smells of roast meat wafted out, fragrant with lemon and saffron, and the clink of weapons and dishes, and Saadi's melancholy songs of war. At the wave of a long yellow hennaed hand, hundreds of white-turbaned servants hurried in, the backs of their silver slippers flapping, with water for ablutions, hot pilaus under red covers, carpets for love games and prayers, and the sturdy Khazars guarding the doors to the harem quailed at the peals of laughter inside.

The bugle sounds in the distance, and our horses clear the ruined walls in one leap, and the soft silhouettes of the arched gates see us off with their silent blessing, like outstretched arms.

The road continues along another plateau to a solitary settlement, a couple of mud huts, with some low tents of a black oily fabric spread out over the earth. Several families live in their shade – children of exceptional beauty, herders and their wives, liberated from their *chadors* by toil and poverty, simple and graceful as women from the Bible, who bring the weary riders pitchers of sour fermented mare's milk.

Every so often we pass wells, hiding their damp palms under pointed stone hats. Morning, midday, afternoon – everything is consumed by the fiery emptiness of the sky, dazzled by its dizzying golden depths.

Aware of nothing but our tiredness, with no idea where we are, our caravan approaches a cleft in the hills, where a spring gives life to a few trees and fields. And in this bare place a miracle awaits us, with tents, carpets and tables.

Stopping the horses with much cracking of the whips, our guards abandon their rifles and absurd cavalry uniforms, and become a crowd of quick silent servants, like ghosts from *A Thousand and One Nights*, setting out dinner, bringing rugs, fans and jugs of water. Spirit lamps are lit, crystal tulips on tall silver stands, their smouldering wicks held aloft in the claws of ancient Persian lions. Stars streak across the velvet black sky, disappearing behind the dreaming foliage of the trees and our encampment of tents, lights and fires, shimmering like a mirage in the desert. It's insanely beautiful!

From Herat to Kabul

Nowhere else does life coexist so closely with the dead rocks. At the bottom of a sheer ravine is the fertile Harirud Basin, whose orchards and rye fields are irrigated by hundreds of little streams. Each branch, each stalk of rye, each purple and blue wild flower growing among the crops, drinks the cool water with a barely audible song for the joy of life. At home in Russia, our fields are a dusty gold at harvest time. Here they are eternally fresh, and the splashing streams mingle with the song of the skylarks, like water and wine in a glass the colour of the sun.

Above the fields, like scalding yellow bubbles, the sandy hills are studded with ancient cemeteries, broken slabs of stones laid on the remains of lives lost in bloody feuds with the Khazars. The path runs past them, beneath the brownish-yellow teeth of the mountains, rising in sheer walls above the valley, their crowns touching the sky. Boulders overhang the edges like giant toads about to leap. Then some soft pink volcanic tuff, like faces leaning forward at a meeting. Then suddenly – blood. Somewhere in the mountains the granite veins have burst, as if the heart has become too full of fire and lava after giving birth to this family of giants, and has ruptured into the rocks. On all sides the slopes are streaked with red. Even the sun-baked clay of the shepherds' huts is soaked in precious vermilion. From this clay, humans were made.

High Up

The sharp shoulders of the ridges are covered in flowers, invisible but powerfully aromatic. The wind is as pure and cold as spring water, and the peaks glint with micre, malachite and marble. Our language has no words to describe them, rising to the sky like banners, each vaster than the ocean, vaster in their totality than anything else on earth. Perhaps a great poet looking down from these cloudless heights could describe the unheard-of colours spilling over the metal armour of the rocks, the puffs of opal smoke rising into infinity in the heat of the sun. Perhaps some wild hero standing beneath the soaring eagles will utter his unearthly war cry, drunk with joy at this world waiting to be conquered, and grief that it can't be conquered forever.

The Living

On the lower slopes are the local wild sheep, with their spiral horns and shaggy fleece and strong legs. Thrifty gophers, tormented by their insatiable curiosity. Square-headed lizards, and countless birds, most of them blue. There are pink mosses and wild roses and honeysuckle, and clumps of pink flowers like thorny carnations, with the same sweet girlish scent, growing from a single stem. Wild mint and lavender cling to the rocks like a light frost and perfume the air.

Everything is weightless under the pale sky.

Our horses scramble down the ravine to the soapy greyish-green river, flanked by tall white limestone rocks, and we gallop for the next nine miles like mad people. The sand couldn't be yellower, the sky couldn't be a purer gold, melting and flowing into the mountain ridges in blinding streams of light.

The Ram

Travelling at the front of the caravan, in a special cage on the back of a pack-horse, is the ram, a gift to the Emir from the Governor of Herat. His kind mournful face, with his yellow eyes and silky ears, pokes through the bars, and he has an ivory crown on his head, with two circles cut out at the top for his horns. He wears his silly headgear resentfully, like a child made to wear a grownup's hat, and knowing the hopelessness of his situation, he is refusing to eat and is losing weight. So this evening a friendly talkative goat will be fetched from the mountains to cheer him up.

The twenty servants attending to him grind his barley, polish the bells on his collar and clear his dung, trembling for his health, knowing if any harm comes to him they'll be flogged to within an inch of their lives. And now this road laid by Tamerlane and Alexander, the Great Trunk Road connecting Afghanistan to India, witness to twenty conquests and invasions, is ruled by a sick unhappy ram, and peasants with fierce Persian and Macedonian profiles angrily drive their donkeys into the ditches to make way for him.

The Rabats

Every forty miles or so are the *rabats*, old citadels perched in inaccessible spots in the cliffs, rocky as traps, which have been turned into caravanserais for passing travellers. They still have their fortress-like appearance, with their moats and crenellated battlements and narrow gates, through which pour a steady stream of caravans, just as they did a thousand years ago. Every inch of these buildings, every watchtower and stable, can be defended separately, and at the corners of the inner courtyards are vaulted galleries, where rooms have been set aside for guests.

The mud walls of our windowless cell absorb the heat of the day. Dusty shafts of sunlight flood through the chimney in the ceiling onto the green velvet mattress on the carpet, covered in dirty blue, pink and pistachio-coloured blankets, where the Ambassadors are bitten by revolting 'camel bugs'.

Throwing off their slippers, our kind robber servants bring in little red flower-patterned bowls of tea, like acacia buds in spring. These Afghan servants are strange people. Their only needs are some kohl for their eyes, a good horse and a gun, to shoot any foreigners venturing onto Afghanistan's roads. The lives of these farmers, herders and horsemen have absolutely nothing in common with ours. The handsome giant Faizmamed puts nothing but salt cellars on the table. He is responsible for these cheap nickel bazaar trinkets with their little holes at the top, and they have eaten into his customs and behaviour. Khudodad isn't Khudodad, he is the plates, which he himself doesn't use of course, but which have taken over his entire life – dirty or clean, dozens of them or not enough, foisted on him by this alien culture with its alien ways. You can ask him with tears in your eyes for a glass of water, and he'll return with a blank hypnotised face and give you another damn plate.

We live with our drivers and servants like grubs in an anthill. They pick us up and take us out to the sun, feed us from their antennae, defend us, and take us from place to place, performing tasks that make no sense to each individual ant, but make perfect sense in terms of the colony as a whole, uniting it in bonds of wise conformity and habit.

Like Khudodad and Faizmamed, every peasant from the Hari Valley is one with his field. Each has inherited from his father and forefathers a tiny scrap of earth, watered by an incomprehensible network of wells, canals and dams. They have never understood the ancient origins of the water system that gives them their crops and vines, and they carry out the great rituals of irrigation like the devout at their prayers, and the earth bears fruit. Until one fine day a watercourse in the mountains will collapse, and then no one will know the reasons for the calamity, or have the keys to the old knowledge. The sands will lose their last memories of their vanished culture. The streams will dry up, the fields will blacken, like the barren earth in the cemeteries, and Khudodad and Faizmamed, with their plates and salt cellars, will no longer be men.

One *rabat* is much like another, and at the end of each day we step inside our clay boxes. Wild pigeons warble in the roofs. The bells of the resting horses jingle, and the cavalryman's bugle sounds the evening prayers. Towering above are the mountains, silent and infinite, leaving their tingling afterglow on the skin, and memories of their mighty yellow-brown slopes.

Evenings are when we write our diaries and letters and drink tea. As Ambassadors, *Safir Sahib Khans*, any kind of work in the normal sense of the word is considered beneath us, with the exception of writing, and my diaries inspire the same respect as the marble headstones on the holy graves that fall onto the roads from time to time, decorated with horsetails and wild goats' horns and indecipherable inscriptions.

The Water Boy

Each morning, through a dream of exhaustion, we hear the sounds of splashing water. This is the Indian water boy, sprinkling the dusty courtyard, with his comically lewd way of shaking the mouth of his water-skin in front of him. His baggy blue trousers are tied at his bare ankles, and his thin beard falls onto the ends of the towelled turban wrapped round his thin dry neck. He is paid four rupees a year, and is fed on starvation rations, and he rides at the back of our caravan on a donkey, which brays rudely and shakes its long ears at him. The water boy is the lowest person in the *rabat*. No one *salaams* him – neither the soldier who brings us our tea, clutching his rosettes of bowls in his dirty lap, nor the stable boy who anoints the horns of the Emir's ram with clay, nor the collector of the horses' dung, which people dry and burn on their fires in winter.

The Summits

Alpine cold. The path winds across a plateau through the high mountains, whose crown is an unbelievable twenty thousand feet above sea level. The metallic grey grass rustles like funeral wreaths, and a few little yellow flowers flutter like dying candles. Far below is the emerald velvet strip of the river, lined with the ruins of sharp-clawed fortresses like those guarding the mountain pastures in Northern Greece. High in the sky is a snowstorm of fighting white eagles.

Rocks

Another sudden drop in temperature. Giant rocks loom over the sands, ancient as time, splashed with a dew of rare grasses. The rocks are so old, it's almost

frightening to look at them. Over the centuries the sharp knives of the mountain ridges have carved fissures in them, spilling their sand over the dusty slopes
like the waves of a petrified ocean, exhausted by its existence. Only what is truly
eternal survives here. There are no young rocks, no new giants. Lumps of marble
like stone bouquets, pink, pale yellow and grey, veined with black, waste their
brilliance. Even the days have existed before, running across the crags and ravines and dying a thousand deaths on the peaks, telling the earth as they vanish,
'We'll return until you're gone forever, and the last of your rocks have crumbled
to dust'.

The Sand-Spout

Between a lavender bush and a lump of lava, a wisp of sand hovers in the tense
still air. The grains sweep up, expanding in the heat into a whirling funnel,
pierced by shafts of golden sunlight. The top spins more quickly, and suddenly
it's a dancing fire, spilling over the turquoise edges of the sky like hot wine
exploding from a bottle. A grey column coils from its blazing depths, tilting
into smoky banners. Then the base crumples, and a grey geni with bound feet
spirals into the emptiness.

Descent

The path drops vertically into the Kabul Valley, the most fertile area of south-
east Afghanistan. The road is shaded by tall green poplars, and lined with
flourishing orchards. Only the crimson frames of the rocks remind us of the torture chamber of the mountains. Our poor horses have descended the burning
thousand-foot cliffs as thin as skeletons, with lowered heads and open wounds
on their legs. But now they revive and speed up, cheerfully swinging their panniers.

Merchants in bright robes ride along on sturdy mules, holding umbrellas
menacingly aloft. We pass camels loaded with bales of cotton, with their naked
swaying necks and soft strong feet, like the arms of giants, and scampering
behind them their thin-legged babies, with their liquid blinking eyes. We pass
women with uncovered faces, and peasants and mountain people with low
dark foreheads and ancient Semitic profiles, their narrow eyes the colour of
amber and rusty iron. These give way to the pale oval faces of the people in the
Kabul Valley, with their flashing agate eyes, powerfully built and extraordinarily
beautiful, especially the children, darting round the clay buildings like birds.

At the bottom of a hill, below a cluster of huts and the ruins of a white fortress, is a clump of trees that resemble willows, with the same pale elongated leaves. And in the middle of these trees is a sacred pond, filled with cold transparent water from a mountain spring, the blueish colour of melted snow. Hanging from a branch above the pond is the cage of a friendly quail, loved by the Afghans for its shrill musical song, seen in all their orchards and bazaars. As it scrapes its coral beak against the bars, a grain of barley drops in the water, and the limpid surface instantly puckers into seething iridescent knots of steel-blue arrows. These are the fish of the holy pond, uncatchable shoals of wild trout, throwing themselves headlong at every scrap of food.

Dangling one leg over the edge, a reaper sits resting from his labours, dreaming with his eyes open, the silver blade of his sickle mirroring the darting fish. A woman leaves her slippers on the top step, throws back her veil, washes her jug in the water and fills it, then walks unhurriedly back. The trees cast their trembling shadows over the water. A scene of utter peace.

Further ahead in the valley, the harvest is being celebrated with an old pagan ritual. Dozens of women move between the boundaries of the fields still untouched by the sickle and bless the crops, their veils thrown back from their faces and falling in soft folds to their feet, bending occasionally to pick the largest stalks as charms for health and happiness.

The wind blows a prickling dust from the fields that have been reaped. The sheaves are piled up like a giant bonfire, blazing with the harvest of a fruitful summer, and are threshed by slowly circling pairs of black oxen, driven by entire families, replacing each other in a chain. Then the women winnowers, in their baggy red trousers and thrown-back blue veils, shake the sheaves high above their heads, releasing showers of the glowing amber chaff.

The sun is at its zenith. Weary sheep shelter under the poplar trees planted along the river to protect the water. The smell of apricots and baked clay wafts from some huts clinging to the rocks in the glare of the heat, and an old man impassively lays out his fiery fruits in the dust.

We have left our last *rabat*, and Kabul's clay walls and towers appear in the distance, like termites' nests. The bugle sounds for the last time as we pass through the gates, and a soldier covers his ears with his hands to drown the piercing cries of our ram, who is to be slaughtered for dinner.

In Kabul

Dawn. A cool breeze raises clouds of dust from our tethered munching horses – everything that makes for peace and happiness in the desert. Gardeners water the wild flowers sown into the grass, plain but very sweet-smelling. The soldiers who guarded us in the night wash in the pond, and without their caps and uniforms on we can see how old they are, grey and ashy as rocks. Their jobs are obligatory and for life.

The quail in its cage in the apple orchard was kept awake all night by the electric light, and glares at it with sleepy bloodshot eyes, cursing this wild country for its modern tricks. Beyond the orchard, at the edge of town, are the roofs of a village, a squalid mud burrow filled with hunger and poverty, which we're forbidden to visit. And here is a white poplar, with its rustling green crown. At night, when the moonlight streams through its narrow branches, it becomes a Russian birch tree, tender and talkative and full of laughter and movement. But we mustn't think of Russia. Last night the terrible word famine was uttered on the radio, a slap in the face to the luxury of King Amanullah's palace, as we sat down to our slices of sweet ram's meat, served by his elderly footman in white gloves. We have arrived.

CHAPTER 2

The Afghan Woman and the Dances of the Tribes

Without being Muslim or knowing the language, it's hard in this cut-off country to be close to people, or get a sense of their family lives. Here, more than in almost any other Eastern country, women are barely visible, separated from the world by their heavy *chadors*, falling from their heads to the tips of their loose backless slippers, which further impede their gait. Their shadows are everywhere – in the bright bazaar crowds, riding on donkeys at the back of the caravans with their sunburnt children, with their kohled eyes and brass rings on their fingers and toes. Their faces are hidden from even the babies at their breast, as if they were held by ghosts. When we pass a group of them in the bazaar, they step aside and follow us with long hidden looks. What are they thinking? Do they judge us? Do they envy us?

Passing riders splash them with mud, and a car drives through, scattering the camels, catching one of their *chadors* in its wheels. She is thrown crumpled and groaning to the ground, and a passer-by helps her up without lifting her veil, and leaves her at the edge of the next field. Half-dead or merely concussed, it's all the same, she is just a woman.

The peasant woman and the herdsman's wife are freed from their honourable purdah by toil and poverty. Water in these sandy mountains is more precious than life. The wheat fields laid out at the foot of the rocks, carefully cleared of lava and granite, are watered by innumerable mountain streams which must be constantly adjusted with new dams and channels to increase or reduce the flow, and women work with uncovered faces, sharing with men the work of clearing and deepening these drainage channels. Sheltering from the heat under the mulberry trees lining these life-giving streams, or in the thick sweet-smelling rushes, they rest from their labours with their brothers and husbands, dark-haired and graceful, their strong arms and necks burnt by the sun, with their baggy red trousers and ancient Greek profiles, moulded from ancient Tanagra clay.

In the mountain pastures, women calmly tend their flocks, and drive them home in the evenings to their rough huts, solitary fortresses built on rocky paths once passed by Tamerlane and Alexander, where they turn their bundles of fragrant clover drying in the sun, and spin long strings of camel hair with their ancient spinning-wheels.

These are the more prosperous peasant women from the mountain regions of Hazaria. The nomad women, without mud huts or apricot trees, are also free of the laws imposed by jealous Mohammed on beautiful Aisha. And the poorer the nomadic clan or tribe, the more beautiful and free the women, giving birth to their babies in the dust, nursing them beside smoking fires on sheepskins whose sour smell repels the insects. Beautiful as gods, free as all outcasts, they go wherever hunger leads the family – to Afghanistan's cool mountain pastures in the spring, to the borders with India in the autumn.

Afghanistan's mountain tribespeople, like those in India in the Himalayas, fiercely guard their independent frontiers and their unique way of life, and they have played a key role in the country's liberation struggle, and in the liberation of its women. When their caravans pass through Kabul with their gleaming rifles, people stand aside for them as for conquering heroes, and as a major military threat to the British. Even in Kabul's Great Bazaar the tribeswomen don't wear the *chador*, and the mullahs busy themselves with themselves with their prayers, averting their lustful gaze from these wives' and mothers' burning eyes.

For over a century, the tribespeople living in the mountainous frontier areas of India and Afghanistan have been treated by the British with exceptional brutality. Cut off by a military cordon and a never-ending series of border wars, with no help from outside, they have defended their independence against the most powerful conquerors in the world, and their uprisings in these inaccessible areas have been the first major challenge to British rule.

Yet even India's epic national literature has failed to give a voice to its tribespeople, and to express their struggle for independence, they must look to the songs and dances of Afghanistan. This flourishing of Afghan creativity is particularly impressive given the general collapse of culture in the East – which sadly includes Afghanistan. The poetry of Persia, passed on from generation to generation, has degenerated into the suggestive couplets sung at male gatherings at the court. Hundreds of Moghul watchtowers in the mountains lie ruined and abandoned. People have long forgotten the art of making pure lapis lazuli, which has been stripped and stolen from Herat's exquisite minarets, and the rain has washed away the old frescoes. The only ones to survive are on the marble shrines to the saints, and even these are being chipped away by the roots of the trees. Yet every Afghan beggar or donkey-driver in his flea-infested rags has a love of colours that puts to shame our most avant-garde theatre designers in Russia, with their drab Western outfits. And the most colourful of all the art forms to penetrate Afghanistan's poverty and superstition are its dances and songs.

In October, the tribespeople performed at the country's Independence celebrations, which were held this year on the fifth anniversary of the Bolshevik

Revolution. Kabul's vegetating social life came to life during the *tamasha*.[1] The town thronged with bright crowds of all ranks and races – Indian money-lenders in their yellow turbans, merchants from Bukhara in their silk gowns, pale-faced Western officials in their black tailcoats, Amanullah's bloated sat-raps, demoted now to mere hangers-on at his court, and the mountain warriors, with their guns and black woollen cloaks, who lent their own wild heroic spirit to the day, leaving the cowering bazaar crowds with a foretaste of a completely new kind of social relations, shot through with the hot bright light of equality.

Police spies rode through the bazaars on bicycles, and were recognised by every street urchin. Horses shied at the sounds of the drumbeats, and soldiers in their European-style spurs and uniforms kept order with their rifles, driving people away from any exalted figure who passed, frantically saluting their cars and carriages. Dozens of flags fluttered in the breeze, including the red flag of the Russian Soviet Federation of Socialist Republics, and Amanullah laid bets on who would be first to bow to his hated British 'allies' – his elephants or his cyclists, the students from his new Military Academy, or his two Turkish gener-als recently returned from the front.

The tribespeople were invited to dance before the Emir – about a hundred of their strongest, most handsome boys and men, among whom hunger, the British, and their nomadic way of life had produced a careful natural selection. Only one looked physically weak, and he was the musician. But what a musi-cian! His tormented intoxicated face was as tense as the bow of his ancient fiddle, and the god of music poured through every cell of his thin body, inspir-ing the dancers with the shuddering beats of his drums.

Their dance expressed the very essence of the tribespeople's fighting spirit. Rocking from side to side, shaking their long black hair and chanting spells, they lunged high in the air, like hunters pursuing their prey, then writhed on the ground like dying warriors, their chests torn open by the same British bullets used to shoot game and insurgents in Malabar and the Punjab. Then finally they conquered, joyfully lifting their arms and taking flight like mountain eagles.

That was their dance. But their songs were even bolder and more expressive. Everyone sat in a circle around the best singer, accompanied by the drummer, as he chanted: 'The English took our land! But we'll drive them out and go back to our homes and fields!'

The others repeat the chorus with a shrill taunting laugh: 'You'll never beat us! We'll wipe you off the earth like cows eating grass!'

---

1   *Tamasha*, a type of popular Indian peasant theatre originating in the nineteenth century in the western Maharashtra province, which dramatised stories from India's history, and was widely used for anti-British propaganda purposes.

The singer is surrounded by a wall of silent listeners, and thousands of mocking eyes are on the British attaches on the platform, who applaud ironically, with pale tense faces.

'But not all Europeans are like the damned *ferengi!* There are the Bolsheviks, who are with the Muslims!'

The singer brandishes his rifle over his head – an English rifle, captured in his last battle with the enemy – and the crowd bellows with laughter and moves closer to the platform. They know all about the 'Bolsheviks', they sing songs about them on the borders with India, at the edge of the world, and the drummer bares his white teeth and cheerfully beats his cunning sticks.

CHAPTER 3

Machine Khan. The Woollen Mill

Hundreds of years ago, the walls of Kabul's old fortress converged over the narrow path from the valley, like joined eyebrows. Then time, trade and great conquerors made a breach in them for the irrigation channels and the highway. And finally on this spot, where to right and left of the road the broken walls snake up the rocks to the searing heat of the sky, Afghanistan's first factory appeared, the British-owned *Machine Khan.*

The new walls are constructed from the stones of the old fortress, carved by slaves' hands into the ribs of the mountains, echoing with the cries of the workers who climbed up to the old turrets with knives in their teeth, and were torn down with bloody knees and broken leather shields. As dusk falls, the factory's gleaming windows are like the mirage of some alien civilisation – mysterious constellations of electricity lighting up the rocks. But by day the valley is grey in the heat, and scorching winds blow great sails of dust through the narrow gates into the town. Little peasant boys up to their knees in the muddy ditches throw wooden shovelfuls of water at the nomads and passing tradesmen, with their donkeys and camels, and the smell of wet dust mingles with the smell of onions from the fields.

The orchards and vegetable beds stretch to the doors of the factory, guarded by sentries. The water that once irrigated the wheat and barley, the clover and maize and the apricot trees, now pours into the factory's troughs and turbines, and the hot breath of the old medieval structure smells of warm lanoline and milk.

A bare-chested shepherd in a white turban leans wearily on his staff, like a Biblical Jacob, as lost and silent beside his noisy machine as the ancient patriarch with his flock. Elsewhere, the East is as silent as the ancient graves littering the mountains. Even the noise of the bazaars, teeming with dusty rainbows of energy and light, appears transient and ephemeral. Here in *Machine Khan*, at the heart of the hottest valley, in this concentration of Eastern silence – behind walls built with centuries-old stones, each with its own forgotten history, where no shadow of life, no moisture or green, protects the workers' slave labour, just a quail singing tenderly in its willow cage – power looms gnash their iron jaws, hammers pound, and the electricity gasps and trembles as it pushes the heavy wooden shuttles back and forth, like the peasants' ancient ploughs.

The noise casts its spell on the poverty, the mountains, the mosques, the Mahommedan sky, and after the midday sluggishness of the fields, the blood rushes to the head. It's so long since we have touched a warm living machine, and for a moment we could be back at Petrograd's Putilov or Kronstadt factories.

Working here are the greatest conspirators in the dusty Kabul Valley. And after the fat Afghan swindlers, the sugary courtiers, and the stiff-backed British with their contemptuous smiles, cutting their faces like the notches on their bullets, the pure proletarian rage is like a miracle, maturing like wine in the stuffy air.

The foreman's stick beats back the group of workers gathering around us, and the fat Afghan manager greets us in a dream, bowing and clutching the place where his heart is, under all the bulging flesh and white flannel.

The first workshop is like a farmyard, wafting smells of livestock and human sweat through its low doors. Swallows fly to their nests under the eaves, bringing in the good smell of the fields, and small boys not yet in their teens sit on the earth floor sorting bales of white, black and brown fleece. These children of landless peasants work as bonded labourers. Yesterday they were mowing the fields, watering the roads. Today they're in the factory, and the foreman beats their bare backs as he beats the donkeys, meekly lifting their strong little hooves under their canopies of firewood.

The boys are forbidden to go beyond the scouring-baths at the entrance, or to touch the looms towering over the next workshop, with the patriarchal authority of a manor-house. The spindles belch out breaths of hot steam as they comb the matted wool, and the bobbins blow soft white flakes up to the rafters, like a lace of winter frost. A mist of fibres clings to the workers' bloodless faces, oblivious to everything but the clattering belts. The machines boil them and swallow them up, destroying the nerves and muscles of their old peasant life. And the more complex the looms, spinning the fleece first into wool, then into soft wide ribbons, the greater the tension on their faces, as they operate the incomprehensibly intricate system of cogs, wheels and belts.

Stripped to the waist, emaciated by hunger, a grey-haired peasant scrapes the threads off his bobbin with his sickle. The manager stands over him, so fat that a frog is said to have died in the folds of his stomach while he was bathing, and he only discovered it days afterwards from the smell. How many generations of workers must rot alive in the folds of this Eastern fat, until its body in turn is fertilised?

An old man in a white turban with piercing black eyes, like the holes dug by small animals around graves, checks the dial on the wall, whirring continuously, which measures the looms' speed. He has been trained to decipher the numbers, keeping one eye on the circling arrow, the other on his trembling threads. And the sign on the dial, in big English letters, says 'MANCHESTER', like a magic greeting sent into the void from the kingdom of exploitation and machines, where labour is taking on the power of capital. 'MANCHESTER' means we will win. 'MANCHESTER' means don't despair, we're your brothers, we'll support you. In fifty, a hundred or even two hundred years, our hands will meet. And the machine mutters angrily 'Yes, yes, yes!' – although no one can hear it yet.

Afghanistan's semi-artisan, semi-European serf economy weighs especially heavily on *Machine Khan's* most highly skilled workers, who have been brought here from all over the country to get industry going. The machine is a cruel master. It will produce only one worker from the hundreds who serve it, sucking them up and throwing them out like slag, with no professional qualifications, just an unhealthy paleness, and itching sores on their skin. Whole villages are destroyed to make one small factory, whose owner is police-chief, army commander, ancestral landowner and absolute monarch, all rolled into one.

The new power looms represent a combination of nineteenth- and twentieth-century technologies. The shuttle flies back and forth, taking the threads wrapped round the worker's fingers, while his foot controls the pedal that adjusts the shades of the yarn to make new patterns. Although his personal taste is essential to this labour, and the main instruments of production are still his expert hands, the demands of mass production and the cruel conditions of factory life, with its interminably long working day, are transforming the living artist, with his skills and customs, into a human machine.

Yet here in Kabul's old fortress, where workers are beaten with sticks, and the living corpses of children and old men cut the cloths of their shrouds with the scissors of Goya's devils, the proletarian yeast is rising. The foreman's stick never appears in this workshop, and even the manager's great stomach fails to win its usual respect here. Nobody smiles or lifts their eyes from their shuttles, as they hurl themselves furiously back and forth. If possessions could bring happiness or unhappiness, I wouldn't envy the owners of the cloaks and blankets made from this cloth, steeped in healthy class hatred.

At last we reach the burning heart of *Machine Khan*, an airless underground cavern so hot that the clothes stick to the skin, and the sweet scent of the almond trees in the courtyard is drowned by the dizzying smell of hot machine-oil. Boilers reach to the ceiling. The open jaws of the furnaces are streaked with circles of white-hot metal. It's as if the whole of this vast boiling workshop yearns for a sea of icy blue water to extinguish the heat.

Tending the boilers in this inner sanctum is the master of the factory's fire and energy. His gaunt face under his neatly tied turban has the soft features of an Indian Buddha, with the paleness of metal at the point of combustion. The noise in this hell makes it impossible for him to speak, but as he turns to greet us, his face has a wistful brotherly expression, as if he is saying some special

human words to us he wants us never to forget. How alone he must feel, surrounded by workers whose class consciousness still doesn't go beyond a hatred
of their tormentors the machines, as he waits hour by hour, year by year, for
his underground fires to blaze up and destroy the foreman's stick and the manager's fat stomach.

The manager sees him smile at us and moves closer, and the man shakes our
hands firmly and turns away, knowing he may not live to see the day when the
fine artists and craftsmen dying in this factory will turn their machines into
their allies, and the slaves of this fantastic new technology will be masters of
Afghanistan.

CHAPTER 4

The Covered Woman and her Child

The snow hasn't completely melted yet, but the bubbling of the water-mills is drowned by the roar of the swollen river, smelling of moss and freshness and the sea. The poplars are silver against the turquoise sky, and the fields are filled with teenagers and children in their crimson tunics, weeding the tender green crops.

During the festival of Nawruz, the Spring Equinox, the start of the Afghan New Year, the whole of Kabul pours out of the town to the roundabouts and teashops. Smells of hot charcoal and roast meat fill the air, and children are carried to the *tamasha* on their fathers' shoulders, holding rattles and whistles, little paper mosques, idols with golden eyes, and purple wooden horses with orange heads and green legs. Crowds line the rocky ledges along the roads, like bright statues against the sky, watching the horse-riding displays and wrestling matches. Camels move slowly along the paths above with their loads of cotton, and the ladies of the court hurry past without stopping, raising trails of dust with the hems of their veils.

As dusk falls, all the women from Kabul and the surrounding villages flock to the gardens of the Emperor Babur[1] to celebrate the new moon, whose fine sly sickle signals the end of the thirty-day fast of Ramadan. Thousands of faceless ghosts, of all ages and classes, hurry along the paths between the tall rye, in their curved slippers, identical dark baggy trousers, and thick knitted stockings and veils – even the slits for their eyes are covered in heavy black mesh. In their arms they carry their rejoicing babies, beautiful as flowers, with their kohled eyes, little bells on their wrists and ankles, and hats decorated with paper butterflies, protecting them
from the dust with the folds of their shrouds.

On all sides nature rejoices, from the purple snow-capped mountains and the fragrant clover meadows, to the burning roses in the Bagh-i-Babur gardens. And behind the high clay walls of the gardens, the veils are finally thrown off.

Thousands flutter in the breeze, like wide black ribbons, as the women climb the hill to Babur's summer pavilion, surrounded by peaceful streams and waterfalls. The little girls and young women run straight to the swings, while their

---

1 Zahiruddin Muhammed Babur, 'Tiger' in Persian (1483–1530), first Mohgul Emperor of India, buried at his request in Kabul.

mothers sit in noisy groups on the grass. Traditionally this is a day of contemplation, and the buzz of conversation gradually drops to a murmur, like the hum of a spinning-wheel.

The more prosperous women rest on rugs on the grass like birds unused to flying, their soft bodies flowing comfortably into their usual cross-legged position. Among them are some extraordinary faces. A large middle-aged woman unhurriedly picks her spot in the shade of an ancient sycamore tree, and sinks panting onto a cushion, exhausted from her few steps from her carriage. Then she lifts her face, and it's the face of a Madonna, calm, clear and beautiful, with a smooth white brow and melancholy gaze, as if she has lived many lives before, and their beginnings and ends are like the stilled waters of the streams, and she submits to their unalterable current. The first snows of winter, the first flowers, the cry of a bird on a spring night, the waxing and waning of the moon – all inspire an animal wonder in her, which her wealthy elderly husband cannot understand. She foretells dark times, like autumn water disappearing under the earth, and she sees the murky shallows of Lethe as clearly as the heat and joy of early spring, unfolding in the sun.

We are welcomed with extraordinarily friendly *salaams*, especially by the poorer women, barefoot in rags, from their hovels on the rocks. The young ones laugh, and the children shout, and the old ones reach out to touch us. Not one asks us for money, as if they understand what sort of *khanums* we are, and feel an instinctive sympathy with us, which the bazaars and the *madrasas* are powerless against.

In this sea of poverty are the tribeswomen, princesses in their bright rags, and the plump merchants' wives, with their tight European corsets, sharp-toed shoes, elaborate hairstyles, and ceremonial painted masks. They sit on chairs in the amphitheatre before an attentive crowd of thousands, who will remember for the rest of their lives the nylon stockings on some lady's pale calf on this holy day, and the feathers on her hat.

Between rich and poor is an unbridgeable gulf, which is patrolled by hordes of small boys of about nine or ten, pupils from the Military Academy, who are allowed to be little soldiers for the day. They're given unloaded rifles, which they poke wherever it pleases them, at the babies, at the women's stomachs, running the show with the animal contempt for their mothers they have taken in with their milk, which fills their entire education. Those in whose honour the festival is held, its heroines, allowed once a year to remove their veils, safe from their husbands, fathers and brothers, who wait respectfully for them at the gates with their donkeys and carts, become prey on this day of their liberation to these over-privileged boys, their own sons, who kick and punch them with the casual cruelty of adults, out of sight of the male members of their families.

A group of ragged tribeswomen, with their light step and golden skin, which has never known the *chador*, sit round the swimming pool singing their national songs. Beside these graceful gazelles, who hunt in the mountains with ancient double-barrelled rifles, the coiffured merchants' wives look like fat-tailed sheep, struggling to support the weight of their udders between their short legs. Smiling angrily at them, they jerk their heads at the boys, who hurl themselves at the pool and beat the women back. The wind throws up blinding clouds of dust, and when they go to splash their eyes in the water, the boys kick them away.

During the entire four hours of their ordeal, women make no effort to defend themselves or their babies against these little defenders of public order, and allow themselves to be pushed around like cattle. None of these strong wives and mothers would dream of fighting back, apart from a mad old woman, who throws herself from the terrace onto the burning dust of the path, and stands there howling, as brown and rusty as the setting sun, fighting off the boys who rush up to silence her.

Meanwhile far from the dust and the howling, the Emir's wife passes through the gardens, gleaming with unearthly beauty, the most beautiful woman in Afghanistan.

CHAPTER 5

The Parade Ground

On the edge of town, surrounded by a scattering of hills like chaff around a threshing-floor, is a hot windswept field dying of thirst, where daily military exercises are held. Flashing trumpets play military marches, like military marches the world over, and soldiers in their heavy boots and hot winter uniforms drill for hours in the sweltering heat, melting like butter in this dusty frying-pan.

It's striking how small and young most of them are. Almost all are teenagers, doing their military service for the sons of the rich merchants, the aristocrats of the bazaar. Afghan law allows any recruit to hire someone to replace him, which means the army consists mainly of landless peasants and the lumpen-proletariat – especially the latter.

The senior officers, by contrast, are cultivated like hothouse flowers. Selected as young children to live close to the court and the Emir's family, these toy cadets of five or six, sons of the *sardars* who serve the Afghan throne, are even allowed to enter the women's quarters of the Palace during religious holidays. Surrounded by the rustling skirts of these ambitious royal recluses, who applaud the cause of progress and enlightenment at their banquets, and fight viciously for the sweets, the little soldiers representing the male half of humanity in the harem take their responsibilities extremely seriously, saluting and clicking their heels and waving their swords, pushing through the women to the sherbets and crystallised fruits.

When they grow older, the sacred doors of the harem will be closed to them forever, as they are to every male not related by blood to the Emir. But they carry into the barracks and the parade ground their childhood memories of precious jewels glinting in the twilight, of laughing women running down the long wide staircases to the gardens to play on the swings.

In a country where women's faces are hidden as something indecent, these pages of the bedchamber remember the intimate side of life revealed to them in the harem as the happiest experiences of their lives. And their memories of living with princesses, idealised over the years like all childhood memories, take the form of a fanatical devotion to the Emir.

Needless to say, the lives of these officers have absolutely nothing in common with those of the hired rabble. The young conscripts are ruled by a savage religious fanaticism. Any who break a fast, gulp some water or eat a crust of bread after their exhausting drill in the sun, are subjected to humiliating public punishment, paraded through town sitting backwards on a donkey, to be spat at and beaten by the crowds.

During the fast of Ramadan, Kabul's workers and soldiers work from dawn to dusk under the watchful eyes of the mullahs, in a state of nervous rage and exhaustion, delirious with hunger and thirst. Naturally the officers, the *makhi*, merely pay lip service to the fast. Enlightened absolutism, which came to Afghanistan with the Emir's first reforms, has inevitably clashed with the clergy in its fight for secular power. The senior ranks of the army, who share Amanullah's mocking Voltairean scepticism about religion, veiled in a superficial observance of the rituals, retire during the fast to their houses outside town, to indulge themselves out of sight of the workers. And their hypocritical piety, peering through their fingers at the conscientious exhaustion of the barracks, widens the gulf between them and the rank and file.

This officer caste, the *maktab-i-kharbie*, Afghanistan's new intelligentsia, is educated at Amanullah's Military Academy. Along with the spurs and epaulettes, the shooting, marching and cavalry skills, boys are taught history, geography, chemistry and foreign languages – all from a Pan-Islamist Sharia viewpoint of course, with silly textbooks that would make an educated Arab from the sixteenth century blush. But nevertheless, these things are taught. And although the Turkish officer running the Academy is the court buffoon and a drunken bloated sadist, he knows what is expected of him, and he beats mangled castrated knowledge into his pupils' heads, along with various foreign tricks with smallshot and saltpetre, and plenty of patriotic rhetoric.

The young officers who graduate with tightened belts, rubber backbones and iron legs have the marvellous arrogance of Robinson Crusoes served by millions of gullible Man Fridays. And between them and the lower depths, there is also a large class of non-commissioned officers, whose roots lie deep in the soldier masses. They live the same lives, and share the same interests, and everything brings them together – their common ignorance, and the modesty of their needs. All drink water from the ditch, eat rice with their hands, pray sincerely at sunset, and cringe before their superiors. Each dreams of somehow bettering himself – of buying a good robe, a good horse and a wife, passing the evenings sprawled on a string mattress holding court to his crowd of barefoot servants, who squat before him with humble smiles.

Impossible dreams! One has a couple of apples, another a hookah made from a soda bottle, another a fly-whisk. And when dusk falls, the long mournful call of the regimental bugle summons them all to prayer.

Virtually none of these non-commissioned officers will ever rise above the level of conscript. Like the conscripts, they are wretchedly paid, and they wear the same ragged uniforms year in year out, summer and winter, putting them on only for parade drill, stripping off immediately they return to the barracks to their underwear. They teem with the same lice, sit on the same dirty sheep-skins, go barefoot in the snow, punch people in the face and are punched back. And if by some fantastic stroke of luck one is promoted to sergeant, there is as much difference between him and the top brass as between a thoroughbred Arab stallion and a humble donkey with its lush crinoline of clover.

The figure of this sergeant in his neatly buttoned tunic, clutching his sword and furtively scratching his hair, is strangely familiar. Perhaps one day he will figure in the new literature of Afghanistan, as a sentimental Dickens hero in a turban. Now, suspecting nothing of his splendid destiny, he sits on the field as the village barber scrapes his hard thin cheeks and bristling skull with a huge razor, without soap.

Quinine and Carbolic

Next to the parade ground, wafting smells of disinfectant and formaldehyde over the cracked earth, is the military hospital. Its small courtyard is filled with flowers, fluttering close to the ground like butterflies, watered with medical slops and urine, but powerfully fragrant. Inside, one of the two Turkish doctors, in his tasselled officer's cap and white gown, shows us round the operating theatre, the wards, the medical school and the new bath house.

The operating theatre contains an urn for boiling water, a wooden table covered in oilcloth, some buckets, and an impressive array of saws and scalpels, which an old servant hastily dusts with the hem of his gown. Then the surgical ward. It must be said that the standards of hygiene are excellent. The earth floor is swept, the bandages on the patients are clean, and there are no bad smells from the beds. In the next ward, patients with feverish red mouths and yellow faces lie next to each other, lined up as if on parade. We stop beside an elderly soldier wasted with fever, and ask the doctor what he is being treated for. 'Typhus and malaria', he replies promptly. 'We give him camphor for typhus, and quinine in case it's malaria. It's my own treatment, and we use it with great success'. The results are plain to see. Typhus, spotted fever and malaria lie side by side, passed from patient to patient. In these circumstances, the doctor is correct in seeing every typhus patient as a future malaria patient, and the malaria patients, deliriously dangling their heads from the bed and resting their thin legs on the pillow, as future typhus patients.

He is a qualified doctor. But what of those who will fall into the hands of the students at the medical school, who a year from now will be opening independent practices? There are fifteen of them, bright young boys picked from the Military Academy, sitting on benches around their sergeant-major, chanting from their hand-written textbooks. Our interpreter translates for us: 'Tuberculosis is an infectious disease, whose microbes are spread in air and water ...' Tuberculosis, microbes. Despite their youth, they clearly possess serious knowledge, and their achievements have earned them several stripes on their uniforms. But when we ask them through our interpreter why cholera is caught from drinking ditch-water, they look baffled, and their sergeant responds with a brisk military salute.

Further on all is well again. The kitchen, the larders, the spacious bath house under construction are all spotlessly clean. Discipline, desperate feverish cries, and the flowers flourishing wildly in the heat of the sun.

Here in Kabul's first European-style hospital, it's a revelation to see a thermometer in an Afghan's armpit, as parched as the stray dogs in the bazaar, too lethargic to move from the riders' whips. For these impoverished people, the Réaumur is the frontier post to a new chronology, an end to the dust and sweat of their endless travels, and the first step to a more settled existence.

An Afghan's entire life is spent on the move. The nomads' children are carried as babies thousands of miles in their mothers' arms, from the mountain passes of the Hindu Kush on the borders with India, to the pastures of Khazaria; from the telegraph poles of the East India Company, climbing like black stakes to the summits, to the dusty citadel of Herat and its Great Bazaar, where they exchange a few gold coins embossed with the head of Alexander for some bread or a handful of rice. The peasants' children drive their sheep to market, lazily shaking their fat tails and leaving their musky droppings on the roads. Men travel miles to sell their bread to merchants whose flour is mixed with dust, resting in the yards of their mud homes to drink water from the ditch and pray, while the mullahs keep a watchful eye on the passing donkeys and camels.

People here travel so far, until the age of sixty or seventy, past so many bones whitening in the sands. Only in the East is old age so quick and dry, like the ticking seconds of a clock. Only on its roads do you see an old woman with an uncovered face, hurrying along with barely perceptible little steps, clutching a pair of silver-embroidered slippers to sell at the bazaar, like two Egyptian doves. The only fear these grandmothers have is of stopping. Stopping means the end, like the gravestones buried in clumps of wild mint, flooding the dusty air with their aromatic scent.

And now here is the hospital, with free food and a bed, and a spotty youth who wipes the chamberpots, plates and enemas with the greasy sash of his turban. For the soldier lying here with an expression of boundless calm, like a road suddenly empty of people, buried in weeds and silence, this is his first rest, his first leisure – true, graced with typhus or syphilis, but even these barely disturb the hospital's sacred peace.

Life in the East is as unchanging as the strip of sky above the hospital's baking roof. But *Hospital Khan* has cut the old life to the bone, like a run-over dog thrown in a ditch. The amputated limbs, the eyelids shrivelled by trachoma under the mysterious folds of the *chador*, slipping with a devilish laugh from the pages of *A Thousand and One Nights* – all these beginnings and ends are brought together inside the hospital's walls, in which syphilis and gonorrhoea have eaten an incurable hole.

The director is Doctor Nurenbek. Twenty years ago, Nurenbek left his native Turkey to study medicine in Paris, and for some reason he ended up in Kabul, as personal physician to the old Emir Habibullah. Abandoning his Parisian techniques, he set up the hospital and a mass smallpox vaccination programme, and dedicated his life to inoculating and operating on his patients, or dispatching them to the next world. He saved thousands of lives with his vaccinations, and Habibullah rewarded him with a young slave girl, who he then felt honour-bound to marry. Wizened as a little frog, her painted brick-red face lined with deep grey furrows like ditches in a field, his *khanum* attends all the women's audiences at the Palace, hiding her crooked peasant hands under her bright pink silk robes, like the claws of a frightened bird. How the two of them live together is a mystery. But somehow from her silk folds she has produced three daughters, lively skinny little *gamines* with lacey pantaloons and heavy-lidded eyes, smiling and curtseying like emancipated Russian serfs.

The doctor has a large library of books. He loves Shakespeare, and is an avid reader, and he hasn't spoke to a European for fifteen years. And his loyal bourgeois face under its black skullcap, as worn by Paris concierges and professors, has acquired a strange lopsided grimace. When he laughs, he stretches his mouth to his ears and screws up one eye, and his round stomach heaves under his waistcoat. But there is no joy in his laughter, just a look of horror, as if kind honest Nurenbek is mocking the farce his life has become.

He loves operating on people. He loves passing through the wards to the operating theatre, where his elderly Afghan assistant eyes him like a sorcerer, casting spells at his instruments, trying to replace the castor-oil and carbolic with his charms and powdered dogs' semen. At these moments, Nurenbek imagines he is a famous professor surrounded by snow-white gowns, and that the cornucopia which shook his illiterate *khanum* into his lap will one day reward him with the *Légion d'Honneur*. Dreaming of Saint Lazaire, he heroically cuts open the dirty naked bodies, trying to ignore the weakness in his hands and the bluntness of his instruments. Without his dreams of turning this slum into a model clinic, he couldn't have spent the last twenty years of his life doing his great and necessary work in these conditions, without proper instruments or dressings, where patients squat on the earth floor to show him a rash or gangrenous lump, then wrap it up again in the same bandage.

The terminally ill patients he generally refuses to treat, so as to keep down the hospital's mortality rate, which his enemies in the clergy would use against him. A man arrives, carrying his ten-year-old son in his arms. The boy's swollen head lolls to one side, and he is just skin and bone, with the lifeless wandering gaze of the mortally ill. There is still life in him, and in his childish cries. But the doctor knows there is no hope for him, and he turns to his next patient, cursing these terrible pauses, as the man wraps up his dying son and moves to the door, then stands there waiting to be called back.

A woman comes in for an operation on her eyes. A month ago Nurenbek removed her cataracts, and after being blind for twenty years, she could finally see. There are just a few minor corrections to be made to the lids, and his assistant decides he can do the job better than the cursed *kafir*, and digs into her with a big kitchen knife, blinding her forever.

'*Ces imbéciles*', Nurenbek mutters with his grimace.

How many poets have sung hymns to the Oriental veil, how many dreams it has inspired! Beneath its magical folds, the flash of a narrow heel evokes images of unparalleled female beauty. Here in the hospital, the veil is lifted.

Three *khanums* have arrived to see Nurenbek. One, small, bent and shuffling, raises her *chador* with trembling hands to reveal an old woman dry as dust, wearing a white shirt whose wide sleeves smell of the wild mint around the old graves. Her eyes hurt. Her pupils are rheumy and bloodshot, and her lids are scarred with trachoma, like leaves eaten by caterpillars. Her eldest daughter also needs to see Nurenbek, but the more he begs her to lift her veil, the more stubbornly she resists. When he shows them the door, the mother becomes agitated and grabs his sleeve, and the daughter finally drops her head to her shoulders and slips from her cocoon. The fine dark skin on her back is blotched with eczema, and it's a torment for the doctor to examine her. To preserve her female honour, she feels obliged to display before this man and *kafir* a hundred wretched conventional gestures of shame, covering her face with her hands, uttering shrieks of nervous laughter. She cannot go through the examination without this, otherwise what would be the point of eternally covering her sinful body?

A few women throw off their veils with light impetuous gestures, revealing beautiful young faces unafraid to look people in the eyes. Despite all the religious laws and prohibitions and the hypocrisy, most of the women patients suffer from venereal diseases – either infected by their husbands returning with their caravans from India, or having succumbed to sin themselves. All are ruled by Allah, crushed between the pages of the Koran – even the laughing bright-eyed young woman with full lips who blushingly avoids the doctor's questions, and in a mocking display of her virtue, uncovers not her graceful back for her injection, but a small hole in her veil.

Yet despite everything, the hospital makes a far less depressing impression than our big hospitals in Moscow, smelling of boiled cabbage and disease, with their sweaty gowns and sharp-faced nurses. Is it because death is easier to accept here under the hot sky, than in the cloacas of the Obukhov and Kalinin hospitals? Patients here don't sit in waiting rooms leafing through the infected pages of *Anna Karenina*, they lie on the hot earth in the courtyard. And before going inside, they take a last look at the snow-capped peaks of the mountains, and the stormy foam of clouds rolling down to the valley, and they carry the memory with them to the operating theatre.

Perhaps the landscape creates a sort of equality between people. Not social equality, of course. Some eat *pulau* every day, dripping fat on their beards. Others run behind their masters' horses, lying on the earth at night to guard their maize, like a glimmering sieve in the starlight. But rich and poor alike build their homes from the same mud, along the same shadeless roads. Some mattresses have more fleas, some less, but everyone sleeps on the floor and eats with their hands. And all women, rich and poor, wear the *chador*. Their strength and beauty, their exquisite hand-embroidered velvet bodices, are all wasted, no one can see them.

In death too, there is equality. Everyone stricken with cholera beats their head on the ground twenty times a day, and rich and poor are buried the same way. Only the saints' graves are honoured with ancient marble headstones, festooned with horsetails and fading streamers. For everyone else there's just a hole in the ground, topped with a rock. The body is carried on a plank to a path in the mountains, followed by crowds of relatives. Then a brief funeral ceremony, and oblivion. The paths are littered with these unmarked graves, which the women, who are banned from attending the burials, have trouble finding next day.

Perhaps in this small Biblical country, where the fields are still tilled with wooden ploughs, there is an acceptance of death that makes people surrender to the hospital, as they surrender to the sun, the mountains and the power of the mullahs. The pus and helplessness flowing from its sewers don't break the dusty harmony of the town, where poverty is as natural as drought, and the flowers in the courtyard mingle with the smell of death, like the stink and brilliance of an Eastern bazaar.

CHAPTER 7

Science, the British and the Tug-of-War

Amanullah is uncomfortable around the British, with their white helmets and high and mighty manners, radiating contempt for these people of an inferior race. His brow burns, and he throws off his caracul hat and puts on a locally made straw one, fanning himself with his horsetail fly-whisk, with its carved wooden handle.

His ministers have sour faces. First he banned the turban and *shalwar kameez* from the Palace, then he forced them out of their European suits and ties into ones made from the rough homespun fabric produced at *Machine Khan*. At his last roundup, he cheerfully took his scissors to their stylish English trousers and cut them to shreds. His Chief of Police had to run home with his knees covered in a handkerchief, and others were even more immodestly attired. It's reminiscent of Peter the Great's dress reforms, when his Moscow boyars would leave his revelries with their beards shaved off, wearing Western dress. But in Amanullah's case, he is using his scissors to affirm his love of everything national, and his forty-stone dandies are now unrecognisable in their scratchy locally made camelhair suits, mixed with sheep dung.

Then after introducing his country to jodhpurs and morning coats, Amanullah turned his attention to its ignorance. The Emir has a fierce will, and a sharp intuitive intelligence. Centuries ago, he would have been a mighty Caliph, defeating the Crusaders in Palestine, trading with popes in Venice, laying waste to Persia and India, burning dozens of towns, and building new mosques and palaces on their ruins, raising the Muslim crescent over the belfries of Granada, Tsargrad,[1] or one of the Venetian municipalities. In these days, squashed between Russia and Britain, he is a reformer. Needless to say he needs peace, if only as a breathing space in which to prepare Afghanistan for new wars. And his main weapons against the hated European colonisers are to be civilisation and progress. You can't fight Krupps and Winchesters with scimitars and medieval superstitions. To beat them, his backward kingdom must be literate and trained in the sciences, and a certain amount of Western technical expertise.

Everything in these small despotic eastern states is ruled by the stick. It beats the ears of the elephants bearing their loads of logs. It drives on the soldiers, drowning in sweat in their camelhair uniforms. During festivals, it makes gar-

---

1   Tsargrad, the old tsarist name for Constantinople.

dens spring up overnight on the bare earth, decked with flags, rugs and lanterns. And with the stick, Amanullah Khan wants to turn his impoverished country into a genuine modern state, like a small Japan, with an army and education system to match – an iron military carcass, with a network of telephone and telegraph wires buried in its old rapacious soul.

Yet for all his astuteness and talents, which distinguish him from the mass of degenerate dynasties in the East, Amanullah's lack of education means he has little understanding of proper teaching methods, and is poorly advised by his aides. In charge of the army and his Military Academy is the Turkish officer (now General) Jamal Pasha, famous for entertaining the court with his pranks. During the last spring festival, the rainwater at the top of the marquee tipped over his scarlet general's stripes, and he sat there in the puddle like a drunken Falstaff, regaling the musicians with his obscene jokes. And there were recently yet more scandals at his wedding in Kabul. But with his pupils at the Academy, Pasha instantly changes, kicking them and punching them in the face, subjecting them to endless humiliating punishments. Woe to the boy who falls off the trapeze, is thrown from his horse, or is late for drill.

With the stick, Afghanistan is to be educated in twenty-four hours, and the sciences taught to hundreds of boys whose roots lie deep in the fat of the nobility and the merchant class, who are removed from their homes to be educated, and are beaten, beaten, beaten.

One is reminded of Peter the Great's education reforms. But Peter knew how to find the best teachers for his students. His young aristocrats travelled to Europe, and studied at one famous university after another. His Arab[2] was taught in Paris by professors at the Saint-Cyr Military Academy, and the Dutch shipbuilders, merchants and bailiffs turned mathematicans who Peter brought to Russia didn't beat the noble sons of the Baratynskys and Sheremetevs – although the boyars' skulls sometimes had to be cracked open with the axe or the knout.

Unfortunately the elderly Palace tutors, mullahs and Foreign Ministry officials the Emir has hired as teachers are totally unqualified to absorb European learning overnight and drum it into little Afghans' heads. And today is their examination day, when they will show off their knowledge.

---

2   The Ethiopian nobleman Abram Hannibal (1696–1781), maternal great-great grandfather of Pushkin, the subject of his unfinished novel *The Arab of Peter The Great*. Kidnapped as a child, he was presented as a gift to the Tsar, who raised him in his household and sent him to Paris to be educated, where he met Montesquieu and Voltaire. Proficient in maths and the sciences, and fluent in several languages, he became an influential figure at Peter's court.

There's nothing more glorious than a Kabul spring, languidly approaching from the mist-topped mountains to the rejoicing storms of blossoms in the Palace orchards. The exams are to be held in a marquee there, its sides alternately roasting in the sun and soaked by cheerful May showers. After a few claps of thunder and a sudden shower of rain, the air is more dazzlingly alive than ever, and the smell of the warm earth mingles with the scent of the cherry trees rustling against the clear blue sky, their feathery sleeves trembling from the passing bees. The British have been invited, and sit in casual poses, exchanging bows, pleasantries and hatred. The Emir's courtiers take their seats in their tight Afghan suits. One slumps in an armchair, in a heap of purple flesh and bad blood.

'Right! Left! Right! Left!', barks a drill-sergeant, as a group of boys of about fourteen in their horsetail-plumed cavalry caps march nervously up to the tent. The one in front stops, his hand held stiffly to his cap. His legs are like jelly, and his insides are like starch, and he is too in awe of his audience to speak. But the sergeant pushes him to the edge of the carpet, and there he gabbles a long memorised speech – about education, the invincible greatness of Islam, and innocent Muslim blood waiting for vengeance. It goes on for approximately an hour, and is delivered in a loud monotone, without sense, expression, pauses, or any chance to reflect on his galloping words. More boys come up to deliver variations of the same bombastic rant, their mouths convulsively gabbling like one mouth. The court applauds, and the Emir is happy as a child, and the mullahs, the speeches' authors, rustle at the back in their long robes, celebrating with the spies and stable-boys of the court. The British Consul smiles behind his programme, happy that the Empire is safe for another fifty years.

Proceedings are halted by a brief prayer, and the crowds drop to their knees and pray to the rising sun, the flourishing trees and the damp grass. Then a bell announces the start of the science exam, and two of the ablest boys demonstrate their chemistry skills, shaking mysterious tubes filled with white, green and red liquids before the popping eyes of the courtiers and mullahs. 'Inshallah, two clear liquids become a red one!'

Gases flash, powders turn into water, water into fire, and several bangs signify success. They create a sensation. Why or how is not explained, no one is interested in the reasons. The bees buzz in the reverent silence, brushing the branches of the trees with their wings, and the young British attachés snigger. The Emir, who loves fire and explosions, is ecstatic, casting sidelong glances at them as if to say 'Our youngsters know all your tricks. Give us time, and we'll blow you to bits!'

After the exam, a choir of little boys of about five or six march diligently past with the correct marching step, singing some long sweet madrigals. Then proceedings end with a tug-of-war. The Emir is a great man, an Asian hero, who like the Romans and Florentines before him, is equally fond of alchemy and the stadium, and the day wouldn't be complete without a trial of strength. Pupils of all ranks and ages are split into two groups, and pull on a thick rope, and the spring sun laughs as the court and the diplomatic corps lay bets on the young Lavoisiers and Mendeleevs.

CHAPTER 8

In the Harem

Examination Day in the Harem

Half-close your eyes in the columned hall, with its solemn instructresses and smartly dressed girls, and you could be back at Catherine the Great's Smolny Institute for Girls in St Petersburg.

Our girls at the Smolny were delivered to their classes in horse-drawn carriages. These girls are conveyed to their exams in rumbling wooden boxes with lowered curtains, pulled by pairs of grey bullocks. Education makes slow progress in Afghanistan, between the bookends of the mosque and the court, but moves just as noisily as these kind-eyed animals.

Our schoolgirls were guarded by virtually sexless monitors. Hovering over the fresh childish faces in the harem are the puffy hairless masks of the eunuchs. There's a brazen free-and-easiness about these majordomos, who bring a whiff of the bedroom to the classroom, gossiping and spying and scurrying unceremoniously among the rustling female skirts, elbowing the girls out of the way as they pass bowls of tea over their heads to their teachers.

Sitting under the stage in their yellow silk uniforms, their loose hair covered in light white veils, are the fourteen-year-olds who have completed their one-year course of studies. They have the piety and primness of the wealthy unmarried girls of the bazaar, with the burning eyes and full breasts of women, and the shy eager demeanour of schoolgirls. Standing over them is their Geography teacher, their *munshi*, wearing an enormous European hat, and what looks like the medal of the Soviet Red Banner of Labour pinned to her large bosom.

About fifteen girls are graduating. The others are younger, aged between six and thirteen. These little girls are delightful. They haven't yet learnt to lower their eyes, purse their lips and cup their hands round the Koran, or peer with unhealthy curiosity at the yellow-faced eunuchs mysteriously allowed into the women's quarters.

Lumbering through the crowd like fat kind elephants are the elderly nannies. Tattooed on their wrinkled foreheads, visible through their transparent veils, are the blue stars of recently emancipated slaves from their distant homes in India, Turkey and Arabia. They still speak their own languages and wear their traditional national dress – snow-white trousers with little bells sewn to the ankles, Kashmiri shawls embroidered in miraculous colours of an unfading brightness no one can make now. For them this first celebration of women's education in Afghanistan is an incomprehensible, unforgettable event, and they push to the front, rubbing their eyes, clouded with age and agitation, aware that the day spells the end of their old lives.

With them are the aging concubines, faded but still beautiful, their fine brows like agate arches over their glowing eyes. The faces of these priestesses of love are filled with grace and wisdom. They have spent their lives serving the tormenting god of desire, creating a whole cult of tender tricks, picking up the nuances of passion like the brilliant colours from the carpets. Now, instead of learning the secrets of a glance or a smile, the art of dancing with two little silver bells tied to their waists, girls are being taught to solve arithmetic problems with sultanas and rice. None of this will produce a new queen of the hive, capable of loving and stinging, squandering death and happiness as in the old songs, and they shake their heads at the alien future lying behind the girls' shoulders, and angrily rustle their silks, like dead leaves.

To our way of thinking, what the girls are being taught is unsound, even barbaric. On the map of the world, they are able to identify only the old borders of the once unconquered Muslim kingdoms, and the ephemeral borders of the new Afghan Caliphate the Panislamists dream of. The girl on the stage taking her Geography exam points to tiny Bukhara and Morocco, Tunisia and Algeria, enslaved under the *kafirs*' yoke, waiting for a new prophet to liberate them from the European heel. Her dark eyes blaze as she clenches her little fists at the two infidel hemispheres. The teachers, nannies, eunuchs and ladies of the court wipe away the tears. We representatives of the despised other half of humanity sit quietly nodding at this little fanatic in her yellow uniform, secretly glad that the days of the great Umayyad and Abbasid Caliphates have passed, and the arrow of time has moved on four centuries. The sands won't yield the blood of the old martyrs, the dead won't rise from the grave, and the rosy dawn of enlightened absolutism is already appearing in Kabul.

A teacher makes a speech, and great words flash by – car, telephone, telegraph, progress, the handkerchief, the dentist, who has recently opened his stall in Kabul's Great Bazaar. Then another girl solves an arithmetic problem on the blackboard. As she applies herself to her work, her serious face is lit with concentration, oblivious to court etiquette or even prizes. Gripping the chalk in her ink-stained fingers, she scribbles some numbers, gets confused, stops, and rubs them out. And behind this first arithmetic problem solved by an Afghan schoolgirl lurks the demon of History, waiting to blow up the columned hall, and the centuries-old walls of the harem.

She kisses the hand of the Emir's wife and leaves the stage. Then Mathematics takes her place, to say a few words about its value and beauty. Yes, Math-

ematics herself, known to all and feared from childhood. Her thin hair is stuck
to her bony scalp, her hard dry fingers are like sticks of chalk, and her glassy
eyes are covered with enormous spectacles like motoring goggles, giving the
science a striking resemblance to death. Yet in contrast with the abstractness
of this figure is her astonishingly colourful attire, her gaunt frame enveloped in
the folds of a pale violet *chador*, streaming over her yellow cheekbones and her
stiff chest, which shimmers with emerald silk.

The girls stare in horror at this mathematical fantom, and the concubines,
who live for beauty, shudder at its ugliness, but are moved by its eloquence. The
spring sun pours through the windows, flooding the girls' lively childish faces
and the mountainous bodies of the nannies, and the past meets the future.

The school's middle-aged director is quite different. Her white lace veil is
thrown back from her face, revealing pleasant regular features and sharp eyes
which miss nothing and are shocked by nothing. She has a calm brisk manner,
and she knows all the subtleties of royal protocol. When a lady of the court
drops her handkerchief on the carpet, she returns it to her with the proper
deference, and kisses her hand.

The hierarchical tone is maintained at the prize-giving. Pupils are called to
the stage in order of their fathers' ranks – *Sardar*, General or *Mustashir* so-
and-so – and the girls listen closely to the ladies as they pass judgement on
the families, laughing spitefully with them when they call the father of a rough
girl from a village an 'ignorant worm'.

The programme finally comes to an end, and Mathematics and Geography
are led away by the eunuchs. Then prayers are said, followed by a display of
European needlework – a thousand times inferior to the Afghan embroidery
sold in the bazaars, or the simple colourful ornaments sewn onto the servants'
trousers. The younger women yawn in their tight corsets, dark Western dresses
and hats, blending with the bright shawls of the nannies, and the girls' white
veils, like lilies-of-the-valley.

Then barefoot servants spread tablecloths on the carpets, and bring in dishes
of food. There are no cushions, and everyone squats on the floor and eats with
their hands. The ladies of the court tear up whole chickens and wipe their
mouths with their fingers, dripping with diamonds and fat. The nannies prefer
the pastries and the sweet spicy lamb, dropping grains of rice on their huge
stomachs. Oh, life is good when the *pulau* drowns in a sticky amber saffron
sauce!

To one side a dancer rolls back a carpet. She is barely in her teens, and unfortunately is dressed in European clothes. But her loose mane of hair is as heavy
as a stream tumbling from the mountain rocks, and her face is enchanting.
Behind her crouches her mother, an old Indian woman, beating a drum with

her red-painted nails. She has spent her life dancing on the roads of India and Afghanistan, and dancing was her a religion, until hunger and age withered her like an old tree.

The girl shakes a couple of little silver child's rattles, rustling like birds in the snow waiting for spring, and how she dances! Her heavy white legs barely move, but her whole body is convulsed by the rhythmic stamping of her feet, and with each shake of her rattles, she lowers her long eyelashes, and her red lips quiver voluptuously, as if the goddess of love had lit a fire on her face. She is as chaste as the toys she holds in her hands, but each movement of her body is filled with a rapture that seems to cause her both physical pain and a wild joy, as Asia casts its spells over Europe and refuses to die.

The dance ends, as old as time, and the ladies of the court resume their conversation in French, and the girl's little slave hands put the hookah to their lips, its playful smoke-rings mocking all the learning and education. This is how Afghan women are when they're alone, away from foreign eyes, marking the inexorable passing of time as their grandmothers did, in the days when Kabul's old walls still reached to the sky.

Paghman

The Emir's summer residence in Paghman lies on the Kabul River, dividing into dozens of little streams, flowing between banks of withered rushes. Miles of windswept sands spread across the barren autumn landscape to the line of hills on the horizon. The only living things visible are a flock of ravens, flying slowly against the wind.

The ladies of the court sit in the glass veranda of the harem, passing round the hookah. Their hair is loose and their faces are unpainted, and they are all dressed in black silk, mourning their captive wasted lives and the dying year.

Then suddenly there is a power cut, and the mood changes, and the East breaks through this sombre gathering. The parquet floor and the Louis XVI chairs and gold-inlaid grand piano vanish, and Europe is forgotten. Servants run in with lanterns, and ancient gems flash in the darkness – precious diadems from Persia and India sparkling on tangled black tresses, plump arms glittering with frosts of silver, marble necks streaming with liquid fires.

Amanullah's mother, Ulya Hazrat, calls for her tambourine, then two little drums and an old harmonium and the six-stringed Afghan *rabab* are brought in, and the young women throw off their tight shoes and uncomfortable gloves and trains and jump from their chairs and become who they really are – carefree and charming. The drums beat a fierce rhythm, and the harmonium majestically draws out the dance tune, like bullocks pulling a cart of ripe grain across the fields at sunset, and they dance in a circle, repeating the same steps over and over again, moving more quickly, swaying and clapping their hands and stamping their feet, throwing back their heads with the wild abandon of the dances of the Bacchic tribes.

CHAPTER 9

Vanderlip

Vanderlip in the Soviet Republic[1]

Vanderlip is in his sixties, but his uncountable millions won't let him stop for an instant to reflect on the salvation of his panting soul. The Dollar runs round the world, flightier than the wheel of fate, pursued by this brilliant speculator in red, white and yellow souls, and the gleaming vaults of his banks never sleep.

But now the value of gold is falling, casting a seductive shadow over the bloody gambling fields of Europe, bubbling in a dark foam over the edge of sensible speculation into riskier investments. Which brings the great American tax-collector to Lenin's office in the Kremlin. And here the old swindler sits with the genius of the Revolution, offering to trade with him for the untapped wildernesses of Siberia and Arkhangelsk, the sturgeon of the Caspian, the oil, coal and precious resources of the vast expanses of Russia – and in those places where the red is pink, and the Revolution doesn't threaten his bourgeois purgatory so much, even for a little of the workers' and peasants' sweat, so coveted by his sunny loud-mouthed Dollar.

No one knows exactly how their conversation went. How the two sat opposite each other, the enormous robber, courteous as a Quaker missionary, with his clean-shaven womanly lips and capacious grey accountant's skull, calculating his profits and losses, his honest percentages from all the bankruptcies, all the graves to the Unknown Soldier. Billionaire Vanderlip, chatting with Lenin as he chats with kings and grovelling presidents. Only his eyes give him away, the eyes of a steppe horse thief.

At the start, he probably had no idea who he was dealing with. No doubt he tried to impress Lenin with his gold-embossed letters signed by the barons of his coal, oil and armaments trusts. But when Ilich laughed, Vanderlip realised he could see through all his secret desires, all the sums and schemes buzzing in his brain, and he became blunt and to the point, and went on the offens-

---

1   Californian mining engineer Washington B. Vanderlip Jr., who visited Kabul in 1922 with his business plans. He had tried his luck two years earlier in Moscow, where he passed himself off as banking tycoon Frank A. Vanderlip. He was referred to in the Soviet press as 'Billionaire Vanderlip', and Lenin agreed to meet him, believing he had the ear of President Wilson, and could persuade him to offer the Bolsheviks diplomatic recognition and loans. He was exposed as a fraud soon after he left, and the mix-up is used here to surreal comic effect.

ive: 'I'll buy your famines, how much do you want for them? How much for the cripples of your diabolical revolution – your dying children, your factories without machines, your destroyed homes, your deserts and snow? How much for your future peace and security? Name your price, Lenin, work it out on your little red abacus!'

The Dollar had spoken, ringing out over the spartan office. In a few words, Vanderlip had stepped back a hundred years from his normal business practices into the realm of golden utopias, in which capital would inspire and fertilise new forces to replace this system built by the workers themselves. The sacred ease of buying and selling in his capitalist International. Forgiveness, reconciliation, brotherly aid to Soviet Russia – not defeated, no, its dignity must be spared, just sensibly accepting charity. In the three years of the Civil War, the Bolsheviks had laid the wreaths of October at the altar of civilised humanity. But for the sake of the starving children, Vanderlip was prepared to buy into some of Lenin's ideas.

Communism would be Soviet government plus the electrification of the whole country, Lenin said. Vanderlip could make it happen! The Dollar could make his workers' republic greater than Whitman's America, with machinery, coal and oil. Lenin, the soul of the factory era, father of the machine, ideologue of workers' power, would be unable to resist the workers' heaven Vanderlip could make in

Russia, in return for dropping his crazy socialist experiment!

Spread out before him, Vanderlip sees the Aladdin's caves of the Urals, with their diamonds, sapphires and radium, the fire of the sun, which brings both life and death. The hills of Astrakhan, drowning in rice, cotton and wine. The cries of the camels straining under their loads as the fields came to life. The orchards and vineyards spreading to the Dead Sea. The yellow shores of the Caspian, iridescent with oil, flourishing like the almond trees in spring. The goldmines of Siberia, until now ransacked and mismanaged, finally under proper ownership. Eureka! A new Eldorado on the shores of the Arctic, pouring streams of gold along the great rivers of the North through the rustling primeval forests. The *taiga*, with its furs and rare trees, thrown to the Western Stock Exchange like a Scythian slave woman, silent, powerful and fertile. Russia would be the salvation of the tired white races. In its virgin mines, its shimmering milk-white rivers, its oceans and forests, lay a new era, a new religion of victorious labour working hand in hand with capital!

Together he and Lenin could build this machine heaven, this Russia groaning under the weight of new railroads, new factories seething with activity. In Petersburg's shipyards, the waves splashing against the granite embankments would mingle with the sunny Petrine sounds of hammers. New riches would pour from the prows of the ships, filling the docks with their bulging bales, and the impatient clamour of their sirens.

'You've always been a realist, Lenin. Be a realist now. Don't sacrifice your workers' state to theories. For three years you've drowned your theories in blood. You've passed your decrees cancelling the treaties made by your frankly idiotic tsarist government – and of course, we were wrong, our intervention against you was a mistake, it won't happen again. But let's be honest. First you must drop your experiment with private property and the Third International. You're a great man, you've a remarkable brain, like an American's. Let's forget our misunderstandings. I accept your gamble with socialism was brilliant, most original. Even my Dollar took a hit, not to mention their francs and pounds and so on. As a practical businessmen, I advise you not to pay any of your debts. Brazen it out, and they'll give in. But in a game like this you need allies. You and I must come to an agreement ...'

The Dollar sang out like the bugle before the attack, the whip cracking over the heads of the creaking world, the key the jailer turns in a rusty long-locked door. The room filled with shadows and the night bells of Moscow, and Lenin switched on the lamp, and there was light. And as Vanderlip's face resumed its pleasant courteous expression, Ilich laughed again from his heathen depths, like Ivan Kupalo,[2] and his bright Tatar eyes were calm and cheerful, and Vanderlip was naked as the Emperor in his new clothes.

Vanderlip in Afghanistan

From Russia, Vanderlip's millions drove him to Asia. Like the ancient warrior heroes before him, he dreamed of new conquests in the East, and the miraculous merger of China, Persia, Turkey, Mesopotamia and Afghanistan into one great banking empire. Of new railtracks laid on roads built by the Caesars and Moghuls, and a single electrical grid connecting all the scattered Muslim states captured in national uprisings. Of new markets for American goods, blazing a trail through the whole of Asia, killing off Anglo-Indian trade in one blow, like a good soldier throwing a dying ox in the dust.

Vanderlip's brilliant venture, this wedge cutting into the heart of Asia, would become a great commercial highway extending to India, the jewel of the British Empire, shovelling up Britain's assets and flooding the market with cheap American goods. In the roar of the trains cutting across the wildernesses from

---

2   Ivan Kupalo, Russian pagan spirit of summer.

Shanghai to Kashgar, from Tehran to Constantinople, hymns would ring out to American matches, stockings, razors and unbeatably priced suspenders, in exchange for Asia's fresh curly cotton, its pearly rice, and the oil of Mosul, the dark heart of all this power and energy. To howls of protest from bankrupted British businesses, American capital would pour in a great torrent through the East, to foist its stocks and shares on history for another century. These were the dreams that impelled Vanderlip to visit the capital of Afghanistan.

His journey to the Afghan border passed with the speed of an express train, blindly listing at the bends, then righting itself and screeching on along the mathematically shortest route. He lived by the watch he carried in his waist-coat pocket, and he was calm, direct, clean-shaven, and a little dusty.

He kept up the same pace in Kabul, and explored the surrounding countryside on horseback. The Afghan cavalry officer escorting him slumped in his saddle, his legs dangling from exhaustion. But the American was a passable rider, and didn't sweat or tire, gripping his stallion tightly with his stringy knees like a bundle of fresh patents and business documents. Handing his reins to the Afghan, he scrambled up the cliffs to sip the murky waters of the mineral springs, stuffing his pockets and saddlebags with rocks. Then it was back to his hotel for a shower and a meal. His iron stomach coped excellently with the spicy cuisine, and afterwards there was his pipe and newspaper and his gramophone, blaring out to Gulistan 'Everybody's Crazy 'bout the Foxtrot!'

It was of no interest to Vanderlip which countries his train rushed through, barely drawing breath at the stations, or whether the mountains, palm trees and tundra were yellow, green or Soviet – just so long as his business was con-ducted without delay. Everything must follow his schedule, without wasted time or words. And then came his long, ridiculous, agonising stay in Kabul.

His train came off the rails in the crumbling sands of oriental hospitality, and the Afghans' maddening sugary sluggishness. He made an appointment at the Ministry of Foreign Affairs, and he went armed with facts and figures and clear convincing arguments, charging through his brain like passengers through a crowded turn-style. His hosts entertained him with tea and a hookah and slices of sweet Kabul melon, and some feathery verses by Saadi celebrat-ing the health of their precious American friend, and his mirage shimmered in a thousand places. He tried to work his mighty levers, pressing the handles with all his strength, but to no avail, the hospitality and hookah smoke were unassailable. The minute he tried to discuss a contract, the Ministry vanished in a puff of pleasantries. For hours his cunning logic beat the empty smiling air, battling with these meek fantoms like an absurd Don Quixote, and his watch showed he had wasted a whole day, and that his train had waited a minute and eighteen seconds for him at the border, and had already left.

Roaming angrily through Kabul's blazing bazaars, he eyed the camels and carpets, the jewellery, saddles and pottery, the rich silks and embroidery from Kashmir, Persia and Bukhara – thousands of dusty trinkets dappled by the sun, under awnings hung with pointed cages like witches' hats, where quails sang of eternal spring. In other countries, he was used to doing his business quickly. For centuries traders had helped themselves to the Afghans' furs and jewels, and had met with no resistance. They didn't even have to steal them, they just unpicked a few threads from their embroidered Scythian coats, and they would fly off their backs by themselves, in exchange for a nose-ring with a fake diamond, a pair of socks, or a bottle of ginger-beer. And now these people wanted none of it, and haggled for hours over their impassable mountains and worthless deserts, their filth, nakedness and ignorance.

And as Vanderlip wandered the streets, gulping ice and quinine, he realised that behind their greed and suspicion, their questioning of every dot and comma, their stubborn refusal to accept what they – and principally he – stood to gain, lay a solid strength that couldn't be bought, despite the poverty and the universal corruption, and the government's need for money for the army.

Sometimes fingers reached tentatively for his pockets like hungry suckers, and success seemed within his grasp. But he was held back by something stronger than his hunger for wealth, even though thousands of desires in him were crying out for gold.

'Still, who knows? Let's give it one last shot', he thought.

Ill and exhausted from all the wasted hours between meetings, he travelled to Amanullah's palace at Paghman for Afghanistan's eighteen-day Independence celebrations. Barely able to contain his impatience, he watched the Emir's jumping elephants and fighting rams, and his grandees' vicious friendly wrestling matches, and his watch ticked by the minutes.

A marquee had been set up for him on the shores of an artificial lake, patrolled by an angry malevolent pelican – not a local breed, with a clear purpose in life, but an imported Western one, revelling in the ghoulish delights of the chimerae. The pelican treated Vanderlip cruelly! For two weeks he had to endure its company, like a reject from some Baudelairean fantasy, flashing its spiteful little white eyes at him like dead fish, shrieking and snapping its enormous yellow beak at his feet. Once, in a fit of temper, it spat the entire contents of its craw onto his boots.

Between bouts of malaria, Vanderlip lay in his tent pondering his next move. Before him he saw clearly the complexities of his historic enterprise, his new trade war for this untapped goldmine around which the capitalist world was circling. And he realised he would be obstructed at every turn by the Afghans, as slippery as the revolting feet of the pelican.

'*Quack! Quack!*' it said, snapping its beak at him.

To understand Vanderlip's lack of success in Afghanistan, it's necessary to understand the significance of its Independence Day celebrations that year. The elephants and the wrestling matches were much like any other eastern *tamasha*, and lacked the compelling power and charm of the previous year's festivities in Kabul. But the presence of the royal family and foreign dignitaries gave them official weight. And on the fourth day, when the Emir appeared dressed not in his uniform, but barefoot in sandals, in an austere grey turban and blue cotton tunic crossed by a rifle, as worn by the border tribes, it was clear that this marked the start of a deeply mystical, national part of the celebrations.

Standing behind him were his armed Waziri and Afridi tribal chiefs, who for a century had been fighting the British to defend their settlements in the strategic folds of the Hindu Kush. They had presented themselves to Amanullah that morning in a state of fighting readiness, which by four in the afternoon had turned to ecstasy. At the sight of them, the British Minister felt suddenly indisposed and roared off in his Rolls-Royce, pursued by their derisive bugles. Then each clan gathered under its triangular banner, singed with the gunpowder of recent battles, and the dance began.

They danced in circles like falcons, fighting fraternities burnt by the sun, their gleaming black locks flying over the battlefield. In the middle of one circle, before crowds of thousands on this sunny afternoon, a dancer with a cold pitiless face and three tufts of hair on his bald skull, like a Chinese warrior, danced the deserts, the solitary pursuit, the killing. Then kissing the blade of his scimitar, dark with blood, flickering with the light of ancient spells, he dried it in the sand and slipped back into the circle, quick and sure-footed as a cat.

Midday, sunset, night, the warriors danced on, unhurried, graceful and methodical. Their swords guarded and punished, stained with the blood of countless enemies, calling them from the earth and killing them. This wasn't simply some traditional tribal dance, passed on from generation to generation. They were dancing what happened yesterday in the Khyber Valley, and might happen tomorrow at the fortress at Michni Point. Their dance wasn't about war in general, it was about their war with the British, the shadows of corpses falling in battle, real living soldiers in their dusty khaki and white helmets – Britain's General Cavagnari,[3] slaughtered fifty years ago with his officers in

---

3   Major General Sir Louis Napoleon Cavagnari (1843–79), English son of an Italian general in Bonaparte's army, Deputy Commissioner in British Punjab, Britain's first Minister in Afghanistan. He arrived in Kabul in July 1879, ten months into Britain's Second Afghan War. Six weeks later, he and seventy-five soldiers of the elite Queens Own Guards were killed by Afghan troops fighting with the British demanding their unpaid wages, who decapitated him and carried his head through the streets to display in the bazaar.

Kabul, the currently thriving Sir Francis Humphrys and Sir Henry Dobbs, of the British mission, and countless nameless British troops hidden in Afghanistan's mountains and deserts, the Pamirs and Himalayas.

From under the dancing Wazirs' feet, hosts of locusts flew north and east, hunting down the tribespeople in their mountain pastures, destroying their crops and poisoning their wells, advancing up the rocks to the eternal snowline. As the dancers trampled them underfoot, millions more flew out. Then brandishing their scimitars above their heads, they broke up the circles and became a single burning naked wheel. Their rage was a pure flame, and the dust was like smoke. 'Burn! Burn!' roared the music, and the platform, the square, the sky, the mountains, the whole country and its people were engulfed in the blaze. And in the thunder of victory, the Emir galloped off with his smoke-blackened face, crying: '*Salaam bad isteqlal-i-Afghanistan!*' ('Independence to Afghanistan')

'This is a dead loss, I'm getting nowhere with them', Vanderlip decided, and after taking some snaps of Amanullah with his Kodak, he retired to his tent.

The embodiment of speed left Kabul in a hideously slow antiquated carriage. Opposite him sat his official escort, his *mikhmandar*, an intolerable character, like all *mikhmandars*, with his excessive friendliness, his inquisitive spectacles and his sharp knees, digging into him however far he tried to move away. Vanderlip had mapped out the shortest route back from his wasted trip, and the loose wheels of the carriage lumbering over the rocks settled into an even, steady rhythm, like the pulse of his train. Gradually his thoughts straightened into a series of parallel lines, fixed now by a figure, now by a horizontal row of balances and totals, like the telegraph wires looped from post to post.

Vanderlip never returned to Afghanistan. But it wasn't so much his lack of success with the Afghans that bothered him, as his total failure to understand them. Outside in the dark night, the rain beat down on the leather roof of the carriage, like a great creature restlessly drumming its fingers, asking 'Why, why, why?'

'No, they can't really be that dumb', he thought. 'They're stubborn, yes, but it's more than that. And Amanullah's a fine fellow, I could use someone like him with my striking miners in California'.

The carriage creaked and tipped to one side, and the driver whipped his wet horses. 'They just don't like anything foreign. Damn right they don't! For a hundred years they've not let the English eat them up!' he smiled, and suddenly everything became as straight and clear as a set of newly-laid railtracks.

'Tell me, *Mikhmandar Sahib*, what does "*istekal*" or "*isteklad*" mean?' he asked.

And laying his hand on his wide stomach and tipping his head to one side, the *mikhmandar* translated for him with his cunning oriental smile: '"*Isteqlal*" means Independence, Excellency. It means Freedom'.

CHAPTER 10

How History Is Written

In Europe we understand the longevity of ideas. We understand why the passions of Goethe, Rousseau and Tasso still have the power to move us. The shades of Giordano Bruno still darken the walls of the Castel Sant'Angelo in Rome, millions still live in fear of the Jesuits' cowl, and memories of distant ancestors who died at the stake. But nowhere is life so ruled by the past as in the East. It is thirteen centuries since Mohammed defeated Ormazd and Ahriman, and nine centuries since Firdowsi wrote his *Book of Kings*,[1] but its pages are as alive as if they were written yesterday.

Bridging the gap between the old and new worlds are wandering scholars, part prophets, part travelling salesmen, who visit their wealthy but backward neighbours preaching ideas of national liberation and a light sceptical liberalism, veiled in piety and gossip. Modestly supplied with money and underwear, they set up their stalls in Cairo, Port Said and Kabul, and shape the reputations of politicians and governments. But they leave Afghanistan feeling cheated.

One such recent visitor to Kabul is the Persian Mirza Abdul Muhammed, publisher of a liberal newspaper in Cairo. Like the British who came to Moscow in the days of Ivan the Terrible, or the Dutch to the court of Peter the Great, Mirza Abdul Muhammed arrived in Kabul in his professorial tailcoat and fez with the authority of a holy man, bearing his seven-volume *History of Afghanistan*, on which he had laboured for twenty years, not without hope of compensation. The Emir received him graciously, and applauded his articles 'The Aspirations of the Faithful' and 'What Will Befall the Honourable Muslim?', but politely declined to pay him for 'The Hopes of the Sons of Mohammed', and put him up in the crumbling palace next to the tomb of the Emperor Babur.

Alone in the Great Moghul's freezing halls, Mirza Abdul Muhammed brooded on his host's vague promises and totally platonic affection, and composed more than one angry article about the true nature of this backward despotic state, which only bribed pens could praise, not freethinkers alien to worldly concerns.

---

1 The Persian poet Abu i-Qasim Firdowsi (940–1020), author of Persia's great eleventh-century national epic the *Shahnameh, Book of Kings*, recording the history of the Persian Empire before the Islamic conquest of the seventh century.

He wouldn't have bothered with this wretched tenth-rate country if it hadn't revealed to him a totally new untapped seam of ideas. But now he cursed it, not only for its treatment of its only true historian, but with an anger born of principles. Its religious hypocrisy turned him into an atheist, its stagnant culture into a reformer, and its virtually pre-Petrine servility (Cairo had long abandoned the low slavish bows still practised in Kabul's Great Bazaar), into a revolutionary. And in the soul of this true Persian, with his learning and indolence, his love of political backbiting and British freedom – if not a free press – awoke new feelings of national pride.

He was a vagabond scholar, but with the blood of the world's oldest civilisation in his veins. And when he reviewed his history of Afghanistan, he found it utterly devoid of culture. It turned out that all seven volumes were a chronicle of ten centuries of obscurantism, with all shoots of poetry, art and philosophy ruthlessly weeded out. Sand, rocks, the sword – nothing more.

Argument followed argument, and from the grub of a servile court historian, a pure-blooded Iranian peered out. What was the Koran? Nothing but crude nonsense and animal sensuality, fit only to grace the tents of illiterate nomads, from which it had risen to the heights of humanity to burn the flourishing cities of Persia, with their art and architecture, their gardens and libraries, reducing the splendours of this once great civilisation to dust. It was the Persians who brought the translations of Plato and Aristotle to the mosques of Mauritania, and saved them from the fire. The Persians who softened the petty barbaric laws of Islam with the humanism of Zoroastra and the ancient fire-worshippers, the world's first Magi and astronomers. The Persians who educated wild Arab caliphs like Harun al-Rachid, surrounding him with brilliant poets and scientists, who embellished his bloody reign with the flowers of their crushed culture. Where did Arab culture come from?

When Mirza Abdul Muhammed lifted his slave's eyes to Harun's court, memories of ancient hatreds flared up, inextinguishable as the flames the Parsees guarded in their temples in South India, and he was rejuvenated by real passions. Harun was a savage. His glorious reputation as a patron of commerce and the arts, like an Arab Medici, he owed entirely to the defeated Persians, whose culture continued to flourish under his feet. The trampled roses of Iran were eternally fresh, and the desert of the Koran was nourished by their fragrance.

Abandoning chronology and logic, the Persian fell into the mischievous muse of legends, which opened their blue enamelled gates to him. When did Persian culture die? It was under the barbarian Harun. His Grand Vizier was an Iranian, the adornment of his reign, who invited great scholars and artists to his court in Baghdad. The conquerors' *madrasas* were famed for their wisdom.

Their language was refined, taking on happy phrases of Persian rhetoric and poetry, and Harun was renowned not only for his wealth and military prowess, but for the lustre of enlightenment surrounding his throne.

But when his Vizier's son, the handsome Osan, fell in love with his daughter, his honour was insulted that this Iranian, a virtual prisoner, who possessed nothing but his education, should aspire to her hand. Since Osan had been seen with his beloved in the palace gardens, and she had violated her Muslim purity by lifting her veil, he finally gave his consent for them to marry. But only on condition that Osan never knew his wife, so not a drop of Persian blood would pollute the blood of the Arab kings.

Osan agreed, and knowing nothing of this sad contract, Harun's daughter suffered cruelly from her husband's neglect. After trying in vain for a year to draw him close to her, the unhappy bride confided her shame to her mother, and asked for her help. The kind queen went to her son-in-law and said, 'You're lonely without someone to love. Tonight I'll send a beautiful Greek girl to your room. Enjoy yourself with her, my dearest son, but don't light the lamp. The girl is pure and innocent'.

Osan agreed, and deceived by the darkness, he made his wife a mother on her wedding night. The conquerors and the conquered could have been forever at peace then – defeated Persia joining its poverty and wisdom to the wealth and power of the Arabs. But Harun did not forgive his daughter. In one night he cut off the heads of Osan, his father, and the finest Persian philosophers and artists at his court. And the newborn baby, in whom the past could have made peace with the future, suffered the same fate.

Finishing the last word of his article, Mirza Abdul Muhammed adjusted the spectacles on his nose, and put down his pen.

About the People Cut Off from the USSR by the Desert, the Mountains, Several Centuries, and the Curved Muslim Scimitar

There is nothing more absurd than the diplomatic corps of an Eastern court, playing out its comedy in the desert. For hundreds of centuries, this strip of land between Turkestan and India has been virtually untouched by the outside world, cut off by the mountains and the radiance of time. The most fantastic sights are the telegraph poles, striding with giant steps across the rocks and rushing rivers, flecked with foam like camels goaded by their drivers to exhaustion. The headlamps of cars cut through the darkness of the Asian nights with a fairytale brightness, and currents of electricity light up ravines Alexander's armies were forced to cross on foot, carefully leading their horses. Yet thieves are still hanged in public, and the fields are still ploughed with wooden ploughs pulled by short-horned bullocks, and people die simply, and are buried simply in the earth, their graves unmarked and unnamed.

All this seems exotic to us in Europe only because we have the tomb of Michelangelo, codes of law, and mechanised American ploughs. Yet when it comes to crossing the Suleiman Mountains, camels are still the best and quickest mode of transport. History has barely touched the lives of these people, rolling on like the stones of their ancient water-mills, timeless and unchanging. And along the rivers, where the nomads rest and burn the reeds for their fires, farmers plant poppies, whole fields of opium growing on the fragrant sticky earth.

Russia in general has left little trace in Central Asia, even in places occupied by force. An ugly Russian post office in the bright poverty of the Bukhara bazaar, a Red soldier in his tattered army coat guarding the frontier between Kushka and Childukhteran – all the rest we have in common. The same poverty and fleas, the same melancholy scorn for life, the same sluggishness, for what is the point of hurrying in these hot remote places?

The only reminder of tsarist Russia's military incursions into Afghanistan is the bridge over the River Oxus (now the Amu-Darya), on the Turkestan border, miraculously suspended between its barren marshy shores like a haughty renegade, resting on nothing but its concrete plinths. Britain has crossed the frontier quite differently. Unlike our fields in Soviet Turkestan, soaked with the blood of countless unnamed soldiers, the land around the Khyber Pass is irrigated with vast filters and Artesian wells, so even the camels and horses can drink distilled water on the roads to the next British attacks. A new two-lane highway has been built along the Grand Trunk Road connecting Afghanistan and India, whose potholes are filled by Afghan slave labour. And against the century-old resistance of the tribal people guarding the Emirate's most threatened frontiers in the south, new telegraph and telephone lines have been laid all the way to the Indian border. This line of communications has even crossed the Durand Line[1] into the Wazirs' settlements, scattered eagles' nests accessible only from the sky, bombed by British planes. In Kabul's Great Bazaar, the wind sings in the wires of this new Anglo-Indian cable, and drivers trustingly tie their camels to its treacherous poles, made from the same metal from which English cannon are made.

The pioneers of this great imperial power stoically endure the hatred of the natives, whose settlements are marked on the secret maps of the British General Staff with a dotted line, pinning them to Peshawar province in the Anglo-Indian Motherland, cut off from Russia by a cool neutral zone marked by a neat circle, linking Kabul to Kandahar, Mazar-i-Sharif, Herat and Jalalabad.

Magical Jalalabad, a fragrant temperate hotbed of opium and roses, was once a showcase for Britain's now abandoned policies in the small despotic Eastern states, watered, blessed and manured by English gold. The tips of the date-palms rustling their fans in the heavens, the white palaces with their fountains and gardens, the scented stocks and tea-roses in January, the mimosas filling the air with gold and honey – all this represented the earthly paradise this scrap of Central Asian desert could become if its ignorant people allowed it to be touched by the wand of British capital.

The last Emir, Habibullah, was bought off by the British. They cultivated his taste for luxury, and taught him to squander his wealth. English engineers arrived at the Shah's court to replace the obliging spirits of the *Thousand and One Nights*, boiling over with fat and debauchery, and began their civilising work in the harem's lavatories, then built a modern European kitchen. They laid new roads, along which their Excellencies' cars could speed from one rough haunt to another, perched on rocks in the desert, exposed to the camels and winds. The dilapidated palaces of the old Emirs were rapidly converted into trading-posts, and a new residential quarter was built in Jalalabad for Britain's future Viceroy to Afghanistan.

---

1 The Durand Line, contested by successive Afghan governments, the 1,500-mile frontier line between Afghanistan and Waziristan in British India (now the Afghan-Pakistan border), established by Britain in 1899 as a 'defence buffer' against Russian encroachment into the Raj.

Jalalabad was the model for Britain's strategy in India – of peaceful conquest through bribing and corrupting its minor maharajahs and their over-fed retinues. Dusty and weather-beaten from the highways of the world, bitter with quinine, pious on Sundays, mean and stingy on weekdays as the Anglican prayerbook, the English have supplied India's aristocracy not only with pornography and whisky, which burns them worse than fever, but with a fashionable new philosophy, a tipsy, playful, hedonistic worldview. In this new religion of the Raj, Hinduism's asceticism and good-tempered aversion to the state have been turned into the drunken cynicism of an operetta, a sacred brutishness. For aren't debauchery and asceticism just two sides of the same coin?

On the deck of an ocean liner, some Indian princesses sit over a third bottle of whisky, swaying to the music of the foxtrot, ashamed of the colour of their skin, like amber and honey, which no amount of powder can cover. One of the whites drinking gin and soda at the next table takes them back to his cabin, so that later at his club, to which none of the Indians but his manservant are admitted, he can tell them how he got Princess Damayanti and Queen Saraswathi as drunk as cabbies, but they hadn't passed out, and had gone on squawking in their native language like flamingos.

This is how the whites make India's ruling families break with their culture and religion, pumping them with poison, paying out of their own pockets for their sadistic games, then hiding from this corrupted aristocracy behind a wall of staggering contempt. This new caste of courtiers, dressed in their outlandish plumed uniforms, showered with gold and diamonds, alien to the people and despised by the whites, infected with all the new diseases and philosophies the British have concocted for their Empire, lurches from scandal to scandal, propped up in the arms of two honest sober Indian policemen.

With the Afghans however, Britain's strategy of crushing the masses by courting the privileged elite backfired from the start, and its three wars with Afghanistan all ended in disaster. After the third war in 1919, when Amanullah replaced Habibullah to declare his country's independence, and Afghans smashed the thousand mirrors of the British residence in Kabul, they were forced to start all over again with an entirely different approach, and their Minister now lives in a more modest residence built by the British government. Which brings us back to our theme.

Flying over Kabul's diplomatic missions are national flags of vast dimensions – not flags, *drapeaux, gonfalons*, royal standards. And the most magnificent of them is that of Turkey.

Living under its hallowed staff is the diplomat Nail, a free thinker, educated in the West, knocked about by life, but with the prudent deference of an experienced courtier. Nail has grown old on the slippery floors of court diplomacy,

and has survived its periodic parliamentary monsoons, and despite not own-
ing a metre of land apart from his family burial plot, he has the bearing and
manners of a wealthy landowner. The virtues of the courtier fit well with the
mocking affability of a gentleman who is in debt on all sides, and deftly dodges
his moneylender, his tailor and his French mistress, paying them all off at the
lowest possible interest rates. These skills have taught him the value of hard
cash in his diplomatic work. He patronises the wealthy, and makes them pay
for their democratic tolerance, and millionaires with petrol and car tyres on
their coats-of-arms find this more congenial than grovelling.

This is the age of the educated government official, who discusses ideas of
democracy and socialism with his petitioners. Communism and clerical reaction are in the air. Tomorrow the country might go the way of Mussolini's Italy,
who knows? For Nail the main thing is not to lose his head in these troubled
times, so no sudden change of government can alter the course of his work,
which he carries out with a rakish tilt of his opera-hat, stepping carefully ahead
in his neatly pressed morning trousers and spotless gaiters.

The first rule of this diplomacy, regardless of the international situation beyond its airless confines, is to agree with everyone, be shocked by nothing, and
express no opinions, political or otherwise. Afghanistan's *corps diplomatique*
is a more or less successful gathering of educated men from the same circle,
thrown together, alas, in the hole of Kabul. Each has a sacred duty to entertain
and amuse his colleagues, and when necessary, to take his cue from the diplomatic dance whose steps were worked out over a century ago at the Congress
of Vienna.

It's of no importance whether this dance takes place with the Papuans or
the Nyam-Nyams, in Honolulu or Kabul, international etiquette exists in and of
itself, regardless of time and place. Somewhere on a patch of hallowed extra-
territorial land – on a waxed floor, or a circle of earth around a campfire of
cannibals – two augurers, experts in their respective religions, come together
and establish official relations. They make visits, bow and retire. They hold soir-
ees, leave visiting cards, change from lounge suits into morning suits, and from
morning suits into tails, finally drowning in an expanse of white flannel, topped
by a colonial solar topee, dazzling the natives with the whiteness of their dress-
shirts and the sharpness of their 'London creases'.

Although unfortunately we can't choose our families, there was a time when
diplomats could choose their partners in this dance. However the world since
Versailles has been full of tribulations. Everyone curses the Bolsheviks, but like
it or not, no major international conference can now take place without them,
and civilised men are expected to sit at the same table with these monsters. Yet
here again, diplomacy comes to the rescue, and it turns out it's not a Bolshevik's

hand they're shaking, but that of a distinguished ministerial envoy. And if by good luck the bearer of this rank isn't a complete orang-utan, and doesn't blow his nose on the tablecloth, they can forget our criminal Revolution, and honour in us the blessed memories of our diplomatic forebears – Gorchakov and Izvolsky, Sazonov and Giers.

It's five years since the tsarist Imperial eagle was replaced by the red flag of the USSR, but Europe still buzzes with rumours of certain Schleswig-Holstein princelings claiming to be the Tsar's heirs. The Ambassador is the disembodied spirit of a diplomatic dynasty that still survives, *quand meme*. Once the Tsar, always the Tsar. He has simply jumped out of the pit in which he and his family is buried. There is no break in his succession, his metaphysical being lives on.

In the legal and cultural framework of this diplomacy, the Soviet government occupies a position similar to some four-legged Ostrogoth, creeping under his barbarian's shield to the Cathedral of St Peter, throne of the Holy Roman Empire, to crown himself Caesar with his knotted horse's bridle. While outside the gates of the Eternal City stand the legions of Teodoric and Marcus Otho – hordes of drunken belching Latins in their stolen silk robes smelling of horse sweat, who know how to burn towns, rule with the sword, and reduce popes to a state of angelic meekness.

Of course Amanullah hasn't invited us to Kabul on a whim, it's because without us he would be totally isolated, without allies. Also in the USSR's favour, apart from Afghanistan's economic interests, are the power of its border armies, and the hatred of the entire population for the British.

Even France's semi-official representative in Kabul, Albert Foucher, head of the French Archaeological Mission, has been forced by the Hague Peace Convention to accept the existence of Soviet Russia, marked for the past five years on the map of the Third Republic by a blank spot, surrounded by the *cordon sanitaire* of the Blockade.

Referred to in an official speech by Prime Minister Millerand himself as *'notre illustré'*, Foucher is the embodiment of civilised French values – cordial and correct, with his bald scholarly skull topped by a crown of snowy white hair, his genial blue eyes and his indulgent smile, revealing a powerful set of false teeth, and the remorseless square beard of a man who has spent his life grinding knowledge into a patent gruel to be pushed down the throats of Europe.

Working in steady bursts of activity, crunching up the rocks and artefacts of his vanished Eastern civilisations, Foucher finally reached Afghanistan, whose wild ruins, numbered and catalogued, vanished into his omnivorous jaws. He completed his progress through the country's archaeological appendices and dead-ends with the Buddhas of Bamiyan, and the mysterious Buddhist inscriptions on the tombs at Jalalabad. And the unforgettable day is recorded when a senior official at the Ministry of Education and Great Opportunities in Paris, guardian of the dusty folders of Alexander and the Great Moghuls, pinned the ribbon of the *Légion d'Honneur* onto Academician Foucher's coat.

Like many bourgeois republicans, Foucher secretly hankers for the days of the monarchy, and the word '*Majesté*', so grand and compelling, flies lightly from his lips. Hovering like an anxious nanny over some belching puffed-up *sardar*, he tilts his head to one side and rubs his hands, expressing his respectful agreement with the arguments issuing from the Afghan's thick cranium, like the knee of a camel. At such moments he is like a thick jungle creeper, wrapping itself tenderly round the pillars of absolute power. But in the grand audiences at the Palace, he is outshone by his wife.

Madame Foucher is from a distinguished lineage, the great- or great-great-great-granddaughter of a famous Paris corn merchant who managed to make a fortune in 1789, despite the tumult in the Faubourg St Antoine. Her family's fortunes have long been in decline, and the millions once made by honest robbery have been eaten up by speculation. But the heiress of the famous bakers still has the sugary whiteness of a fresh-baked French roll, in whose moist crumbs the venerable archaeologist has lost all his teeth. Her face is a pink egg-washed pretzel, topped with a feather. Her pale eyelashes above her small grey eyes, the colour of the whey used to leaven the dough, are flecked with flour, and the powerful folds of her stomach are like slices of steaming rye bread hot from the oven.

She does not enter the harem, but hovers outside, smiling and curtseying in the antechamber. To the hard-faced women of the Emir's family, with their stiff corsages of paper flowers, she resembles a piece of dough slung on a kitchen table, spilling over in the yeast of her husband's Sorbonne honours. The servants snigger and the eunuchs gape, mesmerised by her devotion to this alien despotic power. Amanullah's mother, a shrewd ambitious woman, who has seen members of her family honoured in royal portraits, and with bullets in their skulls, their swollen chests pierced by daggers, stares disdainfully at this republican lady spread out selflessly before her. The thrifty East doesn't understand such obsequiousness, like the joy of the slave at the sight of his bonded collar. Only the poor and weak debase themselves, squeezing a few drops of flattery from their sweat. The powerful are hard, proud and defiant. Wrinkling her painted brows in an expression of contempt, the Queen mentally reviews a few cheap furs and rings to give to her importunate guest, and some old but serviceable horses.

CHAPTER 12

Fascists in Asia

The body of India is infested with white leeches. Every so often people struggle desperately to tear the bloated suckers from their sides. But death-squads, armoured cars and artillery pour along the newly built roads to crush them.

After dinner in the English Club, the dancers smile as the shriek of the foxtrot drowns out the planes roaring across to shower death on the tribespeople's settlements. Over the next week, the Anglo-Indian press will publish portraits of the respectable white-flannelled planter hacked to death with his pink-cheeked family. Illustrated supplements of *The Pioneer* and *The Englishman* will honour the heroes who killed the starving natives besieging the *zemindar*'s veranda, where his family had taken refuge behind a barricade of *chaises-longues* laid out for their after-dinner rest. Engineers will repair the bridges and telegraph lines, and the law will hang the insurgents caught on the blown-up railway tracks.

Then the British Viceroy, with his dry clever smile, son of a Jewish fruit-merchant from Spitalfields,[1] will decorate a dozen aristocratic fools with gold medals, and his wife Alice will marvel at the respect paid to her in her old age. High-born *memsahibs* drop on one knee before her, and titled gentlemen stand in line like schoolboys to meet his Vice-Excellency, who has been admitted into their world, with its Stock Exchange and government posts.

Royal honours are bestowed on the crowned head of the British Raj. But the etiquette of the Viceroy's court has little in common with the harsh protocol of the European monarchies. He is relaxed and informal, and is surrounded by plenty of highnesses and excellencies who consider themselves first among equals, and openly disparage the purity of his family's blood.

India's feudal aristocrats, however, whose pampered arrogance could fill whole pages of Shakespeare's *Chronicles*, are expected to lavish him with oriental devotion, and to lay on garish pageants in his honour, while claiming their independence from the British through the charity of their banks. Capital carries out its business in Delhi in a worshipful silence, attended by genuflecting courtiers, senior members of the army, and noble ladies scraping the floor

---

1 Rufus David Isaacs, Marquess of Reading (1860–1935), Viceroy of India from 1921 to 1926, the third Jew in the British cabinet after Disraeli and the Liberal Home Secretary Sir Herbert Samuel. His wife, Alice Cohen, daughter of a stockbroker in the City of London, was known for her charitable work with India's women and children.

with their aristocratic brows. No one dares cough or move. But far in the distance, Pelops is already pushing his trunk from Asia Minor into the heart of India. Soon the country's veins will pulse with new blood, pouring in fertile streams from its old wounds. The last British shots will be fired, the Viceregal Consort will smile at the diamonds glittering on her crooked plebeian fingers, and Gandhi in his prison cell will call for non-violent resistance.

Getting under Britain's feet in Asia, grabbing every morsel of brown flesh escaping from its devouring jaws, are young entrepreneurs from Italy and Germany and the other less successful European powers. They know they have no chance of succeeding in India, but now these new opportunities are opening up in terrible Afghanistan, so feared by the British. Lack of funds makes them resourceful, and their aristocratic titles give them a brazen insolence. Grabbing their tailcoats and a change of underwear, they hop across the mysterious frontier, pursued by the sullen looks of the guards forced to patrol this cursed wasteland, which has devoured so many English lives and so much English gold.

In Jalalabad, the travellers are entertained by the local potentate, 'King of the Silkworms', resplendent against the bare lines of the mountains. But they find nothing ready for them, no profits to be made – no ivory to be exchanged with the natives for alcohol, no rubies or carpets for rusty razors, glass beads or red calico. The merchants are mean and distrustful, laying out their gaudy wares and testing every coin with their teeth. Not one of them is sufficiently civilised to sit with them at their gambling tables, who after a round or two will give up their stalls at the bazaar, their carpets and their gold, carefully counted and hidden in embroidered Bukhara purses under their shirts.

Peering disdainfully through their monocles at this hostile country not yet ripe for exploitation, they scramble over its inhospitable rocky landscape and the large face of the Emir, and their appetites are thwarted at every turn. Frantic after a week of celibacy – for even the native girls in this benighted country can't be bought – they are soon on their way home.

But not before coming to inspect us at the Embassy. Seeing the red flag of the Soviet Mission in this outpost of British India, they are at first guarded with us, and their hackles are up. But there is nothing hypocritical about these young men, no veneer of bourgeois respectability or shame. They don't mince their words, and they spare no one, and they don't expect to be spared themselves when they're up against the wall.

It's not pleasant having to meet them – titled fops à la d'Annunzio, and hulking thugs with faces like flat-irons, with their eyes like dead fish, their supercilious mouths scored by two hard lines, two highways they rob and plunder, spending the profits on drink and terrible red-haired females, who whip them even harder than they whip their weakest rivals. No wonder little Afghanistan grabs its pockets at the sight of them, and runs to count its furs hanging to dry. What belongs to others is theirs, and no legal, parliamentary or religious nonsense can stop them tearing the coats off people's backs, and beating the life out of them with their clean white hands, which have the strength of two well-fed animals. While any who express the criminal desire to better themselves they kick down the mountains with their boots.

For them the whole world, with the exception of the USSR, lies in an abyss of contempt, a craven herd, offering itself to the rich and powerful, who with a snarl of victory grab the fattest sheep, feeling their soft fleece on their teeth, and smelling their sweet sentimental smell, as they bleat 'Might isn't right!'

They see their meetings with us as the prelude to a war that will leave only one ruler of the world, and they speak of Russia with a shocking, cynical respect. The German count snorts with laughter when we speak of our Soviet Constitution and popular representation. 'Well you've done away with all that haven't you?' he says, drumming his fists on the table, impatient to crush his only worthy opponent.

'I'll be happy to fight you Reds at the barricades', he smiles as he leaves, and the two black Afghan servants bow and run ahead of him with their lanterns through the dark gardens, as if leading him to the guillotine.

Berlin, October 1923

..

Berlin, October 1923

Published by the International Organisation for Aid to Revolutionary Fighters (*M.O.P.R.*), Moscow, 1924

In the Reichstag

What a parliament! If anything could inspire fear and respect, it's the enormous marble boots of Kaiser Wilhelm I standing in the middle of the hall. The old soldier, from whom a constitution was wrung with such difficulty in his time, stands with a disapproving gaze, waiting for the moment he can drive the chattering throngs of deputies from his house. Members of parliament swarm peacefully around his venerated jackboots, promenading singly and in pairs, like schoolgirls on the boulevard. From time to time the carefree crowds are parted by elderly functionaries leading groups of youths clad in thick woollen stockings and hobnailed boots, who have come, sweating from this act of homage, to look over the House of the German People. Screwing up their school caps, they bashfully eye the naked oaken maidens with gilt navels holding up the ceilings, the torrents of frock-coats, and the excellent old footmen who represent, like some lofty personage writing his memoirs, the only bearers of the old parliamentary traditions.

Alas, no trace or semblance of the old grandeur now. Not a single figure who could attract even the respectful hatred of all the parties. Not one distinguished for his personal integrity, or for having a few decades of untarnished political gaming behind him. When old deputy Bebel used to pass through this hall, even his enemies would stand up for him. Even die-hard Prussian Junkers would hoist themselves from their swampy armchairs to acknowledge his pure name. Today, not one face, not one name. In the fog of tobacco smoke is the insignificant profile of Levi, a grey reserved face, trained without stage makeup to endure the scrutiny of those he has betrayed. Everything is from the past – yesterday's men, members of the old ministries thrown into paroxysms of self-loathing, belching statesmen, who bear for all time the stains of an indelible filth on the tails of their deputies' coats.

It's easy to pick out the various types of parliamentary fauna in the crowd. Those who have been put to use and occupy ministerial posts, who enter their obscure names on international forms, or on the many tearful pleas addressed to the Entente. Socialists renowned for shooting down workers. Cabinet members responsible for plundering the gold reserves of the German Republic. In short, men who have been put into mass circulation.

Each player in the game knows the pattern on the back of the cards. Never again will they fall into the hands of the card sharps when a cabinet is being formed. Never again will they lay out their Grand Coalitions on the table. The card snatched from a player's hand and thrown back in his face, a beaten, abused card, lives on now as a backbencher, his great days over. Scattered over the red carpets of the Reichstag are a multitude of these played-out hands. It's the younger enthusiasts, who haven't yet lost their political virginity, who are now reaching for the political honours. Behind the backs of the old buccaneers, they speak with awe and envy of their vast handouts, their imaginative betrayals and dazzling scandals. A gallery of disgraced crumpled physiognomies who somehow still manage to sip from the sweet cup of power. Naked among the naked, they blend in with the crowd with no sense of shame.

Mingling with them are swarms of the more mobile persistent young deputies, tomorrow's rulers. A flight of them alights on Breitscheid, surrounded by the flower of his political camp followers, with a whiff of the black market, although for the most part sweet smelling and well modulated. Clinging to them is the Reichstag's pride and adornment, its only woman political correspondent, a little monster wrapped in the pages of some indecent little Stock Exchange bulletin.

The rightwingers walk about as if at the races – white gaiters, monocles flashing beneath arched brows, triangles of handkerchiefs in breast pockets. On their side of the buffers, which is completely separate from the feeding troughs of the Social Democrats, they can pass up and down with no fear of encountering anything coarse or ignoble. Rolling along with them and their haughty hideous aristocratic Prussian wives, who are in the habit of taking their five o'clock tea in the fug of political tittle-tattle, trailing their furs and withered fox-tails like old lizards, are the Reichstag's banking and industrial patriots, its moneybags, so fat from the luncheons they devour in the intervals of the performance that the pages of *Crusader News* sticking from their pockets have got bent and twisted into the shapes of crosses. Christian Fascist crosses.

On the Social Democrats' tables are sausages, coffee and worries. All the entrances to the building are cordoned off, guarded by police, who grab passersby by the scruff of the neck. Standing in the main doorways are the Reichstag's most senior footmen, eunuchs of its political harem, who know the faces of all its legal wives and its favourite concubines, who check each representative of the people with their own hands, deciding who can be allowed in. Standing inside by the newspaper kiosk is a jovial strapping fellow, Berlin's Chief of Police, who pins his sharp gaze on every deputy's face, searching for the criminal element. Deputies put on an open honest face and hurry past him about their business.

Behind this multitude of security precautions is the fear of the communists getting in. The completely absurd panic-driven fear that the communist Remmele will suddenly burst in, toss in a smoke bomb, and blow up the whole Reichstag. Remmele is an obsession, awaited like a *coup de theatre*, his name chewed over, swallowed, belched up and swallowed again. Yet were Remmele ever to appear, or even a gramophone record of one of his speeches, the great NCO in the hall would give a cough from his marble stump, and his parliament would break up in shame. General Seeckt[1] knows this, he just isn't on his knees yet, like the great man brought low described with such marvellous vividness in Voltaire's *Candide*.

The game being played here bears absolutely no relation to the history and fate of Germany and its revolution. History, like the statues standing by the fountains in front of the Reichstag, has long since turned its cast-iron backside on the building. And inside they plot and bargain and battle for power.

For power. Are you laughing, General Seeckt? Power has long since left the building. Yet relentless indestructible swarms of politicking philistines continue to buzz like flies over the greasy marks left by previous deputies' unwashed hands on the pages of the Constitution, long abandoned.

The debating chamber. A deputy speaks. Jubilant laughter and applause from the right. Cries of indignation from the left. Hollow cynical laughter. The opening performance at the German Reichstag. Its great day.

---

1   Johannes Friedrich von Seeckt (1866–1936), Commander in Chief of the German Army 1920–1926

Workers' Children

Berlin is starving. Every day, in the streets, on the trams, in the bread queues, people are fainting from exhaustion. Starving drivers drive the trams. Starving railworkers drive their trains along the infernal corridors of the underground. The starving employed go off to work, the starving unemployed roam the city's parks and suburbs night and day.

Starvation haunts the buses, shutting its eyes on the spinning upper decks to the advertisements, desolation and motor horns reeling past like drunks. Starvation stands guard over the majestic counters of Wertheim's department store, taking in twenty thousand million a week, when bread costs roughly ten thousand million a pound. Starvation serves fussily and attentively in its hundreds of deserted departments, crammed with riches, golden in the light, as clean and respectable as international banks. A young shopgirl, faint with hunger, waits for the next round of staff cuts. A little pointed triangle of a face, blueish shadows of eyes, a smudge of powder, and an obsequious smile. Pointing her customer like a hungry dog to some ten-dollar boots and a thirty-dollar rug, she sells herself for a couple of pfennigs at the old rate, calculating with German thoroughness and at lightning speed the speculators' billions and trillions, entering them in her accounts book in the exquisite Gothic script possessed by this entire nation of highly literate people. Then resignedly, with the same hungry smile on her face, she undoes her shop assistant's uniform.

The walls of the huge apartment blocks, turning their bare backs on the trains flying past, are plastered with advertisements rejoicing in yesterday's surplus goods. Giant children with round rosy cheeks like buttocks and happy blond smiles, gulping the rich sweetness from tins of condensed milk, holding chocolate bars aloft over the city like lamp-posts. Its real living children have stopped going to school because of hunger. The mothers take them along, and ask the teacher to let them go home if they start telling bad during lessons, for how can a small child be expected get through classes with nothing to eat that morning or the night before?

Infant mortality has made a sudden leap in the last months in the black charts of German statistics. A thick tubercular spittle clings to the Wedding, Riksdorf and Oberschöneweide districts, operational centres of the AEG electricity and motor corporation, scenes of recent massive lockouts conducted under artillery cover, and thousands-strong strike meetings, at which in these early October days, so unlike ours, German workers have been learning to sing the *Internationale*. This late European autumn, slowly waning and freezing in the clear Berlin nights, has carried away thousands of their children.

At no time since the war have so many lives been lost to pneumonia – workers spitting and coughing themselves to death drop by drop in the bread queues, whiling away the hours of unemployment in fever and starvation. Unemployment! Not for weeks or months, but for years, with a wife and three or four children of course, and all the hundred and one misfortunes afflicting people when they're already down, worn out and torn to shreds. Sickness, incapacity for work, weakness at the critical moment in the wild scramble for the last piece of bread.

The lower ranks of the petty bourgeoisie, ruined and deprived of all means of subsistence, do all in their power to adjust to the 'hard times', economising and hoarding money which tomorrow will have turned into a pile of rubbish, stinting themselves in every possible way in the struggle to keep up the appearance of a poor but decent life of toil. Living in poverty, working for virtually nothing, they clutch at the cashier's grills from which a new derisory sum is spat out every few days, soothed by the sight of the fireproof safes stuffed with the boss's money – all that stands between them and the threatening revolution. Anything to avoid the social revolution! Better the bunch of dictators whose portraits adorn the walls – high-cheekboned big-muzzled generals of the Wilhelmine era. The petty bourgeoisie live in hope that one of them, or one of the marble figures standing with arms presented on the Siegesallee, will one day return to deliver the German people from leftwing anarchy, rightwing *putsches*, and economic ruin. Yet even though the desperation in the souls of the little office clerks, office-workers and public servants in Germany's fine civilised asphalt-carpeted cities is such that they're ready to go on all fours and howl like animals, they'll decide at the last minute not to go begging on the streets, but to a cafe, where with a thimbleful of coffee in exchange for the financial leftovers of the week, they'll cheat the rage and despair with a damp reeling waltz, the gilt of the little bow-legged baroque tables, the tobacco smoke and the courtesans' hats.

Every office-worker, from the humblest to top-grade skilled officials, has his own furniture in his flat, collected over a lifetime of rigorous economising and self-denial. Soft armchairs, rugs patterned with the Holy Scriptures, winged angels, vases of dried flowers, and always a 'Vertiko', a sort of truncated cabinet, that altar to middle-class cosiness, on which stand the family portraits, a statuette that's indecent when viewed upside-down, and the wedding bouquet under a bellglass. And until such time as the usurious state takes away the 'Vertiko', and the five padded-backed armchairs, and the heavy curtains at the windows, like giant velvet trousers, their owners won't beg on the streets, or lose faith in the peaceful bloodless social overturn the Social Democrats have been preaching for the last fifty years, at the expense of the German proletariat.

In the depths of the working class, where there are no 'Vertikos', and no money for bread, the unemployed husband spends his hours walking the streets looking for work, while the wife goes from one charitable institution to another. If she's pregnant, the doctor will carefully examine her heavy hungry stomach, and an equally hungry but highly respectable nurse will enter the unborn baby in the register of the poor, give it a number, and inform her that in about two months she might be eligible for milk for the infant at twenty-five percent off the market price.

An unemployed man's wife who is pregnant in the winter of 1923 is already a corpse.

A woman slumps on a chair, her belly sticking out from her dark hungry body, as if the baby's round head was already there on her lap under her dress. The philanthropic young nurse is uneasy at the sight of this living woman with her already visible living child, neither of whom will be alive in a matter of three months, without the slightest chance of surviving the winter in this country where the unemployed live on sixty thousand million Marks a week, and a pound of bread cost eighty thousand million the day before yesterday. The woman and her husband have been unemployed for ten months, since last January. This January, at the coldest time of year, their benefits will stop altogether. And that's with four children.

'Why didn't your husband go and dig potatoes in the summer with the farmers?' the nurse asks. 'He did, but he injured his foot. He spent all summer in hospital with blood poisoning'.

In such cases misfortunes know no bounds or reasonable limit, tumbling in a hopeless heap on the heads of those already weakened by hunger. She has tuberculosis without a doubt, her breathing is noisy and laboured.

'So where do you want to have it, in the hospital or at home?' the doctor asks her. 'At home', she says. He wisely does his best to dissuade her, trying to tempt her with the hospital's cleanliness, warmth and food. And with a totally unexpected and irresistible smile, she replies, 'Doctor, I want to die at home. I want my husband to see the baby and wrap him up himself'.

Another woman, with plaits like ears of rye wound round her young head, and a shawl tied across her full stomach, wearing a clean bright blouse, washed in cold water without soap, as wholesome as the hand-woven linen laid out to dry in the mountain sun of the Black Forest. Her husband, who has brought her, is waiting in the hall. Both have been out of work for a year and two months. An older nurse, her face furrowed with wrinkles, like old-fashioned gothic handwriting, asks her 'What will you live on this winter?' 'I don't know', she says, flashing her large teeth in a generous cherry-lipped smile. 'Either everything'll change or we'll peg out'.

Two young girls, both pregnant and unemployed. The face of the older one is puffy with tears and hunger. The younger one, a bored looking child indifferent to everything, is brought in by her mother, a tiny angry woman wearing a fancy hat and carrying a reticule. The nurse purses her lips and makes to close the door, to avoid broadcasting the disgrace to the waiting-room. '*Quatsch!* (rubbish), there's no need', the mother says. 'We're making new workers, not the ones we want dead!'

The most downtrodden German working woman supports her children, her ruined home and her pauperised unemployed family with the most unimaginable courage and strength. The whole family is starving, has been starving for months. But as long as the baby gets its quarter of a bottle of milk a day and fifty grams of gruel, there's still the possibility of hope. Six people living in one room, two of them with tuberculosis. But the baby she takes without fail to its weekly examination is kept immaculately clean, wrapped in a clean piece of cloth. For months the family hold it in their arms, high above the poverty, until they finally succumb to hunger, and the colour leaves its face, its weakened bones protrude from the thin greying skin, and the doctor's fingers feel the soft still unclosed skull under the thin mat of hair.

In every workers' hospital, and there are dozens of them, scales record the weight loss of thousands of workers' children. An entire generation of proletarian children has been weighed on these scales, squealing and wriggling their thin little legs, twisting their weak toothless mouths in their sickly infants' cries, becoming lighter and paler by the day, with the frothy yellow diarrhoea of starvation.

Germany's working class hasn't been and won't be defeated. But just as its forces are gathering into a strong communist fist, the counterattack is being waged by the most contemptible means, by striking at its future, its children. And the German proletarian woman has risen to her full height in the battle, fighting often alone to save her family. Often a man can no longer bear the screaming unfed children, the poverty and filth, and thousands of working women are abandoned by husbands and lovers after a few months of unemployment. It's easy to spot in a crowd these women struggling desperately to survive, at their own risk and peril, their ashen faces scarred by strain and suffering. Easy to spot which of them became unemployed long ago or only recently, or if it's been broken by a few days' earnings. The babies of mothers who are already starving flop their little heads weakly to one side, with ominous sores behind their ears, under their armpits and between their legs. They're kept scrupulously clean, laid out on pillows, covered with their mothers' warm shawls. But there is a limit to what she can do with her loving painstaking care. They need to be fed, milk has to be bought, medicines have to be paid for when the first sores appear on their feeble bodies.

It starts with small inflammations, little patches of moist skin that have to be disinfected and powdered, until the sickness eventually consumes the whole organism. Lying in his nappy is a little old man of seven or eight months, with an enflamed mouth, the bridge of his nose collapsed, bowed legs and a pot belly. His excrement smells bad. It's the end of many months of heroic struggle.

Every one of the unemployed mothers who come to the hospital each week knows that sooner or later it must come to this. But she fights on, battling starvation and death with all the technical means known to science, all the intelligence and culture of the only working class in the world in whose ranks are no illiterate men, and no illiterate mothers either.

The doctor finishes examining the baby and turns to the mother. 'Let me check your breasts', he says. She opens her dress, with no vest under it, and a little warm milk spurts from her high small nipple.

A Prosperous Worker's Family

The elephant pokes his trunk through the bars of his cage, and looks at little Hilda with wise hungry eyes. No, she's not going to give him anything!

The wisest of the wise flaps his ears despondently and moves away, the folds of his dry skin rustling, white with age. The zoo is cold and empty, and the animals are starving like the humans. The elephant will die soon, as is obvious from his protruding ribs and flaccid trunk. A zoological specimen of a beast, displayed for a hundred years in museums, yet still managing to walk and munch a little hay. This particular one hasn't yet reached the moment of expiring. Hilda is scared at first and closes her eyes. But after taking a peep, she clutches the cold metal rail of his cage and feels quite safe, with the mountain in its prison. 'Oh Uncle, Isn't he sweet!'

Some Russian emigres stand in front of the monkey house, offering empty matchboxes, pieces of litter and dog-ends to the clever old baboon. He is deeply offended. Catching the sounds of some family squabble inside his pavilion, he strains his ears with human curiosity, then scampers off to join the scene, slamming the little door behind him, presenting his purple blue backside to our Russian compatriots.

'Get a move on Hilda, we'll be late for the coffee house!'

'Yes, yes, will you get me some bread and butter?'

Hilda has never gone hungry. Her father is a top-grade skilled worker, her mother knits stockings, jerseys and warm gloves on a knitting-machine. Hers is one of those rare working-class families in which gravy, bread and potatoes, lard and coffee are never lacking from the table. And just as the whole planetary system of domestic worries, conversations, desires and fears revolves around a warm sandwich spread thickly with firm white margarine, sacks of potatoes hidden under the bed, and food hanging up or stowed away in the box-room, so too has Hilda's soul been formed from nice thick sausages oozing fat. When this little soul grows up, she'll have the strong glossy flanks of a carthorse, and will smell of the warm nourishing smell of beer.

Hilda doesn't want to look at the Ibis, or at any of the other sceptical-looking long-feathered Egyptian birds, who carry memories of past millennia in every pleat of their grey plumage. The Ibis struts up and down, with his bald head and beaked nose and long bare legs, like an old man with no trousers on. Suddenly Hilda cries with delight – 'Look, look, the feathers in its tail are like the ones on Auntie Wilhelmina's hat! Auntie came round to see Mummy this morning for a free cup of coffee. Mummy says people are so cheeky these days!'

A snowy evening. By the Brandenburg Gates, a snowy wind slices low across the asphalt like a sickle. The Tiergarten lies in deep shadow, like a dark wind-tossed sea. Parked along the empty pavements, as if alongside a quay, are lines of motorcars with their wet headlamps gleaming.

At half past five there is a Communist Party demonstration. Along Unter den Linden march thousands of the unemployed, musical instruments clanking in bags on their backs, cold enflamed ears sticking out from under caps, jacket collars turned up, with wide bare gaps down their chests. The wind whistles in their faces. In the dark side streets, police rip down the little flyers that plastered Berlin for a day, hitting out at the marchers with their truncheons, and are beaten back by the crowd and carried off with broken jaws. On this blizzard-swept evening, ten thousand workers flood the Lustgarten and Unter den Linden, as far as Friedrichstrasse, and the appearance of an armoured car is greeted with jeers and laughter, and the police can't muster the courage to fire a single shot.

That evening, Hilda's mother sits under the lamp in the warm sitting room darning stockings. Hilda is eating bread and lard, and when she is quite full, she rinses her satisfied tummy with water.

'Hilda', her mother says, 'show us how nice children greet their uncle on his nameday. Sing the *Internationale* for us'. Hilda sings the *Internationale*, then a song about a Christmas tree, and a popular medley of psalms. Aunt Wilhelmina, whose husband is unemployed, nods enviously and lavishes praise on him.

'What would you like for Christmas, Hilda?' he says. 'A doll, a picture-book, or a real live camel like in the zoo?'

'Oh, Uncle, give me some liver sausage!'

'Nonsense', Hilda's mother is saying to Aunt Wilhelmina, 'I don't believe in these demonstrations any more. We need an armed rising, a real revolution, not these street processions!'

The coffee pot sputters quietly on the stove, while the raging wind rattles the shutters behind the windows and howls like a demon.

'No', Hilda's mother says, tapping her darning needle on the white oilcloth on the table, 'they're not getting me out there with their speeches. We need a decisive battle, not demonstrations! All we've done is walk up and down for five years!'

Aunt Wilhelmina is undecided. 'My old man's there with them. Heavens, what a night!'

'You must come to our silver wedding anniversary party Wilhelmina, we'll be celebrating! There'll be cheese pie, meat pie, egg salad, cold potatoes and black pudding. I had to sell the sewing machine to pay for it all'.

'Ooh, Mummy, black pudding! Will I get some?'

'Prices keep going up, life's impossible. All the same you are a bit to blame yourself, Wilhelmina. Everything depends on the woman. If she's frugal and thrifty the home won't collapse. You should take better care of your things. That crockery cupboard and the bed – they're both twenty-five years old! But do you care? You should at least dust the shelves every morning and polish the tables, and don't sit on the soft furniture too much'.

'Mummy, Mummy, her baby just stole a lump of our sugar from the blue sugar bowl!'

'We must bear our misfortunes bravely and not let ourselves go. And don't on any account sell the furnishings. As long as our things are safe the family will survive. And don't fall for the government's provocations. Until the decisive battle, no stupidities like these demonstrations. We women must keep our families going and support each other. Take Uncle Kurt. Out of work for over a year, his whole family having to live in summer chalets out of town. Then his poor Minna got ill and died, and the household fell apart. Like I say, everything depends on us women. Well, naturally we relatives chipped in and arranged a decent funeral for her. I lent the poor old boy my husband's top-hat, so at least he could walk behind the coffin properly dressed'.

Little Hilda is asleep on the corner of the sofa, wearing a little white frock and white slippers, with a half-eaten piece of egg pie in her lap. Life is pure happiness for Hilda, run around and play for a bit, eat her fill, then whistle blissfully through her little pink nose, the big pink bow on top of her head slipping onto Uncle Franz's shoulder. The silver wedding party went off splendidly. And the presents! Soap, margarine, flowers, two pounds of butter. The relatives clubbed together to contribute six table-sets and six teaspoons. The sewing machine had to be sold, and some little boys smashed one of the vases of dried flowers on the ledge under the mirror. But the whole block knows Hilda's mother celebrated her twenty-fifth wedding anniversary really well, and everyone on the street will be talking about it.

'The unions have folded – what's the use of them, where do they get their money from? From the bosses, that's where! They've fooled us, haven't they? Those gentlemen, they know the leaders won't fight for us once management's doled out a few billion in hardship funds'.

Uncle Franz touches his nose with a sly wink. 'No, no, our boys won't be bought off! Yes, they take the capitalists' money, but it's us they're helping, not them. We're closer to them, we've worked with them for years, we know each other! They'll win us our gold pensions, don't you fear!'

One of little Hilda's aunts is the widow of a communist fighter killed last year. She couldn't afford to give them anything, so instead she did the washing-up all evening at her wealthy relatives' home. Taking her apron off and drying her hands, red from the hot water, she stands at the kitchen table drinking her glass of coffee and eating the last sandwich, and asks her nephew, leader of the family band (guitar, violin and mandolin), 'Play us "You fell a victim"'.

In the back room, the older folk have switched off the lamp, and in the light of a street light sing over and over again in raucous voices the songs of their youth – 'The Waltz of the Moon', 'The Rose in the Glade'. Then silence, and the clink of coffee cups. In the front room, which is usually let to a lodger, the young people press close together, dancing to the speeded-up one-step of the revolution's funeral march. Little Hilda sleeps on, dreaming of bread and margarine, and of a raisin and apple pie hidden in Auntie Wilhelmina's apron.

9 November in a Working-Class District

Two days after the sixth anniversary of the Russian Revolution. A vast cavern of a hall, half-empty. A hundred or so unusually subdued silent workers have come to celebrate – members of the Social Democrat Party.

On the platform, with dreadful clarity, are red calico banners inscribed with gold slogans, like the lines of verses and pious proverbs seen on tavern walls, greetings cards, and bridegrooms' braces – 'Long live the International!' (which one isn't said). 'Down with the Tyranny of Capital!' 'Liberty and Labour!'

None of the speakers here believes any of it. None has ever marched into battle at the head of the revolutionary proletariat. Behind these stained holy banners, the colour of fresh blood, lie the five years of the vile disgraced bourgeois German Republic, which has shot down its workers and sucked them dry, under cover of these neutered revolutionary phrases.

No jauntily upturned lids of beer mugs are to be seen on the tables, with just a few wisps of tobacco smoke in the cold damp air. Workers have long stopped drinking and smoking. A piece of dry bread pulled furtively from a pocket is enough to celebrate the day. The workers here with their families and children at this cheerless anniversary look like refugees, sitting forlornly at the quayside in hope of a passage. Husbands and wives chat in low voices, bored complaining children cuddle up to their mothers.

9 November, the day after the start of the fascists' coup, with demonstrations planned in Berlin, street battles, mass shootings of workers, pogroms.[1] These November celebrations may well turn out to be the last time the leaders of the Social Democrat Party meet the masses whose support they rely on, whose interests they're pledged to defend. The last encounter between the party's ruling bureaucratic elite and the workers, against whom the fascists promised to unleash their thugs within twenty-four hours. And what did this 'workers' party' consider it necessary to tell them on the eve of the *putsch*? Did it give them arms? A worked-out plan of defence? Assembly points, passwords, military and political leadership? What would it have cost them to announce a proper revolutionary defence strategy in a city teeming with the unemployed, twenty thousand already dead from starvation, an entire army of women thrown onto

---

1 The 'beer-hall *putsch*' of November 1923, when Hitler and the Nazi leaders Himmler, Goering and General Ludendorff, former Quartermaster of the Kaiser's General Staff, addressed thousands of swastikaed stormtroopers outside the Bavarian parliament building in Munich, then broke inside, planning to force deputies at gunpoint to march on Berlin and seize the Reichstag, before armed police arrived and arrested the leaders.

the streets, the disabled, with their paltry government benefits? What else could the organisers possibly have in mind for this party that calls itself a socialist workers' party, which has just been ignominiously kicked out of government by a soldier's boot?

The audience anxiously awaits the first speaker and greets him in silence, with the unspoken question – what now?

He is aligned with the left wing of the party – not one rightwinger has dared address any of the many meetings today – a cultured intellectual and a sneerer, who speaks eloquently and at length for about two hours. What about? It's hard to recall. Not a word about the fascists' coup, anyway. Nothing about the threat to the proletariat, how to defend themselves, avoid provocations and a bloodbath, just a dull bland parliamentary tract. Some tearful phrases about how the day has proved not to be a cheerful one, how Germany has in fact nothing to celebrate. Bread is getting dearer, unemployment is soaring, wicked generals are scheming against the Republic, the peasants don't want to exchange their good harvests for slips of paper with the ink on one side only.

A funereal silence descends on the hall. Such cold despair and confusion gust from the speaker he knows he should sprinkle the end with a few hopeful phrases, before packing off his audience back to their homes – this demoralised proletariat who in a couple of hours will have to encounter the *Reichswehr*'s machine guns, artillery and bayonets with its bare hands, without faith in itself, or the right to have such a faith.

Oh, what a happy breeze this Doctor of Philosophy could have wafted over his cold hungry audience with a few cheap hopes that fool no one, and have never defended anyone, but crawl into a proletarian's heart like a louse onto a table, to be squashed by the iron fingernail of the bourgeois dictatorship. But this traitor of a party, rotting alive on the shoulders of the proletariat, poisoning it with its sugary poison, gets yet another chance to dodge the clear simple fighting slogans needed – for a break with the bourgeois government, and for the hated social revolution.

'We're beaten, unarmed, unemployed, robbed by the vile bourgeoisie', he says. 'Our celebrations today might rightly be called the death knell of the revolution. But dear comrades, let us not despair! Time, history and destiny are on our side, the wheel of history cannot be turned back! Go in peace, don't fear Ludendorff! He has the guns, we have the logic of history. Goodnight, until we meet again, not at the barricades, but at our next celebrations, which with the aid of providence will turn out to be happier than today's'.

That's it.

Then a choir takes the stage and sings sentimental songs for an hour and a half. A fine workers' ensemble of about sixty, divided into two groups by the flapping coat tails of a socialist sexton, peering at their nice clean sheets of music, singing with zeal and gusto of pastoral bliss and pure love.

'Oh, swallow!' a fit-looking broad-shouldered building worker leads off, his solid Adam's apple bobbing painfully under his sweaty stand-up collar. His voice sounds as if his boots are too tight. 'Oh, flowers of May!' a platoon of joiners and stevedores warble tenderly from the choir on the left, their tight jackets rustling over their magnificent bulging muscles. Not a stumble or wrong note. Clearly the men have been practising their performance for at least two months, despite hunger, unemployment, their howling unfed children, and the fascists' preparations for war. No, nothing can divert the SPD from its peaceful cultural and educational activities.

What follows is total bedlam. Children from an entire working-class neighbourhood are hauled onto the stage with a crowd of teenagers and a detachment of mothers and infants, and proceed to perform a sickening doleful play. At the wave of the director's baton, the children moan and weep before their audience of hungry workers and their hungry children – 'Mumm-ee, give me brea-ead!' Then the teenagers, women and children all join in together – 'Brothers, we're dy-ing!' Hysterical sobs from the women.

The performance leaves the audience in an irritable hopeless mood, its healthy righteous anger, the arsenal of revolution, flushed down the sewer of this debilitating degraded pseudo-art. Cunning, these SPDers! Towards the end, the choir that had heroically managed its top Cs performs a selection of lyrical songs, followed by the *Internationale*. The message is clear, to drum into workers that the song isn't indissolubly linked to the blood and smoke of revolution. No, this dangerous battle cry must be neutralised, so that on the eve of the assault, it doesn't unfurl over their heads like a fresh banner blowing in the wind, stirring them to revolutionary action.

The next speaker then stands up to speak, Reichstag deputy Dr Hertz, and the audience does everything in its power to stop him. On his side are the chairman's bell, statistics, history, political economy and logic. On theirs are piercing catcalls, unemployment, hunger and a healthy class instinct. Hertz reflects that the party has made a number of mistakes over the past five years, but that there's no point discussing these now. The audience however wishes to discuss nothing but these mistakes, and dozens of notes are passed up to him. 'The SPD is a stinking corpse, it's time to bury it!' When the deputy claims he can't read what is written, they spell it out for him word for word.

A communist asks to speak. The platform tries to stop him, but the audience overwhelmingly supports him, and he speaks for forty minutes with the chair's permission, then for another forty despite the chair ruling against him. Then Deputy Hertz surfaces again. Braving jeers, foot-stamping and heckling, he makes frantic efforts to get a grip, then is suddenly triumphantly airborne again. He has his allies in government, and he names them.

'For five years we've been fighting the Whites in parliament, defending workers' rights ... (catcalls and abuse) Ebert and Stresemann[2] did all they could, but our unfortunate comrades came under such pressure from the Black Hundreds ministers they could hardly refuse a monthly donation to Kahr's White Guard government in Bavaria ... (howls of rage) According to Lenin ... (deep silence in the hall, Hertz can draw breath) According to Lenin, Germany doesn't exist on her own, as a self-sufficient political and economic entity. Our fate is inextricably linked with the revolution and reaction in France and Belgium, Britain and Italy. Basing ourselves on Lenin's views, we can state with absolute certainty that the possibility of social revolution in Germany is excluded at the present time ...'

Dr Hertz can be seen to be still speaking as his mouth is moving, but his words can no longer be heard.

---

2   Friedrich Ebert, Social Democrat President of the German Republic, 1919–1925. Philip Stresemann, former Chancellor, leading member of Ebert's coalition government.

Hamburg at the Barricades

∴

Hamburg at the Barricades

Published by International Organisation for Aid to Revolutionary Fighters (*M.O.P.R.*), Moscow, 1924

Author's Preface

A revolution, with its rich pre-history of resistance and struggle, survives with its memories intact, its heroic battles etched indelibly on the bullet-scarred walls of the buildings. An uprising passes without trace. In a few days' or weeks' time, the tattered posters will have been ripped from the walls by the soldiers' bayonets, washed away in dirty showers of rain, along with the brief memories of the battles and barricades.

Prison doors slam on the defeated fighters. Those still at liberty thrown out of their jobs must seek work in other cities, or in remote districts. The children of the unemployed deny everything to the security police, with their smarmy questions. Legends of the rising are thus buried and die away, drowned out by the noise of the returning traffic, and the new life in the factories. The workers now taking over the deserted benches may repeat a name or two, or recall the particularly fine shots, but these memories too will soon fade.

For workers there is no history in the bourgeois state. The list of their heroes is kept by the drumhead court martial and the factory guard from their Menshevik trade union. The bourgeoisie, having cracked down on the rising with armed force, must now stifle these hated memories of the danger it has so narrowly escaped.

Several months have passed now since the Hamburg Rising, but the memories stubbornly refuse to die. All traces of the barricades have been carefully smoothed over. Trains run peacefully along the embankments and viaducts that served as defensive and offensive parapets, with seagulls resting on them. Three battlefield sausage-machines churned out prisoners and threw them in jail. Doctors and prison inspectors have long since returned the last of the corpses mutilated beyond recognition to their next of kin. And still the memories of those October days survive. There is no public house, workers' gathering or proletarian family in the old Free City of Hamburg where the amazing scenes on its streets aren't recounted by its fighters with pride, recalled with awe and admiration by onlookers drawn into the battles. And the reason proletarian Hamburg guards its memories of those October days so fiercely is that although the rising was crushed militarily, it wasn't defeated in a political or moral sense. The masses weren't left with the bitter gall of failure.

The long revolutionary process that drove Hamburg to the barricades in October was broken neither on the 24th, when the entire police force and a crack Black Hundreds regiment of Junkers and *Reichswehr* units were mobilised against them, nor on the 26th, when compact police formations, thousands-strong cavalry and infantry detachments and whole platoons of armoured cars, finally broke into the revolutionary suburbs, already voluntarily abandoned a few hours earlier by the workers' units. On the contrary, the workers' movement that surfaced then to rule the city for sixty hours, cracking the enemy's head everywhere he dared to attack their skilfully constructed and placed barricades, lost only ten dead in the battles, with dozens of troops and police dead and injured. And afterwards the rising's leaders calmly organised the retreat, escorting combatants out of the line of fire, hiding their weapons, taking the wounded to be tended in safe houses, then going underground, ready to return to action at the first call of the German revolution.

The revolutionary upsurge started long before October, and dates back to the previous August, when Hamburg was the scene of a succession of bitter wage disputes, for the eight-hour day, for pay based on the gold equivalent, and a whole range of demands, economic and also purely political – for the arrest of the bosses, workers' control of production, and a workers' government. The strike fever led to outbursts of revolutionary rage, with raids on food warehouses, and attacks on scabs and police.

It was in those months that Hamburg's working women came into their own. More resourceful and politically mature than their comrades in any of Germany's other major industrial cities, they barred their husbands' and workmates' way into the striking shipyards. Neither police bayonets nor the weak-willed crowds of workers who were ready to meet the employers on any terms could push back the chain of them occupying the Elbe tunnel. One of the clashes ended with the disarming and beating up of an entire police detachment, with the lieutenant in charge thrown into the cold muddy waters of the river.

The movement that started last August didn't end in fiasco, as the bourgeoisie crows, nor was it defeated by the full-scale military assaults of 21–6 October. The workers' movement will be victorious or defeated only with the victory or defeat of the entire working class. It's in the continuity and steady growth of the Hamburg struggle, led by our comrades, that lies the crucial difference between an armed uprising and a political *putsch*.

A *putsch* has no past or future, just total victory, or an equally total and futile defeat. A revolution, to be powerful and successful, must be guided by a strong flexible battle-ready party, able to retreat when attacked, and spring back into action at the right moment. A weak, politically untrained proletariat will live in the hope only of a brief sharp bloody blow, which may entail enormous sacrifices and casualties and the utmost effort. The undisciplined masses will face anything, as long as there's a glimmer of hope of some ephemeral but incontestably complete and final success. When such an attempt to seize power fails, the mobilised masses will drop out and abandon the struggle, reinforcing the defeat with bitter self-criticism.

Cadres of politically experienced fighters will return from a storming operation to their old positions in the underground, still equal to the long slow siege, organising fortifications and daily harrying operations. The Hamburg Rising, by virtue of the prolonged political process leading up to it, and the brilliant work carried out in the days and weeks immediately following its liquidation, provides a classic example of a truly revolutionary uprising, involving a quite remarkable strategy of street battles and retreats, unique of its kind, which left the masses with a sure sense of superiority over the enemy, an awareness of their moral victory.

The rising's achievements are unquestionable. Yet never before have the betrayals of the trade union leadership reached such depths. Between 25 October and 1 January, over thirty thousand workers dropped out of the ranks of the Menshevik trade unions. We shall go into more detail later about the dastardly role played then by the union bureaucracy and its right-wing allies in the SPD. Members of the United Republicans Party and the Fatherland Defence League, acting as their guard dogs, were hired to replace the police in the quieter districts, allowing them to concentrate their forces on Hamm and Schiffbek. These bellicose exploits by Social Democracy led to thousands of workers tearing up their party cards and dumping them in heaps on the doorstep of its recruiting offices, then risking arrest and being shot at by *Reichswehr* patrols to make their way to the trade union offices, to throw their membership cards in the treachery-stained faces of the union bureaucracy. A number of major unions in the coastal region, including the Amalgamated Union of Building Workers, came apart at the seams after the October rising; it was physically impossible to stop a mass exodus of members. Eight hundred at a branch meeting of the builders' union voted to leave and set up their own association, among them middle-aged men, not all of them party members, masters of their trade and not short of employment, members of long standing, who had paid their dues for decades.

At another meeting, old men choking with rage demanded a complete break with the union '*Bonzes*' (bigwigs), and the immediate setting up of an independent breakaway union. Members of the Communist Party (the KPD) tried in vain to dissuade members from this strategy, calling on them to build a solid opposition that would undermine the bureaucracy from within, and increasingly extend its influence.

Workers see the unions as undeserving of a single penny of their hard-earned wages. They say a worker who stays in a Menshevik union for so much as a day forfeits his proletarian honour, and becomes complicit in their crimes. Staying in the unions after October, even for a middle-aged non-party worker, has become tantamount to working with the *Sipo* or *Eins A*.[1]

The Communist Party, and the masses behind it, have grown infinitely stronger, externally and internally, despite the crackdowns and arrests. The majority of comrades were arrested not during the rising itself, but when it was all over, often on the basis of voluntary denunciations by SPD members and neighbours. Yet the whole of Hamburg, every crossroads, every public building, was decorated with the ineffaceable slogan 'The Communist Party Lives, We Cannot be Banned!'

Parliament may well vote for an emergency *Ermächtgungsgesetz* (Enabling Act). General Seeckt may well be granted special powers, and a White dictatorship may gobble up the last dregs of the small freedoms granted by Germany's labour laws. Yet the latest communist posters plaster the walls like wallpaper of every hut where the unemployed register. They're thrown from the galleries at SPD meetings, stuck on pub walls, in trams and trains and on buses. The women in the suburbs, where virtually the entire male population is either on the run or in various prisons, demand to be sent posters and leaflets, and if they have one complaint, it's the lack of a cheap communist newspaper.

All this so little resembled defeat that the court-martials were forced to commute the sentences of the convicted, who would go off to the fortress or the labour camp with the pride of victors, and the most profound contempt for the laws of the bourgeois state, knowing its days were numbered, and that the revolution wouldn't allow their five, seven or ten years of solitary confinement to run their course. Such a faith cannot mislead.

So why didn't the whole country support the Hamburg Rising?

In those October days, Germany was divided into two opposing camps, each awaiting the signal for the offensive. By then Saxony had already been swamped by *Reichswehr* units and the police, so that by the time of the rising, one of the main bridgeheads of the revolution had effectively ceased to exist. Crowds of the unemployed were on the streets of Dresden night and day, but hard on their heels, alongside and ahead of them, biting into the asphalt, was the *Reichswehr*, armed and dangerous. A signal for battle given in Saxony then would have been the signal for the mass slaughter of Saxony's workers.

A conference in Hamburg in October of workers employed in its great shipyards, and in those at Lubeck, Stettin, Bremen and Wilhelmshaven, demanded the immediate declaration of a general strike, and the union leaders at

---

1   Respectively the *Sicherzeitpolizei* (Security Police) and Unit A, its plainclothes branch.

this policy-making conference only just managed to win a postponement. At another workers' conference in Chemnitz however, a majority voted against a general strike. By then Saxony was under water, and workers shied away from a collision that could prove fatal to the revolution.

Anyone who was in Berlin then will recall the extraordinarily ambivalent attitude to the revolutionary turmoil. Starving women and the unemployed filled the streets. Cheeky urchins whistling the *Internationale* pushed through the despairing poor in the bread queues and outside the butchers' shops. The collapse of the Mark, the derisory benefits to the unemployed, war widows and the disabled. Wage cuts, soaring inflation, the ruin of the petty-bourgeoisie. The sly mischief of Germany's capitalists, dragged into the light of day by the press. The shamelessness of the Grand Coalition. And overshadowing everything, the spectre of the bloodied coaldust of the Ruhr, now a cash cow for France, and the arrests and repressions by the occupying French forces.[2] All these were clear portents of the coming revolution. The wealthy in their motorcars were avoiding Berlin's poor suburbs, and the police were turning a blind eye to the looting of the bakeries. In the outskirts, artillery rumbled over the stony wastes, edging ever closer to the striking factories. Trucks loaded with neatly formed rows of police roared past the crowds besieging the markets and newspaper kiosks, without slowing down, kindling their fury.

Yet at the same time the vast totally passive majority of the working masses still supported the Social Democrats. Hiding behind the backs of the communists and the unemployed was this new bourgeoisified layer of the proletariat, greedily clutching at its piece of bread, its domestic comforts and its pound of margarine, however many hours' work might be needed to pay for it all. A shrill, cowardly, disgruntled majority, prepared to sit out the shootings on the streets for a few days at home by the fire, with a cup of coffee and the latest issue of *Vorwärts*, until the dead and wounded had been carried away, the barricades dismantled, and the victors, whoever they were – the Bolsheviks, Ludendorff or Seeckt – had put the vanquished in jail and the lawful government in power. Along with the active vanguard was this corrupt swollen rear, ready in the event of failure to denounce a communist neighbour lying in a trench under the windows of some worthy socialist official, hiding behind his net curtains.

In Berlin, as in Hamburg, with the exception of certain solidly working-class districts, the proletariat was having to resist Seeckt's troops and gendarmerie in isolation, without the active support of the broad masses, with no hope of rein-

---

2   In January 1923, seventy thousand French and Belgian troops marched into the industrial
    Ruhr Valley, to seize Germany's unpaid war reparations ordered by the Versailles Treaty.

forcements at the toughest moments, and often, as in Hamburg, with virtually no weapons. Yet the Hamburg Rising, undertaken in such unfavourable conditions, produced quite astonishing results. The fact is that behind the rising stood the whole of proletarian Germany, unbroken by the counterrevolution, who in open battle could materially and morally cover the heroic retreat of Hamburg's pioneers.

The job of a party out to win power isn't just to wait for the historic moment – the so-called 'twelfth hour of the bourgeoisie' – when the clock of history will hesitate for a moment, then mechanically count off the first seconds of the new communist era.

There's an old German tale about a valiant knight who spends his life in a magic cave, waiting for a drop of water glistening from the tip of a stalactite to fall into his mouth. At the last minute some absurdity always stops him catching the agonisingly awaited drop, which falls uselessly on the sand. And the worst part of the tale of course is not the actual point of failure, but the dead hollow pause of disillusioned expectation between one drop and the next.

In Hamburg, they weren't waiting for manna from heaven. What they call so succinctly '*die Aktion*' was linked to a strong unbroken chain of uninterrupted struggle, connected to what had gone before, finding its support in a future that stood under the sign of a victory that would smash the old world like the head of a steam-hammer.

CHAPTER 1

Hamburg

Hamburg lies on the shores of the North Sea like a big wet fish lifted still quivering from the water. Eternal fogs settle on the pointed scaly roofs of the houses. Not one day remains true to its capricious pale, windy mornings. The surge and swell of the tides bring damp, mildness, sunshine. From the grey cold of the open sea come the interminable relentless rains, drenching the glistening asphalt, as if someone standing on the foreshore had picked up an old ship's bucket from the water – the kind used for baling out leaky boats in a storm – and was swilling it over gay Hamburg. Hamburg, waterproof as a pilot's steaming oilskin, stinking like a sailor's pipe, charred with the fires of the dockside bars, standing firm under the torrential rain, legs set wide apart as if on deck, planted on the right and left banks of the Elbe.

All along the shores of this marvellous industrial inlet, nature has been eradicated, like some prejudice expelled from our lives by the German Enlightenment. Not an inch of ground is left bare. Over a stretch of twenty miles are two trees, looking more like masts after a fire at sea than the useless living things they are. The one on the jetty is hunched like an old woman walking against the wind, which tosses shreds of angry foam against her thick woollen stockings and shivering legs. The other stands outside the offices of Hamburg's greatest shipyards, Blohm & Voss.

This tree stays up only out of fear. Beneath it is a black canal, into which factory waste flows from gaping pipes like inky vomit. A bridge, the guard's cabin, and on the opposite bank, in the pale light of early morning, the shimmering windows of countless invisible apartment blocks, row on row of them above the harbour, reaching out with their electricity to touch the dawn.

Arching over the harbour are the greatest of its wonders, the shapeliest forms in this realm of shapely metal, the light shadowy jibs of the world's largest cranes. Lying at their feet like toys are transatlantic liners, fully fitted-out with their brightly lit rows of portholes, hiding their ugly lower parts under the waterline, like swans.

The factories here are working three shifts now, convulsively and ruthlessly, wringing out the workers like wet washing. The German bourgeoisie is making this last futile attempt to survive the crisis paralysing industry, filling the oceans with its black-funnelled white ships, the old Imperial black-white-and-red flags fluttering on their sterns replaced here and there with pockmarked republican ones.

They say Hamburg has everything – the smoking factory chimneys, the elephant-trunks of the cranes, ravaging the holds and filling the stone depositories. The light gently sloping bridges crisscrossing the new-born ships. The howls of the sirens, the coarse yells of the hooters. The ocean tides making sport with the jetsam, which seagulls settle on like floats. The massed square red-brick buildings of the warehouses, offices, plants, markets and customs-houses, all built in straight lines, like the piles of cargo the dockers stack on the quays.

Armies of workers are employed in these shipyards, loading and unloading the ships, working in the innumerable engineering, oil-refining and chemical plants, the vast manufacturing works and industrial installations that cover Hamburg's rear, its marshy sandy hinterland, crusted with concrete and steel.

This ancient dirty warm-water port on the Elbe, forever extending and building onto its concreted backyards, stopping place for sea tramps, is where the sea horses throw down their baggage, gulp oil and coal and get cleaned and washed, while the captains touch up the bills, hand over their bribes at the customs-house, and have a shave before going ashore to their families. The crews get nabbed *en masse* in the St Pauli quarter, with its bars, gangs, ready-made dresses and pawnshops, where the same garish, shoddily-made expensive dresses can be lodged at half their price, famous above all for its amazing brothels.

Ever since medieval times, the back streets of St Pauli have been screened off from the rest of the city by strong metal gates, open only at night, finely wrought, with every conceivable whimsical detail, proudly decorated with the emblems and insignia of the metalworkers' guild.

In the evenings, lighted windows open in the houses giving onto the streets, and smiling into the endless rainy darkness are the queens of these seamen's paradise. They wear low-cut dresses, tight at the waist, trimmed with sequins and feathers, a fashion from the end of the last century that has survived to the present, like sweet-wrappers, and in the men's women-starved imaginations, they embody the supreme joy of living.

The line of living meat is sold with the utmost simplicity. Customers pass from window to window, examining the goods on display, then disappear inside, running out into the street a short while afterwards growling and cursing. St Pauli's doorkeepers are renowned for their muscle.

All languages and all nations mingle in the little taverns, known for their egg-grog, their savage wit, and total immunity from police intervention, a wonderful blend of alcohol, revolutionary ardour, tobacco smoke, and the last hopelessly fallen sinner. Some drunken Adam, without face or name, sitting with his girl at a table soaked in beer, as she tells him divine lies about love.

The language spoken in Hamburg is Hamburg's language, soaked in the sea, salty as cod, ripe and juicy as Dutch cheese, rude, smelly and cheerful as English gin, rich, slithery and light as some large rare creature from the deep, panting among the carps and plump eels quivering their wet rainbows in a fishwife's basket. Only the letter *S*, sharp and graceful as a spindle, testifies to Hamburg's old gothic language, and the days of the Hanse and the piracy of the archbishops.

The whole city, not just the lumpenproletariat, is steeped in the lively boisterous spirit of the harbour. It surrounds on all sides the bourgeois districts situated around the Alster, a tidal lake ebbing and flowing with the sea. Villas hug the shore, with barely enough space between them for their neat tended gardens, clad in flowers like swimming costumes, with their tennis courts and flights of steps down to the shore.

The excited unclean breath of the suburbs blows down the necks of the patricians' homes. A ring of electric trains firmly binds the outskirts, and squeezes them against the smart districts like a steel band. Surging along this line twice a day, filling the carriages with the smell of sweat, tar and winey breath, are streams of workers on their way to and from the docks.

All Hamburg lives by the lunchtime hooter, the boatswain's whistle, the arrivals and departures of the morning and evening shifts, just as the smallest child-packed frog pond lives by the pulsing of the distant ocean, which delivers Hamburg's wealth and its winds, resilient as sails.

Hamburg's worthy burghers are as uninsured against contact with the proletarian masses as are their homes. A lady going to the theatre is squashed between two dock-workers who put their greasy work bags on the seats. On the bus, a young thing from St Pauli coolly sits herself down beside the wife of a civil servant, winks at the other passengers, and gets off at her stop on the arm of one of them. A worker cuddles his girlfriend. A stevedore smokes everyone out with his stinking tobacco. Some friends take a drunk sailor home from a binge, and everyone chuckles with them, speaking the purest Hamburg *Platt* (dialect), which can turn anywhere into a jolly seaman's cabin.

After Berlin, where a worker with his tools has the right to travel only on certain specially designated old buses and trains, where the superiority of the first and second classes is enforced by the police, where an unemployed worker, rubbing his cold blue ears, dares not sit on one of the Tiergarten's innumerable empty benches, after triumphant bourgeois Berlin, the very air of Hamburg, with its free and natural spirit, smells of revolution.

At five in the morning, the proletariat is sleeping, wherever that may be, or being dragged to the police station. At a quarter to six, by the light of the electricity, the first high tide of workers begins.

Running above the tram lines are the gleaming ribbons of the electric trains, which throw an army of dockers onto the pavements, with hundreds of thousands more of the unemployed, besieging the wharves in the hope of some casual work. Crowds of them cluster round the foremen in their tarry jackets, hunched under the tool-bags on their backs, with their oil-lamps like colliery overmen's lights. After the call-over, the regiments of workers are split up and sent off to the hundreds of steamships anchored around the yards and plants. Workers pour in across four bridges. Troops and police keep a sharp eye on them, checking that no 'civvies' penetrate the industrial island. Neither the bridges nor the hundreds of steamers, casting their searchlights on the river, like a carnival in this black oily Venice, can halt the dense surge of the morning shift. Thousands more cross the Elbe along the dry bright tube laid deep beneath its waters, which pumps them from shore to shore every morning and evening. At each end of the tunnel, elephantine lifts, screeching in their towers, raise and lower their human cargo to and from the concrete exits, delivering this living fuel to the docks and factories. Out of this forge came the Hamburg Rising.

Barmbeck

Hamburg's workers live far from their factories and shipyards, most of them in the Barmbeck district, an enormous sprawling workers' barracks where all the dwellings look the same – shared sleeping quarters in rented dormitories joined together by the dirty bare corridors of the streets, opening onto dreary squares, looking more like public kitchens or lavatories, each with a dreary fountain under the tin sky.

Crawling in a semicircle around this foul and filthy suburb is the giant steel caterpillar of the railway viaduct, its bowed legs attached to the ground with concrete suckers. Its head disappears in a wilderness of backyards, blind alleys, and buildings with dizzy little balconies hung with washing and trails of wilting ivy, expiring in the smoke and damp. The station building plants its wide flat feet on the tail, leaving a crack for the stream of passengers to pour through.

Directly opposite the railway station, behind spiked railings festooned with tatters of old government decrees, stands one of Barmbeck's police stations, with blackened windows like a detective's dark glasses. The policeman guarding this pockmarked monstrosity of a building does his job with the usual official's boredom and spite, chewed over like a twice smoked discarded cigarette end picked off the street.

The port of Hamburg is open to workers only at certain times. It sucks in an army of them at dawn, and spits them out in the evening. Police remain in this deserted industrial fortress to guard the swing-bridges, turnstiles and subways through which the flood of workers pour to the quays. None of them lives within the port itself. Only the oldest most trusted servants of the masters of industry enjoy this privilege. The obsequiously twinkling lights of their homes huddle in the vast shadows of factory blocks, slowly exhaling into the night fog the human warmth left over from the day. Police patrol the quays, stopping anyone who happens to pass with their bayonets, shining their lamps in their faces. 'Name? Passport? Business?'

In Barmbeck the unrest started a week before the rising. On Wednesday 17 October, working women stormed the markets and forced the saboteur traders to continue business. On Thursday, they formed a chain in front of the shipyards, and drove their shamed husbands back home. On Friday, fifteen thousand unemployed men and women demonstrated at the Heiligengeist Field. Next day, thousands rallied outside the Trade Union House, then proceeded to the City Hall and broke through into the restricted zone surrounding the building.

That evening, tens of thousands of workers poured onto the streets. The police arrested over a hundred, but the angry demonstrations continued. News of the *Reichswehr*'s assault on Dresden's workers spread like wildfire. The masses were fired with a terrible excitement – it was the start of revolution.

On Sunday 21 October, there was a conference of Hamburg's port-workers, and workers from ports along the whole Baltic coast, from Bremen, Stettin, Schweinemunde and Lübeck. The majority of delegates were SPD, but many were from plants already several days on strike, who had been returning their membership cards to the Metalworkers' Union, which had denounced the strikes as wild-cat strikes. There was a sharp clash at this conference between old SPD delegate Mann from Stettin, covered in moss and mould from his twenty-eight years' party service, and the communist worker T.,[1] square, big-boned, widebrowed, pounding his clenched fists like thunderbolts, grasping the reins of the Hamburg Rising in his iron hands. Like a coachman driving his laden waggon up a steep icy slope, T. had simultaneously to urge on and restrain, to stay on his box while cracking his whip at the social bureaucrats, calming the rearing militancy that could shout no more and was blind with rage, arguing for a three-day postponement of a general strike, to allow comrades to stop up all the gaps through which the rising could have spilt prematurely onto the streets. His motion barely scraped through, but the delay gave delegates time to bring the full-time officials to order.

On Sunday night, a courier brought news to Hamburg (which proved to be false) of the successful rising in Dresden. The order for a general strike was then immediately passed round the various quarters, including the Deutschewerft shipyards, which supports dozens of Hamburg's major enterprises, and had been locked out since the day before. Workers had broken through the police cordons and gone inside, then joined the crowds in the city centre. By four in the afternoon, the harbour was paralysed. A hundred thousand workers were on Hamburg's streets, giving it the appearance of a city already in the grip of the rising. At meetings in Altona and Neustadt, a second courier gave more entirely inaccurate information about Russia mobilising its army to support the rising, and sailing submarines to Hamburg.

In the dead of night, the 'chiefs', leaders of the uprising's Military Organisation, the M. Apparat, received their battle orders with a feeling of deep satisfac-

---

1   Ernst Thälmann (1886–1944), leader of the Communist Party of Germany from 1925 to 1933.

tion. T., who had called for a postponement of the general strike, now lifted all the sluices holding back the torrent of the rising.

The worker K. too was pleased.

A few words about K. A sergeant-major in the war, who hated with all his being *der preussiche Drill* (Prussian army drill) in the trenches, he had been awarded a commission for his bravery. Then in one of the towns in occupied Galicia, there was a major incident that cost him his nice new epaulettes. Four weeks in jail for boxing a major's ears in public. A member of the Hamburg Council of Workers' Deputies in 1918,[2] and of the Communist Party, K. was one of the most active members of the Military Organisation. His military training, his courage, his sergeant-major's precision and speed, his port-worker's joviality, his talent for 'giving someone a rocket', all these qualities made him exceptionally popular with the masses, and earned him the cautious squeamish fear of *die Intellektuellen*. As well it might! Philistines don't like people full of the joy of life, with the smell of *Köm* (Kümmel spirits) about them, and the rough crude language of the port. Gaiety, roughness and a slight intoxication in the blood are considered incompatible with the calling of a true European party hack.

After the August riots, the Communist Party was inundated with spies. One, with the touch of an old provocateur, offered to supply the Military Organisation with a crate of arms, receipt of which would have led to its dismemberment. Charged with unmasking this police ruse, K. drove off with the agent to collect the arms, and on one of the bridges he coolly picked him up by the scruff of the neck and dangled him over the side, saying. 'Own up, bastard!' And the man owned up, got his due and vanished.

In periods of lull, comrade K. is a pub brawler and tyrant, terror and pride of the neighbourhood. When he meets a bunch of SPD men in a bar, Hamburg's famous Köm mixed with its excellent beer sharpens his dialectic to the maximum. The Mensheviks, roused to fury by the taunts of this giant with his benign crafty eyes, leap yelling at him in a fight. Grabbing the ringleader from the scrum of his fellow-thinkers, K. hurls him onto a grand piano. The police are called, noses are broken, and indescribable chords come from the unfortunate piano. Inactivity is dangerous for people like K., but in active struggle they're

---

2 Russian-style Workers' Councils (*Arbeiterrate*), or Soviets, sprang up in late 1918 in major industrial cities across Germany, in the Ruhr and Saxony, Bavaria and Thuringia. The Hamburg Soviet of Workers and Soldiers, established 18 November, declared the dissolution of the local Senate and Parliament, to be replaced by a full Soviet government. Within a month, under pressure from the banks, both institutions were back in power, and by January 1919, leadership of the Soviet had passed to the SDP.

in the front ranks. It was K. and communist official Kb.[3] who led the defence of Barmbeck throughout the rising with their amazing network of barricades. More about them later.

At midnight on 21 October, the leaders dispersed to brief members of the workers' units. Most SPD members, like workers not in the party, learnt of the start of the rising only the following morning, after Military Organisation commandos had seized six of Barmbeck's police stations. The storming of the *Polizeibüros* was scheduled with military precision for 4.45 am, to be immediately followed by the capture and disarming of the Wandsbek barracks. Until then, the military leaders couldn't allow anyone to go home, put a light on, or on any pretext to go off to 'say goodbye to the family'. Only thanks to such precautions were the police caught off-guard and disarmed with the fighters' bare hands. The credit for this must go to T. and other comrades who worked out the battle plan. The game was half-won with this swift unexpected blow by the Military Organisation, whose goals were threefold: to deprive the enemy of its support points, its police stations; to arm the workers at the expense of the police; and to show the masses that victory could be achieved, encouraging more to join this struggle that had barely begun.

The government paid tribute to the dislocation caused by the rising. Here is what Hamburg *Polizeisenator* (Police Commissioner) Hense, a Social Democrat, had to say: 'The worst thing about it wasn't the weakness and inadequacy of the forces at our disposal. What was so terrible (*schrecklich*) was that this time, unlike in all previous *putsches*, the communists were able to carry through their lengthy thorough preparations in such secrecy that not a squeak of it reached us. Generally, we're kept informed of everything afoot in the communists' camp. Not that we need to keep spies in their ranks. The law-abiding majority of workers, in whom I include members of the Social Democrat Party, are happy to report to us what the communists are up to, with no coercion'.

This time, the 'law-abiding' Menshevik informers proved unable to forewarn the authorities about the rising in preparation, to the extent that the state of siege that had kept the police on full alert the previous week had been lifted by the government on Sunday, the eve of the rising.

But let's go back a few hours, to some scenes that show communists' mood at the moment of mobilisation, when comrades were shaken out of their beds and led off goodness knows where. The twilight hour when they're unbearably

---

3 Hans Kippenberger (1898–1937), leading member of the Communist Party of Germany, who found asylum in Moscow after the rising was crushed.

cold, and just want to go back to sleep, and everything is a drab muddy colour – not the time to be striking a heroic pose. As they said, everything was rough and ready.

One of the rising's leaders goes round his *Bezirksleiter* (zone leaders) to pass on the orders for the morning's operations. A lifeless street, a sleeping building, a stuffy snoring flat, the home of a poor worker. He rises and dresses without lingering or asking why. A calm handshake, a cigarette glowing in the dark.

Another home in another working-class street. The wife opens the door and helps her husband collect his things, holding a candle over the kitchen table on which a map is spread. He studies it for a while, then from the depths of his heart, with a sense of deep relief, he says, '*Endlich geht's los …*' (At last it's starting)

In a third home, a wife tells her dawdling husband, '*Nu mock di man fertig!*' (Hurry up and get ready!)

Finally a flat in the St Georg district. No one is asleep here. In the back room a lamp is lit, flickering through a web of tobacco smoke. The landlady answers evasively – he's at home and he isn't, she doesn't know anything. Footsteps on the stairs, then the door bursts open, and grinning cheerfully in the shadows is the character known around the dockland bars as Rowdy (Ruffian), barefoot, his face smeared with soot, a clutch of rifles under his arm, his pockets stuffed with all sorts of ammunition. What's this? He's cleared out an entire arsenal! This *Genosse* (comrade) isn't quite a *Genosse* of course, just a sympathiser. But the speed and dexterity with which he unhooked the bolt and lifted out his treasures is quite remarkable. Rowdy is a great performer, who prides himself on the simplicity of his performances. '*Mensch, den har ick dat jo nicht mehr neudig hat!*' (Man, won't be needing these any more!) says the comrade who has come to show him the plans for the capture of the police stations and their arms.

The first phase of the three-day struggle was directed at Barmbeck's railway line, its spinal column, which insurgents were unable to capture due to insufficient weapons, principally explosives. The situation was complicated by the fact that they were unable to take one of the police stations, on Von-Essen Strasse, which drew off and pinned down considerable insurrectionary forces throughout the struggle, and remained unoccupied through a complete accident. The first assault was led by comrade C., an enormously large man, distinguished by an exceptionally cool temperament, as impervious as freshly rolled asphalt. Breaking in with two comrades, he rapped a stick on the desk, demanding the station's immediate surrender. Then as the Blues and Greens[4]

---

4   Blues – the security police, who wore blue uniforms. Greens – *Reichswehr* troops.

were unbuckling their stout holsters, another group from C's unit came round from the back of the building, penetrated the yard, and puzzled by the silence reigning in the now occupied mouse-trap, opened fire at the windows. The *Reichswehr* and *Sipo* men finally came to their senses, saw three unarmed workers in front of them, and threw two to the ground, catching C. off guard. They then barred themselves in the cellar and bombarded the invaders with hand grenades. The workers' unit retreated, and at the first crossroads they were met by comrade Kb., who already had the first barricades up to halt the enemy.

One officer for the whole of the Hamburg Rising, but how much Kb. did for it! There wasn't a street or alley in Barmbeck not blocked up with a couple of barricades. They seemed to sprout from the ground, multiplying at an incredible rate. If there were no saws or spades, they were found. Workers threw themselves into the construction work, hauling rocks, breaking up pavements, chopping down sacred trees in the parks and sawing them into logs. Citizens brought along their cupboards, chests of drawers, beds and trunks. An old woman, living on her own, tugged at Kb.'s sleeve and beckoned him upstairs to take a wide sturdy board from her washstand – the pride of her household – that would be handy for a barricade. The board was put to use and endured stoutly to the end, although it was an exception.

The old romantic barricades have long had their day. The proud *gamine* in her Phrygian cap waving her tattered banner aloft, braving the *Versaillaises* in their white gaiters. The dying student in the Latin Quarter, pressing a lace handkerchief to his wounds. The old worker firing his last bullet from the long barrel of his antiquated pistol. The schoolbooks are full of this charming romantic nonsense, and the legends born in the powder smoke of 1848. Fighting today is different. The image of the barricades in the old days was of a fortified barrier between the revolutionaries' rifles and the government's cannon. Now they no longer serve as a protection to anyone. Assembled from trees, rocks, upturned vehicles and furniture, their function is to obstruct the enemy, with deep trenches that bar the way to armoured cars, the most dangerous foes of an uprising. The trenches are the true purpose of the modern barricade. Yet the old-time barricade, backed up now by the field-trench that has migrated to the cities from the dead fields of large-scale warfare, continues to serve insurgents well, even though in very different circumstances from the days of their heroic forebears in 1791 and 1848.

Piled up across Barmbeck's streets, their jagged menacing wings obstructing a clear view of what was going on, they became the enemy's only visible targets, bravely catching the blind fire the troops rained down on their unseen enemy. This is another new feature that has totally changed the landscape of civil war and its strategy and tactics. The new method of warfare makes workers invisible, almost invulnerable. Most in the rising fought rarely if at all on the streets, leaving them almost entirely to the police and army, and instead fired from the buildings. Those manning the barricades were in a hood of darkness, which no quick-firing weapon could penetrate. These new barricades, of bricks, wood, rocks and upturned vehicles, were the collective work of the fighters themselves, with their millions of secret passageways, their basements and attics and living quarters. Every ground-floor window in these unassailable fortresses was an embrasure, every attic a battery and observation post, every bed could be used as a stretcher for the wounded. It was this extraordinary network of barricades that explained the disproportionate number of government losses, and why Barmbeck's workers could count scarcely a dozen wounded, and between two and five killed.

The troops were forced to advance along the open streets. Workers joined battle from their homes, firing from windows. All attempts by the regular forces to take Barmbeck on Tuesday were thwarted by this elusive invisible formation of rifles, coolly picking its targets from a first-floor window, while down below the helplessly exposed crowds of police pounded the empty barricades.

Anticipating an armoured assault, Kb. managed to get a concrete bridge blown up, assumed to be there for all time, without dynamite or gunpowder. Workers felt for its most vulnerable artery, the gas main, and set it alight.

An army truck lurched into a quiet deserted street. The driver stopped to fix the damaged engine, and a barricade sprang up in front of him. And as he turned round, the fallen crowns of sawn-down trees were already lying crisscrossed in his path.

Vehicle M-14 moved slowly forward under the railway bridge, with five *Sipos* on board. From behind a pub or round a corner, no one knew from where, but close by, a shot rang out, then another, killing the driver and a *Sipo*. The vehicle was ripped to bits, and Young Communists threw the debris around.

Pitched battles continued all Tuesday. The first heavy assaults started at about eleven in the morning. The hardest fought battles were around the Von-Essen Strasse police station, and along the line of barricades facing the railway embankment. Police detachments quickly captured the railway station, and police and troops then ran along the track trying to pick off the fighters from above, managing to avoid the first two ambushes. Over the third span of the viaduct, a deadly volley broke out. Workers were firing from the cover of the neighbouring attics and rooftops. Riflemen scattered across the roofs kept whole streets, the main crossroads and the squares under fire.

Below was an earthworks and a barricade that had held out for several hours. A *Sipo* detachment was advancing, the position became untenable. From the roof of a building, came the order *'Die Barrikade frei!'* (Clear the barricades!)

People didn't know what was going on. A wounded rifleman, a young worker in his twenties with a bleeding shoulder, went down to them and explained that the fighters on the roof were afraid of hitting their own side. He disappeared into a driveway, and a few minutes later firing from the roof forced the *Sipos* to retreat.

Another barricade put up a stubborn resistance for many hours. A quartet of lone snipers came down from an attic. From their observation tower they had spotted an armoured car approaching in the distance, and decided it would be more convenient to greet it downstairs. With a happy shot one of them pierced the radiator, paralysing the vehicle, then they returned once more to their pigeon loft.

The battles around the railway station were intensifying. Workers dislodged several White columns from the embankment, one after the other, then went on the offensive. The open space in front of the viaduct was under bombardment from armoured cars, but no matter, workers met the fire under cover of some huge beams taken from a nearby timber yard. A whole forest of masts got up and moved forward to form a perfect blockhouse, from which the riflemen continued their steady methodical work.

At this point the first massed attack started below. Six lorries, covered by two armoured cars, threw a unit of Greens onto the road, who cut off comrade Kb. from his men, moving up from the other side of the viaduct some twenty metres behind. Kb. was captured and locked in the railway building. If only the police had known that in the figure of this mild-mannered man who looked like a young schoolteacher, rash enough to go out for a stroll among the barricades, they had in their hands the heart of Barmbeck in revolution! Sitting quietly by the window, Kb. conducted a general review of the enemy's forces. He watched corralled mobs of police go past, urged on by a few brave officers – hapless hirelings cheering themselves on with shots and cries, throwing themselves on their stomachs every four paces, gesturing desperately at an unresponsive armoured car moving several metres behind its 'vanguard'. From his window, Kb. also observed workers' cool self-possession under fire, especially little D., whose handiwork he could tell from the terrified faces of the medical orderlies rushing out eight times from the fighting with their swaying stretchers.

Finally, to the sounds of shouting and gunshots, the last platoon of Greens disappeared down the streets of the insurgent quarter – strange empty streets, devoid of any sign of life, as if abandoned by its occupants and defenders. The waiting lasted for four endless agonising hours. Then at about five in the afternoon, the troops and police rolled noisily back. Their losses were enormous.

Alas, the staff centre that was to have directed the rising in Barmbeck, led by three communist intellectuals, city councillors, was deserted. For two days nobody could find them. The battles were directed by Kb., C. and of course T., who set himself up with his wireless equipment beneath the open sky in one of the public parks.

At six in the evening Barmbeck was still standing, deafened by the stillness. A brief respite. Kb. made his way to a friendly pub. The little marksman D. was lying on a sofa being fed hot coffee. W. and splendid C. were there too for a breather, and impetuous K., as cheerful as if he had just enjoyed an after-dinner game of skittles, or one of his twenty-mile walks, dragging his exhausted grumbling wife along behind him. This was the place where Kb. came to give his workers' units their instructions. Everyone who was brave and good in Barmbeck came here to wash off the blood, shake hands, and decide what next.

What did this silence mean, broken only by the occasional rattle of a window thrown open as a white flag was waved at the street – a signal to help someone who was injured or dying? Silent Barmbeck, with twilight falling like a foggy sheet onto the stretchers of its wounded streets, was now split into two halves. Fifteen hundred troops separated north from south Barmbeck. The insurgents' strongholds – the Wagnerstrasse, Friedrichstrasse and Pfenningsbusch police stations – silently stretched out their arms to each other in the darkness, like a police cordon forcing back some innocuous street demonstration.

All of a sudden the ring snapped shut, and the bulky forms of a platoon of armoured cars drew up hard against the barricades. A solid lump rolled into Barmbeck's throat. True, our posts were still in place, but time was against them. The enemy was gaining ground with each moment of the darkening night, and Barmbeck gritted its teeth. The Whites were just as invisible and therefore invulnerable as the insurgents. And there were more of them.

Slipping along both sides of one of the streets was a double file of patrols. At a gateway, the officer in charge grabbed some intellectual-looking man innocently going about his business, and jabbed a revolver in his ribs. He didn't see the other man standing behind him in the darkness with a rifle in his hands, motionless as a stone. It was the second time that day the *Landsknechte* (mercenaries) had let the mainspring of raging Barmbeckt slip through their hands.

An hour and a half later, Kb. was giving the order to his riflemen to vanish, leave Barmbeck, now encircled, about to be flooded with unseen enemies. Each picked their escape route independently. Some took the mountain path over the rocky ridges and ledges of the rooftops. Not one put a foot wrong, not one was caught.

The following morning, the thirty-five remaining met up again in north Barmbeck, and decided to dig in on the broad semicircle of the railway embankment. More long hours of battles, frenzied shooting, barricades thrown across the adjoining streets, and many, many of the enemy dead. Fifty new rifles entered service – toy ones, alas, from a local sports club – and in the face of this assault, pressed up against the embankment on either flank, three defeated hound packs were forced to depart with broken skulls. That day cost the Reds four men, four excellent comrades. Old Lewien paid with his life for hiding the toy rifles in his back garden. Mrs Lewien, living alone in their little house, with her antique chests of drawers, her cat, her white goat, and her portraits of the elder Liebknecht on the walls, her proud atheism, born in the days of the Anti-Socialist Laws, was first given back her husband's blood-stained overcoat, then his bloodless body. Her elder son, an SPD philistine, arrived to burrow through boxes, sell off the chattels, and demand her signature on some documents. But all she could remember was the old man standing alone on a lorry in a crowd of Greens, and that his face was pale.

On Wednesday the 24th, comrades learnt of the fall of Schiffbek, and of the calm reigning in the rest of Germany. That evening, with no word of the start of the German revolution, the rising's leaders were forced to sound the retreat. Not because workers had been defeated, but what was the point of continuing the struggle alone, in isolation, against the background of the general collapse.

It was no easy thing to order the retreat in a city drunk on victory, its defend-ers ready at any moment to go on the offensive, where tens of thousands were preparing for an all-out assault, and the terrible closing act of civil war – the tri-umphant seizure of power. The first courier arriving at the barricades with the order to liquidate the rising was knocked off his feet with a furious punch in the jaw. An honest old worker, who with his family had kept the dangerous courier service going throughout the whole rising, he almost did himself in after that terrible punch, so unjustly received from his comrade P. And proletarian Ham-burg clutched its jaw and turned blind with the pain. You had to admire the fortitude of the leaders who had to pass on to their units the order to demobil-ise. Younger leaders like comrade T., who had grown up with the organisation, was so inextricably linked to its proletarian core, that he could announce this abrupt swing of helm with impunity.

So they retreated, but with the satisfaction of knowing they had driven the enemy from the barricades for many hours. Taking advantage of the confu-sion, the riflemen quickly abandoned their posts with their weapons, carried away the dead and wounded, and disappeared into the now silent suburbs. This planned retreat was covered by marksmen stationed on the roofs. None of them left their aerial barricades until the last fighter had left his trench five floors below, and the last casualty had been carried by his comrades to the nearest safe house. They held out all day, holding back the Whites, from one rooftop zone to another, jumping past dormer windows and slippery ledges, over chimney stacks and dark stairwells, gaping like trenches, as the police surged upwards, scenting defeat behind the unmanned silent barricades. The struggle turned into a chase. The whole population concealed and saved the heroic rearguard of Hamburg's fighters, the wounded blackened loners still firing over the city, who then dug themselves in with unknown workers' families, dressed in rags, with bloodied hands and parched black mouths, as packs of hunters rushed roaring and cursing past the slammed doors.

One of the last of the rooftop fighters to leave was old party comrade W., collapsing from exhaustion, drunk with the need to lie down and sleep, with no strength left to slither over the tiles. Down below, an exit to freedom opened up in the shadows of a murky gateway, and he stopped and unslung his rifle to fire off his last cartridges. The wall he was leaning against was pounded by bullets, but by some miracle none hit him, and his comrades only just managed to haul him away. Around his neck, over his unbuttoned shirt and sweaty chest, was a dazzlingly smart tie. 'What's with the *Schlips* (tie), old man?' they asked him. '*Ich wollte festlich sterben*', he said. (I wanted to die looking decent).

CHAPTER 3

Schiffbek

A few miles from Hamburg, where a dreary line of telegraph poles marches off in the direction of bare sandy Prussia, is the little workers' settlement of Schiffbek, lying between the Bille brook, smooth and murky as tinplate, and hills where sparse trees run bare-headed and tousled against the wind. Below is the jumble of two-storey workers' dwellings.

In the centre of town the Evangelical Church stands empty, like a rusty umbrella stuck in the ground to dry after the rain and forgotten about. Not believing in God, the cosmopolitan population doesn't visit it. Now after the battles, it stands there with gaping doors and windows and a black eye – a priest who has strayed into someone else's fight.

On an island on the far side of the Bille is the chemical factory, dumping its waste products into the icy black waters – naphthaline and other poisons that cover the riverbed with bright green toxic moss. Some thousand workers are employed there.

Inside, metal as dense as the molten planets is poured from furnaces that never cool, and is inspected through their tiny windows. Sometimes the metal is coated in the white heat with a light film of dust, like coaldust. Usually it's totally white. Naked to the waist, workers charge off from their blazing ovens into the frost, rain and snow to escape the fumes in this factory built on the swamps of the Bille.

Along either side of a narrow stone corridor lie the factory's steam mill and its huge rolling works, known as Tin Shacks. On Christmas Eve, its chimneys, much taller than the others, are like irritable smokers suddenly without tobacco.

Spread out along the edge of this frozen white wasteland, the long legless body of Tin Shacks presses its belly to the ground, its seven chimneys set in a row like minarets, from which the shrill muezzin of labour rings out every morning. Work here is terribly injurious to the lungs. The toughest workers can take it only for a few years. You have to be like the giant S., hero of the Schiffbek rising, to survive working in this inferno. But then S. is famous throughout Schiffbek for his astounding strength. Any little street boy will tell you how he can lift six men, clinging to an iron crowbar, on his shoulder. How his hands are bigger and can hold more than all the purses taken to the markets by the good housewives of Schiffbek. How the whole tenement creaks and shakes when he swings his legs out of bed in the mornings, and the neighbours know without looking at their watches that it's time to wake their husbands for work. Since S. is such a colossus, a bold spirit, a Bolshevik and generally devilish, Tin Shacks haven't done him too much harm. Little c. has come out with his leg cut to the bone, K. with red spittle on his dirty handkerchief.

Further up the Bille are the smoky towers of the Jute manufacturing plant, one of the largest in the Hamburg area. Its workers are predominantly women, poorly paid and poorly organised, on whose behalf the communists have year after year been waging a fierce battle against the Menshevik trade unions, the bosses and the priest, and the women's noisy, inflammable but easily intimidated inertness.

The women at Jute have doggedly resisted any disciplined organisation. They complain about their wages, but after the first few days of a strike they're ready to make peace with the managers, smashing office windows, then informing on the leaders. Yet in the course of its normal capitalist business, the factory has been combing out of this tangled easily exploitable female mass the first strands of a strong proletarian solidarity. However compliant they are, their wages keep going down and down, as one department after another is hit by the frantic inflationary race of prices and wages. Within the bounds of their own homes, their own housekeeping, their own workshop, the women are as united as they're indifferent to political movements that go beyond these bounds. They may be impervious to calls for a General Strike, but they'll never let down their workmates in the next section. Thus for over a year now, basically peaceable Jute has thank goodness worked no more than three days out of six. The rest of the time the factory is out on the street supporting the section on strike.

'O, ha! (a favourite expression of every true Hamburger) Hunger is making good communists of them!' say the workers who for months have been conducting propaganda at Jute.

Many astonishing women have come out of Jute. One, we'll call her Elfriede, is the daughter of a night-watchman, well-known about town as an orthodox Menshevik, owner of a superb carbine, used to maintain order in the derelict buildings in his care, known as the *Hundebuden* (dog-kennels). And so they are. But while the watchman faithfully upheld the laws of private property with his carbine, his daughter in every way overturned these sacred bastions with her amazing beauty.

She was also a perfect communist and workmate, and a hero of the Hamburg Rising, who fought under fire at the barricades, and raised Schiffbek's female population to its feet to set up field kitchens, who took hot coffee and fresh cartridges fastened round her slim waist to the marksmen in the trenches, who with her own hands put her old man under lock and key, adding his trusty rifle to the party's scanty arsenal. Who was finally caught by the police in the heat of her criminal activities, namely peeling potatoes for the insurgents with her sleeves rolled up.

Boundlessly brave, totally dedicated to the party, she was one of the first examples of the new type of woman fabricated so unsuccessfully in the pages of the neo-proletarian novel, and in the homilies of armchair revolutionaries, who brought with her into poverty-stricken Shiffbek the spirit of destruction and liberty. Elfriede refused to be anyone's wife. Her name inspired the furious hatred and timid respect of legal wives whose husbands she would take for a day, a year, conquering whoever she chose, loving as long as there were no lies in the loving, then returning her captive to his freedom. She asked none of them to shield or aid her and her child. Never, in weakness or sickness, did she beg for mercy from the law she despised. And so she went to jail.

But first, the scenes that took place at Hamburg's City Hall after the rising, from whose balcony the leader of the Soviet Doctor Laufenberg was thrown in 1918, where arrested communists were brought on 23 October. On that terrible day, rows of lorries stood in the forecourt of Schiffbek's police station, loaded with captured workers lying heaped on top of each other on their backs, waiting to be driven to Hamburg's jails.

The rebels had fought in open battle according to all the rules of honest warfare, pitting life against life with an enemy a hundred times stronger than them, yet still sparing prisoners and letting the wounded go. After the defeat, they were treated like hunted ruffians, renegades standing outside the law. The police kicked and stamped on the bloody broken bodies, lying crushed under their comrades, their faces squashed against the coal-smeared boards, while the *Wachtmeister* (sergeants) of the *Reichswehr* cracked their necks with their rifle butts.

Superman S., that oak among men, with his astounding physical strength, was knocked unconscious and spat blood. K. was dying. Agile little L., lying under the pacifiers' boots, was ready to leap out of his crushed existence, like an eye slipping from its socket full of tears and fire. It was the first phase of the police atrocities, the bloody and dirty epilogue to the three days of the rising, which cannot be stamped out by a soldier's boot from the history of a new working-class humanity. The shining peaks of the struggle rise above the blood-stained police stations, the vile courtroom offices where proceedings were recorded then torn up and re-written, the reeking lavatories of the illustrious City Hall, where the police forced the arrested to wash, so as to convince members of the city government and the socialist deputies of their kind humane treatment of their prisoners of war, so they weren't made queasy by the sight of the blood smeared on the walls, or the smell of the clothes of a teenage member of Hamburg's Young Communists, beaten so badly he had lost control of his physiological functions.

Every quarter of an hour, the *Reichswehr* brought in new prisoners, picking up those who had collapsed off the floor, beating again those who had already been beaten, reviving those who had collapsed so as to knock them down again. And so it was that Elfriede arrived in the long white corridor of the City Hall, smelling of blood, where the living remains of the revolution were driven by the drunken soldiery, where men cowered by the walls under the lash. And Elfriede, who had lived her dignified independent life free of official morality, but straight as an arrow, stood there naked among wild animals, abused and cursed by each new gang of thugs as they arrived. 'Whore! Communist slut! You're not a German woman, you're an animal!'

And in that terrible interminable torture chamber, which lasted all day and night and another day, Elfriede cried out the name of the great German woman who had died for the German revolution, after whose death nothing had been quite so fine and wise in the revolution. And what's more, she had left behind a small volume of letters, a white cover with red lettering, Rosa Luxemburg's *Letters from Prison*.

When a girl arms herself with Rosa Luxemburg, she is as powerful and dangerous as an armed man – a warrior no man will dare to touch. Elfriede stood in that hellish corridor, shouting Rosa's name until she was heard, and finally a soldier heard her and said he 'hadn't known', and his gang slunk off in shame. And in the moments before the next ones arrived, she was able to help an injured man get away and drag him from the scrum.

That is the story of Elfriede from Schiffbek.

CHAPTER 4

Portraits

A Couple

A husband and wife from Schiffbek, both of them fine old communists. Several years ago they separated, led independent lives, started new families. A superb marksman, he was fighting in Hamburg in one of the trenches intersecting its narrow bare little streets, and it so happened that his former wife was there, fighting next to him. He was caught and arrested, and she gave herself up the next day. And so the two fighters were reunited quite naturally under fire, at the first shot. They will stand trial together.

A Private House and the Rising

She was short-sighted, respectable, a chaste Catholic nurse. Comrade L. was a communist, who had joined the party after the war. An earnest resourceful quick worker, he plugged right in to the party, like those little household batteries that can give light, turn a roller to sharpen knives, or run a model railway, miniatures of enormous miracles of energy, that can emit flashing sparks bigger than itself.

One day, this practical-minded highly-skilled worker was struck down by a rather special and rare disease that afflicts only one in ten thousand, and is incurable – namely, a great tormenting love for the devout gawky nurse.

As is normal in such cases, the feelings were completely mutual, and in no time they were married, vaulting over his politics and her catechism, even forgetting about them for a while. Comrade L., who had never flagged or shirked his party work, now began saving money to build their own little house in the outskirts of the outskirts, close to the oasis of little white villas with red roofs which members of the local authority, five old Mensheviks, had gifted themselves from official funds. All in one spot, like one big family.

Winds gusted around the neighbourhood and its population of spies, living happily in their comfortable homes. L. worked overtime and nights, and on his days off he would rush to the site to toil on his house, patiently, brick by brick, tile by tile.

The first baby came along, then another, with a third on the way. The party faded from his consciousness and became a theoretical outlook on life, an idea locked away in an unoccupied corner of his brain. Occasionally, in moments of domestic repose, he would hear its heavy tread and feel it standing there, at the door of his conscience.

The house was built, and his short-sighted industrious wife could finally start living in her own home, sew by her own brightly scrubbed fireplace, sleep in her own bed, raise her children, look after her piglets, polish the stove's Dutch tilework, and scrub the gleaming floors. And on Sundays L. would read aloud some romance of court life, about the spoilt handsome son of a count – with a wedding at the end.

On the morning of 23 October, L. had just stuck the pig for Christmas, and was draining the blood into a barrel for the black pudding. At that moment the shooting started. And in spite of the house he had put up with his own hands, by the sweat of his brow, in spite of his extraordinary love for his wife, the communist took his rifle and went off to the barricades. Then what happened?

He was arrested, beaten up and released to stand trial in a couple of days. So what then? Stay at home or flee?

The same powerful revolutionary instinct that had driven this well-set up, bourgeoisified, domesticated German worker to the barricades now drove him out to the streets again, into the crossfire of bullets whizzing past the workers' tenements, to confront the two thousand regular troops who stormed this hornet's nest to flush it out. A ruthless class instinct had kicked in: don't ever leave the party again, don't dare desert, you must go underground and continue its work.

The day after his flight, the house and its contents, even Lumpi the guard dog, would be confiscated by the government, and his wife and two children and their new-born baby would find themselves on the street. Added to all this, his wife was going blind, and had started praying often and at length.

That night they turned up at comrade C.'s – she without hat or glasses – and told him the story of their life, including that first wonderful look that had sealed their fate.

Next morning, L. took off.

The Eighteenth Century, the Joy of Living and the Rising

Actually this portrait does not concern the history of the rising itself. But in every gallery there is always *'Das Bildnis eines Unbekannten'* (portrait of an unknown man), and this anonymous figure can often tell us more about the special features of a period than all the signed canvases.

Imagine a house, like a sunken ship slowly settling on the seabed, in a dark side-street, flooded from time to time with the lights of a passing motorcar. The light from the lamp over the gate resembles the glow of a rotting tree. A rank doorway, windows close to the ground, as if eavesdropping on each other.

Inside, the bedroom is as cold as the North Pole, with its numbed window panes, broken cupboard and cracked wash-basin, warming itself on a hot-water bottle stuffed under an icy feather quilt. The dining-room, which is also the sitting-room and workshop, is heated by the fierce but rapidly escaping warmth of an iron stove, with a gawdy silk shade on the lamp, like a cheap tart's petticoat. In the kitchen is a reeking sink and gas stove, and the overpowering smell of dampness. The whole setting testifies to the indubitable prosperity of an aristocratic worker. It belongs to comrade K., an artist in wood, employed in one of Hamburg's biggest furniture factories to make reproduction antique pieces. His speciality is the eighteenth century, which without ever having read anything about art, he feels to the tips of his fingers. With his eyes shut, the master can faultlessly saw the cherry-wood veneer, inlaid with metal and tortoise-shell, and furniture whose effete intricately curved contours emerge from a deal board. A heavy damp block of wood falling into these amazingly creative hands emerges as furniture as effortlessly as if they had come from the workshop of the genius cabinet-maker Boulle. In each of the old-fashioned writing desks at which our great-grandmothers would write their love letters, in each of the card-tables on which the Werthers broke their chalk, scribbling the names of their beloveds, placing a candle beside their weighty pistols, craftsman K. fits for the sake of style and accuracy secret drawers, little recesses with hidden springs, which if pressed, deliver into the hands of his admirable bourgeois customers a couple of yellowing papers, a bunch of dried forget-me-nets, and the rare aroma of past secrets. All these items have been gathered by K. with enormous taste and sense of proportion.

He says communism for him is like a tucked away casket of treasures. Ideas, words and slogans wholly inapplicable to practical daily life, yet the most precious thing in life – political style. Needless to say, K. took no active part in the rising, unless of course you count the boundless hospitality he extended to comrades following the battles.

K. is an Epicurian, a true Renaissance man, in his effervescent irrepressible love of life, its pleasures and its palpably warm human beauty, his sense of which is as infallible as his cabinet-maker's skill. K. believes the very process of life, with all its physiological and profoundly mundane functions, will one day become the basis for the greatest and truest beauty. This social aesthetic gives him an affinity with the best things that Edgar Allan Poe wrote about – the as yet non-existent gardens and palaces to be inhabited by wise men. K. inhabits them with the workers.

If the kingdom of the future were suddenly to appear – a purely German concept: only a utopian who doesn't believe in his daydreams could express himself that way – he would fashion wonderful shelves, beds, tables and chairs for the workers' palaces. This is the purpose of his communist 'casket'.

But now the practical questions. Why didn't he join the fight in October? Why does he smile when we talk of strikes and distributing leaflets? Why his deliberate passivity, his desertion from the civil war? Where does his provocative arrogance come from, his manner of a victor over the bourgeoisie? Why is it that this man, created for great spiritual and physical pleasures, who sees communism as the only road by which he and his class could attain such pleasures, didn't lift a finger or risk his neck during the rising?

It turns out he is stealing from the bosses, almost openly, unimaginably large sums by the standards of his cottage industry, putting his profits in his pocket, while looking his boss and his grovelling assistants provocatively in the eye. Then after a week of the most arduous labour, working ten-hour days with no let-up, out come the bottles of the best beer, the champagne, his little wife Elsa in her black silk underwear, and from the stinking corner where the Roederer's cork hits the low ceiling, like a tall man who has walked in and banged his head, through the haze of a strong cigar, the fog of sweaty sultry dampness, the golden illusions bursting in bubbles on the surface of the earthenware mug in which centenarian grape fizzes, comrade K., with the grin of a conqueror, contemplates the bourgeoisie he has deceived, so cunningly and boldly. These are his finest hours.

The old songs of Hamburg are older and more rollicking than ours. There's one about a craftsman's daughter who loved three boisterous apprentices thrown out by her father, another about sea-horses and women, brawls and dockside pubs. He sings them marvellously. How do you tell him that for the crumbs his boss allows his irreplaceable craftsman to grab from his plentiful table, the drop of stolen wine and those few hours of blissful oblivion, he is as much giving his enemy the marrow of his bone, his life and the mysterious trembling fibres of the brain that we call talent, as any labourer gives his sweat, muscle and bones?

CHAPTER 5

About Schiffbek Again

Schiffbek's police station, packed with armed *Sipos*, its council offices, post office and all the institutions and public buildings representing state power in this small working-class town, with its cosmopolitan population, were seized by communists at dawn on 23 October, with the aid of one carbine and one hunting knife with a serrated blade and horn handle.

Head of Schiffbek's Military Organisation, which worked out and implemented this battle plan, was the giant S., one of those truly revolutionary workers who inspire others and lead by example. Surrounded on all sides by the advancing enemy, pinned against a wall, his armed squads fought as he fought, knocking them off their feet with one blow. And along with his phenomenal physical strength, knowing with one movement of his iron muscles he could crush any adversary, was that innate caution so invaluable in a leader, the ability to calculate the precise effect of every shot. He could come down like a steam-hammer on an anvil, carefully splitting a nutshell without damaging the kernel, then a minute later beat out an iron bar.

After occupying the police station and disarming the *Sipos*, S. and his men left with sixteen rifles and as many revolvers, and his marksmen took up their positions.

A single marksman, *Scharfeschütze*, as they're called, concealing himself behind the shrubs and garden sheds and corners of the workers' barracks scattered along the edge of the hills, was able to cover the central highway linking Schiffbek to Hamburg, the bridge and the railway embankment, and keep the enemy at a respectable distance, even during their final assault on the morning of the 26th, when they were a thousand times stronger than the insurgents.

One outstanding marksman, safely hidden, firing at intervals of every five, ten or fifteen minutes, was able to pick off at least one, and often two men with one bullet. The police responded to one of these isolated lethal shots by sweeping whole blocks with machine-gun fire, mowing down a group of women and children who had accidentally fallen into the sights of their impotent rage. Then after a brief lull, another cold sharp-eyed shot caught the driver of an armoured car, who had just peered out from under the steel hatch, removed a fur mitten and lit a cigarette, as well as hitting a Green who had leapt out from around a corner, and a *Reichswehr* soldier, squatting behind a letter box, who had just stopped a woman in the street whose loaf of bread tucked under her kerchief seemed to him suspicious.

Reichswehr recruits are generally rough country lads, sons of rich peasants, a generation that matured after the war and the revolution. In the countryside they're a burden on their fathers, greedy, lazy farmhands who won't put enough horsepower into the land, and can't count on their inheritance. These youths, political quadrupeds, readily become mercenaries, who see civil war as a pogrom they stand to gain much from, with little risk involved. But instead of terrorising unarmed women and children in the bread queues, or the cowardly city rabble the priests back home preached against with such passion, their fat chins wobbling on their white collars, the well-fed peasant boys were being thrown up against the workers' units, and cold-blooded old soldiers who had come out of the last war with every badge of distinction for accurate marksmanship and sapper work under enemy fire.

The roles have now been reversed in Germany. The revolution is drawing on cadres of former soldiers who defend the barricades according to all the rules of warfare, while on the government's side are these crowds of inexperienced inadequately trained boys, cowardly in battle, but brutal when facing a captive with his hands tied behind his back. It wasn't by chance that an officer found it necessary to drive his detachment of raw recruits, revolvers in hand, to smoke out a lone rifleman hidden in an attic, who was picking off one soldier after another. And as the cannon fodder advanced on the brave lieutenant, he cursed their officer to the whole town – 'Scum! Coward! I can sort out thousands like you!'

Even without the officer's assistance, Schiffbek's workers, under the command of S. and his Chief of Operations and Chief of Staff, the incomparable Fritz, were able to resist the onslaught of the regular troops by adapting to local conditions, constantly switching tactics. In the hilly parts of town, or in the open wastelands where little houses stood like oases, they would split their forces into small combat formations, each fighting at its own risk and peril, advancing, taking cover, moving from one position to another. And where the empty white fields flowed into the narrow streets, they would rely on the old proven strategy of building barricades and digging earthworks, blocking the streets with strong dams to stop the armoured cars getting through to the centre.

By half past eleven, the police were back in possession of the empty police station, and the first phase of the offensive had begun. A detachment of fifty men advanced confidently along the main street, knocking down a few chance passers-by, then moved on to a white building with a long stairway jutting out at the side. Beautiful dark eyed Minna hurried past, flashing her dazzling white teeth at them, mentally making a note of their numbers. They didn't notice the red badge on her ample bosom, and her headscarf tied at the back of her head disappeared calmly down a back street. A schoolboy running along beside her suddenly stopped, hiccoughed, and sat down on the pavement. A bullet had struck him between the eyes.

In the insurgents' camp there was still deep silence. Then from a distance of only twenty paces, several shots knocked out the sergeant-major and half his soldiers. An hour later, some two hundred police closed in, from several different directions at once. Workers drove them back from the barricades and earthworks, and opened fire from the covers scattered along the hills.

The defence of the barricades and trenches was directed by Fritz, of S'.s Military Organisation. Beside S. he was almost short. But while S. had grown haphazardly, branching out on all sides with his friendly powerful crown shooting up into the sky, Fritz was a squat shrub, clinging to the rocky earth under a strong sea breeze. Heels together, a barrel chest, hands in his pockets, one shoulder slightly forward, like a boxer or trained athlete, he was famous for his insolence and audacity, able to make women and policemen blush just by looking them up and down. All this had earned him the untranslatable nickname, both contemptuous and flattering, of 'Didlein' – meaning rascal, smart alec, bold spirit, liar, gunman, rogue. In short, a thoroughly good fellow. In peaceful times, he had rather shocked the sedate communist functionaries with his sharp dockside smell and unruly spirit, but in battle he worked miracle after miracle, rushing from window to window, urging on, holding back, switching tactics, cursing and issuing commands, the essential link between S'.s calm strength and his roving bands of insurrectionaries.

It has to be said Schiffbek was renowned for its Fritzes. Firing from the corner of his own tenement building was the marksman Fritz, surrounded by women holding fresh cartridges in their torn aprons, a classic figure, with his large-peaked cap tied with a scarf under his chin, his tattered jacket over a heavy grey docker's jersey, and his wild tangled hair, like a bandit's. A five-minute pause, then a single shot, and four *Sipos* were down.

At half past one, government forces advanced on Schiffbek – five hundred men, plus a squadron of armoured cars. The battles lasted until six that evening. Two first-rate marksmen might be able to stand fast for a long time, but courage has its limits. To win time, the combatants quietly left the earthworks and dived into the nearest gateways, and an hour later, the steel noses of their rifles were poking over the edges of another barricade, joining battle in the most hard-pressed areas.

Meanwhile the confused enemy was still bombarding the now silent ambushes. From time to time the heat subsided and the blind barrage stopped, and scouts would crawl along the roadway on all fours. Then a solitary shot from a nearby attic, and the bombardment resumed with renewed force against the abandoned fortifications full of cartridge-cases, debris and charred earth. Seizing his revolver with a heroic flourish, the lieutenant led forth his musketeers into the assault, shooting blindly into the air and uttering war cries, tumbling into the empty ditch.

Dusk was falling. Sunset, like a sentry, sloped its long pointed bayonets of shadows across the streets. A poster had appeared on hoardings proclaiming a General Strike, and greeting the Soviet government. Shiffbek's thirty-five communists, beset by thousands of soldiers, were convinced that all Germany was rising behind them, and that the whole population supported the communists. Eight thousand people turned out onto the streets, and if they didn't join the struggle, it was simply due to the lack of weapons.

So what of the role of the sacred intelligentsia in the rising? It has to be said that in Schiffbek, as in old Russia, and everywhere else the social revolution hadn't yet taken up arms, the intellectuals marched with the police and the army. Yet not a single professor spoke up for the fruits of European Enlightenment – for what professors were there in little Schiffbek? Not one school teacher – the teachers here were well-meaning but timid. Not even a midwife – for Schiffbek's women preferred to give birth without medical assistance. It was left to party member old Uncle Paulus, the school janitor, to take a stand, a worker who despised the stench of poverty and the muscular ignorance of his youthful charges as deeply as he himself was despised by the implacable blackboards, the teachers' uniforms, and the plaster busts of philosophers in the headmaster's study. Alone in the empty premises, his head stuffed with schoolroom wisdom, the old man grabbed his gun and was ready to go out to the barricades and shoot his own pupils, who were studying street fighting instead of penmanship and the holy scriptures.

A knock at the door. He hid. Another knock, then the gates flew off their hinges under S.'s mighty shoulder. Stretching out his arm, like Schiller to Goethe on the famous Monument, comical and menacing with his dishevelled hair, the old man fired at the worker's broad chest and missed, and the majestic pose collapsed. He dashed to the door, and S. grabbed him and his gun in one hand, wiping his battle-scorched face with the other, and bellowed to the entire establishment, 'Silly old *Karnikel!* (bunny) What use are you to them? You just empty their chamber pots to support your learning!' And the old man wept bitterly, for all the years he had spent rubbing history charts and algebra off the blackboards that had made a true intellectual of him. S. clipped him round the ears and let him off, cursing and laughing, and old Paulus was forced to tear his desecrated party card to shreds, as he listened to his pupils outside, laughing and firing from the barricades.

By evening the insurrectionaries were compelled to retreat – a humiliating five hundred yard retreat from their old positions, which S. viewed with utter shame and childlike despair. In the rear, troops had managed to penetrate as far as the main square, whose wealthy residents showered them with sausages, margarine and congratulations. The encirclement closed in, threatening to become a stranglehold. A squad of insurgents coming to the rescue couldn't break through the police blockade. By then, vehicles of the military command were racing through Hamburg to Barmbeck, where officers of the General Staff inspected its network of barricades, and found their positioning to be superb.

At daybreak, the insurrectionaries were back in the trenches and attics and behind every possible cover, but with no sign of the enemy, whose three assaults they had smashed the previous day. Hooters wailed pointlessly from a few factories. Workers patrolled the empty back streets that emptied into the fields, relieving each other at regular intervals, standing guard over the barricades from afar, as if over a captive prisoner. A menacing stillness, and they sensed the danger creeping up on Schiffbek, and made ready to meet it. Thirty-five of them against five thousand.

At one o'clock, a unit of four armoured cars and six lorries appeared from the direction of Horn, dropping a large contingent of *Sipos* on the road. From Uhlenfeld in the north, twenty-six lorry loads of Greens. From the direction of Eimsbüttel, a cavalry unit. An aeroplane flew low over Schiffbek, raking its bullet-riddled walls with a grey curtain of fire.

Although beaten by the Allies, the German army goes valiantly into battle against its own proletarians. And the example is evidently catching. Cavalry, infantry, armoured cars, aircraft, and a flotilla of five launches of the river police on the polluted waters of the Bille, and the remaining handful of fighters scoffed at the technology of this bloated rotten shell of an army, living off the bosses' fat handouts. Beleaguered Schiffbek held out until four in the afternoon, throwing the troops back along the sprawling unprotected fronts, driving out the broken columns of blue, green and other gallantly coloured soldiers, breaking through the ring of barricades, finally emerging through that bloody breach to freedom, weapons in hand. It's almost comical to relate how three riflemen, the rearguard of this miniature workers' army, were able to keep the Naval Forces of the Republic at a respectable distance, allowing S. to lead his men to safety, through the narrow gap between the river and the main highway.

Then the victors' celebrations. The pandemonium of denunciations, searches, atrocities and church services. It went on for nearly two months. Insurgents were arrested to stand trial, most considered beyond the law. Families hid away in their dank barracks, and insurgents' wives were thrown out of work onto the streets. Every so often they were visited at their homes by a fast-talking trade union leader with a bandaged head, his face swollen and yellow with iodine, who had been seized by the police at Tin Shacks during the rising in error and beaten to mincemeat, and having replaced his knocked-out teeth, was acting as a spy and go-between.

Hunger, snow, dirty cold beds, the unpaid rent, the caretaker shouting. Winter, beating its white birch rods on the streets between the little dens smelling of gas and dirty lavatories. The grey building of the Labour Exchange, standing to attention and saluting an open field, the back of this constable who had nodded off on duty plastered with our communist proclamations.

Women who had been subjected to every imaginable privation were stopped and searched on the streets, visited by the police in their homes. And all the helpless poverty would bristle its spines and put up the stiffest most courageous resistance to the civil and military authorities, rattling their ringing broadswords on the staircases, slippery with frozen slops.

The wife of an arrested Schiffbek fighter, pressing her arms to her sides, her face crimson from rage and the wash-tub, hoarse from yelling at her screaming children and the dog barking under the sagging sofa, pushes away the papers laid before her, refusing to sign her name to anything, vehemently denying everything, dodging questions. These women, who have no food for their children, who will be thrown out of their homes tomorrow, are past caring, and she rains curses on the departing official, as if tipping a dustbin full of rubbish over his head.

On Christmas Eve, the women get together to sew dolls for the children of communists who have fled. C. makes a dolls house out of old boxes pasted with newspaper and some grubby kings and queens from long cast-off suits of cards. Hungry neighbours come round with presents – a bar of soap, a doll, a pair of warm stockings. At midnight, a detachment of workers from Hamburg arrive with a wheelbarrow full of flour and margarine from comrades in America; fifty kilos of fat and twenty-five pounds of sugar for seventy families, each with three to five mouths to feed. These days before Christmas are always the hungriest time of year.

Fifty of Schiffbek's children are to be boarded in Holland with Dutch comrades of the International Workers' Relief Organisation. A knock at the door. Some workers arrive, trying not to look at the washing hanging over the cold stove, the syphilitic mould on the walls, and they chat about the weather, their health, this and that.

From the mother's vacant gaze, they ascertain which child they should take, a boy or girl, and how old. A quarter of an hour to get ready. No luggage. A few minutes' bitter howling on the mother's shaking knees. But stockings are soon firmly on, boots are laced, and buttons properly fastened, and the mother drags a comb through her daughter's tangled hair, brusquely and peremptorily, but making it last as long as possible, and a quarter of an hour later, the child is torn from its roots in routed Schiffbek.

Two mothers refuse to give up their children. One, thrown out of her factory after her husband was arrested, has four boys and two girls, and keeps the six mouths above the waterline by means of unimaginable economies. The other lives at the extreme of filth, frivolousness and physical ruin. Children of every imaginable complexion, from many ardently and briefly loved fathers. The little girls come into the world unasked for but glorious, like bright sunflowers springing from litter-strewn patches of earth. The little boys are bold and bright, and once left to themselves will be like the firm green shoots of maple trees. clinging to the mouldy walls of an old factory. Cursing her unwanted fertility, clipping her howling children around the ears, standing in the cold with her thin skirt clinging to her knees, an infant sucking the edge of her dirty cardigan then at her exhausted bare breast, this mother refuses to send a single one of her spirited hungry brood into exile.

Among these desperate families in defeated Schiffbek, there is one so happy that the neighbours come round in the evenings to enjoy its unusual tranquillity. A small woman, prematurely aged, with a dark complexion and something southern about her voice, which crackles like chestnuts roasting in the embers. Her four children, as if by design, are alternately blonde and blue-eyed and olive-skinned with dark eyes, little Poles and Germans. During the war, her husband, comrade R., an old communist, was beaten up in the army because of his Polish name and his dangerously taciturn manner, behind which his sergeant-major sensed a pacifist. A member of the Spartacus League, a founding member of the KPD, he was wounded fighting against the Kapp *Putsch*,[1] then in Schiffbek, the Verdun of the Hamburg Rising he so ardently believed in. Afterwards the hunger and cold, knowing that at any moment the six of them could fall under the wheel. But by a miracle he wasn't caught, and he fled abroad. And then another of these rare miracles that do still happen – his wife received a letter from him with a visa.

Everyone in the flat thawed out, relaxed, took a breath, and began to talk of the future. His letter was like the scrape of a distant spade digging those five human beings out of the avalanche that had crashed onto their roof.

---

1 In March 1920, 12,000 troops of the German army marched on Berlin to establish a dictatorship under Wolfgang Kapp, leader of the far-right Fatherland Party. The Weimar government fled to Dresden, and Berlin's workers led the resistance with a General Strike. Strikes and occupations spread across Germany, and within a week the *putsch* had been defeated.

CHAPTER 6

Hamm

The Hamm quarter of Hamburg, with its broad straight streets and avenues, is highly unsuitable for street fighting, impossible to tie into a ring of barricades. The smooth bare frontages of the new workers' barracks fall sheer to the slippery pavements, their walls providing no cover for lone marksmen, who prefer the ledges, bays and lofty porches of the older buildings. Spades and crowbars break their teeth trying to dig up the rolled-out lava. You would need to fell a few fully grown trees to seal off the area, but trees don't grow in slum quarters. The smooth empty streets, like stone channels, can't easily be defended by one machine gun mounted at a crossroads. There are miles of exposed spaces that mercilessly betray to binoculars any crouching figure seeking cover in the shadows of those inhuman facades – a marksman with a cap pulled down over his eyes, a woollen scarf wound round his chin, a rifle in his hands.

None of these unfavourable features prevented Hamm from becoming the arena of brief but very intense battles. Not even the generally petty-bourgeois nature of its inhabitants could stop them. Students, who made up a large part of the population, to a man offered their services to the police.

An armed rising presupposes the presence of arms. The Hamburg Rising was a rising of unarmed workers against a massively armed enemy.

In the Hamm zone were five police stations, permanently occupied by armed *Sipo* units and police. Hamburg's Military Organisation set out to seize the small arsenals in each one. Thus in Hamm, as in other parts of the city, the struggle started with unarmed workers seizing the police fortresses, guarded by sentries and packed with their military equipment and every kind of ammunition.

One of the toughest of the police stations was taken by twelve workers with an antiquated pistol. At the doorway the squad wavered. Then their leader, Rolfshagen, whose name is spoken now with pride – the gates of a hard-labour camp have long slammed behind him – shouted back to his men. 'Nun man los!' (Well, let's go!), and without looking round to see if they were following, leapt over the three steps with his huge legs and burst into the station, followed by his friend, a young typesetter, but no one else. The only revolver, unloaded at that, was jabbed into the crowd of *Sipos*. Seeing his men's indecision, Rolfshagen bellowed at them in an unearthly voice, crashing his fist on the desk. Papers flew around, the holy oil in the inkwells was spattered about, and state power tottered to its foundations. *'Man los, hier wird nicht lange gefackelt!'* (Let's go, no time to hang about!)

The police surrendered, put their hands up, and were disarmed and locked away by Rolfshagen's comrades who had caught him up. What to do now? Hold out in the captured *Revier* (police station), or go back to the streets and dig in, go to the aid of Barmbeck, from which the sounds of gunfire could be heard? And all the while no contact with the centre.

Sitting in his corner at party meetings in his waterproof docker's gear, sucking on his pipe, Rolfshagen would never chatter. He didn't like phrases, the calls to struggle party intellectuals were so fond of spouting. He thought of an uprising as something simple and straightforward, without retreats, without the slightest hesitations or deviations, like the sweep of a crane snatching up its prey, the straightness of a compass needle, the unerring course of a ship. And so, without receiving any instructions, Rolfshagen loaded his rifle, stacked up the cartridges in handy piles, and made ready to fight it out and die beside a window whose ledge afforded a slight cover.

His comrades tried in vain to draw him away, arguing the danger of a position that could be surrounded and cut off. But Rolfshagen had decided to stay. *'Dat is Befehl ich blieb!'* (It's an order, I'm sticking to it!), and he stayed. An hour later, his duel began with the police who had poured into the station. Finally, after firing his last cartridge, he fell, wounded in the head, chest and stomach, and lost consciousness from a terrific boot to the ribs.

Rolfshagen didn't die in the hospital, where they removed six pieces of lead from his body. Confident of the revolution's speedy victory, he refused to go on the run, and accepted with a grin the ten years' hard labour Scheidemann's mercy granted him. In the doorway of the court, he turned round and shouted to his friends among the thick wad of bourgeois in the gallery, 'Don't forget to clean my rifle, I'll be coming out for it soon!'

That was the capture of the Fort Street police station.

Now Mittelstrasse. Charli Setter, a member of the provincial parliament who had been entrusted with the leadership of a combat unit, didn't show up until right at the end of the conflict, and displayed a shameful fainthearted-ness and lack of resolution. He was replaced by a worker no longer young but extremely agile, *aufgeweckt*, as they say, whose narrow anaemic face, framed by a small black beard like a black-edged mourning envelope, continually twitched and trembled with pain. He had sat out the whole war in the trenches, and came out an invalid, gravely wounded in the head, susceptible to agon-ising pains, epileptic fits and hysteria. However his disability hadn't stopped his injured head from reviewing and reconsidering his old convictions as a Social Democrat official. Cursing the war and the workers' party that had acted as its livestock supplier, he courageously broke with the organisation he had belonged to for over fifteen years.

Comrades were reluctant to rely on K., who had been forced to recant some of his wilder behaviour. But during the *'Aktion'*, he remained in the battles and risked the greatest danger, never giving in to his fractured nerves, and his conduct from start to finish was irreproachable.

In the assault on Police Station 23, two remarkable brothers marched alongside K. One was the curly-headed giant Roth, a building worker. I don't remember the exact description of his *Branche* (trade), but it was a short tradesman's formula that included iron, concrete and coal, with a proud ring to it, like an order of labour. In reply to all my questions, this comrade merely shook his head and refused at any price to disclose any information about his personal role in the trade, and a shadow would fall across his stern Siegfriedian features. His brother, L., was a highly-skilled joiner, a man of exceptional culture and courage, one of the finest and most remarkable of Hamburg's fighters. His fiery political temperament, his southern liveliness, his sharp eye for the planed lacquered commonplaces of political jargon, like the craftsman testing the blades of his tools on the edge of his bench, went with a cool inner sobriety. An enthusiast, with a small hermetically sealed icebox in his heart, who never for an instant forgot deep within him that the revolution's most flaming words have been written in crude oil paint on cheap calico, and at times he would cast aside his cool rationality and be overcome with rage.

Three anarchist brothers fought with Roth and L. Brave men who had dropped out of the party a few months earlier, impatient for action, but who took up their rifles the moment the password for the rising was issued. The whole family were communists. The sixty-year-old mother, three sisters and two brothers-in-law joined the movement. In short, a family cell, a Soviet knot, of which there were quite a few in the rising. This group, twenty-eight workers, with two revolvers and one rubber truncheon, overran their local police station quite brilliantly, surrounding it on all sides, disarming the police and helping themselves to their store of arms.

At around seven, day began to break. Street traffic had come to a halt (only for a few hours in this part of the city), and detachments of armed workers stopped their workmates who were going off to work not suspecting a thing, and sent them home.

'What's going on?'

'The dictatorship of the proletariat has been declared!'

'Dat kun jo sen, ook io nich wieder gohn'. (That's as maybe, but it won't last)

'Dan got wi werra nochüs'. (Let's go home)

Not to the barricades, to the aid of the workers' units. And that was typical.

Despite the lack of further orders from the Staff Centre, most of the insurgents left the plundered police stations and moved off in the direction of smoke-shrouded Barmbeck, where the frantic shooting hadn't stopped. The only sensible tactic had been arrived at by instinct. There was no way to break up the pavements, with almost no trees, and too few weapons for them to bring in the wider masses. So the groups dispersed in different directions, to make their way to the embattled quarters separately.

Roth, L. and the anarchist brothers and their detachment (nine rifles and twelve revolvers) proceeded in the direction of the heaviest exchanges of fire. In one of the stone corridors, they were peppered with machine-gun fire from a lorry. The riflemen threw themselves on the ground, then under ever closer fire, they took off down a small back street. One of the comrades dropped on one knee and raised his rifle to his shoulder, and it fell instantly from his hands. L. recalled the stream of blood trickling along the pavement, washing a dropped cigarette-end into the gutter. From one side came the roar of a second vehicle. Not noticing the partisans, it parked at the end of the street, its heavy undefended flank facing them, and they swept it with fire from their carbines. Then the little detachment took up a mobile square formation, moving from place to place for many hours, finally giving real battle on the Central Canal Bridge. It was a collapsible sprawling square, which at the required moment could roll up and disappear like water on sand, with four first-rate marksmen in the middle. They occupied the main junction of several major streets, with lookouts armed with revolvers posted on every corner, with their newspaper kiosk, telephone box or tree-trunk, and fired only at close range, in hand-to-hand skirmishes. This flying squad of fighters, dashing from place to place, defending and surrendering successive nodal points, eventually came together at the Canal Bridge, where the stone creases of the surrounding streets converged in a broad fan. The bridge arched its broad back to step primly over the dank waters of the factory canal, and the marksmen lay down at the top, with just the barrels of their rifles protruding. Their only cover was a flimsy lamp post, and beside it a few sad trees, growing in corsets of iron rods thicker than their own trunks, unable to flee this spot because the concrete had squeezed their roots into the earth.

All along the banks, uninhabitable buildings dropped murkily into the water. Every so often a cellar peep-hole opened up in a wall streaked with damp, like a shivering mouth gaping open to take a gulp of air, then disappearing again. A working-class Venice, whose palaces of cotton, fat and iron lacked marble staircases and embankments, where bricks and concrete lapped by poisonous sewage were coated with deposits of regal beauty – pale greens, greys and pinky-browns, more varied than porphyry, marble and malachite, the blood, pearl and ash of the high *Quattrocento*. The grandeur of these watery cul-desacs was marked not by time, but by glistening coal, its shadows more dramatic than those in Tintoretto's Venice. The lagoon washing around industrial Hamburg knew neither gondolas nor romantic nights. It carried out to sea factory waste, dampness, cold and all the diseases that soak through the walls into the life, dreams, labour and blood of millions of workers.

Like doges, the factory chimneys looked at themselves in their cloudy mirrors, smoke drifting from their shoulders like resplendent robes, betrothed to their grey cold polluted sea not by the golden ring of the Adriatic, but by the wail of the ships' sirens heralding the arrival of precious raw materials. The nereids had long died off in the cold filth of the canal. Sometimes little boys pulled white corpses of fish from the water, floating belly up with painfully distended gills.

Over and around this canal, the squad of insurgents fought it out. The lookouts reported vehicles, and the square had to change position again, with marksmen once more in the middle, and scouts on the corners. A lorry packed with soldiers tore round a corner, and with one well-aimed shot, Roth disabled the engine. The *Sipos* abandoned their vehicle and carried off their wounded. The squad then made a desperate sprint to the next corner, and came under fire from an armoured car covering a line of Greens. The partisans picked off the commander – a plucky but stupid lieutenant, who had bravely sprung forward to rally his men. Panic among the *Sipos*, followed by a numbing stillness, like the stillness of the ghostly realm of the canal, with its silent fluttering banners of factory smoke, and the distant gunfire of the rising being crushed.

The insurgents continued to advance along empty streets, past idle factories locked up like monasteries, and eyeless houses with their mouths tightly shut. At the crossroads they broke their formation, as light and adaptable as a nomad's tent, and heard the rumble of wheels again across the dead roadway. This time though it was only a loaded newspaper truck. Forgetting danger, they grabbed at the tightly lashed bundles and thumbed through Hamburg's *Fremdenblatt*. Nothing in its pages about the revolution in Germany and the new Republic of Soviets. Not a word of the news they had been waiting for with more tension and torment than victory. Roth tore up a paper and grabbed another. L. went white. Otto wrapped his wounded hand in that dirty rag, contemptuously nodding. Yes, it couldn't be otherwise.

Then they threw the bundles on the ground and set fire to them. The wind snatched up the blazing sheets and carried them off over the canal, where they drifted like flaming birds, swans set alight.

Gunshots in the nearby streets. The squad retreated slowly, lit by the ruddy glow of the great bonfire the soldiers were trying in vain to stamp out and break up with their rifle-butts.

German Mensheviks After the Rising

Hamburg's dock-workers, who had already been on strike for several days, did not join forces with the fighting masses during the rising. They roamed the streets, hands in pockets, questioning with innocent curiosity their comrades returning from the districts under police siege, 'What's it all about then?' Thousands of workers organised by the Social Democrats remained peaceful spectators of the events in Hamburg. The port-workers, with the exception of those working in the shipyards and the plants processing petroleum waste, where earnings had fallen to ridiculous levels, were aristocrats compared to the mass of the Hamburg proletariat.

They were paid more than the most highly paid inland workers, such as building workers, engineering workers and rail-workers, and of course several times more than the pariahs of the port of Hamburg, those employed in the shipyards. During the war, this contented layer worked zealously for the War Department, earning excellent rates of pay. They were exempt from military service, and entered the revolution as a cold reactionary current, perfectly combining their flabby, cosy petty-bourgeois way of life with an innocuous SPD card. In 1918, this Menshevik-organised mass of well-to-do workers fought tooth and nail against the Hamburg Soviet, weak and wishy-washy as its policies were. Their response to the demonstrations of the unemployed, the banning of bourgeois newspapers, and the wrecking of the SPD rag the *Hamburg Echo*, which had plastered its yellow pages with daily slanders against the Soviet, was a powerful reactionary counter-demonstration, demanding the arrest of the Soviet's chairman and the restoration of the bourgeois Senate. A rail strike then prevented the dispatch of strong volunteer units mobilised by the Hamburg proletariat to aid the city of Bremen, under siege by General Herstenberg's officer division. In short, not for the first time, dockers and other workers in Hamburg's innumerable port warehouses rendered invaluable service to the German counterrevolution.

And well they might! Merchant vessels from throughout the world converge on Hamburg's convenient harbour. Ship-owners have no time to waste, no time to haggle over a few pfennigs. Every day's delay has to be paid for, freights can't wait, rail charges lapse. For all these reasons, the stevedores and warehouse workers enjoy unquestionable economic privileges, while other categories of workers have long since lost the eight-hour day and half their pre-war wages. During the first two years of Germany's revolutionary upheavals, reactionary forces in the port never ceased to make themselves felt, coming out against the socialisation of industrial enterprises, restrictions on private commerce, and any social unrest that might weaken the Free City's credit-worthiness abroad, strengthen its foreign competitors, and depopulate a port that lived on the ebbs and flows of the capitalist world market.

Back in 1919, Hamburg's Mensheviks imagined that Britain would spare the capital of the coastal region (the *Uferland*), in return for their suppression of communism. Today nothing remains of such hopes. The Entente has chewed up the remnants of bourgeois socialist Germany, destroying not only the communists but the most moderate Mensheviks. Their wealth is slipping, their trade unions appeal for donations, and the leaders, now chucked out of the Grand Coalition, vote for the dictatorship of the bourgeoisie. Yet the old traditions die hard. The port has been pauperised, but it's still the best-fed of paupers, and the grateful labour aristocracy assists the police in clearing the barricades, and attends SPD meetings and rallies *en masse*.

Yesterday was a field-day for them. The Free City of Hamburg was honoured with a visit from the eminent Berliner, *Vorwärts* editor *Genosse* Stampfer. Hundreds of workers came to hear him speak. Hard to imagine Russian workers having the patience to listen to a single word of the distortions of Marxist thought this experienced Menshevik had the temerity to present to his working-class audience. In a city, moreover, where trenches that had crisscrossed the suburbs in every direction had only just been filled in, where the tenements in the working-class quarters were scarred with bullets, where dozens of police had died, and dead and injured workers were numbered in their hundreds. It's necessary to have a clear understanding of the total decay and headlong decline of working-class and petty-bourgeois Germany, corrupted by half a century of emasculated pseudo-socialism, to appreciate the great act of heroism Hamburg's armed uprising represented in these conditions. To rise up from that swamp, that cowardly deeply reactionary quagmire, was a thousand times harder than under our old tsarist soldier's boot.

Doctor Stampfer wasn't trying to be particularly logical. He felt himself to be in the provinces, where a good player can cheat without embarrassment with a clearly marked card. Germany's misfortunes stemmed from its endless multiplicity of regional parliaments, he said, which must be abolished. Only strong centralised state power was capable of protecting the working class from the offensive of capital, and upholding the eight-hour day for workers. Catcalls from the audience, shouts of 'what kind of state, ours or the bourgeoisie's?'

Even portly greying SPD members were beginning to feel uneasy. But German Mensheviks have an ingenious way of dealing with dissent. As soon as the gallery begins to whistle, and old men nudge each other and mutter 'Pull the other one!', the speaker drags Kaiser Wilhelm onto the stage, alive, with his moustache, in full battledress. The speaker need only punch him on the nose, tell a couple of anecdotes about the ex-emperor's stupidity, and have the unprecedented courage to abuse Wilhelm as a fool, idiot and maniac, and he'll have the philistines quaking in rapture at such blasphemy, and the audience will be his. Having spat out Wilhelm, the speaker will then pass on to the communists.

It turns out it's the communists who have smashed the sacred chalice of the Republic. Lacking any respect for the legal forms of democracy and the noble philanthropic methods of parliamentary struggle, they have sullied the skirts of the innocent maiden the Republic with the blood of their own proletarian brothers. Amid a deep hush, Stampfer hurls his accusations: 'In Prussia, communists brutally tortured two police officers. Isn't the poor *Schupo* (policeman) as much a proletarian as we are?' Shrill mocking howls from the gallery. 'Down with Scheidemann! Hang Ebert from the lamp post!', drowned out by virtuous grunts.

'Ebert', says the *Vorwärts* editor, beating his starched breast, 'Ebert, that son of the people, has attained the supreme responsibilities of state thanks to his talents! The German proletariat can be proud that a son from its own depths has reached such a position!' Pope Ebert appears aloft in clouds of parliamentarism. The Republic stretches forth to him the crown of victory, and signals to the ballot box, democracy's divine lottery. One out of a million can win two hundred thousand Marks or become president.

Stampfer admits to some of the SPD's mistakes with a disarming frankness. The party has been learning. Nothing is gained without trials and suffering. 'But why must we always condemn our party – it debilitates us. We should make our criticisms in private, face to face. Take for example Dr. Her.tz, Breitscheid and myself'. A note of confidence and intimate simplicity. 'They voted against the motion of confidence in the Marx government, but I was for it. So what? Did we fall out over it? You just don't! We travelled in the same train compartment together and didn't talk politics – we were up to here with it! Think how we'd argued in the faction, almost coming to blows! But at the station we all had some sausages together!'

Electors are always flattered when they're allowed to peep through the keyhole into the kitchen of big-time politics. A dozen speakers, one after another, speak against the worthy *Vorwärts*, and demonstrate the following elementary truths: 1) that the Social Democrats have safely delivered the dictatorship of the bourgeoisie; 2) that such a dictatorship is being directed exclusively against the working class; 3) that the party leadership bears the sole responsibility for this.

All the speakers in their ten quickly passing allotted minutes, punctuated by the chairman's bell, attempt furiously to substantiate their profound disillusionment with the party and their rage at its crimes, and are met with loud applause and ovations. Then with exceptional uniformity, a motion of confidence in the SDP's parliamentary faction is passed by an overwhelming majority. Having given their deputy a chewing-over, shoved his nose in the sins of the SPD and revealed their complete understanding of his sharkish tricks, the electors wipe Stampfer's broken nose clean and let him go off home with a vote of full confidence. A card-sharp mustn't cheat his own side, or he'll be beaten. But cheat for the benefit of his precious middle class and outplay the hated revolution – that he can and he must.

Coal Iron and Living People

∴

Coal Iron and Living People

Published by the State Publishing House (*Gosizdat*), Moscow, 1924

CHAPTER 1

Bilimbay

The Iron Mine[1]

The cart bumps along the track, humped and twisted like the roots of a tree. The earth is a rusty metallic red, damp with dew, bright with clumps of pink mosses and violets. The hills above are dotted with pine trees, like the handles of giant shovels stuck in the ground. Running past, barely glancing at them, is the happy blue-eyed river Chusovaya, on its way to the mining settlement. Then it turns back, and is filtered through some chalk streams, before breaking through, pushing before it a runny porridge of mud, and descending into the mine.

The tunnel is propped up by struts bolted to the trunks of ancient conifers. Beaten into the dark underground earth, the old forest continues to grow, without leaves or roots, just the trunks, supporting the walls with their broad chests, covering the gaps where the ceilings have caved in, straining up to the light they'll never see again. Water drips in the darkness, leaking through the cracks in the rocks and trickling along the floors, stopping to collect itself, then running on and vanishing again.

Further ahead, some logs nailed to the wall have buckled and fallen to their knees, defeated by the all-pervasive wetness. At the end of the tunnel is a small cave, lit by a kerosene lamp. It burns evenly, and doesn't smoke or poison the air, but it gives a weak light, like the eye of an invalid on their sickbed. The flame glimmers through dense clouds of steam, filled with the hoarse even breaths of the miner laying the dynamite, and the sharp-toothed blows of his axe.

Working on his knees, he hacks a soft strip of clay from the base of the wall. Above him three metal rods poke from their blast-holes, three fingers pushed between the teeth of their iron barricade. The preparations are complete. A haulier loads the clay and shale onto his cart and drags it off, bent double, dripping with sweat, trying to avoid the slippery walls, crawling almost flat on his stomach over the puddles. The dynamite-layer sits on a pile of rocks and rolls a cigarette. His matches are wet, but finally he lights one, and the damp smoke

---

1 Now Belebey.

mingles with the steam of this human body, smoking its stinking 'goatsfoot', enjoying its few moments of rest as if in a bath house.

From the next tunnel come the steady blows of an axe, like a heart beating under heavy clothes. There's nothing like this underground silence. It's as if the ears are filled with water, muffling the sounds of the metal woodpecker tapping in the next hollow, and the gently subsiding earth.

The dynamite-layer finishes his cigarette. Sweat pours from his face, deathly pale in the darkness. To make more light, he puts another match to his spare candle and attaches it to the wall. The soft grey dynamite can be cut with a knife, like yeast, and he must make holes for the fuses so they don't blow up in his hands. 'Every day we risk our lives in this pit!' he grins, spreading out the steel wires like silver dandelions, to help them light in the damp.

Thirty yards away, miners sit smoking, waiting for the explosion in the shaft above. The crooked steps of a ladder descend vertically to the bottom. Icy draughts waft up, smelling of indescribable mustiness and decay. Miners must scramble up and down this ladder every day, shift after shift, when they arrive and leave, treading carefully in their heavy boots, slimy with mud, dislodging showers of loose pebbles, which clatter against the walls and explode with a deafening crash into the blackness below.

The guttering candles drip burning wax on our fingers as we move along the tunnel. Lamps glimmer in dark openings, and if you listen closely, you can hear through the weeping underground water the muffled blows of an axe, and a miner's rasping breaths. They seem to come not from a human chest, but from the living mine, its lungs streaming in the darkness, its lamps like the lesions of tuberculosis.

At the drift, the gallery between the shaft and the earth's surface, the foreman checks his watch. A moment later, there are three powerful muffled explosions. There's no hurry. A little smoke wafts down the shaft, but it won't reach here for another half-hour.

'What's this about them increasing our hours to eight?' a haulier asks Bilimbay's Party secretary, Comrade Volegov.

A former haulier himself, Volegov joined the Party from the bottom of this pit, and fought to throw out the old owners, then fought to defend it with a rifle.

'We're against it, but they probably won't', he says laconically.

'But what if they do?'

'Then we must lump it'.

A young miner speaks, his voice breaking like an empty bucket dropping into a shaft on an unwound chain. 'Forget it, we can't do eight! You work here yourself, you know we can't! We're treated like dirt, those letters you get from the Party are hogwash! Everything's falling down, there's no air, and where are our work clothes? There's no rubber, just canvas. You catch your breath after your shift and your shirt falls off your back. Son of a bitch, you promised us vodka! At least give us cigarettes!'

Another miner goes off to check the smoke. It's coming closer, it's time to leave. We move down to the tunnel below the drift, where the ceilings are too low to lift your head. Fresh molehills of fallen rocks lie underfoot, with more tangled splintered trees bearing down, crushed by the weight of the earth. Finally we're crawling on all fours, between cross-layered timbers lying on their sides, supporting each other with their shoulders. There's no air to breathe. Miners are bent under the folds of the earth's stomach, which threatens at any moment to come down and bury them, with their lamps and axes and the playful thunderclaps of their explosions.

Then suddenly, beneath the boards under our feet, there's the glint of water, no longer in drips or rivulets, but a deep underground lake, as flat and grey as a field of sagebrush. The mine has reached the water-level.

After the miners discovered this underground lake a year ago, they set off to explore, carrying their baskets on their backs like snails, following the seams of metal through the thick layers of wet clay, hacking at its fat antediluvian molluscs, advancing step by step along their wet grave, widening it and repairing the collapsed joists as they went. To go further would require electricity and new machines, and all sorts of technical innovations costing huge sums of money we don't have, and won't have for a long time. But with their special hunters' instinct in the darkness, they have sensed a major seam in the catacombs close to the water-level, and they'll probably find it too. And the entire cost of this search, all the fruitless hours spent by these underground explorers in the slippery depths, is borne by the workers themselves.

Meanwhile this ancient mine, lit by kerosine lamps, held up by rotten planks – where for centuries political prisoners were sentenced to long terms of hard labour for their crimes, and where the tsarist government tried to conscript German prisoners during the war, but failed, thanks to their brave resistance – now produces the iron for Bilimbay's foundry, and is one of the main hubs of the industrial regeneration of the Urals. In 1920, our government wanted to close it, but the miners refused outright, enduring the desperate conditions, even voting to go without electricity to keep costs down.

For six hours of his inhuman labour, a faceworker is paid one rouble twelve kopecks, which he can top up through exceptional effort with a bonus of thirty to thirty-five kopecks. A haulier is paid less, fifty to seventy kopecks. And even so, the new currency reforms[2] mean they're not always paid, or

---

2   The NEP's currency reforms of 1922 and 1924, to tackle the hyperinflation of the Civil War, and bring the rouble closer to the currencies of Russia's new capitalist trading partners.

are paid late, and five hundred of Bilimbay's workers have had to cancel their donations to starving children in Germany.

In another of Bilimbay's pits, more voices are raised against the longer hours.

'It's always the same story', one says. 'Wait a bit longer and we'll fix things, they keep saying. But what can they do? There's the currency reforms, and the English won't give us loans ...'

The speaker is a communist, so there's nothing remarkable about his knowledge of world events. But his few words are filled with a deep consciousness of our Party's responsibilities in carrying out its programme, in whose name workers endure their punishing labour. And the extraordinary paleness of the man, speaking of the fate of the world at the bottom of the seventy-metre shaft, pickaxe in his hand, clouds of cold sweat steaming from his shoulders, gives them a special seriousness. Every hammer blow, every strike of the axe, is carried out to achieve the speediest possible advance to a more just, more human life.

'Just write this, Comrade', he turns to me. 'A lot of us have bad lungs. We're sent to local sanatoriums in the Urals for sulphur baths, but they're very cold. We need to be in the sun. The mine can only afford to send one of us a year to the seaside, it's not enough!'

The Foundry

Bilimbay is an ancient industrial town, whose foundry was built three centuries ago by serfs, and was owned first by the landowners, then by the new merchant class, with their huge resourcefulness and wild extravagant ways. Seven serfs' settlements sprang up around the factory, and it acquired vast tracts of forest, which have remained its property to this day. The trees stretch for miles – pines, firs, spruces, cheerful silver birches in their pale-green farm girls' shawls, mischievous Cossack junipers stealing their shade, and closer to the town, garden species of mountain ash and wild apple and cherry trees, running from the maids' quarters, dangling their dewy white tassels over the fences.

As well as the foundry and the forests, the landowners' patrimonial estate included their private church and summerhouse, and the stables where the serfs were flogged. Their filthy living quarters were hidden from outsiders' eyes at the back of the masters' mansion, delightful and imposing at the front, with its white-columned Empire-style facade. The church still stands on the slope above, flooded with sunlight under its dressing-gown of birches. The lacy white cuffs of its gates open into the lush green gardens, and the house lacks only a breakfast table and samovar on the veranda, and a lady pouring tea with her marble aristocratic hands.

Those wasteful times had a weakness for the latest adornments, which survive in the plaster wreaths above the foundry gates, and in the ornamental columns at the entrance. But a different life soon came to Bilimbay, less lavish but even more brutal, in which the new merchant masters violated the girls, and sent the strongest boys into the mines, and the serfs were punished not in the stables with the bailiffs' fists, but in jail, with the big clumsy bullets of those times. The golden age of private property in Russia has left terrible memories of its first industrialists and self-made millionaires, who ruled their slave workforce with a cruelty that far exceeded the slovenly tyranny of the old nobility.

The foundry's wood-burning furnaces and its fifty-year-old turbines, encased in their ornate cast-iron grilles like ancestral tombs, would make a Western engineer laugh. But after decades of honourable service, Bilimbay's ancient machines have been recalled to duty to support the Revolution in its time of need.

Foreman and master of the boilers and ovens is Alexei Alexeich Kashin, a small man with the most good-natured face, loved by all for his friendliness, and a true 'specialist', who knows his work inside out. Peering through the little window of the furnace at the thirty-pound lumps of metal and charcoal fluttering into milky cast-iron, he can detect at a glance the subtlest variations in the burning qualities of the different woods – whether to throw in more steady-burning pine, if there's too much quick-burning birch, or enough resinous cedar, with its small crackling flame.

Comrade Kashin has worked at his furnaces for thirty-five years. He left them briefly during the Civil War, to fight with Kolchak's White Cossacks. But he hadn't gone more than a mile before he stopped at the place where the ore left the mine, and something greater than his everyday fears and prejudices drew him back.

He points out with pride the special high-quality blades (or 'feathers') at the base of the turbine, which drive the water. To my shame, they look to me like the ordinary blades of a water-mill, glimmering in the patch of moonlight on the floor. But fortunately Alexei Alexeich doesn't guess my irrelevant observations as he leads me round the heart of the foundry.

Tending the furnaces is punishing work. The stokers throw in load after load of timber and iron, moving the flames from pile to pile with their long rakes. Jets of hot smoke gush up through the flues or escape-pipes (sorry Alexei Alexeich, I forget the correct technical term!), liquefying the metal at the ovens' fiery core, releasing showers of sparks in a flashy fairytale suicide.

Only Alexei Alexeich knows when the blaze has reached the right temperature for the flux to be added. Then all the sick blood in the metal comes to a head in the heat, flaring up with the impurities in the alloy, before being thrown out with the seething slag to give up its independent existence.

The stokers are soaked in sweat, and their shirts steam, and what is good for the furnaces is fatal for their health. They work in tropical temperatures, but their backs are chilled by the icy winds of the Urals, and they alternately boil and shiver as if after a hot shower. They are on the lowest pay rates, categories four to six, plus bonuses and overtime – in other words their wages are wretched. Yet at no other factory have I met the same deeply political approach to the current policies of the Workers' Republic, whose ruling class is condemned to endure these cruel conditions until the state has been established.

The lack of new equipment, the low pay and the pressure to work longer hours have exposed the glaring deficiencies in the Budget. But workers have cut the cost of ferrous metal production in the Urals with their blood and sweat, and at many factories, including Bilimbay, productivity has reached its pre-war levels, and even outstripped them. How has this happened? At what cost?

Bilimbay's old machines were worn out decades ago. Jobs have been cut, and one worker must now do the work of three. The quality of the ore has fallen, and miners are too exhausted even to make the walking-sticks they used to sell to make a bit of extra money. Shouldn't productivity have dropped? Yet the foundry's ancient samovars, puffing their smoky nostrils next to the mine, have already produced half a ton of cast-iron above their quarterly quota of seven and a half tons. Clearly this isn't due to any technical improvements, but to workers' unbelievable heroism and endurance, as they labour to save Russia from economic ruin. And all this despite their anger and protests, and on empty stomachs. The swans and thistles of 1919 and 1920 have disappeared, but the factory hasn't seen meat for months.

The one question they ask, as they put down their rakes to wipe their blackened foreheads, is 'Will things get better soon?'

What can I reply?

All that remains at the end of the last shift is the casting of the metal, repeated every day, but always a happy anxious time at the foundry. Calmly and grandly, the molten ore flows into hundreds of waiting casting-moulds, twitching with purple shadows as it cools and hardens. Then the stokers damp down the fire, raking the embers to the sides like gamblers cashing in their chips.

CHAPTER 2

Revda

'On the twenty-eighth day of January, in the year of Our Lord 1774, a band of brigands entered Revda',[1] the town's priest reported to his spiritual superiors. 'To avoid falling into the criminals' hands, citizens left for Ekaterinburg, where they remained until the twenty-eighth day of February'.

The foundry's owner, Count Demidov, was meanwhile writing to his factory board: 'When the insurgents invaded Revda, the guards and bailiffs sought shelter in the forests, and the villains through their thievish efforts laid waste to the factory. After many battles with the aforesaid villains, numerous peasants and factory hands were shot or beaten to death'.

But the illustrious Demidov needn't have worried. Already on 20 January, brave Captain Erapilsky was writing:

> Three workers escaped from Revda to Shaytanka, and informed our military commanders of the weakness of those occupying the factory, whose leader, retired soldier Beloborodov, a former lieutenant of Pugachev's, has fallen into extreme poverty, and is resolved to grow rich from robbery. Sergeant Markov marshalled his forces, and twenty local farming men, fifty factory hands and a hundred reservists advanced on horseback to Revda in the correct military formation. The criminals, weakened by fear and hunger, had little expected to be thrown into battle, and gathered round their cannon. But after our first shots, they fled into the woods, from which they returned fire. The harshness of the terrain forced them to remain there, and our forces shot two dozen dead, and took many more captive.
>
> On the twenty-first day of January, all who had fought in the campaign were rewarded for their loyalty to Our Most Gracious Empress with gifts from the Imperial Exchequor. Colonel Bibikov then led a new detachment against the criminals. Weapons and men were as follows: 4 muskets, 4 falconets, 2 cannon, 60 soldiers, 216 factory hands, 202 peasants.

---

1 In 1774, in the reign of Catherine the Great, units of the Cossack Emelian Pugachev's 100,000-strong serf army in the Urals occupied the foundry at Revda. The rising was crushed a year later, leaving over ten thousand fighters dead, and the survivors were sentenced to hard labour for life in the mines. Village settlements were turned into penal colonies, which would be used as labour camps for Russia's next revolutionaries, the Decembrists, then for successive generations of tsarist political prisoners, and in the 1930s as the base for the *gulag*.

At seven in the morning on the twenty-third day, a hundred mutineers left the forest, and were driven back by Bibikov's forces, who then advanced on the factory and fired for four hours at the plunderers and the assembled rabble outside. Without inside information, it has been impossible to establish how many of these monsters were killed. But the evil they have inflicted on the State casts them into eternal damnation and contempt ...

The stokers at Revda's foundry are the descendants of these last units of Pugachev's dying uprising, crushed here two centuries ago. Another chapter in Revda's history was added a century later, in the extraordinary diary of a literate serf named Umnov.

Umnov worked first as a farmhand on the Demidovs' estate, then in the factory office, and finally, thanks to his excellent penmanship and wonderful bass singing voice, which shook the walls of the church, he was moved into the masters' house as bailiff. He lived for a long time, and wrote infrequently. But all the most important events of that difficult century are recorded in his diary – apart from the Emancipation of the serfs. He passes over the cursed year of 1861 in angry silence, and forbids those close to him to speak of 'it'.[2]

His diary opens with the French:

1812   'Patriotic War. Napoleon 1 entered Moscow'.
1830   '1 September. Snowed for two hours. Continued all week'.
1835   '13 April. Barges left Revda on seventeen-day journey'.
1836   'His Excellency Alexei Petrovich Demidov left Revda for St Petersburg'.
1840   'Midday 2 May, 510 buildings on the estate burnt down'.
1843   'Midnight 3 June, theatre and riding-school set on fire. Cost: 4,000 roubles'.
1844   '22 April. Snowed this morning. Continued until 17 May'.

And finally, 1848. 'In Saint Fomin's week, an insurrection broke out at the gates of the foundry. On May 15, military detachments were sent in with orders to shoot. The dead were 160 men, five women and four children, two girls and two boys. Forty-eight were wounded. The soldiers were two hundred in number, led by police chief Colonel Stepan Parfyonych Kuraev, Inspector of the mine'.

How briefly Umnov evokes the repercussions in Russia of the revolutions sweeping Europe. The floggings and killings in the masters' stables next to the

---

2   As a relatively privileged house serf, Umnov would have seen little change to his life after the Emancipation, and unlike the farm serfs, would have received no land.

empty coal sheds, their shutters banging in the wind. The gaping jaws of the two disused prison mines, flooded with water, with the blue Sorokovaya Mountain and the towering peaks of the shaggy Wolf Mountains in the background – mapped eleven years earlier by the geographer von Humboldt, who calculated their height as 2,271 Parisian feet, 2,420 Russian.

The next Umnov, father of the two communists who left this terrible place six years ago to join the Red Army, continues the diary with bailiff's records of fires, expenses and the weather, and accounts of drunken brawls. His story breaks off when he is conscripted into the great brawl of 1914, leading his men in a drunken delirium to the station with cherry blossoms in their caps, dancing and fighting on the platform to the frenzied music of accordions, and the weeping of their wives. After that there is nothing, and a year later he is killed at the front.

Almost eighty years after 1848, Revda is in Soviet hands, and the Demidovs' white mansion is now the headquarters of the Factory Committee. Only the ground floor has survived. The upper storeys were destroyed in a fire, and the stables, kennels and laundry have all fallen down. But the entrance to the foundry is still intact, between the old office and the gates where Count Demidov ordered 169 men, women and children to be shot.

Hidden from view behind the gates is a small brickworks, where the workers are exclusively women. Nobody likes the place, neither the Factory Committee nor the Trust's directors or 'specialists'. Its messy manual labour brings down the tone of the foundry, and outsiders rarely visit. Temperatures hover between those in a greenhouse, where the soft young bricks are germinated, and a kitchen, where they are baked, and every part of the process, from beginning to end, which no man would touch, is injurious to human health.

In the first workshop, the wheels of the first crusher feverishly scratch great lumps of quartz with their iron nails, raising clouds of smoking dust which the women breathe in and out. Two millers rake the stone flour into piles and sift it through a sieve, before it's ground to an even finer dust in the second crusher, mounted on four cast-iron legs. The mouth burns, and the throat is as dry as sandpaper.

In the next workshop, workers knead the clay for firebricks, like dirty curd cheese mixed with granulated stone sugar. The air is unbearably damp and clammy, and smells of wet cement, like a newly built house rented out before it has dried.

Finally we come to the low two-story building housing the kilns, like a kitchen, bath house, laundry and prison all rolled into one, with its own suffocating fumes. Rows of damp bricks and hollow pipes with holes in their sides lie on shelves waiting to be fired, and women's work here doesn't stop for a second, kneading the damp dough into pies and sausages for the ovens, whose greedy bellies are hot enough to incinerate their own walls.

Unlike other workers in the factory, they're on piece-rates. In her long eight-hour shift, a cook is paid fifty-two-and-a-half kopecks for her first two hundred and sixty bricks, plus a bonus for any extra, and the same for sixty pipes. All the women are either widowed or single. Three have new-born babies at home, and almost all joined the Party in the Lenin Enrolment. Two sisters, aged forty-five and forty-nine, joined in 1914. The older one lost both her two sons fighting with the Red Army.

'How many bricks do you produce?' I ask their forewoman, popular rosy-cheeked Comrade Natasha.

'Three hundred', she says, pushing her barrow of clay to a special mincing machine, then returning to her table. 'We move a ton a day – why won't they give us any soap?'

One of the managers appears, and tries to step quickly past her, but she blocks his way and shakes her fist at him. 'You took our soap away! It's not fair, not fair! A bit of soap won't break your budget!'

Two of the kilns are already full. Jumbled piles of newly fired bricks lie on the floor, red as raw meat, smoking as if from the depths of the underworld. The heat is unbearable. People say there's no job more exhausting than this in summer.

The great machines in the casting and rolling shops look down on the brick-works, with their primitive charcoal-burning ovens and lowly artisan labour. Technology knows nothing more complex or demanding than the operation of these machines. Human hands aren't displaced by them, they're connected to all the different stages of the productive process, demanding of workers the greatest imaginable skill, speed and concentration.

Heating the metal ingots in the furnaces before they're rolled and cast involves the stokers in dealing with volatile minerals that may react dangerously to even the finest vent-wires aerating the fire. Propped up on either side by two helpers, the foreman moves his visor over his face with a flourish, then scoops a quarter-ton log of wood into his giant shovel, like an outsized sardine-tin key, and hurls it into the white-hot flames. A minute later, he places his terrible forceps on the soft red skull of the new metal, pulling it from the blazing womb in one swift movement, and tosses it into the iron pram of a wheelbarrow, swaddled in bands of steel. This is then wheeled to the dark nursery next door, filled with the clash of giant rattles, where it's sliced by the mechanical cutter, its blade remotely controlled by an operator in a special cabin that protects him from the hot spittle.

A group of stokers stand round the furnace between two contractions of its empty stomach. 'How much are we paid? Twenty seven roubles a month for the most skilled, eighteen roubles nine kopecks for the rest', one says.

Those nine kopecks are the bright quick little lizard of a boy who opens the door of the oven, deftly dodging the melting bars as the stokers pull them out with their huge tongs and throw them in the water tank to cool their heads. Soon hundreds of black bars are queuing up like iron sheep, waiting to be kicked into the fire with their steel-capped boots. 'They cost twenty-four roubles. We can't afford new ones on what we're paid, we have to look after them!' one says.

A few minutes later, the bars are pulled crimson and screaming from the flames, and are rolled into long strips in the first rolling machine, then moved to the cutter. Three blows, and the red tips smoulder with ashy shadows like cigar ends. Then it's on to the next machine for the second rolling. Angry heads leap from the rollers like writhing serpents, and the foreman pushes them back, jumping away as the tails whistle to the ground and coil round his boots.

Another bar is being removed from the water tank, and a third is waiting. Then disaster strikes. One has become jammed in the rollers. A bell rings and everything stops. The machine throws out its mangled lump of metal, and the foreman gloomily counts the wasted seconds as it's carried off on a stretcher, like a corpse from a burning house.

Meanwhile all hell has broken loose in the foundry. The all-powerful State Trust has returned several deliveries as underweight, and the director, Comrade Yushkov, has announced that the weight of the bars is now to be increased to thirty pounds, and cut into four parts, instead of three. Unless work is speeded up, the factory will lose the contract, he says; it's up to the workers to decide.

The drive to increase productivity is demanding of workers yet more seconds of precious concentration, and Yushkov can hardly make himself heard as they mob him on all sides. Sweat pours down the older ones' thin beards and pale bristled cheeks. The faces of these factory elders have long exceeded the limits of the human body, and are impervious to colour or expression, bony, bloodless and indispensable. Standing with them are the younger ones, who replace them every half-hour at the ovens, their faces skinned red by the heat. It's hard to control the old rebellious blood. Objections are flung at Yushkov across their whistling telegraph wires, and they're well-informed too. What does the Factory Committee say? What about Kozyrin, Gorlanov, the Mokretsov brothers?

As these old Revda names are called out, I'm reminded of Umnov's account of the 1848 insurrection, and of the punishments meted out to the whole village – even to the 'good' bailiff Umnov himself, who the masters had nothing against. In those days, the bosses would send in the army at the first sign of trouble. Now workers and managers are pitted against each other in this labour battle, close comrades and bitter enemies, with the Factory Committee and the union standing between them.

'You want our pre-war levels? On empty stomachs? On just potatoes?'

'You can explain all you like, we can't do it!'

Yushkov's tousled grey hair sticks up on end, but he doesn't back down, he can't. 'You say you can't? You're lying, I worked on these machines myself!' he says.

'We know you did, otherwise we'd have knocked your face in!'

'It's a stitch-up! Tell that to *Rekai*[3] with their gramophones!'

On the wall behind Comrade Yushkov, this red director and communist planner, is a graph showing that rolled metal is 27.25% below target, despite the new twenty-four-hour working day, and the twenty-nine extra workers thrown with superhuman effort onto the bookkeeper's scales. On the table before him is the thick Blue Book of the Urals Industrial Bureau, with its brief three-line instructions to the Labour Front, its dry figures and pitiless totals for the past quarter, and almost buried in these pages of business, its even dryer few words of praise.

For Revda's workers, with their inexperienced foremen, their exhaustion, their lack of food and desperate living conditions, this is the culmination of three uninterrupted centuries of labour – first forced serf labour, then worse than serf labour, and now voluntary, but just as punishing.

Later that evening, Mokretsov, one of the angriest of them, sits smoking at the gates, ticking off on his fingers the great minuses of his life at the factory, and his life in general. Occasionally he is interrupted by the bells from one of Revda's three churches, chiming with the voice of the foundry's old furnaces, or he stops to chase away a pig rooting under a nearby birch tree, wrapped against the cold in its green Orenburg shawl.

Ashamed that I've nothing to say to all his 'whys?' and 'how much longers?', I stupidly ask him, 'But don't you keep pigs yourself?'

'Even pigs have to eat', he says.

A cold wind blows across the steppe. A man passes playing an accordion, followed by a cart with a stinking barrel of fertiliser, slung on two poles at the back like a body being carried to a funeral. Then he says, 'Will you write about it?'

'Yes I will'.

He spits out his cigarette, and suddenly all the anger seems to leave his voice. 'Good, people need to know', he says. 'Well maybe it's the only way'.

---

3 The RKI, the Worker's and Peasants' Inspectorate, or *Rabkrin*, headed by Stalin, established in 1919 to tackle economic inefficiency and corruption, described by Trotsky as being as much use as giving a peasant a gramophone instead of a cow.

CHAPTER 3

The Shaytanka Steelmill

Heat gusts from the furnace. Glimmering behind its half-closed lids are the wandering whites of its eyes. Bent double, their faces covered by the visors of their helmets, the stokers hurl shovelfuls of scrap-iron into its white-hot depths, like hunters throwing rocks at a wild animal, driving it into a trap. The iron takes on the colour of the blaze, and the dead metal flares up, melting and turning into new forms, revived by the blood flowing through its fireproof veins.

It's highly skilled work. The stokers tend the fire like a woman in labour, and at the end of their six-hour shift, the old foreman must judge if the alloy is hardened. A boy opens the mouth of the furnace, pulling on a rope threaded through its upper lip, and a lump of blazing spittle flies out, cooling instantly on the metal floor, turning an indescribably pale colour. The foreman shakes his head, his face colourless from the heat, 'No, not yet', and a stoker chips the hardened sample from the floor and throws it back in the oven.

All the stokers are young and strong. However punishing their labour, working here under the clean Urals sky is infinitely less unhealthy than in our stinking factories in Moscow and Petrograd, and they have a rare ability to use every brief break in their labours to recharge their energy. As the oven's juices digest the last load of metal, a group of them stand a little way off, with a loose, slightly slouched gait, smoking and dozing with their eyes open, noticing everything between two drags of tobacco, ready at any moment to straighten up and go back to work. This was how they must have stood at their ovens two centuries ago, complaining of their suffering at the hands of their master, Efim Alexandrovich Shiryaev. 'There are enough god-fearing men to get rid of Shiryaev', they said, and plotted with the renowned Urals brigand Ataman Ryzhanko to have him killed.

At the end of the shift, a bell rings for the pouring of the steel, and everyone runs whooping and whistling to the furnaces, as if to catch a horse thief, or drop the first caravan of barges into the river in spring. The stokers and their helpers are all in their places. The director in his leather jacket paces round the burning coals. The engineers peer into the flames with the confidence of young doctors, casting frequent glances at their illiterate but most experienced midwife, the foreman.

Then finally a little of the blindingly radiant liquid, incomparable to anything but the non-existent human soul, trickles into a row of small iron cups, hissing like champagne. The stokers beat them rapidly with iron rods, and the frothing wine solidifies and turns gold. As His Majesty Steel appears, the windows of the foundry blaze like the ballroom of Count Demidov's estate, but lit now with whole trees of light instead of candles, and with a more glorious firework display than any the Count arranged for the Empress Catherine. Nowhere is metal further from its dark origins in the mine, filling cup after cup, wreathing their cast-iron edges in sparks.

Soon just a few blueish black chips of metal are left in the dust of the foundry floor, the colour of the workers' unwashed gloves. The show is over. The masters' theatre has burnt down, and the serf actors in their bast shoes go back to their quarters, the cattle-yard and the stables.

CHAPTER 4

Lysva

The wind combs hairs of smoke from the office of the Factory Committee, looming over the square like a brow yellow with fever. The white screen of the open-air Triumph Cinema sticks out its tongue at the bulky church of glorious Saint Sophia, its bricks encased in rough home-made iron which cost its donors nothing. Herds of goats and grunting pigs graze behind the market, trading resentfully in the shadow of the new three-storey cooperative store, the finest in the Northern Urals. On the potholed road from the factory, the steel mushroom of the water-tower gazes loftily at the crowds of workers rushing straight from their morning shift to a meeting about the new pay deal, without stopping to wash the dirt from their faces. In the distance, far from the buildings and bustle, are the rolling foothills of the Urals mountains.

The offices of the Factory Committee are in turmoil. The senior bookkeeper, Mylnikov, pushes open the door of the manager, Ivan Dianych, with a look of resigned despair, and is instantly besieged by workers demanding a few roubles from their May wages.

A sheet-metal worker hovers over Ivan Dianych's desk, clutching a small hand in his broad palm, his little witness. 'We've nothing to eat! Our kids are starving!'

'We're broke. We're only surviving thanks to those fifty roubles we borrowed from the co-op', Dianych says.

He breaks off to answer the phone. It's Kildebakov, chair of the Factory Committee. Workers in the sheet-metal shop are calling for strike action.

Dianych turns aside, his sharp nose twitching, holding the mouthpiece to his thick sunburnt neck. Oh Dianych is worried, although his mouth still curves up in a smile, like the blades on good figure skates. A brainy peasant, the workers call him.

Outside the window, the whole factory is running in the rain to the meeting – women with little bound steps, men tearing through the puddles and along the railway tracks, barely looking where they're going.

A worker's power is measured by the strength of his chest, and the power of this factory is measured by the workers in the sheet-metal shop, with its vast rolling-mills and open-hearth furnaces. Under Kolchak, Lysva lost hundreds of its citizens, and the dead were laid in a fraternal grave. The factory was robbed of its machines, which were finally rescued from a distant railway siding and returned to the workshops. But two of the furnaces perished, and at the heart of the once living factory were roofless walls and wrecked machines, overgrown with a few sad wild flowers.

Engineer Guerin climbed over the ruins in his brown raincoat and peaked cap, camouflaged against the leaves of rusting metal like a clever beetle, and everyone, from workers and factory-school students to directors and engineers, was fired by the spirit of resistance. Ivan Dianych gazed tenderly at the machines, his smile a downward semicircle with just the tips up, and allowed himself to dream out loud: 'We'll clear up this mess and get the furnaces working, then we'll rebuild the right half of the building and fix the roof. We've orders to meet ...'

In the roof-metal shop, heat shimmers over piles of slag where the workers have put their teapots, and one of the two surviving furnaces has just poured its smoking wine into the moulds. The metal is then lifted into the arms of a crane, which lumbers off, creaking like a giant boat, to cover the holes in the roof at the far end of the hall. The second furnace is being loaded with fuel. The stokers open the door and shovel scrap-iron into the blaze, and are instantly driven back blinded, with burning faces, and the salty taste of sweat on their lips.

A powerfully built fair-haired man removes his hands from his face, his eyes like eggs dropped in a boiling samovar. This is Alexander Terentich Ermakov, who helped build these furnaces twenty-eight years ago, and nursed them through their brief childhoods, and has spent three quarters of his life with them. He left them only once, in 1918, when he went off to fight with the Red Army at Vyatka. Then he returned to defend them against the Whites.

Grasping a hot billet with his giant tongs, Ermakov carries it to the steel rollers set in the floor of the next workshop, before another worker passes it to the cutter. As the blade slowly pulls its long body into its mouth, slicing piece after piece, it rears up like an angry tapeworm, drawing its tail to its head in golden loops, spitting sparks at the metal floor. The worker stumbles, but instantly rights himself with a convulsive effort of his muscles, like a cat thrown out of a window.

These workshops are ruled by the supreme punishment. Falling means death. Delay means death. Clumsiness means death. Metal has no colour at 800 degrees, just the colour of death. But workers' supreme mastery of their machines gives an extraordinary lightness to their movements. All have their job to do, and they work unhurriedly, with perfect timing, jumping over the sparks sniffing at their ragged bast shoes, grabbing the blazing half-ton billets and throwing them in the cutter as easily as throwing a lazy dog in the river in summer.

Working at their steady measured pace, which to an outsider might look like idleness, each keeps a keen eye on the other, and at the critical moment, never a second too late or too soon, will share the weight or beat back the fire. Poverty forces us to keep these barbaric long-obsolete work practices, yet each part of the process is connected, like the cables carrying the electricity. And a year from now, instead of two rolling-machines in this workshop, there'll be three.

The Sheet-Metal Workshop

At first sight, the whole of this magnificent workshop resembles a giant wheel. The first of the great wheels, clanking like the anchor chains of a battleship, is behind the two next to the entrance, one working, the other dismantled and collapsed on its columned plinth. Another, the pressure-wheel, turns silently in the gloom, like a foggy evening creeping in from the marshes. Maybe it has a voice, but it's drowned out by the surrounding din.

Only the most highly skilled workers here operate the big machines, with their stinking breath and dirty black mouths dripping toxic sweat. They have been picked for their youth and above-average height, and they have the muscular grace the machines teach their understudies. The senior foreman, Vetrikov, stamps on some hot metal flung from the rollers, then takes a brief break between tasks, propping one of his steel-tipped boots on an upturned box. His fair hair under his black peakless cap is dripping with sweat, and his voice is barely audible, dried out like the water he throws at the machines' enflamed joints.

Asked how much he puts through a day, he wheezes in my ear, 'A ton to a ton and a half, maybe half a ton of underweights'.

'For how much?'

'Sixteen roubles a shift'. His shirt, blotched with wet sores, gives off the smell of metal at the point of combustion.

Kuraev, one of the workshop's most skilled workers, pulls a sheet from the pile, flicking off every speck of dust with his hands, barely protected by his torn gloves, then throws it in the rolling-machine for the next part of the process. It turns gold and tries to fly off the rollers, but is pushed back by these barechested warriors, stripped to the waist, in their Red Army caps, felt boots and bast shoes, made from the peasants' birches in the workers' forest.

Jumping to avoid a piece of hot metal flying past, Kuraev moves another sheet to the machine, throwing himself at the pressure lever like a bear tearing at a tree. Half an hour later, drenched in sweat, he is relieved by Vetrikov.

His gloved right hand firmly grips his tongs, but his left hand hangs by his side and trembles slightly, as naked and yellow as his streaming face. The machine blows acrid fumes in his eyes, like an insolent smoker, and this communist, who volunteered with the Red Army in 1918, puffs and gasps as he shouts 'We're burning alive, it was easier at the front ...!'

The rest is lost in the roar and screech of the rollers. Each strip is cut into two, then four, then sixteen, then thrown back in the oven like a prisoner between interrogations, before being returned to the machine to be tortured again. Among the machines and the wheels and the stacks of metal, in the noise and fumes, where it's hard to breathe, someone has pinned a note to the wall saying 'Remember Lenin!'

In charge here is the communist Comrade Palkin. His bushy moustache is the reddish colour of hot cinders, and he has a broken jaw and fresh burn marks on his face. Seeing Ivan Dianych in the doorway, he hurries over to him in his bast shoes, clutching the holes in his overalls, chewing a piece of bread. 'Our foreman's no good, he's rough and ignorant, you must sack him!' he says.

'So who will you give me instead?' Dianyich asks.

High above the pressure-wheels, cranes move around like drunken giants, with their loads of scrap-iron. Dianych sweated on one of these cranes himself as a boy, and he knows he can't pull one over on Palkin. Palkin says they need someone strong for the job, and between two crashes of metal, they come to an agreement. Meanwhile next door in the clean engine room, a haven of peace, the desperate people running the factory without a kopeck in their pockets – any fool could do it with money – are discussing with grand audacity its speedy electrification.

But those who want to see the achievements of our great Revolution should visit the factory not only in the peaceful times, but on the days marked on its calendar by disputes and flare-ups. And to end this brief sketch of Lysva's workers and their heroic sacrifices, we must return to the meeting in the sheet-metal workshop against the new pay deal.

Comrade Shadrin, a middle-aged worker with a small clever face, stands at his machine like a cashier handing out money, passing through sheet after sheet for their final rolling. He started working at this machine as a boy of fourteen. In 1914 he was conscripted into the army, and in 1917 he deserted, and for three years he fought with the Red Army, and was wounded three times at the front. Then the fighting ended, and Comrade Shadrin returned to his machine.

The rollers' insatiable mouths swallow up the sheets, and he works at incredible speed, broken every so often by a smoky cough. Each shift, he pushes through a ton and a quarter of metal. He has two children, and is paid ninety-three kopecks a day, plus bonuses for exceeding his quota. What happens though is that as soon as his output increases his quota is raised, making his surplus mandatory, and his bonus vanishes somewhere closer to the limits of his strength. 'Year after year your pay gets eaten up and you're in debt again', he says, coughing up a lump of black soot. 'I'm too old for this work. Gorshkov, you do it!'

Comrade Gorshkov's job is to adjust the pressure-levers on the rollers. A communist, who fought to defend Perm and many other cities in the Urals, he has large hands and a broad face, with full lips and clear eyes, and his whole figure is as straight as a pine tree. 'All our work with the Lenin Enrolment shows we'll live better with a majority in the Party', he says.

Yet even Gorshkov and Shadrin have now downed tools for the meeting.

Comrade Kildebakov, of the Factory Committee, stares wretchedly at the workers, like a man broken by their quarrels with the workers' state. Maslyannikov, chair of the trade union, doesn't look happy either. Only Dianych is still smiling, his mouth curved up like a croissant.

The machines have come to a standstill. The wheels have stopped, without an atom of life in them. Dianych speaks first, about some damaged rollers. 'They're as moody as women, leave them for a second and they crack!' He goes on to discuss the factory's new Czech director, Professor Pyznov, an outstanding engineer, who is supervising the new orders, and has saved the Trust many tons of metal. The workers skim over all this like a clever preface no one reads, and wait until he pauses to hammer him.

A worker in a torn coat and stained cap, sitting high on the main wheel by the entrance, asks what everyone wants to know. 'So you want us to work longer for less money?'

'We've no choice! Do you think we're millionaires?' Dianych says, irrelevantly, but from the pit of his stomach.

'If the rouble crashes, we're done for!' another says.

A mood of thoughtfulness and responsibility sets in. Soviet power must survive. That's the starting point, these are the terms under which everything must be discussed.

Dianych takes advantage of this mood to touch on sore points – competition from the south, and from the factory's main competitor in the Urals, the Goujon Metallurgical Plant, which is driving down prices. The workers knew all this, he needn't have said it, and more arguments flare up over the details of the deal.

'What about the foresters? Are you cutting their pay too?'

'Yes I am! I've been on at them for months!' Dianych smiles, hoping he has disposed of their questions with the foresters. But the discussion now gets down to business, with more voices raised against the pay cut.

'Forget it, we're not doing it!'

'We're done in! We put all we've got into what we earn, we can't work harder!'

'The place is filthy! The ceilings let in the rain!'

'Flour used to be two roubles forty kopecks, now it's three fifty!'

'Why is workers' pay higher in England and food cheaper?'

'The Party's screwing its own people!'

The walls are barely visible through the clouds of greasy smoke, and flakes of soot flutter in the air and settle on their faces. Their anger is mixed with a deep sadness, which Dianych has difficulty responding to, and he flounders. But the workers ranged against him are pitiless.

'Stuff your deal! What do you take us for?'

'You can't fob us off with your bits of paper, they're all lies!'

'Why are you managers paid twice as much as us who do the work? Where's the justice in that?'

'Our casting shop has dozens of specialists with their hands in their pockets!'

'Ours has no "spets" and it works fine, just as good as the rest!'

'Just one "spets" in each shop!'

They surround Dianych like a black forest. But his round face is still smiling as he dodges their attacks, just as he dodged the hot metal flying past his heels when he worked here as a boy.

He finally compromises, and agrees to sack a few specialists.

Then someone shouts, 'Give us the Trust's figures for the shops!' and they read them out: 1,020 defective sheets – seventeen roubles forty-eight kopecks deducted; 1,100 – twenty-three roubles ten kopecks deducted; 752 – eleven roubles one kopeck deducted.

Finally the storm bursts. 'They've knocked half the price off, we've been robbed!'

'We've increased our output like good citizens – you can't touch our pay, we can't eat as it is!'

'What use is the union? It should be on our side, not sucking up to management!'

'What's the Factory Committee playing at?'

They turn on Comrade Kildebakov in his battered cap, who looks as if he's come off worst in a fight. 'See, he's ashamed to look us in the eye!'

Dianych's nose quivers. An old porter sitting on the main wheel stands up and stretches like a bear, clawing at a beam with his gloved paws. His striped peasant kaftan is filthy all over, and his bent back under his leather waistband exudes infinite power and exhaustion. Above him, three awakened slaves of Michelangelo prop their heads on the wheel's shoulders as he shouts, 'And when it's time to elect you again? It's two months since the Lenin Enrolment, and nothing's changed! We've old peasants here who should be retired who've been sent back to their hammers, and they support the rest of us!'

'Strike! The rollers won't work without us!' someone shouts.

'Strike? Close the factory? How would we explain that to the working class?'

The man in the torn coat sitting high on the wheel has again raised the general over the particular, and everyone is silenced by his calm quiet voice and the bright wall of their responsibilities. And with these words, 'How would we explain it to the working class?' it seems the deal is accepted – along with more months of increased work, the angry reproaches of their wives, a hard winter, and growing debts.

'How would we explain it to the working class?' means not a day more of this hell than is necessary. Accept the deal, but don't forget the human cost of each day, each hour of the new pay rates. Don't let the managers, directors and specialists line their pockets and grow fat. Don't waste a single kopeck on unnecessary overheads, adding their own cruel burden to every ton of coal and ore, every Lysva dish and spoon.

Maslyannikov of the union gives a good speech, summarising everything that can be said in defence of the present in the name of the future. Tall, severe and incorruptible, hero of the Civil War, in his high miner's boots, leather cap and black shirt buttoned to the neck, the uniform of the industrial Urals in the Civil War years, Comrade Maslyannikov commands everyone's respect. The anger disperses, and the fog of fumes seems to lift, and it only remains for the deal to be voted through.

An elderly worker shuffles back to his bench in his old tin helmet covered in holes, like the holes in the roof. Workers' protective clothing, their pay and conditions, the machine oil so injurious to their health – all this has been pushed aside by the need for a collective agreement.

The Enamelling Shop

Only the main workshops were against the deal. It's a different story in the kitchenware departments, where virtually all the workers are women, on the lowest pay rates.

In the stuffy circular hall of the enamelling shop, topped by a damp dome, they dip low-grade tin into vats of enamel, from which it emerges gleaming, beautiful and dead, leaving them with red blotches on their cheeks, and their hair plastered to their heads with sweat.

Rows of utensils, created to sit lazily in one place, dry on shelves as if in a buffet. It's still early, seven in the morning, but the dry heat is already spreading through the whole building. At first it lies on the shoulders like a comfortable knapsack, and you don't feel its terrible weight. But as the heated floors warm the soles of the feet, the body gradually fills with a burning exhaustion, and you long only to lay your throbbing head on the nearest workbench and rest. Anything to sleep!

Yet women's work here demands an enormous amount of concentrated energy and attention, consisting of an endless series of small quick movements. During her eight-hour shift, a dipper lowers hundreds of saucepans, mugs, plates, basins and spoons into the vat – all these everyday objects we take for granted, unable to enter their long kitchen lives without their blue and white glazes, which she gives them just once, to last for ever. Pressing her damp apron against the side of the vat, she stirs them with her tongs for fifteen to twenty seconds, as carefully as if bathing a baby, making sure they don't swallow water. Then she shakes them in the air, until their blue dresses and white pinafores are spread evenly over their plump bodies, before laying them on the shelf.

In some of the other workshops, the machines have been cleaned up, which helps a bit. But there's no way workers here can avoid the toxic fumes. However mechanised the work elsewhere, these women still stand for hours in puddles that burn their feet, dipping the tin into the vats of hot sulphur and tin oxide, choking on the foul stink. The scientific evidence is that the lungs can only withstand this work for four years at most. And they aren't just statistics on paper, they involve living people who know nothing of this fatal limit, and go on breathing the air for five or six years, however long they have to.

In its final transformation, the tin is turned into cheap toys and spoons, to be stuck into the mouths of patients at the free hospitals. The sulphur burns Comrade Gorbunova's stomach through her apron, as her quick hands decorate pieces of tin with sawdust and plaster of paris, turning them into royal mirrors, so the first things they reflect are her white shawl and matchless shoulders. She lost her husband fighting with the Red Army, and she has two children, and earns sixty kopecks a day.

At the next vat, Comrade Sorokina pulls items of kitchenware from the acid and rubs them with sand, then dips them in water and rubs them again until her fingers bleed through her rubber gloves. And if at the end of the day her output isn't too bad (who would put themselves out for this stupid woman's work?), and if a commission visiting the workshop tells her she must produce a hundred more pots for her sixty kopecks; and if Comrade Sorokina joined the Party in the Lenin Enrolment, and knows quite well what is expected of her, but still tries to keep back a bit of her strength – from a sense of self-preservation deep in her bones – then it's not surprising her face isn't cheerful, and the commission makes the saucepan lids bang in her soul. What do they care about her?

And now all these tireless frail-looking women are cursing like hell, and civil war has broken out between them. Not only is their pay being cut, the helpers, who have to hold the wet items to their chests, have had their aprons removed, while the dippers, whose work is fractionally cleaner, have been allowed to keep theirs, in honour of their backbreaking labour and burning feet, which are barely cooled at night by a few hours' sleep.

The helpers angrily stumble off with planks of damp utensils on their shoulders, holding out their arms to balance themselves, glaring at Shurochka, their Factory Committee delegate. But with Kildebakov they're more out-spoken.

'Give us our aprons back! We need soap! The enamel gets under our clothes and eats our skin. When we rub it off in the bath we're like sandpaper!'

And Kildebakov smiles at them with that air of superiority which so offends women, but they secretly like – in other words, like a man.

As soon as he leaves, they tear into Shurochka.

'Where are our aprons? Have you no heart?'

'Don't take it out on me, I don't count for anything here', their delegate says. 'You can tell me how you feel, but not as a Committee member, as your friend'.

Men rarely take women's complaints seriously, especially in this workshop, where the senior dipper's job, which no man would touch, is on the lowest pay rate. 'The girls are moaning again', they say.

A group of them stands round a handsome young stoker as he gracefully pushes a griddle into the furnace, then pulls it out with its jumbled heap of half-finished items. 'Hey sweethearts!' he whistles at them.

The Stamping Workshop

It's noisy, drafty and dark. Running between the open doors at either end of the huge barn is a narrow-gauge railway track, whose construction in 1905 provoked workers into an angry strike, which was brutally suppressed by the factory's owners, the Sheremetev brothers.

On both sides of the rails, moving belts carry electricity to dozens of machines. At one end are those producing the larger cookware, the proud aristocrats of the workshop, their movements as varied as hand gestures. Squatting beside them like a primeval potter is the ancient punching-machine, filling the air with its monotonous blows, giving birth to new utensils, hurling them from its knees. A bent withered little man in a shabby waistcoat and bast shoes diligently feeds it with iron cakes. 'No, it's too early to join the Party yet, reckon life'll show us', he says, angrily chewing the stump of his pipe like a gnarled root.

Great words echo through the din: '... after Octyubi we takes forty thousand Cossack prisoner ... We cut off the Tversk Regiment at Gunib fortress, and we saves it!'

This is Sekirin, a native Udmurt, uprooted in October from the northern swamps to fight for the Revolution, who after several months in one of Kolchak's jails, went on to defend the Workers' Republic in insurgent Georgia and Daghestan. He arrived in Lysva after the 1922 demobilisation, and he now has a wife and three children, and is paid at the lowest rate – fifteen roubles a month, thirty with bonuses.

'Hey switch the machine off, it needs fixing!' he shouts, and the punch thuds onto the waiting piece of iron, then slows and stops, and a heavy casserole clatters into the basket.

Other machines give the utensils their final shapes. One quietly buffs their rough sides, giving a little yelp as it drops the finished products into the basket. Lining the windows are machines like sewing-machines, where rows of women sit stitching handles onto cups, jugs and teapots. Only they sew not with thread but with fire, and their needles are the fat metal fingers welding the metal.

Marusya Shilova has worked at her machine for seven years. The best years of her life, her entire youth, everything a person can experience in seven winters and springs – loves, successes, losses – Comrade Shilova has spent sewing handles onto millions of frying pans and chamber pots, sitting on her iron stool which shakes like a gun-carriage in battle, and has caused numerous complicated female complaints over the years. For every shift, for every thousand items she produces, she is paid eighty five kopecks. 'But that's only if you work flat out. Not if you take a break, and you have to sometimes, you really do. We're not treated like the others, we can't stop for a second'.

The machines flash lightning on the dirty walls, and sparks fly over her small hands and her severe kerchief and apron. Sitting next to her, sewing handles on teapots, is Comrade Mushkina. The workshop has etched into her fine graceful figure the flat chest and bearing of an eighteen-year-old boy. She is one of the few workers here who still subscribe to the newspapers, for which she pays two roubles thirty kopecks a month from her wages. 'We have to push ourselves to do a thousand', she says. 'And no, Marusenka, there's no way they'll let us women onto the big machines!'

Not everyone in this factory expresses their anger and exhaustion in fiery words. And those whose shoulders are so crushed by toil can suddenly drop their burden and be overcome with sadness. It might seem strange that the pay deal was voted through less acrimoniously in these workshops, where conditions are hardest. But beyond a certain limit, sensitivity to pain is dulled. Life must look very different through a fog of fumes that cause severe chest pains, nosebleeds and dizziness. All this, so unbearable to begin with, soon becomes constant and familiar, and reduces the will to fight. Take pity on these workshops in the new factories of the future! They must be the first to be opened to the light, with the sunniest windows, the freshest air!

The women's defender and union organiser in this workshop is Comrade Anna Balkova, a tiny woman they all love and trust, who wears her black headscarf knotted to one side, like a wise hare with one ear up, and lives on nothing but dry bread dipped in slops of weak coffee, and flourishes like summer – a truly new kind of woman, who lost her husband and family at the historic crossroads of the Revolution, in the years of hunger, typhus and Kolchak, who found her way to books and the Party, and calmly endures the poverty and hardships, making life easier for others, cheerfully bearing on her shoulders her great and necessary work for the factory.

CHAPTER 5

Kytlym

Kytlym in the Udmurt language means cauldron, and that's what it looks like, a giant circular bowl cut high into the mountains, just below the eternal snowline, where clouds leave shreds of their whipped up hems on the jagged summits.

For centuries, hunters roamed these mountains shooting bear and grouse. But the landowners jealously guarded their plots of land, and the treacherous *taiga* and forest fires meant they could never shoot enough.

Count Vorobyov was thoroughly sick of his neighbour Duparc.[1] For days he hid in the bushes, listening for the little bell of his *troika*, waiting to load him with a round of smallshot. If the Frenchman was a gentleman he would buy his own land, not trespass on his.

Duparc was equally sick of Kytlym life. After sitting at home for weeks without going out, he would make sudden sorties along Vorobyov's forbidden road, dashing over the potholes with the flaps of his Udmurt fur hat pulled down over his ears, his buttocks protected by a feather mattress. Vorobyov kept missing him, but got a good shot at his Borzoi dog running beside his carriage. Then finally he shot through Duparc's mattress. He was an excellent marksman, whose bullets were cast from the dense white metal found in such abundance in these backwoods, most of it in the mossy marshes and wetlands that formed the greater part of his property.

Naturally he didn't run around collecting this gold that wasn't gold himself, he paid some boys a kopeck to do so, and they brought sackloads of it back to the house, which his wife would throw out with the rubbish. She hated this common local metal that made holes in her husband's strongest pockets by midday.

But Vorobyov's metal was strong, and his eyes were sharp. And when Duparc finally built a road across the mud to his land, he was glad to see how cheaply it was constructed, from thin logs. They quickly rotted and collapsed, and in the first year his best stallion fell in the mud and broke its left foreleg. Then in the same year Vorobyov's bailiff disappeared, after drunkenly buying a bag of smallshot for fifty kopecks from some peasants. Fools sometimes get lucky, and tales of his fabulous wealth soon spread for miles around.

---

1 Louis Duparc (1866–1932), Swiss Professor of Mineralogy at Geneva University, who visited the Urals in 1900 to study its mineral deposits.

For the next two years the *taiga* sucked its paws, until one day Vorobyov made an astonishing deal. For three gold roubles, a hunter told him two secrets. First, that the bullets that had shot Duparc's dog and mattress were made of pure platinum, 'white gold', the rarest and most precious of all the metals. And second, that some of the richest deposits in the world were to be found to the north of his property, around Sosnovka, closer than you could spit. French and English prospectors paid him over five thousand roubles for his mud, cash down, and for his 'special services' to their companies he was set up for life in a comfortable apartment, with firewood, electric lights and a latrine.

Cut off from the world by the rolling mountains under the clouds, Kytlym was soon shaking the world with stories of its platinum – of foaming rivers tumbling from the mountains carrying tons of the metal, hiding it under layers of moss and rocks, or carelessly dropping it to the bottom. And it wasn't only the strong hands of the foreign robbers that created this platinum kingdom in the swamps, where barbarians used to shoot wild duck with gold bullets. Russian capital too was involved, just not very much of it, generously allowed to join the triumphant march of the foreign shareholders.

Five giant excavators crossed the landscape, each costing over three hundred thousand roubles, like the old machines used for mining gold, but on a massive scale, pulled by up to twenty horses. Sinking in the mud under the weight of their engines, the iron caravans moved along the bear trails with the pomp of the wedding processions of Saxon Anhalt-Zerbst princesses, travelling to our kingdom in their golden carriages, their knees covered in sable rugs, unheard-of in these parts, with the latest prices for snuff, meat and vegetables in their virginal account books. Their encampments on the *taiga* resembled the camps of the invading Moghul armies, and the foresters threw burning branches into the darkness to ward off the wolf nights, setting fire to thousands of miles of forest.

By 1904, the companies had already covered the cost of their machines, and were extracting staggering dividends from the earth. Distinguished geologists travelled from Europe to prospect the mountains, and although their findings were kept strictly secret, stories soon spread of the deposits discovered in the alluvial marshlands around Kytlym.

In 1905, the year of the virtual collapse of the Russian economy and our first revolution, wild *troikas* galloped from Kytlym every week with their spoils, totalling millions of roubles. Russia controlled the world market in platinum, with ninety percent of the mined metal in the universe, and it was with this easy money that Europe bribed our rapacious tsarist government waiting at its doors.

Profits reached astronomical levels before 1914, and platinum madness took hold in the years of the Imperialist War. Armies of prospectors tore up the earth, opening new mines at Sosnovka, Kosva, Tylai, Ragged Hollow and elsewhere. Most of the platinum extracted consisted of small nuggets that fell into the hands of private brokers or the police, and prospectors lacking the funds for further excavations would jealously hide their finds under rocks and branches, like abandoned tombs.

But not everyone fell victim to the madness. Kytlym was seized by something greater in those years. At the heart of the cauldron were the people who did the work, for whom it was just a job like any other, allowing them to buy a crust of bread and some books. Working on the company's excavators, reading and studying, were Kytlym's first partisans, its future commissars and economic planners. And in 1917, the Bolshevik Boris Didkovsky, whom the tsarist concession had initiated into all its plans, not suspecting that this highly qualified geologist, future Rector of the Urals State University, was seized with ideas of social justice, dealt the company a severe blow.

Foreigners will never forget October 1917. What profits they had made from their Russian colony, with its well-disposed government and cheap labour – thousands of workers cut off from the world under the total control of the entrepreneurs. Then suddenly it was all over.

It was for Kytlym's millions and billions that Russia had fought this war, which we then had to pay for all over again. It was for platinum that Admiral Kolchak marched his Cossacks on Kytlym in 1918, armed to the teeth by Britain and France, choking on the forest fires, littering the mud with their corpses, urged on by imperious cables from London and Paris over the wires of his field telegraph, looped from tree to tree – 'Dammit Admiral, what are we paying you for!'

The cables hiccoughed out the foreign words as Europe hurled itself at the platinum, dreaming under its blanket of pine needles and snow. By December, Kolchak had reached Kytlym, and its workers, who for the past year had dared to deprive the criminals of their spoils, were taught a cruel lesson. Orekhov, Sergeev, Ikanin, Shumaev and Naimushin were shot, and their bodies were thrown down a disused mine. Also Gribenkin, Yaroslavtsev, Zenkov, Beloglazy, Dyldin, Novoselov, Alexander Startsev, the Ismogilovs, father and son, young Vanyushka Sergeev, Kasatkin the blacksmith, Korobkov the baker, Kryukov the carpenter, Poloznikov, Pokryshkin, Rogachev, Mansurov and Kolodkin. The entire mining population was forced to flee. Whole villages left with their children and animals in the bitter cold. Those at Sosnovka had just five horses to pull their carts through the snow, and Kytlym's workers helped harness them up. The families were soon forced back. But the Bolshevik Didkovsky formed his men into a partisan detachment, and they went on.

I was told the story of their escape by Comrade Ermakov, a powerfully built man with a large round face bristling with thick blonde stubble. They had ten rifles between them. Most were just boys, still wet behind the ears, with nothing but their bare hands to fight with. They went down to the valley, but the Solikamsk Highway out of the cauldron was cut off by three feet of snow, so they had to bypass it and struggle through the drifts to Kosva, narrowly avoiding a reconnaissance unit of Dutov's White Cossacks.

> We leave the carts and split up, cavalry and infantry one way, seventeen of us and Didkovsky the other. Hours go by. Will anyone find us? A mile ahead we hear gunshots. No food, not a soul to be seen, just the trees and snow. It's coming down heavier, and we kill one of our horses and chop up the meat. We line up the ones that can't go on, and the old men stay behind with them. 'You're in charge, we'll come back for you', Didkovsky tells Sakantsev.
>
> Thirteen of us are left. We trim our snowshoes and go on, I don't know how but we do. Then on the sixth night we hear more shots. The others are past caring, but Didkovsky says 'They're ours!' So we head in that direction. By morning we're on the road to Molchanovo. Our snowshoes are packing up, but Didkovsky orders us on. Next minute bullets whistle past, and the youngsters throw off their snowshoes and sob. Then we hear the creak of a cart. We ask the driver where he's going. 'To Kosva, to the army', he says. 'Which one?' we say. 'The Red one', he says, and he shares his bread with us, two loaves between thirteen men.
>
> We reach the Reds' camp. Didkovsky shows them our papers, and we fall in the snow, all black and terrible looking. A woman tries to heat curd tarts for us on the fire. They can't make a proper fire, but we warm ourselves in the smoke, and the commander Silin lifts up the unconscious ones and pours broth down their throats. We're not soldiers, we're dead meat …

A year later, the Republic occupied Kytlym for the second and last time, and since then the mines have been under Soviet control.

Platinum mining is a filthy, dangerous, ridiculous business. The massive two-story electrical diggers are erected in hollows in the mountains, surrounded by millions of tons of mud and bare rocks. First the subsoil is excavated by locally made ploughs, then a pit is dug, and a floating platform is lowered into the dirty yellow water for the digger. In this place where industry is barely developed, thousands of kilowatts are thrown at the uninhabitable swamps, brutally cold in winter, swarming with mosquitoes in summer. Machines blast the landscape day and night, bellowing and shrieking, devouring miles of trees and rocks, ending up with a barely noticeable handful of metal. Mountains are moved to produce a few ounces of platinum. The whole valley is turned into a graveyard for the sake of these fragments humanity considers valuable for some reason. Forget its notional value, and it's a picture of insane waste and destruction.

The diggers work frenziedly in the sludge, like idiots swimming in their own excrement, swallowing up the banks, piling them in neat ridges of digested rocks. They play a strange game in their murky pits. Surrounded by miles of mud, they act like ocean liners, gazing loftily at dry land from their captains' bridges, while wide grey scoops dip in and out of the water like steel frogs, raising their wet shovels over their heads, somersaulting under the surface with a little splash, then floating up with their mouths full of mud.

Each scoopful is deposited in the sluice-box in the digger's entrails, then moved to a perforated cylinder, where it's given a cold shower to hose away the sand and gravel. The large rocks are then hauled up on a narrow mechanical rubber belt, scattering lumps of granite, and the remaining sludge is sieved into special trays, and moved up to the surface for its final rinsing.

The wash-plant is surrounded by a high metal fence, and the gate is locked with a special lock, guarded by a communist, who opens and closes it at the beginning and end of each shift. The workshop comes to life, as workers wrapped in leather and tarpaulin pour into the lion's cage where the priceless nuggets are buried in the mud. The communist controller sits on a beam with a loaded revolver, dangling his dry legs over the rinsing tub. The trays float up from their watery bed, shaking off their hard blankets and spitting out particles of grit. Then the taps are turned off, the metal grids are lowered over the tub, and the trays are moved to the rinsing tables. There would be total silence if it wasn't for the digger thundering like an earthquake, and the howl of the scoops dipping up and down.

Like the rest of Kytlym, the workshop is drunk on the metal. The peasant who comes to Kytlym to make enough money to buy a new bath or plough, and is lured back year after year by dreams of platinum. The communist worker, formerly a brilliant student at Moscow State University, unable to support himself and his family, touched forever by the platinum, who has fallen hopelessly back into the barracks. The strange workers who aren't workers, exiled political prisoners and ex-*Chekists* sacked for their crimes, cursing Soviet power under their breath, burning their throats with cheap brick tea that tastes of urine. All are drunk on the metal, drunk at the sight of the water flushing the grit from the mud. Blind drunk, secretly drunk, without noticing it, without alcohol.

Only the communists have been saved from the platinum fever, devouring Lenin like quinine for malaria, reading him late at night under the weak electric lights of the remote Urals, escaping the diggers once a week to run five miles to a party meeting, following great world events through the blurred mirror of its communiqués.

Old Guryan Maltsev joined the Party in 1918, and has worked in Kytlym's wash-plant for six years. Only he can see the platinum hidden in the mud. Flushing away the excess, he methodically smears the remains on the bottom of his tray, and scrubs the sides with what looks like an ordinary kitchen scrubbing brush. Then carefully, with his quick sensitive hands, like two little white cats, he chases the silver mouse under the water. The platinum still isn't visible, and he pursues it gently, tickling it and playing with it like a lover. The whole workshop is mesmerised, you could watch him for hours. Finally he's holding the platinum, patting and stroking it and spreading it out. The heavy blueish-white metal gleams in the water, emitting faint sparks, and everyone trembles as the controller scoops it in his ladle and dries it by the stove, like a chandler drying his grain.

Guryan watches with the detached look of a gambler whose luck ran out long ago. His life hasn't been easy. He lost his whole family when his village burnt down in a forest fire, and afterwards he set off alone across the Urals to pan for platinum.

Each year fires set the *taiga* around Kytlym ablaze. They burn themselves out and come back. They devour hundreds of miles of primeval forest, then return to snap the slender trunks of the young fir trees, their crowns cursing the sky as the smoke licks their feet. They're as unpredictable as a wild animal. Today they won't touch you, tomorrow they destroy you, streaking across the scorched *taiga* past a rider on a frightened horse, wafting soot over the earth, then racing up a tree and hurling their fiery squirrels through the branches. They can't be trusted. They spell death. They grow angry over nothing. Suddenly a monstrous red face pokes from behind a birch tree where it's been hiding from the rain, and runs up the trunk, gripping it with its red hands like a sailor, unfurling its smoky banners at the top. All around is devastation. Thousands of trees with torn trunks and charred roots fall gasping across the paths, and the forest throws out little black butterflies, like the special stamps issued after disasters.

Parts of the woods barely survive their injuries, but here and there leafy saplings appear to replace the old pines. The fires take a special joy in returning to these reviving woods, like a conquering army to the ruins of a destroyed town, snatching all those who escaped and unwisely decided to return. It seeks out its old haunts, overgrown with wild roses, where the trunks haven't had time to rot, the partridges haven't fled, the hares don't jump up, and the horses don't bolt.

Guryan saw the fires, and he fled from them. He spent years searching the Urals for platinum, and he found it. He didn't bother with the small deposits, just the finest samples, selling half to the Imperial Exchequer, losing the rest on his next unsuccessful gamble. Then in 1917 he was seized with the desire to search for something better. He left the Urals and fought with the Reds in Siberia. But he found nothing there, and the old hunter decided to return home and gamble everything on one last find. And what he found in Kytlym were people like him, crawling around in the mud, and he stopped searching.

He never returned to prospecting. The Revolution had cured him of his platinum lust, and he went to work on a Soviet digger, bending his gambler's face over the metal, grasping it in his intrepid hands, stripping and washing it like a baby.

Guryan is one of six hundred miners in Kytlym who return from their shifts to sleep in its flea-infested dormitories, which are so filthy and disgusting one doesn't want to write about them. Six hundred workers dependent on a wretched cooperative store that sells women's face powder and hair dye, but no flour. Six hundred workers cut off from the world by the mountains, permanently wet and most of them ill, for the climate here is cruel and inhospitable. They complain bitterly about their housing, but the truth is they don't complain enough. It's a scandal that we still house people in these terrible places we inherited from the old companies, with their broken windows blocked with rags and sheets of metal, their sewage and age-old filth seeping through the walls. They save mere kopecks, and fuel more counterrevolutionary propaganda than the Whites could dream of.

Living a few yards away in his comfortable brick-built house with his family and his embezzled platinum is a former prospector, who plays his two-keyed harmonica and milks his two fat cows every day and mashes their feed. Meanwhile Didkovsky's partisans, who almost starved to death for three years, who suffer rheumatic fever and tuberculosis from their work on the diggers, must rot in their fetid cells, unable to afford the wood to build new homes. The *taiga* blazes for hundreds of miles, millions of roubles go up in smoke, but they're not allowed to take the timber or buy it cheap. It's an insane situation. The work of our so-called Forestry Commission, which we aspire to in a dream, consists merely of stripping the branches from the fallen trees so they can lie flat on the earth and rot more quickly, and workers are trapped in their barracks because we've decided we must save the forest economy, destroyed by the Revolution. What if some new criminal concession appears near Kytlym, and cuts down enough timber in twenty-four hours to build warm bright cottages for workers, and gives them boots and overalls and jam? They'll either escape there, or they'll be consumed with envy. The partisan Ermakov described with a terrible seriousness the looming counterrevolutionary threat this poses.

Then there are the famous new railway lines running between the mines and factories, which cost the Republic over three million gold roubles, as flimsily built as cheap toys. The slow moving trains are frequently derailed at the cuttings by a cowpat or nutshell, and no self-respecting railworker is without cuts and bruises on his face. A decree was recently issued ordering the engines to be fitted with special muzzles, to protect the forests from flying sparks. Needless to say, lack of funds means these will never be bought, but the bureaucracy has done its job. Meanwhile the old paraffin stoves continue their arson campaign, and workers who are paid eleven roubles a month, and end up with minus six roubles fifty kopecks, are charged eighteen roubles a log.

Kytlym's workers have made inspiring sacrifices to rescue the economy, and have achieved miracles. They've got the old excavators going, and have brought in two new ones. Despite the shorter working day, they've more than doubled the kilowatts at the power-station, from 1,400 to 2,900, and platinum output has been restored to the high levels achieved by the old company between 1913 and 1914. More importantly, platinum mining is developing into a proper industry. Instead of the old speculation, work is now carried out in an atmosphere of calm collective ownership, with clean hands. Platinum is no longer stolen in Kytlym, and that's that. Its crazy allure is still in people's blood, with its sinful smell and dangerous aftertaste. But its flesh was killed five years ago, when the communist Didkovsky was elected chair of the soviet.

The mechanic Shlyakhtin, secretary of Kytlym's Party cell, described how many workers unfamiliar with the Party programme had been against him, and how the company's shareholders put pressure on them, terrified that the Bolsheviks would nationalise the mines. 'But we saw how things were going, and we put out word that everyone should vote for the Bolsheviks, and Didkovsky was elected. We had to take over the machines, and we needed him!'

Kytlym has been healthy since then, thanks to Comrades Shlyakhtin, Didkovsky and others. Director of the mines is Comrade Gavrilov, a man of exceptional integrity, a former sailor and political prisoner, sentenced to hard labour in Kytlym, who stayed on to work here after the Revolution and joined the partisans. Head of the militia is former partisan and Red Guard Comrade Solovyov.

Yet Kytlym's miners still live in poverty, sitting on this Soviet platinum that belongs to everyone and no one. And along with the Party's heightened sense of discipline and responsibility, is its shocking neglect of workers' most basic needs, and a reluctance to spend just the small sums needed to give them the new life they can and must have. Nor is this to single out Kytlym alone for blame. Workers are housed no better at the splendid Nadezhdinsky Metallurgical and Engineering Plant, pride of the Northern Urals.

In the light of the sleepless nights, the marshes around Kytlym gleam with uncountable riches. But we can't be sure that every rouble sunk into the bog will produce a hundred, or risk hauling diggers up to the small pockets high in the mountains, which may not cover their costs. We don't have a spare three hundred thousand to borrow from the earth at exorbitant interest rates, under the security of the mountains of pure platinum, the rivers of metal pouring into the valley. And where we can't afford to put new diggers, the claims are being leased to private speculators, mainly wealthy young peasants, our new 'mining Nepmen'.

There are some twenty of them in the 'Wild West' around Kytlym, and the thefts have spread to Kosva, Konjak and Sosnovka, high in the mountains. The skulls of the old mountains are tangled in rocks and forests which soften their brains, and the horses stumble along, lowering their heads to sniff the boulders under their hoofs. Only in late June, when the corncrakes shriek and the grouse sit warming their eggs, do these parts of the *taiga* open up to people. Then Comrade Solovyov slings a rifle on his back, takes his revolver and his silver whistle for luring game, and makes a tour of inspection of the prospectors' nests.

Girls with cheerful knowing eyes greet us in the swamps outside Kosva, and take us to meet the mine's elderly controller, former bailiff to the industrialist Prince Abamelek-Lazarev, a thief who has never been caught, with the severe saintly face of an icon. He treats us to fish soup, and agrees to show us the mine, but he has no horse. 'It's only two miles, you can go on foot', Solovyov tells him, mounting his Siberian stallion. And although we cover the distance at a brisk trot, the old man reaches the 'American' mine just minutes after we do, wiping a few drops of icon-lamp oil from his face, and the dust of a silent reproach from his eyes.

Clutching his revolver and rifle, Solovyov tethers his horse loosely, so he can make a quick getaway, then goes to inspect the camp.

The road from the power-station is lined with platinum, but the prospectors lack the money for new excavations. The foreman has told them they should look for new spots and wash the samples. But they grudge spending a kopeck more than necessary on the unknown, and have ordered the digging to continue in the exhausted pits. The crews work slowly, picking at the mud like bears at a raspberry bush, hoping to rake in a new pocket without having to move. In the hunt for these invisible riches, everything is ruled by an animal instinct. The prospectors cluster round the foreman, needing his secret knowledge, but hating his thieving restlessness, with the hatred the native peasant feels for the gypsy.

Today's finds are higher than usual, almost double those of yesterday. But the controller claims it's a weak strip, which produces only so many grams of platinum per ten square metres. Ten metres or five? Solovyov asks him, without raising his voice. The young men sprawled round the fire digesting their lunch, staring woodenly at the controller's scales, sit up and turn their greedy eyes on him. 'And by the way you're getting a new controller, a communist', he tells them.

Just then a man in a Red Army greatcoat appears through the trees. His face under his sweaty forage cap is sunburnt and square-jawed, and he carries a briefcase and a revolver. The prospectors, who live like animals, with no interests but those contained in the tortoiseshell cases of their pocket scales, roll on their sides and stare at him, wondering how much of a threat he poses.

The workers here don't welcome outsiders, and they don't look up from the mud. The older ones dig with their sons and their sons' wives, whole families of peasants harnessed all day to the prospectors' heavy barrows, stopping only when darkness falls. It's heavy, dogged, repetitive work, unrelieved by songs or conversation. Women with closed greedy faces tear at the mud like the udders of a sick cow. The men hack frenziedly at the rocks, hating the mercenary earth which gives itself to everyone but yields nothing for days on end. The older single workers are like alchemists, dried by the sun, light as feathers from their constantly changing fortunes. They sit smoking at the edge of the pit, dangling their legs over the sides, urging on their young apprentices. 'Dig lower, Mityukha! There, under the water!' And driven on by youthful greed, Mityukha hacks metre after metre, strains sieveful after sieveful, and finds nothing. Streaming with sweat, he hurls himself at the mud with new fervour, and the old men laugh at all the fuss. Even great luck has left them with nothing. It's a long time since they stopped gambling in earnest and totting up their wretched debts.

God deceives no one more than he deceives the true believer, and as often as not, this isn't a Russian but an Udmurt. For years he chases the platinum, patiently enduring failure after failure, convinced that one day his luck will change and take pity on him. And over the years he comes to accept his losses, and happily amasses more, each new setback increasing the dizzying sum of his debts, bringing closer the miracle of miracles when his gamble will finally pay off. Until in his old age, after decades of this fruitless exhausting search, he is completely alone, and he drives away uninvited companions. What does he need them for? He doesn't want to share an iota of his misfortunes, which promise at any moment to deliver his dreamt-for happiness.

Then one hot summer day, when the air is filled with sweet birdsong, and the marshes steam under their carpet of green, his eyes are too swollen by mosquito bites to see the treasure in the mud. And as he stands weeping before the controller on his swollen rheumatic legs, asking to be sent to the hospital, he is still convinced his happiness lies at the bottom of the pit he has to abandon, where the frogs croak in the mud, lazily bursting the bubbles with their legs.

Kosva's most successful prospector is the peasant Pichugin. He looks like a horse thief, with his sharp wolf's ears and cunning eyes, smiling craftily at Comrade Solovyov from a safe distance as he grills him, sniffing round his questions and taking them in another direction. When Solovyov briefly leaves the room, he draws back his lips and bares his teeth, winking at me with the silent laugh of an old hunter. 'You know how much I've got? Twenty pounds! He'd better not find out, or I'm in trouble!'

Generally when a prospector grows rich, he builds himself a comfortable brick house with a green roof. Pichugin's family still lives in their old tin shack, eating sour bread and cabbage soup, and he's waging a fierce battle with his daughter's fiancé over her dowry.

'Why do you still live in poverty Pichugin? Don't you like being rich?' I ask him.

'This way I'll put enough aside for my sons and grandsons', he says, and speaks lovingly of his family, who from generation to generation will live on their wretched embezzled inheritance, like bedbugs on a wall.

'Did you know Pichugin has twenty pounds of platinum?' I say to Solovyov when he gets back.

'What are you talking about girl? God is my witness, I said nothing of the sort!' he says, and lifting his shining eyes to the portrait of Lenin in the corner, where the icons used to be, he removes his cap and crosses himself.

CHAPTER 6

Kyzyl. Black and White Coal

The woods lie open like a book, with the blue bookmark of the river Kosva running between them. Beyond its steep shores, veiled in a haze of blue smoke, lie coal and ore, ore and coal.[1] Industry is still barely developed here. So far only a tiny fraction of the deposits have been extracted from the vast Egorshinsk mines, or from the shafts at Kyzyl, Gubakha and Chelyabinsk, and there can be no thought of developing them yet. In twenty years' time, Kyzyl's Bear Hills will be a great industrial centre. Now it's still the *taiga*, where people pick raspberries, and cut down the majestic pine trees to build homes.

The largest of the working coalmines are at Kyzyl, and to be sure this is a massive operation, consisting of three shafts at the centre, including the one at Polovnika, and three more at Gubakha, some ten miles south of the town. The underground workings cover dozens of miles, and yield many million tons of coal each year. Kyzyl is an entire kingdom under the earth, with its own capital, 'Lenin', the main pit, whose broad sloping passages drop to tunnels 120 feet deep, with their low ceilings and narrow difficult seams, where miners work on their knees, bent double, ingeniously hacking the coal up from the ground.

Buried in the shafts of Kyzyl's dark subterranean *taiga* are its highways and country tracks, its centres and outskirts like Polovnika, its wagons like electric trams, with their bells like real tram bells, pulled by shortsighted pit ponies stumbling through the eternal night; its squares surrounded by glistening ten-foot walls of fuel, regular as granite embankments, gripping the shores of this sea of coal.

Underground Kyzyl has its own time, unlike that on earth. There are no seasons, no night or day, just labour, broken into three eight-hour shifts, each sending tons of coal to the surface. On the earth it's summer, and the dew dries in the morning sun. Under the earth the dew never dries. The ladders to the bottom are wet and icy, and the rails sting the flesh. And the lower the tunnels, the wetter they are. The silence is broken at first by a few drips of water from the walls, which swell to a soft babble, then to the noisy chatter of a passing stream, and finally to a deep reverberating splash at the bottom of the shaft.

Underground Kyzyl has its own time, its own humidity and temperature. Heat and humidity coexist happily here, and support each other in the dark-

---

1   White coal, the fuel used for smelting iron, made from drying chopped wood over a fire.

ness. In the mud and dead ends of the deepest wettest faces, with their broken ladders leading up to the light, miners are heated from some invisible source that soaks them in sweat, and makes the flames of their lamps flicker in the acrid air.

The air in these pits is unlike the air anywhere else. However lost a miner is, if he stops and listens in the darkness, he can always hear through the dripping water the hiss of the ventilation pipes. If his lamp goes out, his hands can always reach for the long perforated cast-iron tubes through which the air is pumped under the ground. They're everywhere. When he goes into battle with the glowing walls, plunging his creaking mechanical crowbar into the coal, hacking at the seams with the iron claws of his drill; when he lifts his lamp at the ladder to count how many more steps he must climb, drenched in sweat, fighting for breath, his chest heaving in its swollen rib cage – the life-giving pipes are his constant companions.

The coal-fired compressor pumping the air in at one end and out the other is housed in quiet clean quarters in the storey above. Everything is done to make this precious machine comfortable. The room is flooded with light, the ceiling is high, the coals lie securely behind high concrete walls to stop them escaping. For miles the wet gloom below is ventilated by this invisible machine, and the earth pressing down on the pipes hears through its eternal sleep the air bubbling from its door.

Yet for many years Kyzyl's overloaded power-station barely had the energy to support the mines' lungs, and there were increasingly frequent power failures. True, they were repaired quickly, after many hours of desperate work. But every day the lower faces were choking on thick green fumes. There's something malignant about their bitter sweet vanilla smell, which grips the throat and overwhelms miners with dizziness, making their lamps flicker and go out. And then there was another hitch at the power-station, and at the Volodarsky Mine, where miners worked without lifting their heads, like Christmas trees bending their tops against the ceilings, there was no ventilation. The lamps ran anxiously from gallery to gallery. There was no power! Workers hurled all their weight at their drills, which fell weakly from the coal. The blood pounded in the head, and a hot sluggishness filled the pit. The whole mountain was choking. Angry miners lay on the coals, smoking and gasping for breath. Others tapped the walls, checking the exits. The older ones crawled a few feet higher, covering their eyes with their hands to protect them from the fumes. The young ones, irritable from lack of oxygen, stripped off their shirts and cooled their chests in the sulphurous water dripping from the walls, which at first puckers the skin as if it has sucked a lemon, then turns it cracked and blistered.

The first asthma attacks[2] in the Kyzyl mines were recorded during the Civil War. But people were too hungry then to notice them so much – all that mattered was staying alive, and keeping the mines alive. Then after the fighting ended, when everyone from hauliers to directors joined the battle to raise production; when cheap coke from the Kuznetsk Basin was suddenly flooding the market, and was being transported thousands of miles by train across the country, and Kyzyl had to knock twelve kopecks off the price of a ton if it was to survive – then any holdup was a catastrophe. Time was money, and its value increased by the minute. But miners were still overcome with choking and vomiting, which made them throw down their shovels and crawl to the exits so as not to pass out. Air, air, air!

Then the day finally came when Polovnika seemed to be dying. Engineers checked the pulses of the sick machines with watches, predicting the hour of their death. Managers hung on telephones. Messengers galloped off on horses. For days the electricians didn't leave the mine as they carried out urgent repairs. The small generator was still working, but increasingly erratically. Then at the moment of the greatest danger, when the suffocating vapours had reached the lowest pits, a sudden surge of power, no one knew from where, shot through Polovnika's flabby cables and brought them back to life.

Two years ago, in the midst of typhus and hunger, the new hydroelectric power-station, *Kyzylstroi*, was built in the Bear Hills, ten miles from the town, where the river Kosva falls headlong from the mountains. This new Regional State Power Station, or GRES, was intended primarily to power the mines' decrepit machines, to provide Polovnika and Gubakha with the extra six hundred watts they needed, and increase the six thousand watts the Trust used in total. It was also built to allow the Republic to supply the entire region, for hundreds of miles, with cheap energy. *Kyzylstroi* won't just keep down the price of the extra half million tons of coal the mines' director Comrade Sazhin estimates they'll produce this year. It will lead to the development of a vast new industrial complex here in the near future, with dozens of new highly mechanised cheaply run mines and factories.

To the left of *Kyzylstroi*, its glass roof looks out over the bristling forests of the mountains, through which a wide clearing has been cut for the new road to Kyzyl. To the right stretch the rows of workers' barracks, where single people and families live piled on top of each other, and eat, sleep and choke in filth without a moment's peace – living in other words like the proletariat

---

2   'Miners' asthma' and 'black spit', as lung cancer, pneumoconiosis and silicosis were known then, caused by the inhalation of coal dust, were also commonly mistaken for the symptoms of tuberculosis.

throughout the Urals, if not the whole of industrial Russia, as they work with superhuman endurance to drag Soviet industry out of poverty.

In a few years, the forests will all have disappeared. Perhaps a new railway station will be built to replace these slums, or a new factory in the place of the red roofs of the wretched little field hospital, like wild strawberries in the grass, on whose bunks over three hundred workers died in the construction of *Kyzyl-stroi*, which a decade from now will have given birth to new factories. But what if workers were rewarded for the three hundred who died with a new Palace of Labour, where they could take a break from work, enjoy some culture and entertainment, and do some studying? Or are they too crazy with pride to care, running around their magnificent new power-station, gazing from its vast windows at the hacked down *taiga*?

Work on the outside of the building isn't finished yet, and the square is piled with rubbish, which is dragged off in barrows by gangs of emaciated Chinese labourers, staggering from hunger. The foundation piles poking from the river are a reminder of the most difficult part of the work, when a seven-hundred-foot concrete channel was dug to divert the water to *Kyzylstroi*. Constructed forty feet below the river, against the pressure of the mountain waters, it was built on the pay and brutal rations of 1922, virtually without machines or protective clothing, and in Kyzyl's harsh climate and living conditions, in which despite the vast improvements in workers' lives, ninety percent of babies are still born with symptoms of tuberculosis.

Work on the inside of the building is already completed. At its heart are the four new boilers – the American Babcock-Wilcox marine type water-tube model. At present these power only half the palace, and their huge bright hall has been built to accommodate the two new ones that will soon be arriving to join them. Beside the boilers are the two turbogenerators, each carrying eight thousand volts, resting on their concrete plinths like lions, caged in by a mass of tubes and pipes. Every machine has its own voice and rhythm, but there is nothing like the steady throb of these generators, filling the building with power. All they need are foundations strong enough to support their massive weight and their barely audible vibrations, which can shatter rocks. As soon as the plasterers finished the floors, they crossed the threshold, threw off their heavy winter coats, and set to work against the huge windows exposed to the sky.

Despite the coal fumes and the soft rain of ashes at the boilers' feet, the air is fresh and easy to breathe, and the whole of this two-storey building, from its dusty cement floors to its glass roof, rustles like a forest, throbbing under the weight of the new machines. Armies of workers carry in heavy machine parts, hauliers drag in wagons loaded with hundred-pound loads of fuel for the boilers, and the stokers grumblingly shovel up the trails of soot the dirty day-labourers scatter over the floors. Before long the wagons will have disappeared; new iron pipes are being built through which the coal will be moved mechanically to the boilers.

A small temporary forge thunders from the upper floor. Carpenters sing on platforms, surrounded by saws, lathes, timber and damp plaster, and a handsome electrician in his high Urals boots climbs up a ladder to inspect the water tanks in the roof, from which the full magnificence of *Kyzylstroi* can be seen.

Yet for the peasants working at *Kyzylstroi*, the triumph is mixed with a bitter sadness for their fields and villages. 'Two years I've worked here, it was easier at home', a bricklayer from a village near Kazan complains quietly as he finishes off a ledge. 'Old Yakimov from our village helped lay the foundations and finish the floor, then he dropped dead of a chill. People born on the land should return to the land. Who'll make the bread if we're all proletarians?'

Most of *Kyzylstroi*'s workers aren't peasants but proletarians – builders, plumbers, mechanics and electricians. The bricklayer Comrade Shevrin fought with the Red Cavalry in Ukraine and in the assault on Perekop, then he helped dig the river channel to the building; he's no use to the army now, his legs are too swollen with rheumatism. Comrade Anyapov fought at Polotsk, then helped build the ceiling of the furnace room, lay the floors and reinforce the foundations. Both these old soldiers, in their cotton aprons covered in mineral dust, are now preparing the floor for the sixteen thousand extra volts *Kyzylstroi* will be taking on in two years' time.

And now for *Kyzylstroi*'s holy of holies, the main control-room, with its panels connected to locked rooms containing its superchargers, or *Umformers*. How else is an ignorant journalist to describe these secret places outsiders are forbidden to enter, with their forests of cables carrying power and light? Warm breezes of energy waft from the panels, and only the most highly qualified technicians work here, deciphering their switches and flickering arrows, all bending in the same direction, like sunflowers. The silent figures hunch over the dials, their faces bathed in the blue light, logging every movement of the volts and amps with their sensitive mathematician's hands. Looking at them, you would never guess that most are old soldiers of the Revolution, who carried a rifle for two years. The engineer in charge of the main switchboard, Comrade Orekhov, a communist since 1918, fought with the Fifth Army in the Urals, from Glazov to Lake Baikal. The mechanic Pshennikov fought to drive the Whites from Ufa, then in two desperate years, with hundreds of others, fought to get *Kyzylstroi* going.

Like them, *Kyzylstroi*'s director must possess a rare combination of qualities – communist ethics, and the expertise of an outstanding technician. This is Comrade Tiszevski, one of Poland's most brilliant engineers, a longstanding member of its party central committee, who has taken his place with them in the control-room, whose blessed peace will soon be broken by the extra six thousand volts waiting to course through its cables.

Among the piles of rubbish being burnt outside *Kyzylstroi* is a small wooden cabin, which used to be towed from place to place wherever it was needed. This is the old office of the Factory Committee. Many not only worked in this portable shell, but slept there too, not wanting to leave the building work for a second. There is no space here to do justice to all these comrades and their work – exceptionally hard work, begun in 1922 and finished two years later, not only phenomenally quickly, but to an exceptionally high standard. One of those who has sacrificed his health to *GRES*, whose two years on the labour front have left an invalid, is Polygalov, Chair of the Factory Committee.

Typically, Comrade Polygalov never mentions his exhaustion or his shattered nerves, but his record speaks for itself. A Party member and Red Guard since 1917, he fought with Blyukher's partisan army in the Urals, then as Assistant Military Commissar of the 23rd Regiment. In 1921, he was appointed chief Military Commissar in the Anti Banditry Campaign. A year later he arrived at *Kyzylstroi*, and either he will spend 1925 recovering in a sanatorium, or he will die.

CHAPTER 7

Underground People

There is a limit beyond which the last thread connecting life on the surface to the underground breaks. In Kyzyl's Pit 46, miners have to crawl on their stomachs, clutching at the rows of posts supporting the timber roof. There is no exit, no chink of light above their heads, just streams of rubble and dust, and an overpowering muggy heat. The ceilings bear down on them, and between them and the slippery walls, there is barely room for the lamps strapped to their chests.

The hunted coal runs away, upwards, sideways, in all directions, before finally collapsing in a hot black heap, open to their axes, which circle it like kites over the carcass of a horse. The team's leader is Mikhail Matveich, his stern face covered in youthful fluff, known for getting on with the Tatars, who all want to work with him. Unstrapping his lamp from his buttonhole, he hooks it with a dirty fingernail next to a row of others, hanging from a beam like glowing bats. No one smokes or talks. There are no faces, just eyes staring into the darkness, the narrow strip of a forehead, the gleam of a mouth.

Before arriving here the men were working in the spacious Lenin Pit, and they still haven't got used to the cramped collapsing tunnels and the lack of air. But although output has fallen drastically, they don't blame this on their working conditions. Anyone who has spent an hour in this hell knows that fulfilling the quota here is incomparably more difficult than elsewhere, if not impossible. Yet as long as they feel the 'blame' lies with them, and that their reduced output has less to do with their working conditions than with their inability to adjust their breathing and the movements of their hands, none of them says anything. This is miners' etiquette. The body will soon adjust to the new demands made of it, which play around the edges of slave labour, and only then will they complain.

Further ahead, a miner turns from the wall. One side of his face is white, the other completely black, as if it had been growing into the coal and broken away. The flame of his lamp is blue under its mantle, almost extinguished by the vapours from the walls.

Another, bent double, raises his axe and plunges it angrily into a seam. His lamp flares up, licking the ceiling with its smoking tongue. 'I joined the Bolsheviks in 1918 and volunteered for the front, then in 1919 I went home and left the Party', he says, and explains how this came about, when he loaded his cart with potatoes instead of 'comesticles', and was arrested by the 'meddling Party brat' brought in to run his village cooperative, who he curses loudly and at length.

The lit-up patches of tunnel resemble cages, in which the miners are buried alive with their axes. And working at the far end, in Pit 25, dripping wet and pitch black, is the remarkable Comrade Derevnin.

He is still quite young, just thirty-four, with cunning white teeth gleaming through his coal mask, and he is an underground fanatic, who hates sunlight and fresh air. Nothing would induce him to abandon the darkness of the shafts for the shadows of a summer morning, creeping over the soft green earth. The Revolution called him up to the surface, and the Reds and the Whites argued for the right to put him under arms, and he fought on one side then on the other, and found them both equally alien. Riding the trains, out on patrol, lying in hospital, at his political education classes – run first by his communist teacher, then by a dashing speechmaker from the Whites' propaganda unit – he would dream of the mines. If only all the fuss and bother would go underground. The wind and fresh air made him nervous, and he longed for the cramped safety of the underground. Who needed the wide open spaces, the empty fields, the storms and dangers and bullets? When it's deep winter outside, and workers in their thin greatcoats grip their rifles in their frozen hands, the coal faces are eternally warm. Even in the Epiphany frosts, the air is as hot and dry as at harvest time, and day after day Comrade Derevnin throws off his soaking shirt and reaps the black harvest.

Needless to say, he wasn't much of a soldier. 'I had a hell of a time up there, I nearly died', he says. Perpetually mobilised and on the run, he finally found refuge in Kyzyl's welcoming shafts. Up above he was timid. Down below he is a fearless fighter, persistent and indefatigable. Up above he was short-sighted. Here he is a sharp-eyed hunter, who hasn't once dropped his axe. Leading his storm column of miners, he feels himself blessed and protected, and he has a deep distrust of outsiders. He lives in fear that they will track him down and drag him back to the light, and he lurks in the coal shadows with the watchful look of an eternal deserter. 'You're safe down here. You can see what's over your head and avoid it', he says.

At the Volodarsky Mine, below the smooth level gallery at the entrance, which drops imperceptibly to seven hundred feet; below the silent underground cell of the explosives room, where the Chinese hermit with his fur cap pulled over his ears weaves sandals from damp strips of birch bark, bending his head from time to time to check his dynamite; below damp wooden tunnels whose ceilings are flecked with foam, as if after a great flood; below all these is Pit 61, a dwarf pit, with stubborn, narrow, agate-hard seams, locked in a cavity of granite, where miners work on their knees. And here the true masters of Kyzyl are found.

They're drilling a long narrow seam just above the floor. Their lamps glimmer through clouds of wet soot, and their machines work with a steady tearing pulse that bursts the eardrums, like a steam engine crashing into a wall with its motor running. Comrade Ivan Egorych Motorgin, in his buttoned-up sleeveless jacket, kneels over his drill, guiding its metal arm into the holes in the seam. He is no longer young, in his fifties, with sagging shoulders and blackened fingers poking through his torn gloves. His beard is caked with wet coal, and the soles of his bast shoes are soaked and filthy, and his pale ribs poke through the holes in his shirt, like the rungs of a ladder worn down by generations of miners, bumping their exhausted heads on the sides as they go up to the surface. 'Twice the air pipes came away in my hands', he says, but that is the limit of his complaints.

A weak light shines on the shovels of the two hauliers struggling to clear the pile of coal he has left for them. And with a look of deep shame, he explains how he was expelled from the Party, breaking off occasionally to check on their work. 'The Party, well we all want to be in it don't we?' he says. 'I went to night school and passed my School Certificate, and worked hard for it. But I'm getting on. I get home from work and I'm too tired to move. Then one weekend I was coughing soot and couldn't work'.

In other words, the old man had broken Party discipline and missed a compulsory meeting or Saturday labour day through illness, and his membership had automatically lapsed. It was a mistake of course, and will soon be put right. Older workers like Ivan Egorych aren't meant to be penalised for such things, and there are always extenuating circumstances for miners. Those on the surface, the communists living on the happy earth, have little understanding of the infinite exhaustion of life underground. At the end of their shifts, miners resemble the dying flames of their lamps, which they blow out as they climb up.

The hauliers sit astride the wooden chutes, gripping the sides with their wrists, pushing up the heavy rocks of coal with their legs and backsides, their 'protective clothing' for this work consisting of strips of sheepskin sewn onto the backs of their jackets, and they run home in them, blinded by the sun, like exhausted animals chased from their burrows. It's hard to talk of 'Party discipline' in these conditions!

One of the simplest most effective ways to increase productivity has been to draft in new reserves of young energy to support the older generation. Most of these new miners are drawn from the command staff of the Red Army, and they're assisted by thousands of hauliers turned miners. You often see a young haulier desperate to move up in the world and become a miner, who after gaining himself a few extra minutes by unloading his cart at fantastic speed, throws himself at the nearest seam and hacks at it like a madman, testing the black bones with his puppy's teeth, while his weary horse drops its head to its knees and tries to sleep.

There are almost none of the old miners left now, and the fewer there are, the more valued they are. These elders of the mine follow no timetable. Even reducing their working day from ten hours to eight, and from eight to six, which has immeasurably improved the life of every living soul at Kyzyl, is a matter of indifference to them. They work to their own rhythm, and can stretch or compress time like elastic. They can fit eight hours' work into six, and produce six hours' worth of coal in four. They are artists and experts, whose work moves around the clock like a well-trained horse on tight reins.

The younger engineers don't take a step in their explorations without consulting these old men, who can sniff coal from a distance, sensing it like they sense winter in their bones. What would they do without Tatarinkov, foreman of the Lenin pit, who has propped up its drifts and faces for twenty-seven years? How would they manage without this old miner, who knows and respects every seam? A tall imposing figure in an old-fashioned peaked cap, his long thin body squeezed through a tight leather belt, like a napkin through a napkin-ring, Comrade Tatarinkov has three deep vertical furrows on his high-domed forehead, and his eyes are as colourless as the miners' lamps extinguished in the daylight. If you looked under his skull, you would see the whole mine, depicted in the angular matchstick patterns of their maps.

These old men aren't keen on the Revolution or the Party. Ask 'which of you comrades are communists?', and they'll reply with choice curses. Why bother to recruit him? Tatarinkov grins. With his knowledge and expertise, is there anywhere on earth he is more valuable than down here?

Of all the laws and decrees of the Revolution, it seems only one has reached the Tatarinkovs of the mine, making the miners its sole legal owners, and however much they grumbled and tried to avoid politics, this transfer of ownership was passed. And now these new owners with full rights must initiate the ignorant young into their fine old trade, hovering anxiously over their successors, as they train the next generation for their new role. 'What will happen when we old ones go? Who'll teach them then?' Tatarinkov says.

The newly qualified young miners don't think like this, or care who does the work after them. Which is why the lower in the pit hierarchy workers are, the greater the importance of political education. An engineer or head of a rescue team may be non-Party, but a brave, resourceful, highly qualified worker. But with the new young mining teams, the importance of Party membership can't be overestimated. When a pit has a communist foreman, he'll build up a layer of young workers around the older ones who are both technically and politically qualified. And the old miners, who form a separate caste, cut off from the outside world, will pass on their knowledge to them, and take to the grave their contempt for life on the surface. Then the young will pick up their axes and carry on the work they started on a new drift, and there will be a different spirit in the mines, ruled by living people.

At the Volodarsky pit, the nature of the seams makes working conditions exceptionally difficult. There's nowhere to stand up, and the lower levels are filled with water and stifling heat. But politics are less cursed here than at the comparatively easier Lenin pit. Workers at the Lenin are exhausted too, but their exhaustion here has a more complex, qualified character, if one can put it that way.

Working at the end of one of the Volodarsky's tunnels, through a silent *taiga* of coal, connected to the drift above by a low winding gallery, is the Tatar Comrade Mindulaev. He is as dark as if the gloom had closed door after door behind him, and never in my life have I met anyone blacker or more exhausted, or with a more joyful face. Woken by the Revolution, he joined the Party in 1919, and was released to the surface to fight with the Red Army. He loved his new freedom, became addicted to the sun and wine, and married a woman from the pale earth-dwelling race. But his party and professional duties called him back to the mine, where despite working to the limits of his strength, from seven in the morning until six at night, he earns a pittance. Yet every word of Comrade Mindulaev's is measured, he stamps out every irritable remark like a cigarette end to avoid a fire. And this man greedy for the joys of life, good-natured and long-suffering, is passionate about his work, driven by the iron discipline and self-sacrifice that made him abandon the sun for his airless cell.

If the mines are to throw their extra half-million ton of coal onto the market, and reduce the price by twelve kopecks a ton, and if Kyzyl's Party organisation is to grow stronger in the process, it will be thanks entirely to those like Comrade Mindulaev, who have kept their faith in communism, despite the exhaustion and suffering and the shortcomings of the transitional period. 'We've been waiting since 1919 for things to improve, and I hope to god they do', he says, attacking his drill with his powerful hands, raising a black plume of coaldust like a mad horsetail.

The broad face of Comrade Suslov, the senior foreman, still has some of the colour left from his years at the front. In the daylight, despite his powerful physique, his miner's pallor makes him look like a soldier recovering from typhus. Underground, in the light of his lamp, he looks like a partisan, as broadshouldered as the beams propping up the ceiling. Not only has he a vast knowledge of the technical aspects of each coalface, he knows each worker by name. Working at these faces, digging at the coal from every direction, are three hundred men, and he knows all of them. He knows their problems at work, how much dust is in the air they breathe, how much water is on the walls, how many feet the seams are above their heads, how many children they have at home, whether they have a goat or a cow, and the thoughts that go through their heads, light or heavy, during their shifts.

For a communist like Suslov, the Lenin Enrolment is like a call to arms to deal with a fire or flood. Every worker in Russia, of every age and nationality, has been called to join the Party, and Suslov must remember all those who have heard the call, and those who have stayed below. There are no more insulting words for a miner than 'he stayed below', and only the foreman can discover if this is due to demoralisation or some personal misfortune. Suslov knows how far it is to the light, how long it takes through the exhaustion and poverty to hear the quiet voice of life calling them up. And as a result of all his work, there are now a hundred and fifty communists at the Volodarsky.

Comrade Malyshev, in Pit 61, also fought to win the mine for the Bolsheviks. In 1918 he joined the Red Army as a machine gunner, and for the next three years he fought from Vyatka to Irkutsk, and in the battles for Sivash. He was expelled from the Party because of what he calls 'White Guard tricks' in the town of Kansk, near Krasnoyarsk – which the Whites flooded with vodka, 'to undermine the proletariat'. Everyone knows that people are completely different under the influence of drink, and Comrade Malyshev was one of its victims.

He returned to the mine, but he hasn't reapplied to join the Party – 'and if you saw the room where I live, you'd know why'.

So what are these rooms like, which stop people joining the Party? Kyzyl's Industrial Trust inherited the workers' barracks from the old owners, the famous Abamelek-Lazarev princes, whose architect was blessed with a powerful sense of fantasy. In the middle of each block, a few feet from the entrances, he artistically laid rows of latrines, filling the air with their stink. And at the far end he put the old jail, still known as the 'clink', from which convicts used to be led to the mine in shackles.

After 1914, German prisoners of war were drafted into the mine, but they proved uncooperative, preferring to put their arms under trains than submit to this slave labour. So after the revolt of the white slaves, Kyzyl's pits were flooded with yellow ones, and three thousand Chinese were moved into the barracks. These children of the sun adapted poorly to their new living conditions. As soon as one shift left for work, their warm bunks would be occupied by the next one, and hundreds were cut down by syphilis and tuberculosis.

The Revolution relieved their lordships of any further responsibility for their workers. But the curse of the old slavemasters still weighs heavy on Soviet Kyzyl. Thousands of families still live in these rotting dwellings. Hundreds of rooms without a stick of furniture – not a chair or table, wash-basin or shelf, not a single book. Only the older workers have their own quarters, tiny huts with low ceilings where they snatch a few hours' sleep after work, wrapped in blankets on the floor.

For workers' families, a cow is a real blessing. But there's no room in these huts even for a small bird. In other words, they live in scandalous poverty, which can only partly and with difficulty be explained by the economic crisis and our lack of resources. If a worker stagnating in these nine-foot cages manages to lift his head, bent by the ceilings of the mine, and say in the voice of someone who has been stranded on a desert island for years that he wants to join the Party – 'all the young ones are joining, you can't stay behind!' – it means the Revolution has pulled a truly great human being from the mud.

The mood is less steady in the Lenin pit, possibly due to the somewhat random nature of its workforce. But close to the bottom, below a wide dripping tunnel from which a new connecting corridor is being dug to the gallery above, is the extraordinary Pit 3. The whole of this underground landscape will soon be mechanised, and the hauliers and horses replaced by electricity. But the pit now is as cold as ice, dripping with sulphurous water, where workers shuffle through the rusty puddles in their soaked bast shoes, clutching their heads: working at these depths causes terrible neuralgia in the face and teeth.

The foreman here is Comrade Osipov. A communist since 1905, he worked underground in the mine and in the revolutionary underground, and was sacked in 1907 for attending an illegal Party conference. During the Civil War, he was commander of a special battalion fighting the Whites, while simultaneously working to rebuild the economy they'd destroyed. After the fighting ended, at the height of the fuel crisis, he was sent back to the mine to boost production, while continuing to work in the town for the local soviet. In the mine, he cleared the flooded pits, timbered the walls, and mobilised miners to the Party. In town, he battled against typhus, hunger and illiteracy, and organised teams to repair the burnt-down railway bridge in fifty-two days of voluntary Saturday work.

But the mine was jealous of the soviet, and demanded his exclusive attention, and forced to choose between them, he again chose the underground, this time the labour underground. Shovelling coal is an intolerable burden on his fifty-three-year-old back, but he insists it wasn't the mine that destroyed his health, it was his work for the soviet.

Another communist in Pit 3 who chose the mine over life on the surface is Comrade Yuferov. He earns just thirty roubles a month, and his family shares their small hut with four single workers. 'We've peace now, but life's no easier', he says. When asked about the thought processes that led him to join the Party in the Lenin Enrolment, Comrade Yuferov's reply makes the pit arch its dark brows, and all the pegs on which a worker's life is measured – the wet shoes, wretched housing and low pay – pale into insignificance. 'It was to show the foreign capitalists we counted for something', he says, throwing off his fur cap to cool his face, and his high Asian cheekbones gleam like a thought rubbed in butter.

CHAPTER 8

The Nadezhdinsky Plant. A Story of Two Workshops

The Blast Furnace

Coal is stupider than metal, and goes uncomplainingly to the oven. When the wagons at the front are held up, the ones behind shove it on, impatient to be moving. Haulier Esin and his helper grasp a sack in their clamps, and it swings happily over the mouth of the furnace, oblivious to its fate, before dropping into the flames, roaring and struggling to grab the sides. Esin shovels up some scattered coals and throws them in the fire, while his helper leans against the next wagon to catch his breath. Then they swing another sack over, beating the coal against the suspended blaze-rods, until it falls unconscious from their hands and continues on its airy way.

Metal is afraid of light and people, and is harder to lure into the noisy tower. It hasn't forgotten the blows of the axe that took it prisoner, or the stone jaws of the grinder grinding off its dust, and it's left to rest for a while under an awning, on boards that have taken on the crimson colour of the ore. Then gently, so as not to frighten it, it's laid in the wagons that take it to the loading-bay, where it's weighed on scales under the floor. After this, still suspecting nothing, it's carried in a special lift at the base of the furnace to the platform at the top.

Through its mesh, the entire factory can be seen – the skyscrapers of the main buildings, the mountains of scrap-iron, the cranes and smokestacks and narrow-gauge railway tracks, the shriek and roar of machines in unknown workshops, raging like madmen trying to break down the walls. As the wagon approaches the thundering oven, it feels the treacherous heat beneath it and breathes in the icy rain of coaldust, and tries to jump back. But Esin and his helper grab it on both sides and drag it on, like a ram by the horns, keeping its steel hoofs on the rails, as muddy as a country track. Then when they reach the furnace, they tip it slightly to one side, and a wall opens to become a door. This is the last trick played on the metal, and it crashes defeated into the fire.

Esin slams shut the heavy door, leaning all his weight on the levers that release the coals from their prison, while keeping a close eye on the fire-gauge, whose rods lie deep in the oven's stomach. The fire instantly swallows its 'galosh' (three wagons of coal, two of metal). The needle rises, the dial gulps, the furnace is full.

Little flames shoot through chinks at the top and whistle through the cracks, greedily licking the edges of the pipes, reaching for Esin's helper, who has moved too close as he urges on the blaze. At the heart of the fire, a charred lid screwed insecurely to the wall has come loose. What if it falls? The furnace is very old, with holes that make traps for the slag porridge. Several times in the past fifteen years, it has had uncontrollable fits of vomiting, pouring in burning streams over the water, rocks and metal the workers threw at it, before finally subsiding and disappearing back into the oven.

Esin and his helper are now pulling the next wagon from the lift. This dirty dangerous work, carried out in the open air, with its constant changes of temperature, from tropical heat to Siberian cold, is classified as unskilled, and both are on the fifth and lowest pay grade, of twenty-two roubles a month. To look at Comrade Esin, with his thick red beard and powerful fists and shoulders, you would call him the embodiment of human strength. But one side of his beard has been singed off by the fire, and the heat and cold have weakened his muscles in their battle to possess his body. He is still a fine worker, able in all sorts of clever, barely noticeable ways to shift the weight of his work onto the machines. But the sweat dripping from the collar of his thin overalls is as cold as the damp on the walls, and his pale face under its coal mask exudes exhaustion. When the ruddiness from the fire fades from these hauliers' faces, they have the blueish pallor of skimmed milk.

At the base of the furnace are its huge windpipes, driving in the hot breath and pushing out the waste gases from which the fire has extinguished everything living. They rush up, desperate to live again. But they have paid the price for their freedom, and have no oxygen left, only their heat, and even this must be surrendered. Their path to the light is through endlessly long brick-lined tunnels, which they heat with the warmth left from the flames. Only after completing this final task do they raise their smoky hands in defeat, and fly off to the sun.

Comrade Pelnik works at the pipes pushing the air into the oven's lungs. Weakened by heat and thirst, it flies through catacombs of blackened tubes thick with mineral dust. But before entering the white heart of the fire, it must be cleaned in special 'saucers' on the floor, where it quietly has its face washed while it drinks from the deep clear water.

Every so often Comrade Pelnik opens a small window in a pipe, and is almost knocked off his feet by the heat. Turning his face away, he pushes in a long metal fork and rakes the ashes and cinders, and is instantly boiled and gasping for breath, with a bitter taste in his mouth. He has served at his post for fifteen years, five of them for the Soviet Republic, and like Comrade Esin, he is on the fifth pay grade.

The Rolling-Shop

In many of the workshops, it's hard to tell the peasants from the born factory workers. All wear the same bast shoes instead of work boots, the same scorched greasy shirts. All have the same burnt hands and blackened faces, their eyes hidden behind thick blue goggles, or buried in folds of skin, like silver coins in the folds of a Tatar shawl. The Kazan Tatars are easiest to recognise, proudly carrying their sacks of coal on their backs like their best gowns, waiting for the iron to be cast as if waiting for prayers at the mosque.

The differences between peasants and workers are more marked in the foundries and rolling-shops. The peasant throws his iron into the fire slowly, raking the bars like fresh hay, raising his hammer like a flail as he threshes the iron rye, scattering grains of sparks. At the stamping machine, which stamps the ingots with the special die they need for the next stage of the process, the factory worker pushes them through quickly. The peasant grips them carefully in his tongs, like a blacksmith shoeing the hindleg of a horse, and his conscientious hands wait a few seconds before allowing them to be branded by the little monster, twitching like an angry horsetail as it hits the anvil.

For the born factory worker, his machine only has value in his hands. When the factory fell to Kolchak, the workers fled, so as to arm themselves against the thieves, and take back the instruments of its production. The peasants stay at their machines whoever is in power. They are tied to them as they're tied to their ploughs, and the fields bear crops regardless. For the worker, the Revolution means fighting the great battle for production. For the peasant, it means drought, crop failure, the hail beating the winter crops. If his cooperative store is run by a scoundrel whose potatoes cost more than at the market, he's afraid to speak up and complain. If his wages are pitiful, if the laws protecting his labour are regularly flouted, and he lacks even the most basic protective clothing, the poorly workerised peasant sees all this not as due to government necessity and the crisis of the transitional period, but as a divine punishment, a continuation of the old regime.

At one rolling-shop, a team consisting entirely of peasants from the same village takes the metal billets from the entrance, separating them first with their tongs and sprinkling them with ashes – an old Urals trick to stop them sticking, so they heat better. One peasant moves a sheet to the furnace for its first heating, then another throws it in the first rolling-machine, where it surrenders, crimson with rage, to a third, who hurls it crashing onto the metal floor. After this it's returned to the oven again, before it's moved to the next rolling-machine for its second rolling. As the melting dough falls between the clanking rollers, it jumps out and tries to break free, leaving behind golden scraps of its skin, and has to be pushed back again and again. Standing high above them is the peasant who turns the wheel that increases or reduces the torture, unable to leave his captain's bridge for a second to join his comrades drinking and cooling their faces at the water-tanks.

Workers in this workshop must endure not only the heat and fumes, but the noise – the shriek of the crimson skulls hitting the floor, the murderous roar of the rolling-machines. No voice can shout over these machines. The only sound audible through the din, as soft as the squeak of a mouse under a giant's feet, is the foreman's whistle, calling workers back from the bench where they've collapsed exhausted. No matter how soaked in sweat he is, or how numb his hands, a worker always hears this signal of labour discipline, this call to come and help.

The peasants in this workshop are all elderly. They escaped from neither the Reds nor the Whites, and they arrived here three years ago from the Budinsky factory in the south, after the old masters left. Under the Tsar they had their own little huts and plots of land, and they can't forget their abandoned village, where for generations they lived under the knout, but with their own apple tree, their goat and piglets and spotted calf with its babyish wet eyes. They were flogged, but they were fed. And now they stand at their machines, thrown out onto the proletarian street like old men thrown out by their families after losing at cards, and they yearn for their fields and ploughs, and the first green shoots pushing through the earth in spring.

They are fossilised peasants, without land, forced to work in the factory, but with their roots still deep in the earth, the Almighty Father, and the tiny allotments leased to them by the masters. They have given not a single worker to the Party in the Lenin Enrolment, they have silently boycotted it.

Comrade Legotkin joined the Red Army in 1917, and fought for two years at the front, before he was invalided out with typhus, and sent back to his machine. Pinned to his thin chest, as bent and crooked as a Chinese worker's knee, is his badge of the Red Banner, awarded for taking five White officers prisoner while he was out on patrol. He was in the Party too once, before it lost him in the typhus-infected trains, as it lost his memory, his residence permit and his name. And now his fellow peasants stand like a wall between him and the Party, which has no time to notice this man who has fallen overboard, no time to reach out and pull him up. 'So you got your medal. You fought for them and they promised you the earth, and you live worse than a dog!' they say, and only the wild blows of his hammer can silence their nagging, which is wearing him down.

Another former communist in this workshop the Party has lost is Comrade Furin. He too volunteered for the Red Army, and fought for three years at the front, but he left the Party after an old unhealed grievance which has distorted his whole being, like a scar on his face, and he hasn't rejoined in the Lenin Enrolment. Yet at every meeting, this honourable old peasant, a Bolshevik to his core, speaks and votes for the Party.

CHAPTER 9

Gorlovka. Eastern Ukraine

From the window of the train, it looks as if the entire Don Basin has been redesigned with pyramids, identical geometrically regular cones, breaking up the flat grey fields of sagebrush, towering over the factories and smoking chimneys of this industrial landscape, with little wagons scuttling up them like ants, tucking their iron legs under them, to feed the tops with tons of industrial waste.[1] The steppe below is crisscrossed with railway tracks, the great trade routes for the black caravans passing between the mines and factories.

The land here is rich in coal and iron, and the slag-heaps have built up over the centuries. One of the oldest and largest of them in the Donbas is at Gorlovka. The black cone of the pyramid lies on broad foundations of crimson rocks, like cooling lava, and the sulphur at its tip smoulders at night like a dormant volcano, with little flames wandering across its slopes like beggars searching for food. Despite its malevolent glow, the mountain isn't dangerous. But two years before the miners took over the mine, the pits lying half a mile beneath the surface were as unsafe as they had been a century ago. Locked deep in their bowels were muddy lakes of firedamp – methane – leaking through cracks in the seams and gathering in the coal pockets like rainwater in a bucket, triggering underground explosions.

In 1918, three hundred miners died in the worst disaster in Gorlovka's history. The hewer Comrade Senichkin told his foreman he refused to work at a face where his lamp had gone out twice, and the air smelt of death. But in those days, any interruption to work was harshly punished by the mine's Belgian owners. Desperate to avoid the expense of tests, the managers put out fantastic figures about safe air-levels, and the man who drove the ponies, for whom unemployment and the sack were a cruel and tangible reality, believed them. The glass of his lamp was cracked, with a big black scratch down the middle, and his foreman told him to take it back. But he ignored him, and drove his noisy wagon towards a lake of methane, and as his short-sighted pony turned the corner, the lake rose up and took the whole pit and everyone working in it. The ignited coaldust gave the explosions exceptional force, and seven followed one after the other, at brief intervals.

---

1   Gorlovka is now Horlivka.

There are hundreds of heroes in the history of mining whose stories have survived the Revolution, and one of them is the engineer and scientist Chernitsyn, head of emergency rescue work in Ukraine. Three times he led teams to the bottom of the poisoned shaft to save any miners who might still be alive under the rubble, and not one survived. Those in the first team were rapidly overcome with vomiting, and Chernitsyn struggled back above to collect more. But after a few steps through the toxic gases, they too were overwhelmed with nausea and had to drop their stretchers. He returned to the surface once more, and with tears in his eyes, this man who had twice escaped death begged the third and last team to go down for their lost comrades who might still show signs of life. He led the last eight back into the reddish twilight, and only now, six years later, have the bodies of the three hundred and this hero and his comrades been brought up and buried by the new Soviet Russia, born while the lethal fumes were dispersing at the bottom of the shaft.

In those six years, Gorlovka's workers had to fight not only for the survival of their comrades, but for the survival of the mine, which faced total ruin when they inherited it from the Belgians. It's hard to imagine the state of the pits then. All the equipment was wrecked, the ventilation and water systems had collapsed, the main shafts were filled with methane, and coaldust flew through the tunnels like moths through an empty house, threatening to give a more terrible force to even the smallest explosion than the glorious explosion of 1917.

At the head of these ruins was Comrade Korobkin, a big polar-bear of a man, who had risen from pit boy to lamp-carrier, pony-driver and faceworker, communist and Red Guard, and now Red director. Workers went back to the pits, unlit and unventilated, flooded with water and toxic air, and Korobkin fought for every lamp-screw, every inch of reinforced cable, somehow getting supplies sent from the front, often doing the work himself. Each day, miners risked being blown up or drowning in the underground water. And all this on the rations of 1920 and 1921, which will one day be displayed in museums – a pound and three quarters of flour per family a day, a pound of sugar a month, a quarter of a pound of meat, a twentieth of fat and vegetables, and four cigarettes. After two or three hours' work, they would be knocked off their feet by exhaustion. Yet despite everything, the turning point came. Within a year, Gorlovka's main Pit I was producing seventy tons of coal, and output is now just over twice that, while outputs at Pits 5 and 8 have tripled.

Although working conditions have become easier, the Gorlovka mine is still considered one of the most dangerous and difficult in the Donbas, if not the world. The main shaft drops in a sharp diagonal corridor to a depth of almost half a mile. Branching off it are perpendicular drifts, and between two of these drifts is a solid wall of coal, three hundred feet deep. But the seams all lie at angles, and cannot be worked horizontally, and miners have to leave the comfortable drift to follow them, squeezing down through narrow chimneys to the faces below.

Someone dropping down to a coalface from a central corridor above, gingerly feeling with their legs for the timber footholds cut into the sides, feels as if a powerful wave on a ship has suddenly swept them off their feet and thrown them onto the lower deck. Once the underground ship has stopped heaving, it can be seen that instead of shaking a leg in the famous Mazurka seam, the fantastic figures hanging from the thin crossbeams over the emptiness have just cramped three-foot-high cubby holes to work in, their walls and ceilings propped up by wooden struts. But the whole pit lies on its side, making 'walls' and 'ceilings' meaningless, and instead of the floor beneath their feet is a bottomless open pit, into which they hurl the hacked rocks down a hatch to the wagons that carry them to the lift.

Between this hatch and the next one, plugged with coal, there must be some ventilation. But there is no air in the real sense of the word, and dangerous levels of carbon dioxide accumulate around the air vents connecting the pits to the outside world. The dirty underground breath is sucked in and out by the steam pump at the mouth of the shaft. Sometimes you catch a little fetid air escaping from the drifts, which have frantically gulped it in, slamming shut the doors of the horses' stables behind it, barring its way to those working below.

A heavy weight of gases coils round the chest, like a snake warming itself in the sun, and the miners are barely visible through the fumes of their underground slum. Their trusty lamps, which guard their peace of mind while there is just an atom of oxygen in the air, hang on beams across the void, flickering like stars in the outer darkness. The smell of sweat oozes from a hundred armpits, trickling along the walls like machine oil. Soot clings to their skin and flies into their eyes, which learn to see through the stinging grit, and their lungs at these airless faces are like sacks of coal.

Each has his own patch, and his own way of working. One spreads his body across his black cage, hacking at the coal with his even worker's cry, as clouds of dust fly up, biting like swarms of mosquitoes. Another grips the wooden handle of his pick and hollows out a seam with its flashing steel blade, releasing showers of sparks, then leaves the pile baring its teeth at him, and moves on. The dust grows thicker, and as he stops to catch his breath, he drops his pick. He searches for it, gasping and cursing, and is sprayed with water from the walls as he stoops to pick it up. But its curved beak is soon flying over his shoulders again. Here the coal resists him and refuses to move. But after another blow it finally loses consciousness, and comes crashing to his feet in a shower of rocks.

The dust behind him is like the dust raised by a galloping cavalry, and his lamp smoulders like a camp fire trampled by the horses' hooves.

This is Gorlovka's master of all trades, Comrade Gondar. He pushes on, opening tap after tap, and the black dams collapse, and the ceilings slip and groan. These cleared spots must be immediately timbered up or filled with waste rock, before they crash on the miners' heads. Gondar throws his pick at a beam, leaving the blade quivering in the wood, then hammers a stake into the open jaws of the coal, slipping in a narrow tie-brace to secure them, as neatly as a tram conductor slipping her thick timetables into her bag.

Nothing holds up. Everything is crumbling and collapsing, and must be wedged and shored up and darned together with big wooden stitches. Gondar strikes the wall with his fist in a word of command, showing the others where the work must be done. Then he grabs the handle of his pick, still clinging to the beam like his faithful dog, and after testing the endurance and obedience of his legs, he lowers himself onto a foothold, spreads his chest over the wall, and hanging upside-down, starts hacking at a new seam. At any moment he could be hit by falling rocks, and the flame of his lamp is as pale as the muscles of his powerful shoulders, visible through the holes in his torn shirt.

Working in the pit below Comrade Gondar are nine men, separated by a row of narrow ledges. The air here is virtually unbreathable. Nine streaming patches of coal, nine clouds of impenetrable dust, nine throats coughing black spit, relieved by much soul-soothing cursing.

Work is only slightly easier at the Magpie seam. The same thundering avalanches of coal pouring down the chutes. The same dust and laboured breathing and lack of air. The same steady tapping of the steel woodpeckers hollowing out the rocks.

Perched on narrow girders, attacking the seam from above, are four miners as different from each other as you could imagine – in other words, as different as people are everywhere. Working at the bottom is an old soldier from St Petersburg's elite tsarist Preobrazhensky Regiment, with enormous ears like crab shells. At the top is a boy, a former *gimnazium* student, stirred by the spirit of adventure to join the Red Guards, then the Russian Communist Party. Mayne-Reid and the Revolution, *Captain Grant and his Children* and the Bolsheviks. Working between them is a real old Gorlovka miner, who fought to defend the pits against Shkuro's White Cossack Cavalry, and was jailed for two weeks, 'sitting in his drawers', waiting to be shot. He escaped, and went straight back to the mine. Like most miners, he soon grew sick of life on the surface, with its bright empty days. He couldn't live without the coal or his lamp, lighting the tunnels with its even spots of brightness, like the lamps people love on the surface on dark winter nights, writing at their desks surrounded by silent piles of books.

The fourth worker's voice is hoarse with phlegm. He is a communist, who left Gorlovka to fight Kaledin's Cossacks in Ukraine, then at one front after another, until the fighting ended and he returned with five wounds, his longing for the mine undiminished by his years defending the great Revolution. And no wonder! For twelve years he had driven the underground wagons, shaking the shadows with his fearless bandit's whistle. His ponies' powerful hind legs flashed in the darkness, and the miners would cling to the walls, waving their lamps at them as they passed, whistling 'These communists go like the wind!'

Sooner or later, all the hewers, colliers, hauliers, mechanics and drivers who leave the mine end up going back.

Each of these four has their own way of holding their axe in their eight-hour shift, their own way of being alone with their thoughts. Yet whatever the differences in their ages and political backgrounds, all would agree unquestioningly on two things. The first is their elemental, blood connection to the workers' state. This means something different for each of them. For the Preobrazhensky soldier, striking the coal with grand sweeping gestures, as if taking the salute on St Petersburg's Palace Square, his Soviet citizenship is a badge of honour, guarding him against each new hardship and setback. For the dreamy provincial schoolboy, whose punishing work in the mine has turned him into a man, the Revolution lies deep beneath the surface of his consciousness, like a rich new seam of social experience. For the communist intoxicated by the underground, and for the miner who has worked here fifty years, for whom rest is unthinkable, the Revolution has become part of the life of the mine, like the face of Lenin drawn by a miner on the arch of one of the deepest and most dangerous horizontals.

The second point on which all four would agree, and at the heart of all their grievances, is that the masses who defended the mines with rifles in the hungry years of the Civil War, littering them with their corpses, achieving what the economists and 'specialists' thought was impossible, have the right now to expect the Party to pay the same detailed scrupulous attention to their needs as they pay to the needs of the mine.

The mine teaches a tireless watchfulness. Detail is everything for the highly skilled faceworkers in Gorlovka's most dangerous pits, where the slightest error could cost thousands of lives. No detail is too small, and any carelessness is punished instantly, with explosions, maimings and death.

Miners are labouring to the point of exhaustion to drag the mine out of poverty. All this gives them the right to make the widest criticisms. And the sharper these criticisms are, the closer to industry and its needs, the more clearly we will see the face of the new post-revolutionary Russia.

The familiar 'this or that was better in the old days' has become a completely innocent way of making a justified practical point. Ask workers to say more about the recent past and the old regime, and for most those days have dropped forever from their consciousness, and no longer have any reality. Seven years have passed since 1917, and few can barely even remember the Whites. Only a small number of the older workers, like the former tsarist political prisoner Comrade Isichenko, keep alive memories of the 1905 revolution, with its shootings and gallows and mass funerals.

For twenty years, Comrade Gutsev has been in charge of the mine's lamp department, checking that a thousand breech-rings are screwed securely to the glass, and that none of the thousand mantles lets in an atom of air. And if everything runs smoothly in the mine, it's because Comrade Gutsev, surrounded by his smoky flowerbed of lamps, hasn't neglected a single one of the details essential to his work. Miners have declared war on fate and chance. There are piles of nails, rivets, wires and scraps of copper, iron and steel, lying in drawers in the repair shops, guarded by the older workers like treasure, waiting to take their place in the machines to make them strong and healthy and avoid needless accidents.

Above the main tunnel is the lift, delivering a constant supply of workers, wagons, engineers, timber and water to the bottom – everything the mine needs. Its construction is very simple, a pully with a steel cable which winches two cages suspended at either end up and down the shaft. They hurtle down at terrifying speed. Water gushes from the walls like a mighty waterfall, the blood rushes to the head, and the underground lamps flicker on, as if everything around them had died.

Far above the pits, in the quiet machine-room, next to a machine resembling an old grandfather clock, making feathery lines at varying speeds on sheets of paper, is the machine that controls the lift, connected to the clumsy old day-labourer machine at the loading-bay, which rings the bell calling the miners to their cages. Engineers hunch over the dials, oblivious to everything but the lift's movements, recording its loads, checking that no one jumps out before it stops, guarding against the thousands of possible disasters on each trip.

Workers at the power-station are all ruled by the same single-minded attention to detail. A stoker swinging his shovel over the flames knows if he blinks for a second he could blow up the whole town.

It would be easier for Gorlovka's workers to bear the hardships and sacrifices and the new pay cut if they knew these were due to necessity, rather than mere neglect. But the town's impoverished medical services, its lack of proper housing, its rundown cooperative store – all these chafe the bloody corns of their psyche.

Their homes, which we inherited from the mine's Belgian owners, were so shoddily constructed that they were falling down by the time we liquidated the concession in 1919. Yet these slums, standing in crooked rows like dirty warts, sinking up to their windows in mud, are still occupied by families of six or more, or by three or four childless families, all crowded into one room with a tiny kitchen and earth floor. The walls are built of wattle and clay, and ooze mould, and in the winter the wind blows away the moss and sand they have patiently stuffed in the cracks. Snow falls down the chimneys, and the gabled roofs have no ceilings, and workers are woken at night after their long shifts by the rain dripping on their necks.

Gorlovka's air, polluted by the waste products of the mine, is a breeding ground for tuberculosis. The lungs of a dying miner in the hospital are streaked with inch-thick seams of coal, with a few pale shadows of fat marking the brief times he lived on the surface. This wretched scrap of a human body is a record of years of heroic struggle against hunger and exhaustion. Yet Gorlovka's housing crisis is so acute that dozens of miners lack even their own bunks to return to after work, and have to sleep on the floor of the boiler-room or the bath house, avoiding the eye of the cleaners.

Workers are less angry about the situation though than might be expected, due to the emergency building programme finally being carried out. After getting home from their shifts, they go with their families to inspect the bright new brick homes going up, with their own front doors and fireplaces, and their own shelves on which to dry their wet clothes. For hours they stand admiring the cellars and cowsheds and outdoor summer kitchens, with their gleaming silver roofs of fireproof Urals asbestos.

Yet although Don coal is hungry for new homes, it unfortunately hates to spend money, and Comrade Plushkin, of the State Building Committee, has applied for only twenty new homes for families this year, and four hostels for single workers. They are certainly well constructed, but totally inadequate for a population of twenty thousand, seven thousand of them miners, who watch with hungry eyes every nail and plank they use. If the Party fails to put the same energy into tackling the housing crisis as it did with the food crisis during the Civil War, and Gorlovka's workers are not supplied immediately with decent accommodation, built with three-foot walls of healthy brick and wood, their rotting tuberculosis-infected slums will continue to be hotbeds of counterrevolutionary agitation, right under the nose of the GPU.[2]

---

2   The Government Political Administration, the political police force set up in 1922 to replace the *Cheka*. Subsequently the NKVD, then the KGB, now the FSB.

The town can afford to send only fifty miners to rest-homes each summer, and no more than four or five percent go to the Crimea or the Caucasus. Most go to Donetsk, whose damp forests are hardly conducive to their rest and recuperation.

Gorlovka's medical services are stretched to the limit. The hospital is desperately poor, with beds only for the most seriously ill; anyone able to walk is sent home to be seen at the clinic. A miner arrived recently in the town who was already ill, and had nowhere to live, and when he dragged himself to the hospital there was no bed for him. He got a job at the mine, and worked there for two days, before collapsing in a corner of the screening-shed, where he lay with his agonising cough, getting under the miners' feet.

And this ruin of a man, this pile of blackened rags seeking refuge in the pits, wasn't just anyone, he was Comrade Trofimov, who had fought for two years with the Red Army, before he was invalided out with a serious injury – one of those miners who fought to put the great mines of the Donbas on their feet, working until his dying breath to drag productivity uphill. Hooters signalled the beginnings and ends of the shifts, miners came and went, the bottomless earth gave up its tons of coal, and the victorious march of labour stepped over the head of its fallen fighter.

Much more must be done too for those seriously injured in mining accidents, so they can be carried up quickly on stretchers to the hospital to end their days in peace. At about seven one evening, at Horizontal 260, close to the bottom, a miner was injured in a rock-fall. The lift had broken and couldn't immediately take him up, and the only way to the surface from these horizontals is through a few 'winzes', wet narrow tubes cut as emergency exits, barely wide enough for a human body. The murky smell of the mine rises from their depths, mixed with the smell of horse sweat and manure. The feet struggle to grip the wide-spaced ledges, and even a small piece of coal falling from above, gathering momentum, has the power to kill someone.

By the time we got there, shortly after midnight, the lift had been repaired, and the invalid had been taken up to the small infirmary above, and was lying on a straw mattress, his head wrapped in bandages. The paramedic had arrived just fifteen minutes earlier, and for five hours the man had lain at the bottom of the pit, surrounded by the lamps of his frightened comrades, flickering in the darkness.

None of this can obscure Gorlovka's mighty achievements in improving workers' lives. But wherever you turn, whoever you talk to – at the pits and furnaces, at the cooperative store, at Party meetings – people repeat the same thing over and over again: that the thousands of bureaucratic abuses that blight their lives can and must be dealt with.

Take the workers' cooperative, which has only just begun to stand on its own feet, after years buried in debts like a field of weeds. People remember how in the months after October, its meagre resources were squandered in the most scandalous fashion on trainloads of expensive jackets, fancy notepaper and cosmetics, and how the director ordering these purchases took five thousand roubles for himself. They remember the bread shortages of 1918, when miners returning from work had to hunt down the drunken distributor for their rations. Emergency stalls were set up, but were unable to operate because they had no scales – although there were plenty of scales at the mines, and any worker would have happily lent theirs. Many in Gorlovka will remember 1918 as the year of the all-night bread queues, when women and children slept on the pavements outside the stalls.

In the pits and at Party meetings, howls of rage go up over these 'details', which are assuming elephantine proportions. For heaven's sake, if workers approached their duties so frivolously, they'd be sacked on the spot!

These are all the minuses. But the beaten defeated pre-revolutionary face of Gorlovka is gone. The town's youthful life-loving Party and *Komsomol* work modestly, without bureaucratic arrogance, and their meetings are always packed, most of them organised by the workers themselves, without a single senior official involved, often in direct opposition to their inert bureaucratic will. The Lenin Enrolment is bringing the best most experienced workers into the Party, fifty percent of them former Red Army volunteers, often with a higher level of education than those who have had no time to study. This January, 144 workers in Gorlovka were in the Party or had applied to join. By August, these had risen to 536, with twenty-two more applications in the briefcase of the local secretary, Comrade Gorsky. Twenty two applications, calmly considered and delivered, waiting to be processed.

A last memory of Gorlovka – the meeting organised by the *Komsomol* to discuss the new family life of the Revolution. The whole town packed into the *Komsomol* building, and a brass band played, and a young communist spoke first, saying we must 'educate Mum and Dad', and was warmly applauded by the elderly couple with him on the stage. A woman in the audience rocked a noisy baby, and the band broke into a speeded-up wedding march version of the *Internationale* to quieten it, and everyone happily stood up and sat down to much laughter. Then another *Komsomol* spoke, with a passionate attack on marriage. 'We don't need it! We should be free to love and live happily after our long hours of labour, without having to turn every experience into a life sentence!' 'But what about families and children?' women in the audience protested.

And isn't this all part of our new life? The glorious long-legged *Komsomol*, throwing his heavy economics books aside, not knowing what to do with his hot blood in the long days of summer. The shy young woman worker who has just defied her family to join the Party. The old miner discussing politics and his marriage problems with our smart clever *Komsomol* organiser Comrade Shishov. The old man says he finds it hard to get through *The History of the Communist Party*, though he has honestly tried three times, and he finds it even harder to divorce his wife, as they have so many possessions between them in suitcases he doesn't know whose is what, and Shishov goes into the details with him, and questions him about his sheepskin coat, and quietly draws him to the Party. And the old man is surprised to discover a completely new admiration and respect for the shy new woman Party member, asserting herself against her family's prejudice and gossip.

Questions of great importance were discussed at that meeting, about love and marriage, and our new social relations and responsibilities for each other, questions directly involving each individual and the collective as a whole, as we square off the hard brick of the old life with our new collective tomorrow.

Gorlovka was extraordinary that night. The mine was like a dark harbour against the warm moonlit sky, with the giant triangle of the slag-heap towering above. Angry little flames swept its slopes, and the red-eyed gypsies spat clouds of smoke at the wagons running to the top. From the streets of the dark town came the sounds of a mouth-organ, and the smells of fresh bread and the flowers from the park, filling the air with the fragrance of the south. And in the shadow of the mine, where there was once drunken animal poverty, there are now its *Komsomol* and brass band, its clubs and meetings, its old miners' songs and the *Internationale*, the wagon-drivers whistling at the girls, the schoolboys outside the theatre, eagerly sucking up scraps of a new play like melting five-kopeck ice creams. Peace and struggle, light and shade – all the strength and creativity of this little Soviet town in the fourth year of victory.

CHAPTER 10

Salt

The Bahmut Valley is like a loaf of black bread dipped in salt, a vast salt kingdom under the black earth, stretching a hundred miles, with beds a hundred and fifty feet wide in places, ten times wider than the widest coal seams in the Donbas.

Until four years ago, seven of Bahmut's nine salt mines were owned by Dutch and French companies, whose peasant workers clung to their local ways, speaking Ukrainian and growing watermelons, driving around in their slow old bullock carts. The other two mines belonged to local capitalists, Ukraine's new bourgeoisie, liberal and highly educated, with their barristers' tailcoats, Oxford degrees and dreams of a Russian constitution, who waged a constant war with their foreign competitors for their share of the profits.

The brilliant banker and entrepreneur Mikhail Tereshchenko, later Foreign Minister and Minister of Justice in the Kerensky government, cursed by every schoolboy running to the head of Petrograd's 1917 demonstrations, had his own modern well-equipped mine, now named the Sverdlov.[1] The first bed was only forty feet beneath the surface, but the salt was of inferior quality, so Tereshchenko had tunnels dug to the massive hundred-and-fifty-foot horizontal below. His enterprise was built on secure financial foundations, and he spared no expense on his Ukrainian colony, importing the latest scientific equipment, and a new mill to grind the best quality table salt. He built a modern power-station and good homes for the workers, the best in the Donbas, and before long he was earning a healthy return on his investments.

But it was all doomed to end in naked avarice. With the outbreak of war in 1914, prices of essential goods shot up in the race for quick money, and it was the age of lucrative speculation, in which Tereshchenko had no choice but to play an active part. He lost interest in buying new machines, put a stop to all maintenance and excavation work, and ordered the new tunnel to the horizontal to be blocked with rocks.

Salt mines form perfect vaults, whose underground structures seem eternal. No cathedral to Saint Sofia can match the glorious extravagance of their snowy domes. But you would have to be either hugely arrogant or ignorant of the basic

---

1 Named in memory of the popular Secretary of the Party Central Committee, Yakov Sverdlov (1885–1919).

laws of mining to neglect the mines as Tereshchenko did. Why else did the speculator state ruin the internal architecture of the Sverdlov mine? It hadn't even been re-lined with fresh concrete against the pressure of the underground waters, which flooded in for three days at the rate of eight thousand buckets an hour. Then forty-eight hours after the flood, despite the warnings of one of the most experienced miners, Comrade Rudchenko, the drainage pipes were closed, and water gushed out to the first salt pillars. All the old masonry caved in, and to this day the cages of the lift lie submerged in water at the bottom of the shaft.

Rudchenko is now director of two of Bahmut's mines, a burly indefatigable man with an earth-stained face like a clump of freshly dug potatoes, running round the pits day and night in his unbuttoned Ukrainian shirt, like a tramp lost in a forest. Two months after workers took over the Sverdlov, a learned commission of engineers arrived from the Supreme Economic Council, and proposed flooding and closing the mine, arguing that as Russia's total salt consumption was no more than a couple of million tons a year, it would be no great loss. But that would have meant losing the salt forever, and as one old Sverdlov worker said, 'You just banged in a nail and hoped the Commission wasn't looking'.

For all sorts of technical reasons, it was necessary to abandon the huge Artyom mine, next to the Sverdlov, with its hundred-and-fifty-foot seams and mile-long passages, and enough unmined salt to last a hundred years. But the miners and the chair of the Trust fought to save the Sverdlov, and this unique mine, fully repaired and mechanised, now provides the Republic with its cheapest salt, just a rouble eighty seven kopecks a ton, and has already produced over four million tons this year, exceeding all expectations.

The Shevchenko mine[2] is less modernised than the Sverdlov, and the cost of salt is slightly higher. Its main chimney, 'Old Jeanette', has been there for over fifty years, as has its primitive Dutch grinding-mill, crushing the blocks of salt with its clumsy belts like a Dutch girl flapping her starched skirts. The cast-iron sump is an honest old Russian farm labourer, which hasn't had a day off in thirty years, working unhurriedly, raising and lowering its powerful shoulders as it fills its stomach with water and belches it out into the mine. A whole ocean of salt has passed through its entrails, and everyone visiting the Shevchenko will be shown this remarkable piece of equipment, a model of workers' power.

First you pass through the room of its new assistant, a small Swiss electric 'Sulzer' pump, installed earlier this year, a polite well-behaved machine, work-

---

2   Named after the great Ukrainian national poet Taras Shevchenko (1814–61).

ing quietly away in the underground like a foreign technician who doesn't know the language. Operating it is a highly qualified engineer, as modern and youthful as his new machine. This is former Red Guard Comrade Belorus, with a sensitive intelligent face and the ear of a musician, listening to check that it sings its working song evenly, like a fluttering snowstorm. On his stool, next to the oily rag he uses to wipe off its sweat, lies an open copy of Paul Bourget's novel *Cosmopolis*.[3]

Below this room, at the bottom of a short flight of stairs, water bubbles in the darkness along a narrow brick-lined pipe, spilling yellow mud over the floor. The ground drops, and the water runs on, uncatchable and undefeatable, to the great brass pump at the bottom of the deep damp shaft, known as 'Old Thunderer', oiled and polished like a big country clock.

Generations of workers at the Shevchenko were pampered by these ancient machines, as industrious and reliable as servants in the old days, often leaving them for hours at a time, knowing they could manage perfectly well without them. Nothing had to be checked or adjusted, they did the work all by themselves; the piston turned the water, the mill ground the salt. Some developed strange quirks in their old age, but they were used to them. The Dutch grinding-mill for instance, the respected grandmother of the mine, refused to work in the summer without cooling compresses and lotions, so a special worker familiar with her needs had to hack a block of ice from the ground each winter, to be attached in summer to the roller connected to her main shaft.

When Comrade Rudchenko took over as director this spring, the Shevchenko was in a state of almost total collapse, and the whole workforce was up in arms when he banned the grinding-mill's special regime and the valet administering it. 'You want to take away what's best about her!' a good old worker said, with tears in his eyes. 'Twenty years I've stood at that machine, and because of you she'll die. Sack me if you like, I don't care!'

Another commission of engineers arrived from Donetsk, and established that the mill's 'anomales' were quite normal, and even helped to protect the bearings from wear and tear. But the authority of Soviet power was at stake, and Rudchenko stood his ground. He stopped the mill for six days, and established that the 'anomales' were a disease of old age, and had been affecting output for decades. The old woman was defeated, the ice blocks disappeared into the realms of myth, and afterwards the battle against the old habits became easier, and there is now a new labour discipline at the Shevchenko.

---

3   Paul Bourget (1852–1935), poet, journalist and novelist, often compared to Zola, whose *Cosmopolis* painted a picture of cosmopolitain life in Rome in the 1890s.

For forty years, water had been hauled up from the remote shafts by hand, singing its ancient songs of women's grief and snowstorms and frozen buckets. Miners now have a proper water supply, powered by electricity. To deal with the staggering waste of fuel, the old steam boilers, corroded by salt water and damaged by irregular stoking, have been repaired and relieved of their secondary duties, and workers no longer treat the machines like their nannies, responsible for caring for them. The former tsarist technicians and specialists, demoralised by the old government dragging itself through the autumn mud, were told to shape up or lose their jobs. And when one carelessly attached a wire to the bearings and fused it, damaging the pins of the rollers, he was sacked on the spot.

As a result of Rudchenko's work, the Shevchenko produced close to three million tons of salt last year. The price was screwed up to two and a half roubles a ton, then dropped to two. But even this is too high; the mine must cut the cost by a half or face closure.

Between the ceiling and the earth's surface lie the dangerous waters of the Bahmutka River. The mine itself is as dry as a salt-cellar – if one can describe this heavenly white city as a mine. The lift drops down a steep narrow shaft to a depth of 150 feet, and stops at a vast glittering square, surrounded by wide empty avenues, arches and palaces. Sometimes you have a sense of this vastness alone on dark winter nights in big cities, after the traffic has stopped. But the night in these underground Nevsky Prospects is eternal, like a black jewel in a case as black as itself, gleaming with crystal vaults, galleries and stairways, whole districts of windowless skyscrapers, immeasurably tall. And in the motionless sky above, a Milky Way of incomparable brightness, gleaming with stars of sparkling salt.

The underground city is still growing. 176 new salt chambers are being carved out, which in six months' time will have reached the height of the working passages. Work has just started on fifty new chambers in a deep cavern, where an overhanging ledge loaded with explosives has brought hundreds of tons of salt crashing down. The whole tunnel is piled with loose boulders, which the hauliers drag off on their trolleys, drunk on the smell of the dynamite clinging to the grains, like cigar smoke in hair.

Late at night when the thunder stops, the cutters arrive, the bravest and most experienced of the mine's workers. Hooking thin ropes to the tops of the crumbling blocks, they pull themselves up by their armpits, then hack at them with their unmechanised metal drills, no longer used anywhere else.

The Shevchenko's drilling tools are as ancient as its old machines, and like them, Comrade Orlov hasn't had a day off in thirty years. For thirty years, Comrade Orlov's life has been a perpendicular metal stake driven into a block of salt, cutting into it like a boat tacking across a wave, making the same zigzag lines cutters have used for centuries. The Revolution broke out, and the Germans came to the Artyom mine, with their discipline and good brandy, and he drilled salt. Petlyura came, then Denikin, and he drilled long and hard. 'I was sweating fat', he says.

Between the Artyom and Red Sverdlov, the Shevchenko belonged to no one, neutral and still unclaimed. While the next shift stood guard above with their rifles, Orlov drilled, and every night he took a communist with him down to his spacious palace at the bottom of the shaft. To avoid bandits, he said good-bye to his wife and children, and left home to sleep at the Soviet power-station, 'Salt'. Sometimes he speculated in salt, sewing little bags of it into the linings of his overalls, haggling with his workmates over the price. And he drilled, drilled, drilled. When Denikin's White Guards seized the Shevchenko's fuel supplies, workers went home and told their wives to bring all the slag they had saved for winter to the ovens, and to chop up every scrap of spare wood from their huts. Then they returned to work, and Orlov returned with them, and he drilled on.

Denikin vanished into thin air and Petlyura perished, and the Whites have disappeared into the past. The Dutch grinding-mill and 'Old Thunderer' have been retired, and Orlov's hard old hands, which have built the palaces and galleries of this salt city with his rusty crowbar, will soon be working with a new pneumatic drill.

The old man has just finished his morning classes, and he sits hunched on a block of salt with his hands on his knees, waiting for the foreman to arrive. He looks worn out. All the light seems to have gone out of his eyes, and his neck is as thin and dry as a withered vine twig. He drives away exhaustion by teasing his young helper Babenko, perched on the block below him.

'You let that woman of yours run all over you', he says, in a mixture of Russian and Ukrainian. 'Trust me, women need to know who's boss!' Then looking around proudly, he says, 'We found treasure here, but we blocked it up to save it from the Whites. They'd have hung us if they found it, and we didn't want trouble. We Ukrainians are peaceful hardworking people'.

'Damn right we are, so put me in charge here!' Babenko grins.

And from the top of the white mountain the wise old voice says, 'Don't be daft son, you're soft as a girl. Just stay close to me and mind you don't fall'.

In Hindenburg's Country

..

In Hindenburg's Country

Published by the *Pravda* publishing house, Moscow, 1926

Preface to the German Edition

I have travelled through Germany, 'Hindenburg's Country', and have seen it with the unclouded eyes of a visitor from the country of workers and peasants, Lenin's country. You have castles and museums, government palaces where ministers sit, victory avenues and victory monuments, madhouses, war memorials, barracks, schools, prisons and factories – millions of people sucked dry and a bourgeoisie with culture, technology and all the comforts of a good life.

But I didn't want merely to learn about German streets, and who was begging, starving, strolling, motoring or parading in them, I wanted to see the places from where it is all being invisibly ruled, where the millions of threads come together: the power centres of public opinion and the industrial workshops of the German spirit, German culture and German guns. I have looked for Germany in her national sanctuaries.

Krupp and Essen

The streets, plants and pits in the Ruhr are all marked with the name of Krupp, like the teaspoons and pillowslips of some propertied family. The city of Essen is a hereditary estate, a family possession passed down from generation to generation. The family, as if in its own home, puts up its memorials to its deceased members in public squares and gardens. Grandma on one monument, cousins, sons, grandsons, all with their own interests and pleasures, on another. At every crossroads, a bronze Friedrich Albrecht or Albrecht Friedrich. Buildings, tramlines, people and vehicles meekly give way to their iron masters.

The cult of the ancestors reigns over the greatest of Europe's industrial centres. The last male of the reigning family died long ago, and the outrageous scandal accompanying him to the grave is long forgotten. His daughters then inherited thousands of millions by right of blood, and became the autocratic sovereigns of hundreds of factories, pits, shipyards, railways and harbours. Husbands were found for them for the continuance of the line, petty officials turned prince-regents, who took their wives' names and multiplied, so the great city of Essen wouldn't be left without thoroughbred masters. Hundreds of thousands of workers and millions of machines could then settle quietly to work for real pure-blooded little Krupps. Although life of course has long since outgrown the patriarchal economic forms with which old Adolf started half a century ago. Business is now managed by the board of a joint-stock company, not a monarchical lord, and the Krupp colossus strides out in a direction fixed and ultimately guided by an army of expert officials, rather than by the will of the brilliant organiser and builder old Krupp the Second.

Thirty years ago, on the site of this city where the giants of metallurgy now work crammed together, where plants jostle against each other, and factory chimneys crane their necks into the soot-black sky, streaked with thick strips of smoke; where far beneath the city's feet, pits gnaw at every piece of coal between them and the black covered ways, stretched like cables, each colliery grabbing for them with a hundred hands and pulling them over to its side; where the great smelting furnaces that knit the Ruhr into the body of one giant plant are never extinguished – here on the site of this Essen were once open fields and scattered peasant farmsteads. You can see today how the city has grown up. Concrete and asphalt have merely overlaid its age-old disorder. Streets have formalised the winding crooked paths trodden by the first miners between the pub and the works. The city is reconciled to its wild ungainly buildings that recognise no discipline, lolling around like tramps turned millionaires, without gardens, with the winds beating their bare stone chests. Overwhelmed with wealth and the smell of money, Essen rushes on its way, seeing nothing there, and building on it. Essen has a passion for construction and large useless earthworks. It loves to sit down and sort through its bag of odds and ends, its old kit-bag, pulling forty-pound rocks from the road, digging up the soil so the stench of bare earth that hasn't removed its stone shirt for decades hangs over the city, then putting it all back again, opening new tramlines, installing new street lights, building bridges so the miners' feet in their rough boots won't be crushed in the traffic.

Like the webbed foot of a goose, Essen lies mostly between the works and its workers' dwellings, squeezed between the factory blocks, huddling against the fences, afraid to take an inch of vacant land without permission from the coal syndicate. Every narrow multi-familied back street has only to take a few paces forward to find at the end a factory chimney standing like a watchman waving a smoky flag – 'Go back, this is Rhine Steel'. 'This way to Herkules'. 'This way to AEG'.

These dwellings have a cramped look and bulging eyes. Black, half-blind, round-shouldered, capped with tiny roofs, they cling to the walls of banks, plants and commercial premises, pits full of people, creeping upwards, because of the terrible pressure forcing them up from the ground.

All the plants in Essen belong to Krupp, its housing is the property of Stinnes. The ineffable squalor of the latter was until recently still entered in the company's fabulous account books as an asset. But even where factories are compelled to move aside to let streets and tramlines through, they still remain masters. The alleyways are so narrow that women can hang their washing on lines thrown from a window across to the one opposite. The works stretch their pipes, cables and bridges over the pavements, striding across roofs and blocks of flats like giants over Lilliputian cottages. Without shame, the lords and masters throw their waste straight onto the street, spitting steam, ash, gases, water and grime onto the heads of passers-by. Everyone passing the wide windows of the steelworks can see it beating with hammers its constant wife, pliant but unyielding. Children are woken in their beds by her shrieks. Day and night, the dormitories hugging the factories hear iron crying out like an infant in pain. Every object in workers' homes shudders like an anvil, however far away the blows, and adjusts its breathing to the sounds borne on the wind. The worker unconsciously sets his heart and his watch back or forward by the works' hooter – a silver miner's watch like an onion, with a fat black hand like a finger. Everything keeps the same time. Hundreds of thousands of miners and metalworkers move about, sleep, work, wake up and have their dinner without missing the pace, falling out of the column or breaking their march, and never, even in moments of deepest oblivion, cease to hear the martial music of labour booming from the factories into the city, its outskirts, and all its people.

There is only one spot in Essen where deep solemn stillness reigns. This isn't in the works' so-called 'estates', long ago swallowed up whole, with their flower-beds and bees, dying from the coal-dust. Nor is it in the country club, where a speck of nature with grass, leaves and a fishing-pond has been specially set aside for loyal office workers and their children, looking at everything with one eye tightly shut, so as not to see the factory chimneys wafting their dirty clouds of smoke over this garden of delights for sixth-grade officials. No, the real deep stillness, so deep that not even the modern lifts gliding silently up and down can plumb its depths, shut off from the outside world by impenetrable glass walls, is in the main office and boardroom of the Krupp works. Not so much an office as a ministry of government, with its portraits of its kings on the walls, and their wives and grandmothers. The places of the greatest honour are occupied by guns, steel samples and certificates awarded at international arms exhibitions. Something about these expanses of officialdom, these deep pools of secrecy and staid respectability, is more reminiscent of the Quai d'Orsay or the Foreign Office, the gloomy building of the *Reichswehr* mission by the canal, or the Embankment in old St Petersburg. Job applicants who gulp in this atmosphere fall lifeless into armchairs. Virtually all of them, even specialist technicians with top references, go away with nothing. There's an international crisis on, and Krupp can take his pick.

The inner life of his firm is known to very few. Even his own people make mistakes.

'May I see Major R.?'

The old functionary grins, 'You mean Colonel von R.?'

'What, since last week?'

Officials move up the ladder of ranks that's not supposed to exist since 9 November. They walk in single file or overtake one another in the slow promotion race, while someone in the shadows shifts its faithful servants from one step to the next. Second lieutenants become lieutenants overnight, lieutenants become captains, captains become majors. Quite young men take up the vacant posts in this army that has no fighting men or lower ranks.

Krupp has his own General Staff, and naturally his own diplomatic corps. This has shrivelled in size over recent years, and is now sharply reduced. The cannon king recalled most of his ambassadors long ago. Today they live in the small houses built by Madame Krupp for her old domestic retinue, receiving tiny salaries and eating herring tails with the dainty family silver, crown princes with horsey faces and glass bubbles for eyes reminiscing about the old days, when one word from Krupp's representative in Peking meant more than all the assurances of the official envoys. Yuan Shih-kai would make regular trips to a little Chinese house far from the hated European quarter, where he would purchase advice and order guns. Then came the war – and all was lost! Yet to this day what contacts and sources of information Krupp has! Brief items in the *Essener Zeitung* on foreign, and particularly eastern, affairs are revealing a vast operation quietly in hand. While the Foreign Ministry gropes to find a route for German exports, here in Essen they have long understood what a Chinese market can mean for German industry. China's revolutionary struggles are followed with the closest attention, prices offered, relations renewed. They watch and they wait. I happened to get into a disagreement about China with one of the Krupp managers, and to add the final telling weight to his argument, he opened a desk drawer with an impatient gesture and pulled out a fresh report – a resume of every movement and word of Comrade Karakhan in Peking!

The rectangular tower on the roof of the works' main administrative block has outgrown all the other buildings on its skyward path, outreaching the sharp pinnacles of an old monastery, which laboriously sends up to heaven its peals and laments about the machines whose constant vibrations are crumbling its walls. 'Oh Lord, who shall come unto Thy house when a 25,000-ton blast furnace is smoking next door? Oh Lord, grant this be not so!'

Essen's heaven has changed. Now it's just the cloudy vault of the railway station, the ceilings of the factories. Sometimes where the glass panes have been smashed you can see a bit of blue. But high above, a celestial ventilator quickly slams it out again.

The lift cuts a thick slice off the house of Krupp like a razor. First it leaves behind the job applicants, then the lower floors fall away, and finally it reaches the crown of the building. The young girl with a yellow complexion, who goes up and down in her box for ten hours every day, pushes back the door. The corridors are still and grey, like the coils of a brain. And how strange, here is a dining-room, set for ten people, as bright as a lighthouse, around which the whistling wind lashes rain and soot against the glass walls. 'Here', our escort whispers, a former officer with a scar across his mouth and a black glove on his wooden hand, 'here dine the demigods!'

Seated at the table, you can see the whole of Krupp's kingdom. The history of German imperialism written in the lines of the factory blocks, with their chimneys as punctuation marks. The horizon is scribbled over with them, like notes in the margin of a stock-jobber's ledger. The wind rubs them from the sky's board every minute, washing them off with a rainy sponge, to write up new signs and figures. Smoke creeps up in long zigzag lines, like Krupp's yearly dividends. The sky is playing the stock market, buying and selling.

Far below, in the concrete and granite, is the little wooden house with two windows where the first Krupp set up business a century ago. He planned to take advantage of the weak state of British industry during the Latin American Wars of Independence, and to forge a powerful rival on German anvils. But he lost all his fortune, was ruined and died in the little house, while Britain ruled the world steel market undefeated. The crisis had come too soon, while the German bourgeoisie was still in nappies, and its prophet who lacked both credit and cash was crushed, together with his experiments and his one blast furnace. His son then had to start all over again. For twenty-five years he worked to prepare the world for steel's victory over iron, the victory of the steel gun cast in one piece over the old bronze cannon.

He sent a top-quality steel ingot weighing 2,000 kilos to the London Exhibition of 1851. That lump, which won a gold medal, was a warning no one understood then, and was destined twenty years later to flatten the French war industry. Within that ingot, before which thousands of visitors had stood in ecstasy, lay Germany's victory in the Franco-Prussian War.

By the eve of this war, a prototype of the modern steel gun was already complete. Krupp had become a world name. Short and cast in one piece, like his steel, it boomed out first in Europe then in Asia. His name was uttered wherever thunder clouds gathered. Krupp meant war. A new war whose horrors were still unknown to mankind, a new mode of death and a new strategy, unlike those before. On the Ruhr, plants smoked day and night, furnaces blazed, and metal was poured and cast to produce heavy guns, rifles, mortars, howitzers and explosive devices for anyone who could pay. The Ruhr was the arsenal of the world.

Krupp was born a German and a patriot – in as much as any businessman can be a patriot of any one country. Accordingly the Kaiser would be received at his court more frequently and informally than others seeking his friendship. Any new invention would be offered first to him. The Fatherland was the most important of all his customers. But if the Fatherland couldn't pay or requested a deferment, the goods would pass into the enemy's hands. The journalist Felix Pinner writes: 'In the days when Krupp threw the barrels of his guns onto the market for the first time, nobody was tormented with pangs of conscience or prejudices of a political nature. Everyone without hesitation bought his instruments of murder, both friends and foes. Bismarck's wars were but a proving ground, the ordeal by fire, for his guns'.

Had the French government realised the superiority of these guns and hastened to re-equip its army, the war of 1870 might well have ended differently.

The subsequent forty years saw the coming of age of German industry and German imperialism. Krupp turned into a whole state, who reconstructed his coalmines, engineering plants, ore deposits and power-stations in the form of a vertical trust. Everything in one place and at hand, everything his own product. He secured his rear, and waged war against middlemen and whole alliances of middlemen for the independence of his raw materials – ore, fuel and chemicals – and his furnaces, plants and workshops acquired their own foreign colonies. Krupp conquered vast territories and seas of oil. He strangled his neighbours like chickens, swallowing up their assets and forcibly merging them with his own in the form of joint-stock companies.

At a press banquet In 1913, on the eve of the war, Krupp made a brilliant observation, which passed as unnoticed then as that lump of steel sixty years earlier: 'A factory must create its own demand and its own customers'.

Krupp made guns, and war was his customer. And in 1914 it broke out.

Never had the works flourished as in those first years of the war. 130,000 workers employed in his factories, manufacturing arms, 40,000 sitting down at a time to eat in the canteens. New buildings shot up at incredible speed. In the first year alone, profits rose from 33.9 million gold Marks in 1913 to 86.4 million in 1914. And in Essen's outskirts, where the occupying French troops now have their firing range and sing their merry songs, there appeared the vast flat-roofed dark red barn of the greatest gun plant in Europe – the Hindenburg Works. The works were built to realise the celebrated plan for the militarisation of all German industry, of which the Field Marshal was considered to be the father. Simple, this plan: flood heavy industry with gold, cram the country's last resources into its maw, and force it to turn out more guns than all the Allies' plants put together. However Krupp was beaten at this game. Vickers Armstrong and the Bethlehem Steel Corporation proved more powerful. Nowadays, the day the Hindenburg programme was implemented is seen as the start of the Mark's final decline, the beginning of the crisis, and the years of inflation.

No one had been so enriched by the war as Krupp, and no one was dealt such a blow by the Versailles Treaty, which forced him to switch to peacetime operations. The machines that had produced his arms were blown up. Tools in his ammunitions shops were wrecked or confiscated. Whole districts fell silent, dozens of chimneys stopped smoking. The pits and mines in Alsace, Luxembourg and the Saar passed mostly into the hands of French industrialists, who treated them exactly as Krupp would have done in the event of victory. The sites of the now destroyed or paralysed installations are gaping gaps. Fresh reserves of raw materials, lost for ever at home across the Rhine, had to be found abroad.

Hitherto Krupp had never made things in the accepted sense of the word – you couldn't make soup or sew dresses with any of his products. Now he must grab what he can get, nothing is beneath him. He is forbidden by Versailles to make guns. All right, he'll make false teeth – light, durable, stainless, odourless, tasteless steel jaws, ten times cheaper than platinum and just as good. He fell upon the dairymaids, took away their cloths and strainers for pouring the milk into bottles, and gave them lovely separators for twenty Marks each. The great Krupp has struck up a friendship with the smallest darkest cinemas, where the owners' daughters play the piano, and now they'll buy their projectors from no one else. He has induced doormen's wives, little post office clerks, old maids, schoolteachers and chemists to buy his magic lanterns. He has supplied thousands of groceries with their cash registers. Yet all this isn't enough to stop the gap. Krupp has been caught off-balance, and must take a new step forward and carry out a technical revolution if he is to beat his foreign competitors without guns and bayonets.

Now he is largely following his original path. His plants produce not only goods for consumption, but the means of production. Krupp is a nursery for pedigree horsepower, the breeding ground for machines that will in turn beget countless generations of new ones. His power looms are like queen bees, from which springs the life of the entire beehive. Their slim steel bodies throw out millions of tons of cloth, shifted by his cranes and lorries. Locomotive wheels, self-emptying wagons, diesel engines, struts for overhead railways. Harvesters, machines for planting potatoes and spreading fertiliser. Rakes, shovels and boilers, oil-storage tanks and pipes – embryos of new factories, the sperm of new airways and towns, new tonnages of fleets that will carry the crops of the next decades.

And here it all is, visible from the tower. At lunch every day the directors count up the dead shells under the long flat roofs of the Hindenburg Works, with a smell that seems to grow fouler each day, like the carcass of a rotting whale. A silent polygon resembling a cemetery. A dead building beneath a dome looking like St Petersburg's old Admiralty building, headquarters of the Tsarist Navy. Here are the innumerable workshops of Krupp's old arms plant, spread out like the barrel of a gun, sealed up on the outside and empty within, with flights of stairs visible through the glass walls like bones through skin. Somewhere there booms not a cannon but a hammer, or a hydraulic press stamping out cisterns and boilers for chemical plants. But very soon this work will come to a halt. Today it's boilers, tomorrow it will be cannon again.

The plant that suffered so cruelly under Versailles now works at half capacity, but is still the largest in Europe, occupying an area of 47,000 square metres. Its last big order was for locomotives for Russia. But many months have passed since then, and Russia is now making its own locomotives.

To the west are the open-hearth furnaces, and a square grey lake of water from underground. Gasometers, garages for hundreds of thousands of vehicles, towers over the pits still working, with the racing wheels of their winding gear. A low hunchbacked building, the laboratory where a new rustproof iron was discovered this year, steel mills, blast furnaces, chemical works, textile machinery plants, all fanning outwards. Some of these have been snuffed out, some are half-empty, while others are working three shifts flat out, setting world productivity records with the lowest possible wages and the longest possible working day.

From this height, it's plain that these plants, factories and workshops aren't standing still at all, they're moving, and their movements are as coordinated as on a chessboard or in a battle plan. Some edge round their own corpses, stepping over the empty yards and structures. Others, weakened and unable to stay on their feet, are assigned to the rear to re-arm and replenish themselves with new energy, shifting the burden onto the shoulders of the stronger ones, which now have to bear double the load, and the clouds of smoke hanging over Krupp's camp are like the banners of his armies.

A crisis. Yes. For Krupp's creditors and his workers, at whose expense this silent technical revolution is being prepared, it's a palace coup by machines. And at the root of it all is Germany's acute coal crisis. Apparently German coal can no longer compete with British. The Ruhr's newspapers are full of reports that Russian coal, which no one took seriously before, is beating German and British coal in the Balkans and throughout the Near East. Production costs must be driven down, or the economy will collapse – that's the catchphrase of all the right-wing and Social Democrat press. So down with miners' pensions, down with their leave and public holidays, away with national insurance and pit safety legislation, away with all the proletariat's rights gained in the battles of the last fifty years.

To demonstrate to workers the gravity of the crisis, the Krupp family has resolved to take drastic measures. No less than forty footmen have been dismissed from its palace, as large and ugly as a covered market, and moved to a well-appointed town house. The magnanimous gentlemen are sharing their travails honestly with their workers. By saving on the wages of a couple of stable-lads, Krupp can throw another few score thousand onto the streets with a clear conscience. Heavy industry's wounded body is convulsively shrinking. It rationalises production and discards everything superfluous, everything with little or no profitability. Over the last few months some forty thousand workers in Essen and the surrounding district have been thrown onto the street, and Krupp feels no need to conceal the fact that a hundred thousand more will be sacked this winter. The state – meaning the taxpayers, meaning the workers – will feed these armies of unemployed and their families at its own expense, so as to give Krupp and Stinnes the chance to hatch their conspiracy without undue losses: a conspiracy for an uprising of manufacturing industry. The uprising is being planned for the control of coal. Coal is the black bread of Krupp's industrial plants, which for over a century has kept the world dependent on its prices and quality. In order not to be overthrown, it must now adopt a constitution, accept concessions, dissolve itself, turn liquid, and share equal rights with the brown coal it had hitherto held in contempt.

Versailles exploded and halted half of Krupp's works. But it left in the hands of the German bourgeoisie the great and inexhaustible source of its wealth – the sinewy backbone of the Ruhr's miners and metalworkers. Supporting himself on this spinal column, Krupp has now embarked on a struggle to the death to drag himself out of the crisis. Not just to darn holes, but to take a new step forward. German Social Democracy and its trade unions are assisting Krupp's stabilisation as loyally as they assisted him during the war. For only under their cover can the uprising of the machines be carried out. Metallurgy's Ninth of Thermidor.

A Concentration Camp of Poverty

As they say here, unemployment benefits are too little to live on, too much to die on. Workers thrown out of their jobs are not immediately threatened with starving to death, but will exist for a while on the brink of utter poverty, with nothing but a piece of dry bread. Unable to afford a flat on their assistance, they must flee from the block, neighbourhood and district where they have lived for many years, and where a communist might maintain dangerous contacts. In Essen, they'll be moved to accommodation in the distant outskirts, in the abandoned unoccupied barracks of an army ordnance depot, turned into a hostel for the unemployed – a vast godforsaken stone barn built by the Empire for its soldiery, where the Republic now settles unreliable workers. A concentration camp of poverty.

No grass grows here, trampled by decades of Prussian drilling. Ragged children play in puddles of sewage around the sentry-boxes. The huge structure that once spat entire armies onto the battlefields is now murky and desecrated. The soldiers who lived here have been moved to the nearby *Reichswehr* barracks, and workers trundle hand-carts piled with their shabby goods and chattels across the fields to this dismal hermitage.

The Barracks and the Cobbler's Wife

The lame red-haired cobbler, eighteen months out of work, 'because of politics', drags a soldier's old stove out of the ruined barracks and saws it in half in the sunshine, making ready for a hard winter. The women have attached washing-lines to the old Imperial eagles on the gates, and dry their rags on the sacred window ledges of the former officers' quarters. But all efforts to make this dead building designed for soldiers warm and human are in vain. Objects taken from their natural intimacy are spread out and stand heavily to attention along the naked walls, swallowed up in the emptiness.

A barefoot bandy-legged little boy shuffles across the dirty wooden floorboards, half of them chopped up for firewood last winter when there was no fuel. His baby brother died last week. Two beds side by side, where the child and his father and mother and fourteen-year-old sister sleep.

Every morning the communist cobbler's wife washes the long corridors, out of fear and a desire somehow to appease this hostile building, to pay the barracks a pledge of human warmth, which it accepts with as much indifference as a field-marshal accepting a bribe from a raw recruit. And Frau Schumacher need only lift her head and see the messages on the dead walls to lose her last hope: 'Lerne leiden ohne zu klagen' (Learn to suffer without complaining). 'Ordnung regiert die Welt' (Order rules the world).

Wherever Frau Schumacher turns with her bucket and floorcloth, these barrack-room virtues greet her like a fist to her head. Living here on this island of the dead, on seven Marks a week for the four of them, knowing that at night in the cramped room her little girl will be unable to sleep, listening morbidly to every movement, every sigh of her parents. And all day Frau Schumacher must listen to this incessant voice from the past, prattling away with its sluggish tin tongue about valour and obedience – yellow Uhlan uniforms and dashing Hussars who have long rotted away in the Marne or in the snows of Russia.

This winter perhaps another rickety little boy will no longer be alive. Perhaps the cobbler himself will pass away, for it's hard for him to drag himself along in the ice and rain to the Labour Exchange on his skidding crutches. But these spectres from the past will live on, and another proletarian family arriving in this unlocked prison, where the gates have been torn from their hinges, where the wind from the fields sweeps the crumbling stonework down the corridors, from which there is as little hope of escape as from any other prison, will be greeted by the same drumbeat of dead bones: 'Furchtlund os treu für Gott, Kaiser und Vaterland'. (Fearless and True for God, Kaiser and the Fatherland)

Only one window in the building shines in the dark, one gold tooth in its big dead jaws. When it's dark and cold, the eagles painted on the ceiling fly out to the black yard, dipping their pedigree heads adorned with the bald down of the old Empire to peck at the scraps left in the rubbish by the cobbler's hens.

Frau Fritzke

Frau Fritzke runs along the corridors in stockinged feet so as not to wake anyone. She is the Ninon de l'Enclos of this wasteland, whose love life is packed up in big grey bags on her face. The damp of the building smudges her 'Kazan' face-powder, and her thin dress flaps damply around her knees.

Frau Fritzke was widowed in the war, and everyone must sell what they have. Hundreds have tugged at her breasts since then, like pulling on a lavatory chain. In this way she saved her two children from starving to death in the years of inflation. And now the state that took their father from them, and spent their orphans' benefits on subsidies to Krupp and Stinnes, has decided to take them away from their immoral mother. In a few days' time, a policeman will arrive and remove her naughty plump little boy and her twelve-year-old daughter, who is disabled and has constant fits, and place them in a Catholic orphanage.

Frau Fritzke's friend August offered to marry her, to save this relic of love and her family, and she went to the registry office with him in triumph, skipping over the dust in her lacquered slippers, he in a paper collar reeking of petrol, as solemn as fate. This heroic measure was the talk of the barracks, but was of no avail.

She collected references going back over many years, showing she had also worked as a charwoman, and with all the filth, muck and cobwebs she had carried out of people's homes on her back they could have built a pyramid in honour of her scorned labour.

But her tormentors were implacable. Frau Fritzke wept. The rings around her eyes are like rings drawn with an umbrella in the sand.

The Iron Cross

If you land in the barracks, it's best to stay down in the depths and not move. It's all right for Frau Fritzke to wear her fancy dresses, because it's her profession. The cobbler's wife is entitled to heat her curling-irons on the communal stove, until her hair and her nits crackle, because everyone knows she married the cobbler out of pure love, when he was already lame. But no one else dares lift a comb. There's no point putting on airs here, trying to impress people. Everyone lives in complete nakedness, like snails squashed on the road, weakly twitching their horns, topped by their never despairing eyes. So when Mr Boss doesn't allow people in his room, ashamed of his pawnshop receipts and his leaking feather-mattress and pillows (which everyone knows about anyway), they find it offensive.

In this building, as in paradise, or the precincts of a country church, middle-class shame stays behind the gates guarded by the fiery sword of the angel of poverty. Anyone who feels shame will upset the others, and then they too will have to waste their energy on fig-leaves of pretence that fool no one. The building despises Boss, along with the medal on his chest, and his voice, which sounds as if he'd dined well today.

If only they knew how much hurt and humiliation and bitterness there was in those former field marshal's quarters of his! If anyone had slept on nails and gone grey with hot ashes, it was Boss, who for thirty-four years had worked in a War Department powder-mill.

All his life he was separated from ordinary men by a solemn oath. Men who took this soldier's vow of silence didn't join trade unions or political parties or go to the workmen's pub. Even reading newspapers of any political tendency whatsoever was seen as improper and suspect within the gates of the powder-mill. What the General Staff kept quiet about for big money, high ranks, plumed helmets and rows of decorations on their chests, workers in the powder-mills and munitions plants kept quiet about for nothing, happy with the confidence being placed in them. It made them feel like partners in government, not merely hired workers. The Kaiser was indebted to the armaments workers for their tact and discretion, and they loved the dynasty, like paupers whose hard-earned pennies a millionaire has deigned to accept from them as credit. And so when the war came, and gold was smelted into powder and iron, the government paid Mr Boss the great honour of reaching out for his savings book. When the manager's most confidential adviser, his wife, visited with her daughter and servant to offer the old worker a few war-loan bonds, with what joy Boss threw all his savings into that abyss!

Ten-pfennig pieces vanished into thin air like dew. Marks turned to smoke before he had time to wipe away his tears of emotion. As for gold coins, 132 of them, no one heard a sound as they fell to the bottom of the inflationary pit. But Boss was happy.

Five, no, more – seven whole years passed. The world was drenched in blood, made a desperate bid to free itself, and was finally skinned over with the thin skin of stabilisation, broken by the black ice-holes of starvation and unemployment.

When his dresser and rocking-chair were taken away, Boss still believed in God and justice. When his wife came home from the pawnshop with the receipt for his personally inscribed silver clock with the Imperial monogram, awarded to him by the works for his twenty-five years' irreproachable service, he still held out, and he forbade her to talk of their son killed in action.

But when all the sacrifices had been offered up, and the still patient and devoted Boss began to be overcome by the great tiredness that suddenly descends on a worker when they're nearing sixty – his eyes were growing dim, his hands were weak and dithery, and the alcohol in his blood was making him cough up rank yellow spittle – then Boss received his marching orders. Two billion in fake money, and a room in a workers' barracks. And for the first time it hit him he was a worker too. The horror, the loneliness! Stripped bare and crushed under the wheels of the blind machine, Boss, a grain of sand, Boss, a splinter, fell headlong into the great sea of his class, right to the bottom, where there was neither light nor hope.

Above him rolled the dark waves of 1919, then 1921. Boss lay still, and from time to time revolutionary ships wrecked in battle came down and settled beside him, with flags on their broken masts and the best of humanity on their shattered decks, its stormy petrels, the bravest of the brave Rosa Luxemburg and Karl Liebknecht.

In those long hours of miserable idleness, Boss would pull a box stuffed with now worthless money from under the bed, and he would sit over it in the evenings, sit over it for days. The wallpaper in his room was grey with red specks faded with time, like spatters from a fountain of human life run dry. The veins in his legs were swollen, and his tired blood was begging to go back to the earth.

Through the walls of basements and attics and factories seeped the quiet still waters of labour solidarity, gathering in streams, streaming into rivers and seas, lapping at the prison bars, breaking them down bit by bit, ready to surface at the right day and hour in a great torrent of rage. Such a day came for Boss.

Tall, leaning on a stick, dressed in a coffee-coloured jacket, with a medal on his watch chain, he went to meet his wife, who despite her grey hair, had started working at the tobacco factory. Everyone knew Minna. There was no face like hers, a whiter than white mask of such beauty you wanted to stand before her and bow to the ground. In his youth, Boss had been imperious and impatient with her, considering it his duty to keep her in order. After work, her face with its little beads of sweat on the forehead shone like plaster-of-paris.

Their neighbour the cobbler made his way up to the first floor, took a rest, got himself up to the second, knocked at the door and went in. He had come to offer Boss a copy of the communists' paper *Arbeiter Zeitung*. Silence fell on the room. Pale Minna turned even paler and hid in the corner. The cobbler sat down. The paper cost twenty pfennigs. Almost choking on his tie, Boss handed over the twenty, then threw on the table another coin, grey and spiked, with a little ring at the top. 'Take this sh-t! It's all I've earned in my life!'

The Iron Cross. *'Für Kriegshilfsdienst'* (For war service behind the lines), with 'WR' and a crown.

Milk

Soaring food prices mean milk can't always be bought every day, and each drop is precious. While there's milk for the baby there's still hope. Today it's wasting away, tomorrow it will be sucking at the fat teat with its rosy cheeks.

The milkman sees everything on his rounds of Essen's tenements – births, marriages, who's working. His steps on the stairs are the first herald of the day, and get people out of their beds. They drowsily open the door to him wearing just their vests, without embarrassment, and he'll see inside – the lard gone cold on a plate from last night's supper, a piece of stale bread on the oilcloth, dirty beer mugs, a thin sediment of acorn coffee. Aha! A heap of dirty work clothes in the corner, the stink of a miners' boots drying on the stove. To his nose they smell sweeter than incense. It means father's working, so they're living.

'I'll pour you first grade, shall I Madam?'

And he's not wrong.

With enough to eat comes joy. At the next flat bare feet patter gaily across the floor to the door, which is opened to the smart milkman with a cheerful smile. Behind her on the table is a pale slab of margarine, which always makes its appearance when the money is coming in. Warm sleepy eyes hit the bib of my starched apron. 'Oh, Mr Milkman, you're late today! I didn't know you had a new helper!'

In most flats there is no margarine on the table. At first it had seemed to me that Essen's miners and metalworkers lived better than ours in Russia. A collar and stiff shirt front, clean shoes and a smart hat. Lunch in a tidy bag. It wouldn't hit you so much now that workers and peasants in our country are getting more comfortable. For us, growing prosperity means new boots, fur coats, warm shawls and mittens, a heavy comfortable sheepskin. In the West, shiny department stores with their annual sales are at workers' service, with their mountains of smart hastily run-up rags. Five roubles for a coat, 80 kopecks for stockings, three roubles for a decent looking pair of boots, which turn to dust the minute you put them on, fade in the sunlight, and have a mortal dread of air, wind and rain. German workers will deny themselves the most basic necessities and go short of food and sleep if only to dress smartly and not stand out in the crowd with their shabby clothes. Their day-to-day living requirements are infinitely more sophisticated than ours, and as long as poverty doesn't destroy them and break their bones, they wouldn't dream of putting on a dirty shirt, or tolerating a bug or cockroach in their home.

'You wanted to meet the Lokführer (train-driver)?' the milkman asks. 'He's on the third floor, they take six bottles and one of cream. Twenty years on the railways. His old woman is a comrade of ours. Go on up, the old dog probably isn't back yet'. And indeed he wasn't. A charming young lady opened the door.

'Comrade ...'

Her plump pale unlined face, the face of a thirty-year-old girl who hadn't given birth or been close to the heat of a kitchen stove, winced and turned hostile. 'I'm not your comrade. Go and see mother, she's in the kitchen'.

After all the poverty, this labour aristocrat's warm spacious flat with its bright kitchen was paradise. Shelves, chairs, cupboards, towels, tablecloths, all spotlessly clean. A delightful fragrant cloud over the coffee-pot. Butter, ham and white bread on the table. A grand piano in the sitting room, paper flowers, curtains, carpets, two magnificent beds in the bedroom, with mountains of feather quilts and snowy linen. Frau Rotte, the mistress of all this prosperity and abundance, was a stout anxious-looking woman of about fifty, with a kindly face, her left eye twitching with a nervous tic. Her husband wasn't in. Lying on a chair was his old formal work dress, a blue jacket with red cuffs, and a sword presented to him for his quarter of a century's service on the railways, which Frau Rotte said sourly had 'made a man of him'.

Frau Rotte had been a communist since she was roughly three years old, she said, when her mother, the widow of a labourer, left with little children on her hands, would have to entertain the priest on whom she depended for financial assistance. As soon as his heavy steps sounded on the stairs on Sundays, the whole family would settle down around the Bible and sing psalms. This comedy went on for many hateful years.

Ever since then she couldn't look at a priest without shuddering. She had married young, and the local women said she couldn't have done better – a *Lokführer*, a man of honest character, in good standing with his boss. Depression gripped her after the first children arrived. Her husband religiously brought home all his pay, keeping nothing back for himself. But although he never missed a day visiting her at the clinic, Frau Rotte was filled with such bitterness and despair that even after thirty years she couldn't forgive him. Herr Rotte held the whole family in an iron grip. He would force them to go to church on Sundays, and not allow them to read a single newspaper. Often it seemed to her she was re-living her mother's life – the priest's footsteps kept sounding in her head. Old Rotte kept his sons at their studies with his fists and the lash, and they all ended up as technicians or accountants. Heinrich handled the correspondence at Mannesman's engineering works, Otto was a cashier at a big bank. All of them loyal servants to their masters, their class instinct firmly stamped out by their father – pen-pushers who felt nothing but disgust for the workers. Back in the war her son Heine had gone along to a workers' meeting, and the poor lad forgot to take off his monocle – which he really did need to wear for short-sightedness – and he got beaten up. He never forgave his class for the mis-understanding, and didn't repeat his shy attempt to return to 'his own'. Over the years Frau Rotte had quietly watched her husband crippling her children polit-ically, selling them off one by one to the employers. Then in 1917 she chanced to run into a communist rally, took a gulp of revolution, and came home drunk from it. It was too late now for the older children, but she managed to save her youngest son, who became a metalworker and joined the Young Communist League.

Since then she and old Rotte had agreed not to argue about politics at the dinner table, to keep the family peace. But the loss of her daughters caused her untold grief. In this family, like a cross-section of the social stratification of Germany's highest-paid workers, the girls worked as typists and clerks, rep-resenting all the bourgeois republics from Scheidemann to Seeckt. They hated their father, who hadn't given one of them a proper education – hated his uni-form, his voice and his fist. But their mother's communism was infinitely more hateful to them. Their father's broad back had at least lifted them up and set them on the next rung of the ladder; they hadn't to choke on factory fumes or black bread. Admittedly, Frau Rotte's daughter said her boss treated his secret-aries no better than he did his labourers. The beautiful girl in her office who could type in three languages and knew book-keeping was out of a job now because she dared to reject his advances.

Frau Rotte tried to exploit the situation. 'Come with me to the meeting, Minna!' she said.

Minna stiffened her soft smooth neck. 'You get such horribly common people there, Mother. A girl who earns 125 Marks can't be involved in such idiocies, I'm going to the cafe!'

The old woman lost her temper then, and with a special feminine sensitiv-ity, struck her in her most painful well-padded place. 'You're thirty now, just you wait, in five years you'll be finished! None of those rich men will marry you, and no worker will want you either! You'll be going from office to office like a lost dog! You'll see yourself in the mirror – tired, grey, worn out! You're worse than your father. The old man's got some convictions, even if they're wrong – you've got nothing! You'd happily give up the work you despise, and your body too, just to get a man to give you a comfortable life! *Du Klassenlose!*' (Class traitor!)

It's the strongest abuse a worker can throw at another, and through the powder on her mealy-white cheeks Minna blushed ...

Slippers

They're comfortable camelhair slippers. Everyone thinks they're foreign, probably English, because of their chequered pattern. Four Marks fifty pfennings a pair.

In fact these 'Anglo-Saxons' are made in the town of Hanau by special slipper seamstresses, who sew them at home. The slippers are afraid to breathe, for fear of betraying their lowly origins. They reek of poverty. Frau Kremer is paid four Marks for a hundred, and in an hour she can complete five. Her daughter, in just her second year in the job, can sew seven in fifty-five minutes. To work for forty years, and be beaten by the automatic advantage of youth, Frau Kremer says. Like a cabman's horse, however many years it clatters its hooves on the road, its skill won't increase. However fast she works, jabbing her needle in at lightning speed with the corns on her fingers, it makes no odds. Any country foal can outjump her. She can push herself to the limit, but it won't increase her earnings. The faster the needle flies, the more often the cheap weak thread breaks, and her employer gains too. It's all calculated and measured out so meanly she can't save a pfennig, and often has to put in some herself.

It's tempting to sew the warmer thicker-soled slippers, padded with cotton-wool. A young working girl ignorant of the craft easily falls into this trap. But you won't catch Frau Kremer out. Let others burn their fingers, she knows it's all a matter of needles. For the warmer ones, the factory-owner pays not ten but all of fifteen pfennigs. But it's harder to push through a double sole than a normal one, and for both types you're supplied with exactly the same number of needles. Three per hundred. As if she didn't know that with the cotton-wool ones the best seamstress will break at least ten. The tricks the bosses use to squeeze the last drop of energy out of a human being are boundless. It's easier to sail a ship round the Cape of Good Hope than to stitch a bulky sole so not a single stitch shows. Add it up – how many plain ones can be sewn in an hour? Five. But with the padding, just three, and an extra pfennig on needles. So for the same sixty minutes the boss will give ten pfennigs less.

With her hunched back and black rags, Frau Kremer is a monument to sorrow. If life came to her today with outstretched arms, she would just purse her lips and hide her store of unfinished slippers out of reach. Frau Kremer lives in her room, with its broken window, its mattress leaking feathers, its unemptied chamber-pot, its tap with no water, like a mouse fallen into an anthill, half gnawed to pieces. She has only one means of defence, total distrust. She is against everything. The SPD are rogues, every word they say is a lie. The communists are cowards, they let 1923 slip by. What does it matter to her if the party was ready for the struggle or not, or how many more months or years are still needed to lead the proletariat to victory? And when might that be? Frau Kremer doesn't believe in strikes or socialism, or smallpox vaccinations. Everything that comes from the masters is a big swindle. Didn't she hide her little grandson for a whole year from the municipal doctor? Then one day they came and dragged him off to hospital and pricked him all over – and there, wasn't she right, four pockmarks up his arm!

'The union doesn't want me', she says. 'They'd stop me working for such low pay, I'd lose the job'.

But today is a big labour holiday. Her only son, fifteen years old, employed at the cigar-box factory, is out on strike for the first time in his life. The strike has only just started, with 135 workers involved, and no hope of succeeding – strike breakers are already pouring in from the surrounding villages.

No grumbling, not a word of complaint. She acts as if it means nothing to her, and she doesn't even notice his presence. But how she gazes at him as she puts his food on the table, sitting there with his tall manly back. How proud she is of him, for being true to his class, for the solidarity that passes from generation to generation, for the young courage that doesn't remember past defeats. 'My boy's on strike you know', she tells all the neighbours.

He a Communist, She a Catholic

Factory workers robbed of their livelihoods by their politics tend to belong to the older generation. The young peasant lad, who lives at his father's for free, will go off to the factory whatever the pay, however long the hours, just to earn himself a few Marks for his beer, a new bicycle, and a smart suit with knee-breeches for Sundays. Older workers who have lived through long years of trade union and revolutionary struggle are less compliant, despite their comparatively high wages and their status as the aristocrats of labour, less likely to give up on their demands without a fight.

The result of even the most moderate cautious resistance however is generally the sack. At first the worker is not too depressed. He has excellent references going back years, his trade is picking up, and tomorrow if not today there's bound to be a vacancy somewhere. Anyway his wife is working, and earning a decent wage.

No one tells him about the cruel laws of unemployment, they come into force by themselves. The one who feeds the family is head of the household. Returning from a hard day's work, father likes to sit down to a good spread on the table in a clean and tidy home, the children washed and brushed before he returns, their noses wiped and homework done. Now it's mother slamming the door shut every morning, and he must put her apron on and start the housework, washing the dishes, rinsing the cloth he cleaned the pots and pans with, doing the dusting, cleaning the windows, taking out the slops, sluicing down the kitchen floor, making the bed, hanging the feather quilt over the window to air in the sun, then putting it back in its place with meticulous care.

We Russians haven't the least conception of the ritual of cleanliness and order the wife of an average German worker, even the poorest, performs every day in her home. You could watch her for hours, cleaning, washing and scrubbing her kitchen, crockery and linen. Not just flipping a wet rag round now and then, like we do. No, under the sofa, behind the stove, along the windowsill, and in the furthest corners where no one ever looks. All this must now be carried out by her husband. And just as in good times past he would run a finger along the stove to check there wasn't a speck of dust, and not forgive his wife if a single spot was missed, now it's he who must answer to her. She is head of the household now, who works to feed the family. He is her subordinate, her obedient domestic help, her nanny in trousers, who must change the children's nappies and check their homework and clean her shoes, a washer-up in his own hearth and home. And as he pushes her mop into the corners, or sits over a bag of potatoes with his sleeves rolled up getting dinner ready, he feels degraded to the depths of his masculine being, and attempts to redress the balance in his own way.

On her payday he is sulky and irritable, and a furious scene breaks out when she bashfully lays her week's earnings on the table. The crash of a fist. The old lash comes off the wall. 'Who's master here, you or me?' The children cry. Mother begs his forgiveness. After dinner they go off to the bedroom, and he makes her beg for a long time, and takes her with hatred, making her cry out so loud she can be heard on the staircase. Then he sends her out to buy cigarettes. Never, even in the days of good money, has he loved her with such a jealous love as when it has to be bought.

It has to be said most German men see their wives as their servants, and look down on their work. Even many communists deep in their souls see things this way, like any petty bourgeois. 'Look what I've been reduced to!' says comrade Kamm, out of work three years. And adding to his humiliation is that he's being supported by his wife's family, wealthy Catholic peasants, with portraits of the Kaiser on the walls and masses on Sunday, whose father-in-law is standard-bearer of the veterans' association of the 166th Regiment of blue-and-yellow Uhlans. They had been against the marriage from the start. What had possessed their tall fine honest peasant daughter to marry this short restless former foundry worker, who changed bosses like gloves, and was incapable of supporting her and their child? And now he'd fallen into financial dependence on them, they were seeking to review the whole family constitution to her advantage, at the expense of her shiftless husband. Yes, little Lieschen can spend the whole summer with grandma and grandpa, and it won't cost a penny, and on Saturdays we'll send dumplings, lard and goose to town. But only if she goes to church every Sunday and doesn't miss a single mass. If father wants us to support him, he must tell her God exists, and the godless will go to hell.

What could he do? He must just go along with it, and luckily Lieschen shares his sceptical way of thinking, and they understand each other. 'Lieschen', he says, sitting her on his knee, while the old folk stand there watching, 'Remember I told you there was no God, and heaven was just a silly tale for children? Well I was wrong, I made a mistake. He really is up there sitting in the sky, and he sees and knows everything'.

The little girl nods, 'Yes, Daddy'.

Kamm knows his own kind. It's a good thing she has a nose as cold as a dog's for their tricks.

For three years he has done the washing, baked bread, learnt to darn his wife's stockings, and all he's got from her are reproaches. How he was fit for nothing with his stupid communism, how the communists made use of him now he was unemployed. 'What have they ever done for you? They don't even pay you for working for them!' You could go out of your mind.

Sometimes he escapes from her for a few days, and goes round the villages with his satchel of communist papers, climbing the hills to remote upland settlements where no communist has ever been before. But all the tracks lead back down to the valley, and he must go home to his beloved daughter and his beautiful pious imperious wife.

And when he gets back, and they're alone together in the bedroom, who would have thought it of this devout respectable girl, with her perpetually downcast eyes, it's as if all is forgiven. But when it's over and she's had her fill, she says 'all that' changed nothing. 'And don't forget to remind me, tomorrow we must buy Lieschen a new prayer-book, are you listening! The Old and New Testaments!'

Junkers

Like any true scientist, Professor Junkers had to break out of the university and leave its walls forever to devote himself to science. This he did in 1909, along with his old colleague and assistant Doctor Mader, whose stern gaze was fixed on the internal combustion engine, as it still is today, nearly twenty years later. The university required them to teach a limited number of subjects to ignorant young men, and they were glad to be free to pursue their research in peace.

Junkers hadn't left his *gymnasium* at Aachen intending to take up aviation. The flying machine interested him no more than any other machine. If flying had ever been an art rather than a science, it was surely in those years. It engaged dreamers, sportsmen, adventurers and martyrs. They constructed funny little boxes out of sailcloth, wires and matchboard, and on these paper kites they flew or fell at the will of fate – from the standpoint of 1925, a year of calm reckoning, irrationally, brilliantly, and in profound ignorance. Almost every attempt to fly ended in disaster. Every day, spectators were running across fields and jumping over fences to heaps of smouldering wreckage. As many frontline aviators lost their lives in a single day then as die now in a whole year. Humanity was clearing its path to the sky on paper wings spattered with blood.

Junkers had nothing to do with this noble madness. After many years' toil in the quiet of his office in the little town of Dessau, he just decided to take a look at the comparatively unresearched field of aeronautics, and his research brought about a world revolution in its study and application.

The guiding principal of his research was extremely simple. Think of the bird or insect in whose image a machine could be built that flew without skin, and was just bare bones and nerves, like a living creature which carried its innards on the outside. Those early flying experiments had done just that. The heart lay on top, but with no protection at all. The wind whistled through the extensive rigging, clogging it with dust, soaking it in the rain. And despite the machine's obvious lightness, all the webs, strings and boards increased its surface area and air resistance tenfold. Junkers decided to cover the plane's nakedness, make a chest for its heart and a stomach for its guts. Count Zeppelin's stupid giant sausages, made partly of aluminium, still commanded the attention of the public and the Imperial Court. Kaiser Wilhelm greatly fancied the scale and militaristic look of these contraptions, and launched whole fleets of them into the air. Professor Junkers took out a patent for the first machine to be made entirely of aluminium, in which pilot and fuel tanks would be hidden inside a silver oblong body.

The war brought the Professor resources and world fame. Satisfied that he could at last work without worrying about the pennies, the kindly Junkers, who looks more like a vicar than a scientist, sent model after model and flight after flight to the fronts. His fighter planes became, after submarines, the favourites of Admiral Tirpitz. The buzzing of his silver aerial dragonflies left indelible scars of fear in the memories of millions still alive and the millions who fell.

Then Versailles forced German heavy industry to switch to peacetime production, and work halted. His plans for a torpedo-carrying plane went to Paris, and Entente commissioners came to his factory in Dessau and smashed with their hammers everything that could serve the aims of war. At the height of Germany's inflationary crisis, when anyone could become chief of any concern if they were smart enough to send a couple of thousand dollars with their visiting-card, the big sharks Stinnes and AEG gathered in the murky waters around Junkers. But he had had enough experience with War Department officials to have no illusions about the fate awaiting him in the pockets of private businessmen. The merchant is an enemy of any innovation not forced on him by competition. He must make the most of what already exists, and milk as intensively as possible any idea that has already won its market. It wouldn't enter the merchant's head to compensate the Professor for experiments that had by now swallowed up most of his means and his government grants.

At this difficult time, God sent Junkers two guardian angels to deliver him from the voracious jaws of the speculators. One was his advanced aluminium smelting workshop, which had survived Versailles, and to this day repays his costly ventures into the land of the unknown. The other was the pilot Sachsenberg.[1] Every Don Quixote needs his Sancho Panza. To allow the scientist's thoughts to range freely, make mistakes, drop what has been started and start all over again, whatever the cost, a devoted donkey of practical common sense must follow behind him. Its broad back will carry him out of any situation, and on days of setbacks will seek out its hero in a roadside ditch, and lick his muddied face with the heavenly caress of its warm rough tongue.

The post-war economic crisis, which forced Krupp to make milk separators and false teeth, and big Stumm the battleship king to go into children's toys, was easier for Junkers' factories, and allowed him to take his work in new directions. The tiny bird of prey, fleetingly glimpsed in the war as a barely noticeable spot in the sky, now descended and grew bigger, and gradually its whole body was reborn. The head was enlarged, the trunk extended, and the wings threw

---

1   World War 1 naval fighter ace Gotthard Sachsenberg (1891–1961), with 31 victories. In 1917 appointed commander of the world's first naval air wing.

themselves into an iron cross. Impelled by hunger, the eagle of war then entered the service of the post office. It was then that Sachsenberg, an outstanding organiser, came up with his scheme to expand post office operations into an international commercial airline, and offered him his services.

The waves of revolution rose high, and aristocratic officers with thorough-bred noses had their epaulettes ripped off, and left Germany to join foreign legions, or were hired by the armies of the small Baltic states to do their dirty work, hunting down Bolsheviks. The governments of small shopkeepers had no intention however of allowing these agents of German imperialism to settle in their countries. Latvians hadn't forgotten the agrarian riots of 1905 against the hated German barons, and the peasants hanged on the baronial estates, or how the head of the Baltic nobility had handed over the keys of Riga to the Kaiser. In short, the mercenaries were used then booted out.

In 1919, a group of officers from the old Imperial Fleet made their way back to Germany, virtually on foot, and to avoid serving the hated Republic, they took up farming. They planted potatoes and carted muck, and would lift their heads from the plough or spade to follow with a longing gaze Junkers' mail planes flying over the fields. It was Sachsenberg who saw that these men from the old officer caste, his former colleagues, no use to anyone in Germany, hated by the proletariat and the finance aristocracy alike, could take to the sky as the first pilots in Junkers' new airline operation. Russian emigres in Paris are known as first-class hairdressers, waiters and chauffeurs, and Junkers' pilots soon became known as the best chauffeurs of the international skies, travelling the horizons of Europe and Asia in his planes as calmly as if driving the Paris boulevards.

The commercial side of the business required that boarding an aeroplane should be as simple as boarding a lift or a train. Aviation had to be dethroned and demystified, stripped of all its old romantic features, so as not to scare off the nervous bourgeoisie. The interiors were made to look reassuringly famil-iar, with cabins like railway carriages, seats from the smoking-room of a bank, mirrors from a middling restaurant, handy spitoons and clean lavatories. Obli-ging paper bags for queasiness beckoned from nails. But so rare were accidents, so calm the pilot's mittens on the control column, that passengers could relax. Aviators will soon be the equals of Paris chauffeurs, and flying will become ten times more popular when they're wearing livery and can accept tips.

The irony of all this demystifying of aviation is that it has attracted some of the last great romantics of the old regime, coolly stepping out of their machines after flying the world to wipe the passengers' vomit off their silver wings, many of them wounded war heroes, carrying their wooden legs from the cockpits when they land.

Germany belongs to the Republic, its land cut up and divided for many years to come, with none to spare. The stitches put in by Versailles and Dawes won't be unpicked by a bayonet for the time being. But the great blue continent of the sky is still barely discovered or conquered, with unsounded depths and untravelled roads, clouds moving across like opulent caravans open to plunder. And what is plundered will never be returned.

Command of the air will be decided by the changing balance of power, but the very boldest flights leave no trace. The Great Powers launch fleet after fleet into the air, but their ships are swallowed up in the world's expanse, their journeys infinitely small against the millions of miles that have yet to be covered. The sky is the stage for new wars. To shower Russia's snowy expanses with dynamite and nail China to the ground, the enemy's planes will have to rise like stars over the entire universe.

Furrowing through foreign skies in empty space, Junkers' planes are continually expanding an empire that no longer exists. China has been lost, Kiaochow seized, the Congo gone, the Baghdad railway torn from Germany's hands. But the skies of China are still open to the winds. High in the sky, the routes of the airways will cut across each other in this struggle for new colonies, which is only just warming up.

Junkers' planes are bound tightly by the knots of Versailles, working for any client anywhere. The tentacles of Deruluft[2] have reached Italy, Scandinavia and Switzerland, and Sachsenberg is now conducting an offensive into the Balkans and through the Balkans into Anatolian Turkey.

Not long ago Dessau began to stir like an alarmed beehive. Pilots who had just flown in from all parts of the world gathered at the bar, speaking strictly in order of rank, according to the list in the officers' mess. One was back from Persia, another from the sands of the Gobi Desert, a third from the dust and sunburn of a Russian summer.

'I hear the Crown Prince has a new horse'.

'How is His Highness's health, sir?'

'Very well, thank you. The King of Saxony ...'

Then the bombshell. 'Have you heard? Junkers has signed a concession with the Poles. We're to build a fleet for those scoundrels!'

For a week the airmen drank gloomily to the news, put their chauffeur's accounts in order, measured out miles to the nearest metre, chopped pieces of space from infinity. There was nothing to be done, such were the laws of capitalist development. The aviation trade was international, a member of no party or nation.

---

2   Deutscher-Russische Luftlinien, the joint German Soviet airline operating in the 1920s.

Homeless German imperialism was now running little fighters' nurseries for its friends and enemies alike, hoping its pupils didn't grow into teachers too quickly, that its own people would at the decisive moment find themselves at the helm, and the machines built by German engineers would one day rule the world. A vain hope. Foreign nations' war industries were learning avidly from Junkers' pilots and scientists. And having barely learnt to walk, they were driving from their command posts those they saw as irreconcilable enemies. The better Junkers' schools were, the sooner his pupils reached maturity and cast off their foreign tutelage, the more they endeavoured to be free of him, and his efforts to strengthen his position by honest and entirely disinterested work was proving futile. No one suffered their youthful ignorance and arrogance more painfully than Junkers, and however conscientiously he fulfilled his obligations, the gates of the factories he had built and put into operation kept slamming shut in his face. After the first disquieting telegrams, he redoubled his efforts, investing ever more resources into his threatened enterprises, and he was brought several times to the edge of ruin, with angry unemployed aircraft contractors descending on his quiet little house in Dessau.

Junkers is the purest of pure scientists, who runs his airline services to support his research, perhaps not fully grasping the huge political significance of the international organisation he has created. Of course he gives his contractors more than they give him. For what is money compared with the culture, knowledge and experience he spreads around the world, like Mechnikov with his yoghurt.

But in the final analysis the Professor can't complain of lack of success. Whatever countries' flags his airships fly under today, no government in the world has at its disposal such a well-integrated team of magnificently trained and educated airmen, engineers and scientists. Not one of them arrived ready-made. Most started out as volunteers, receiving no pay for months, suffering hardship and hunger. They have grown up with their machines. Each step forward and each new invention is checked in practice. And the pilots are a sensitive monitoring apparatus, without whom he couldn't function. How invaluable to him is indefatigable Jüterbog, endlessly circling the East. He flies low, hugging the earth, and in stormy weather the Caspian Sea spits foam onto his wings. He crawls through fogs and windy deserts, over the telegraph poles of the East India Company, but never have storms or fogs halted him on his flights. He'll roam for days on end, but he'll get his mailbag and his three Persian merchants, yellow from the pitching, to their destinations without fail. That's Jüterbog. There's nothing he doesn't know about tropical dew, desert dust, and the effects of air, sun and humidity on a plane's organism.

Then there's Herr N., promoted from junior mechanic to one of Junkers' best airmen. An ex-sailor, he's happy in thick fog, and isn't attracted to the East, he prefers the lushest, dampest, cheeriest bits of Europe. Over hundreds of miles, the damp winds of Holland beckon to him, the bright lights of Amsterdam's bars. N. is a night pilot, extraordinarily sensitive to danger. His bulging eyes, flush with his face, can see in the dark, and the night sky beneath him is like the sea-bed under a fishing boat.

For speed and altitude records there are the cold desperados, masters of space, who board their machines without changing their suits, and emerge with them uncreased. Demoted titled aristocrats and risk-lovers, overfed with life, frozen like bottles of wine in the rarefied atmosphere, whose value equates for them with the maximum amount of acute nervous pleasure to be squeezed from it. The result is immaterial. The object once achieved isn't worth talking about. Yet how exquisite those moments of single combat at a height of 5,200 metres, where danger dissolves in the air like a diamond in a glass of water.

But it's not in the new airlines that the roots of the Junkers enterprise lie, or in the agents' offices or the aerodromes, swept bare by the propellers' wings, or even in the main workshops of the famous Junkers aircraft factory in Dessau. Its heart lies in a modest little single-storey building standing apart from the commercial offices where Sachsenberg and his men run the business side of things. Here is Junkers' scientific research institute, his chemistry laboratory and archive. Experts say there's nothing like it in Europe.

All the work of the scientists gathered here is founded on the deepest mistrust of materials. The laboratory is an arena where metals fight for supremacy, like champions. Anyone can take part in the contest, specimens from the best known firms down to unheard of young fighters coming onto the market for the first time. Krupp's proud steel must prove its worth here every day. Any tramp met on the road can challenge it to a duel. The metal to win first prize in Junkers' laboratory today will be a celebrity by morning.

Bright aluminium triumphs over all its rivals, and the Professor won't be happy until all his aeroplanes are made from it. To date over twelve competitors are scrapping over this tough material – for engines, heat-resistant wheels, axles that don't snap on landing, a steady frame and a light wing. The metal skin of an Eskimo, fearing no amount of cold, and an African, surviving the tropical heat.

Research into raw materials begins with atoms. The metal is examined under microscopes and X-rayed. The slightest irregularity in the alignment of the crystals means the whole batch must be scrapped. Steel is the biggest thief. It needs only a fraction of a second to catch an alloy. A machine forces it to yield everything it has gathered and concealed. Stolen carbon is burnt up in its stubbornly clenched fist.

Priceless scientific material from this laboratory has been accumulated over the years. Meticulous records of its research are kept by outstanding scientists, and every young scientist before setting to work will study the relevant literature in these archives, standing on the shoulders of his predecessors.

No metal passes unrecognised through the laboratory's monitoring section. Any alloy can be detected from an imprint in the testing apparatus, like a criminal's fingerprint, and materials that pass the first purge must then go through a second and third. Every line of research proposed, however persuasive on paper, must be defended in practice on the metal body. Long thin pipes are being produced to sustain the whole weight of a wing. An improbably heavy load is lowered onto a fragile-looking reed. It withstands 9,000 kilos, over 40 per square millimetre, and breaks only after that. Steel veins twang on the torture rack, and snap at 5,200 kilos (50 per square millimetre). Mechanical scissors bite through threads used for sewing up parts of the apparatus. From thousands of skeins, iron hands select the one that will take 127 kilos, 25 kilos per square millimetre of cross-section.

Metals are like sinners in hell, cut, ground, stretched, torn and snapped. A little machine runs day and night, not letting them sleep, shaking the strips under trial, trembling with a light feverish tremble, like a plane travelling at full speed. In another corner, a skittle-like valve jumps up and down hour after hour, while a scientist observes its glowing core through a special tube, noting the slightest changes. Here every possible accident that could happen to an aeroplane is simulated and recorded. The plane is dismantled into thousands of its smallest parts, tested for the impact of wear and tear, heat, cold and stress. In its journey around the world, it fights storms and fires, crashes, drowns and burns, experiences a thousand perilous adventures without moving from its spot in the small laboratory.

Even the Chinese don't cherish their ancestors as this laboratory cherishes its bits of metal, mangled and twisted in experiments. They are safeguarded in the most perfect order – set out along the path of aviation like rows of unforgettable warnings. All errors must be corrected, and science's retentive memory must be forever alert to the one unsuccessful experiment in a hundred thousand successful ones.

The aeroplane is still very young, and its life expectancy hasn't been determined yet. There's a machine at Dessau that's been flying since 1919, and no one knows how much longer it will hold out. What does it eat? What kind of food is best for its delicate constitution? For years Junkers' chemists have been hovering around the issue of fuel, without coming to any definite conclusion. There are old men working here who've been led by the nose all their lives by frivolous fickle petrol, who in their old age are now coming round to the idea of divorce, and are turning their attention to heavy reliable uncapricious diesel, the fatty oil consumed by motor vehicles in the Alps, Russian snows and the Arctic.

'*Das sind nur Anhaltspunkte, Wir wissen noch nichts!*' (It's only the start, we still know nothing!) says the quiet little man who reports to the Professor every day on the behaviour of the oil.

Nothing! After so many years of toil and discoveries! Look at the scientist X-raying some microscopic membrane, and you suddenly go cold inside. How on earth did those first pilots fly with no *Anhaltspunkte*, just willpower? Junkers has many brave scientists working for him, but which of them would have dared go up on those iron wings, hanging on the walls now like the scabbards of medieval knights?

For all its perfection, Junkers' plant still resembles a university or a craftsman's workshop more than a factory. Production is barely mechanised. The machine is the worker's spare hand, assisting and taking over one of his many actions, but not carrying through a single operation to the end. It's impossible to maintain strict uniformity of type using the hand. One rudder-cable guide must be absolutely identical to another. One claw under the rail on which the machine rests when it lands must in no way differ from another. Workers can't turn away for a second from what they're doing. They must be totally focused on each seam, each nut. The engineer with the close-set eyes, flat face and infantry officer's cheekbones can walk round as much as he likes, beating his brow against the unknown, tracking every item arriving and leaving the workshop, scrutinising them as if in the barracks. There is always the risk that some slight act of neglect will lead to a catastrophe, a day, a month, a year from now. The work is slowed dreadfully by the fears that go with this responsibility. Scientists will sit for hours over a trifle, not daring to let it slip from their hands. Accustomed to relying on themselves, they're becoming as individualistic as the airmen. Each hammer speaks its own language. Benchmates don't understand each another.

Why am I reminded of the Professor's house, with its light rooms full of his scampering children, here in this section of the works ruled by such a reverential stillness, broken only by the faint scratching of a drawing pen, like the rustling of silk? Why am I reminded of his children now, outside the hangar, where twenty machines stand on an earthy meadow like swans. Not one looks like the next. Each has evolved from its own special embryonic idea, waiting to grow up and test its strength. A scientist's enormous patience is required to rear children, machines and ideas the way Junkers does. Of course it's hell for him at home. If one of his assistants calls with some papers, he has trouble finding a corner free of the lively chatter of his marvellous, self-educating, model children, growing up as their inner logic dictates. Any serious conversation at the table is unthinkable. There's always an age at which any situation seems madly comical, and one child dances a wild tribal dance over his father's wise head.

Now take a look at this same principle in the drawing-office. Several dozen highly talented designers employed to think, draw or do nothing all day at their benches, undaunted by their assignments. Any one of them can take any detail or basic principle and stand it on its head. The work creates an artificial selection of workers unafraid of independent thought. The engineers and designers in their white coats stand like anatomists before their silent drawing boards, a font for their new-born ideas, a registry office for their findings. A meticulous clerk writes out the birth certificate of each new idea as soon as one lifts its head from the formulas and figures.

The most talented engineer in this section is a pale, thin, unusually sensitive-looking young man, a former apprentice, who vaulted over his more professionally qualified contemporaries in the feverishly competitive promotion race. In appointing him to one of the section's most senior and responsible posts, Junkers was showing his appreciation of not only his talent but his whole physiology, which is filled with a sharp aversion to brute force and brute physical toil. No one will eliminate the remnants of the aeroplane's animal nature with greater delight than the upstart ex-worker who despises his 'lowbrow' class. The future belongs to the brain. Aeroplanes, like engineers and scientists and all creatures of the higher ruling strata, shouldn't have a body. And now before him, on a wide sheet of Bristol board, he is already putting the finishing touches to Junkers' latest precious project. The machine's body is to be drastically pruned. Its trunk, first long like a dragonfly's, is now short and fat like a bee's, reduced to almost nothing, its passengers and cabin hidden away in the wing, tucked under its arm.

In this shipyard of the air, the new fliers stand almost finished, filling the hangar with the heady smell of paint, drunk on the oil and spirits with which they're rubbed and fed in the final preparations. The day isn't far off now when they'll be rolled out onto the field.

The banging of hammers echoes like a victory march. An armless machine tries on its wings and feels for the first time the unprecedented toughness and flexibility of its shoulders. Then, without knowing what to do with them, it suddenly realises what the patch of sky in the square of the doorway is for.

Workers with nails between their teeth crawl through the empty eye sockets in the skull, upholstered with soft leather on the inside, and there's a pool of petrol on the bare ground. It's peeing, so it's alive.

Ullstein

No need to run to the telegraph office for the news, it arrives on its own. A little bird drops it on the editor's desk, already translated into the human language, printed out by a small gadget onto a narrow ribbon of paper. Ten small machines tap away night and day. A dark monastery with a hundred cells. A hundred telephone booths, a hermit in each, invoking the god of sensation with wild cries: 'Hallo! Hallo! This is Berlin, *B.Z, Berliner Zeitung*, Ullstein! Hallo! Speak up!'

Messengers doze on chairs, like passengers waiting for trains forever arriving and departing, never standing still. Trains full of news, circling the globe. Many have been waiting since the previous evening. They have already met the specials from America and the Entente Express, packed with flighty little Stock Exchange bulletins, those bewitching adventuresses slipping unnoticed across the borders with their scanty luggage packed with fake news, the precious contraband so hunted by newspapermen.

Ullstein's house is big enough to accommodate all comers. 4,500 rooms, six floors, staircases like elevator chutes, a dozen separate printshops – the best mills in Germany, grinding their daily harvest of lies and truth. Six newspapers that bake the daily bread for Berlin's millions, and for Germany as a whole, catering to all layers of the population, to both sexes and all ages, and to each of its cities individually. Cologne doesn't eat what Berlin likes. Dresden's favourite dish won't find customers in Frankfurt. For the Hamburg docker, it's Knackwurst and beer. For Dresden, pickled ham and sauerkraut. For southerners, anything light, nourishing and tasty.

Nobody travels on foot in Ullstein's house. Stairs are for idlers, here people fly by lift, racing up the floors in open cages. The door has been done away with, the lift man has gone the way of the ichthyosaurus. The lift stops nowhere and waits for no one. People leap on one of the platforms while moving, and leap off while moving. Proofs, copy and telegrams follow a similar course in practical gymnastics. Leading articles, weighty feuilletons and paunchy political commentaries have all become acrobats and circus artistes, running from building to building, snatching the electric postmen's wire baskets, crossing yards on a wire, flying up and down at hair-raising speed.

The Ullstein corporation has grown immeasurably since the days the first Ullstein built his first small printshop, a shed on the Kochstrasse. Yet once the business reached a certain level of perfection, it always had to stop for a while to gobble up its old innards. The day the ever self-renewing spirit of industry dares not club its own skull, or digest obsolete production methods in its own stomach, it will become breakfast for a more powerful and flexible competitor. Take the first Ullstein publication, *Berliner Morgenpost*. It grew out of a cemetery, not of old production methods, but of Bismarck's destruction of the entire Social Democrat press. It was then that Ullstein was able to produce his paper aimed at the broad masses of the petty bourgeoisie, throwing hundreds of thousands of copies onto the deserted newspaper market – into the breach made by Bismarck's Anti-Socialist Laws.

How work methods have changed since then! From hand-setting to mechanical setting, from drawings to photography, from smudgy anaemic photos to artistic montage. After each technological revolution, a brief sickness, as after a vaccination, then a frantic leap forward. The prey – hundreds of thousands of new readers, with new buildings, workshops, staff, drivers, lorries and telephones. In the recent post-war years, appendicitis hit the newspaper industry from the old English typecasting machines that ran on gas and kept having to be topped up with molten tin, or they wouldn't work. German machines have now been brought in to replace them, which devour plain simple coal, and can be topped up whenever you wish. From one cardboard mould you can now get thirty metal castings.

The printworks know no gratitude, acknowledge no past services rendered. Life has left the old section now. It's cold and empty, its dead windows reflecting the fire lit in the furnace of its successful rivals. The cheerful clank of matrixes and files brushing their hot edges drift over to the now banished section, like the clatter of knives on plates.

To begin with, the first Ullstein produced only one newspaper, fearing an evening one would reduce its circulation. Today, like a clever madame, Ullstein sends dozens of papers into the streets, distinctly dressed, speaking different languages, landing on the pavements at different times, not getting in each other's way. Like streetwalkers, they share the streets and don't quarrel, each with her own customers. In the morning, *Vossische Zeitung*, for the Stock Exchange and the banks, latching onto the smart operators standing in Aschinger's restaurant with a sandwich and a mug of beer in hand. She gets into the taxi with them, and they have time to do their business with her in the five minutes between the restaurant and the office or Stock Exchange. A clever well-informed paper, edited by one of Germany's top journalists. Every speculator hopes he'll get something useful for his fifteen pfennigs.

While the husbands are at work, Ullstein's *Die Praktische Berlinerin, Die Dame* or *Blatt der Hausfrau* call on their wives, running from door to door, enflaming appetites with whispers about the cheapest coffee-pot, a housecoat for 3.70 Marks, a double-bed, a pregnancy remedy. *Blatt der Hausfrau* is a miracle of typographical technique. In one shot, the machine not only prints the

96 pages of the magazine's text and its cover, but cuts, collates and folds them, ejecting the finished product into a tray. In this way, 3,500 copies can be produced in a single hour. For subscribers to *Die Dame*, there's the needlework section, with patterns for cheap nightcaps supplied free of charge. Before she has time to think, a woman will be putting money aside for future purchases, like a bird gathering straw for a nest, her daydreams anticipated and snipped out by Ullstein's cutters. Spirits of future overcoats, blouses and tablecloths beckon to her from the fog of the future and the tinsel neverland of fresh clichés.

There are horses that can solve problems and dogs that know geography, but what intelligence a machine may acquire no one yet knows. Hoffmann's mechanical Olympia sang romantic songs and took her curtsey – but that's nothing. At Ullstein's, a worker sits in front of a machine and types on a keyboard. He presses a letter, and it breaks out of its place and lies down at the beginning of the line. Then next to it a second, a third, and in two seconds the whole line is moulded from the tin and jumps onto the galley. Once the word is on the galley, the letters are no longer needed and they demobilise, go off to their homes. The machine lowers its long black arm, snatches up the used composition and places it on a special track along which the letters tumble like keys into a keyhole.

Old Ullstein's youngest daughter, *Berliner Zeitung*, comes onto the streets at noon, the fastest, most persistent and accessible of her sisters, like a fly or lizard, with a readership of 16,000,000, and growing. Anyone can catch her on the wing for next to nothing. She has neither her own opinions nor her own voice, she is a little puddle, in which the whole world is reflected. In two minutes, in a language intelligible to anyone, she can re-state in the simplest crudest way what the big press is saying and thinking that day. No need to chew the news over, it's been chewed already and is fully digested. One swallow, and you're informed. The man who has no time to think or collect his own information can't live without this handy intermediary, this echo of the big cities, this flying street gramophone. She is born of the wastepipes of all the other newspapers, and she lives for half-an-hour. Her appearance is eagerly awaited. Millions of people check their watches awaiting their rendezvous with *B.Z.* Yet no paper is so quickly forgotten or abandoned, on bus seats, cafe tables, the floors of trains, as this little tigress with over a million readers, queen of the leftovers, emerging every day from the froth of the streets.

12.10 p.m: the first Stock Exchange bulletin is posted. 12.12 p.m: the last telegram is taken in the composing room. 12.15 p.m: editors stop taking copy. 12.16 p.m: the rotary press puts on its armour of gleaming plates. 12.17 p.m: the duty engineer switches on the current. The continent's largest rotary presses are starting their morning's work.

The pages flow like water on a mill-wheel. A word is no more than a microbe in their torrent. The first finished collated copies edge into view, and off they trip into the world with the crack of machine guns. This is the morning assault, the crossfire of the press, shots that never miss or misfire. Every sheet will be read by someone, every shot will hit someone. The boom of the offensive hangs in the air. Bales of papers cover the floors, giant cocoons of lies, from which will flutter millions of ephemeral butterflies.

The building is like a fortress, its deep yards, separated from the city by mountains of granite, resembling those of a prison. In the event of siege, a fortress must have stocks of water and bread. Ullstein has an energy source independent of the city's, which can feed his besieged machines for a week in the event of a strike. At the first sign of unrest, the armour-plated doors will slam shut, and within three minutes of the alarm, generators will be pumping thousands of horsepower of electrical strike-breakers to the machines. No employees will go in or out of the gates unnoticed, the doorkeepers have been drilled on who or what to let in. And at 12.18, strike or no strike, eight minutes after the last telegram, the sluices will be raised, the doors opened wide, and newspapers will overflow into the street. Conveyor tubes throw bundles straight onto lorries. Light motorbikes stand throbbing, waiting their turn. Cyclists hold open their bags. The couriers who travel with the newspapers to the station to deliver them to the provinces abandon their unfinished lunches. On Saturdays 400 tons are loaded. Twenty mail trains taking a single lunchtime paper. Counting the other publications, that's 75 mail coaches in three-quarters-of-an-hour.

A newspaper outstrips time. A newspaper overtakes the hands of the clock. A human being sleeps for half his life. He steals the night hours for himself. Clearing the hurdle of speed, the newspaper stumbles over an insuperable obstacle, a barricade of snoring nightcaps. But in the cities everything is relative, dawn can put on pyjamas. From now on Europe will be like Greenland or the Arctic Ocean, its electric day will be continuous. At 8.30 p.m., the news vendors turn up for their evening shifts outside Aschingers. By 8.40 p.m., provincial editions of *Vossische Zeitung* are out in Berlin, minus the final telegrams that are printed and transmitted at night. A piece of tomorrow, a piece of the future, with football results, the names of dreamers who've fallen under motor-cars, debates in the English House of Commons, all for fifteen pfennigs.

Ullstein is one of the great powers levying a duty on any vulgarity that can be imported into the human brain. He is like a wharf, where ocean-going liners discharge phrases that fit neatly into the consciousness, like rubber protectors on down-at-heel boots, unloading witticisms as flat as the soles, smutty anecdotes and political slogans. The masterpiece in this genre, without par, is of course his *Berliner Illustrierte Zeitung*, the most widely distributed magazine in modern Germany. Thirty-two pages of laxative ease. A peephole drilled into the boudoir of a celebrated filmstar, a chink through which anyone can spy on a beautiful woman in the bath, from Spitzbergen to the Cape of Good Hope. Fragments of banal racy novels you read in the lavatory. Adverts. A prince's wedding. Another advert. Ten pages of adverts.

But *Illustrierte* has never been an enemy of Soviet Russia. It publishes interesting unexpected stories about its streets, demonstrations and crowds, its children's homes and hospitals, its leaders and the army, and German workers probably learn more from it about the true face of the USSR than from anywhere else. Russia, like everything else in *Illustrierte*, is a sensation.

B.Z is a cipher on Russia. Its sober practical minded businessmen readers will more readily accept an established stable government there than one still existing only in the heads of Russian aristocrats on the Kurfurstendamm. If the Bolsheviks can hold out another five years, *B.Z* will treat Berlin's White emigres just as it treated Russian students in Berlin after the 1905 revolution, as criminal subversives. For now Ullstein is hedging his bets, quietly printing the writings of the White Guard Rul in one of the secluded corners of his house, mixing *B.Z*'s bland editorials with headlines lifted straight from the far-right press – and when repeated 16,000,000 times, they echo more loudly than Moses' commandments from the mountain of the Hebrews.

Illustrierte doesn't deliver its politics in headlines or editorials, it tattoos them on a music-hall artiste's velvet skin, a celebrated ballerina's underwear, or a bottle of scented water for removing foul odours from the armpits. *B.Z* too likes to stay light and entertaining, with stories of yachts and motorboats furrowing the seas, of racehorses jumping fences, of an American boxer getting his nose cracked, of *B.Z* motorbikes setting speed records. Dog shows, prizes for the best pedigree bull, tennis and football matches, swimming competitions. Europe pays close attention to such things, sports champions are better known now than the most important political figures. Every decent paper now has a sports page, and *B.Z* was the first to cash in on this goldmine. Ullstein introduced a special sports section while others were still sending their crime reporters to cover the matches and races. He took on a special sports editor, dispatched plenipotentiaries to all Europe's totalisators, and attached correspondents to all the famous racing stables.

Ullstein knows nothing about art, and has hired an assistant, a gentleman connoisseur of old porcelain and all the eighteenth-century snuff-boxes in the world, to edit his small monthy magazine *Querschnitt*, printed on vellum paper, for a few hundred subscribers. *Querschnitt* is like a lily, floating on Ullstein's millions, far above the midden beneath that gives life to the vulgarities of *B.Z* and *Illustrierte*, smelling fragrantly of African sculptures and very artistic very

naked drawings, intended for experts. Ullstein snorts with disgust at the aesthetes and their antics, but he leaves them alone. Let them root around in their
business. They bring no money in, but they attract people of taste and circum-
stance to his house, and it's good to have a classical Venus in the hall.

For his *Die heitere Friedolin*, with its dog on a bicycle on the cover, he needs
no assistants. No one knows better how much sugar and suet to stuff into his
little ten-pfennig daily paper for young children, a mixture of cops and robbers
cartoons and sentimental slush. 35,000 copies sold a day, 700,000 a month, its
hero a cycling police dog, with the soul of a *Vossische Zeitung* Sunday supple-
ment reader.

Lastly, there is his wildly popular fiction department, and his stable of best-
selling authors. None of the 'Immortals' stand a chance against them. Goethe
and Tolstoy have nothing on Mr Weber, author of *Yes, Yes, Love!* Good old Ullstein is like a camel with a date with his potboilers, to be chewed, spat out and
chewed again. Reading them isn't enough, you have to see them, and immediately on publication they get turned into films, made in German studios.
The shopgirl, the schoolmistress and the postal-clerk need happy endings. The
petty-bourgeois needs to believe an honest man can achieve anything, a villa,
a motorcar, his own shop, without bloodshed, violence or struggle. Anyone can
go along and see how honest little Alice, with her neatness, her good figure
and pretty face, finds her way into the world of German high finance and ends
up marrying Stinnes. Only this Stinnes is young and handsome, like the assistant in the outfitting department at Wertheim's. You can see workers and petty
clerks winning the lottery and marrying the boss's daughter. How people who
work hard all their lives die rich – look at their funeral processions, isn't it worth
being obedient all your life if you can be driven to 'rest' with all those pompoms
and top hats? What's the point of politics? Why make a revolution? Millions of
workers dream of revolution, and cling to their hopes for Russia. Ullstein sends
his readers to the pictures instead to see the promised land.

There are many Ullsteins now, increasingly monopolising the publishing
industry, threatening to overtake him. New press barons like former Krupp
manager Hugenberg, who has taken over many of the old 'non-party' newspapers to which the average German philistine has grown accustomed, turning
them into mouthpieces for the most rabid reaction. The services these factories
of bourgeois ideology rendered the government during the last war cannot be
overestimated. There were no pores in the social organism, no cells in the brain
they couldn't penetrate. Without the aid of the newspaper trusts pumping out
their cocaine for the masses, the government couldn't have squeezed out of its
citizens the millions they needed for the War Credits, sending millions to war
to be slaughtered. And now their heavy guns are pounding away at Russia: 'War

on Bolshevism!' 'War on World Revolution!' 'War on the Murderers of Innocent Shortsighted Whitehaired Kindermann with his Travelling First Aid Kit!'

Ullstein knows if he is to survive he must join them, no longer a cipher but a dangerous political weapon, whose power and reach are virtually unmatched in Europe, preparing the world for new wars, propping up the great wooden statue of Hindenberg standing by the Victory Column opposite the Reichstag.

The Ruhr under the Ground

'Sit there, don't move! If anyone tries to talk to you keep your mouth shut!' The door of the Works Committee office slams shut, and my guide's lamp tilts in the direction of the screening-shed. Shafts of light from its windows lie like white leaves across the desk. The office is bare, and loud snores echo from the shadows – or that's what it sounds like. In fact it's the noise of the compressor, driving the air down under the ground. You measure its breaths with infinite jealousy. Is it better than ours in Russia? Engineers pass through on their way to the night shift, their shadows waving sleeves across the floor, and my guide returns. 'Let's go. Take longer steps. Right hand in your pocket, push your cap further down'.

The lift hurtles down to the abyss. A modest little cage, for the pit isn't a large one, employing no more than about eight hundred miners. It has survived only because the coal can be loaded straight onto the Rhine.

Two hundred, three hundred metres down the shaft's black gullet. Golden fissures mark the different levels, and the cage stops, clanking like the wheels of a pit-tub, then drops again, the damp slime of the walls rushing to meet it at indescribable speed, longer than a flight of stairs, yet lasting only a second. It pulls up, groping blindly for the floor level, then settles carefully on the levers stretching up to meet it. The air stuffed into the ears like cotton-wool leaks out, and we're in a brightly lit underground station, with miners standing around, waiting to get on.

My guide leads the way to the first gallery, and it's as if someone is calling out in Russian in the darkness, so familiar are the sounds – the clatter of the ponies dragging their tubs, the quiet singing of the water streaming in plaits over the coals. No matter where they're from, a foreigner will feel a thrill of recognition in this German mine. Mines have their own language, shared by the whole world, one even simpler than the tapping of prisoners on prison walls, its alphabet formed from the branches and crowns of tough pines and old oaks. You find yourself smiling! What thin trunks they use here for the pit's backbone, slender graceful trees, standing as though in a forest glade in the calm before a storm, bent to one side. Above them lies the weight of the mountains, and they follow the course of the ranges, and are bent by the earth's imperceptible movements. A cavity has opened up behind the bulkheads, and must be stopped up with boulders without delay.

The gallery becomes a cramped narrow coop, woven from twigs, brushing our jackets with their wet animal snouts. Can't they make more space here?

Can't they widen the walls of the grave, stick their feet in the earth's belly, push it back with their hands? And this is the Ruhr, the most technologically developed region of Germany, if not the world!

Achtung! One warning sign after another appears on the damp joists, like a deaf-mute making letters from matchsticks. Cold leaks from cracks, distant coals fall with a hollow ring. Over there is a dangerous gap in the seam, and everything is pressing, pressing down unbearably.

It's only gradually you realise how badly the work is being done. At first glance, the mine seems to be well maintained. No luxuries or extravagances, but everything in its place. The concrete areas are bright and clean, with fresh straw gleaming in the stables. The plump well-fed ponies can each pull fifteen loaded tubs, and push up to four in front with their chests. The water brought up from the lower levels murmurs peacefully like a village mill, with a new concrete dam standing like a bastion at the end of the western gallery. Behind this a well has been sealed off. A few years ago a drunk drank himself silly and fell in and drowned. They'd tried to push forward in that direction, but snakes of water shot out with such an evil hiss and at such unexpectedly high pressure that the breach had to be plugged immediately with this concrete cork. The drivers of the ponies, like shepherds, have stopped driving their flocks that way, and since then there has been order and calm in the sector.

But the alarm signals continue along the first offshoot branching from the main trunk. Why hasn't the timbering been replaced for so long? Close to the entrance are some dry trunks that have been treated with a special compound protecting them from damp. But this costly treatment was dropped many years ago. Everywhere else, dampness flowers happily in frothy sponges, whole rows of trees suffering from it like a bad disease, and the water quietly sniggers as my guide unpicks some porous bark with his lantern-hook to reveal the soft wet reddening flesh beneath.

Keep walking. Stumbling past the upper joists, legs wide apart, we reach one of the older corridors leading off the tunnel where coal is no longer mined, weaving from side to side like a drunkard, getting booted back by the mass pressing down from above, barely managing to reach the exit, where it drops its rotting crutches. The ground is littered with crushed props, as if after a pogrom. A naked imprint of miserliness and neglect. You stumble at every step on traces of criminal thrift and fear of expenditure.

Passing behind the wall are the heavy footsteps of the boss's son-in-law. In the staff cuts and sackings following the 1918 coal crisis, this young man, a former Prussian officer, who knows nothing about mining, and didn't even manage to complete his course and get a qualification, was drafted in to replace one of the overmen. Drastic economies on wood, nails, even lamp-oil, are increasingly driving him underground to berate miners for wasting materials. Then as soon as they turn away, he rushes to the faces with a quaking heart, checking for new dangers, studying the seams, squeezing himself into corners, tapping props and joists. Miners never know when he'll appear, and it's hard to say what they hate most about him – his barking Prussian officer's voice, and the affectedly cool way he orders them to work at the most dangerous poorly reinforced faces, or the terror and infinite lack of confidence oozing from every pore of his pale puffy face, which saps the confidence of others. A boorish brute who cared about nothing but himself would be better than this superannuated sergeant-major with his antiquated sense of honour, stinking like a bad tooth.

We run into him at a crossroads, sitting slumped against a wall, his lamp between his sharp knees, while two workers silently clear rocks fallen on the rail tracks, to the accompaniment of his monotonous droning: 'Let me tell you, if you hadn't stabbed us in the back in 1918, things would have been different! Yes, the seven-hour day too, and we wouldn't be having to save every pfennig! Look at that ceiling, it could collapse any minute and kill the lot of us. And who'd be to blame then? The boss, you'd say. No, not the boss, you yourselves. You shouldn't have made the revolution ...!'

He stops suddenly, and pricks his ears like an animal. What has he taken fright at? Is it the boiler nearby that feeds the compressor, without which the mine can't breathe? It hisses as if rocking a crying baby to sleep, then falls silent. He must have just imagined something was wrong, but his fear is contagious. A nauseating fear. A miner is throwing up, and you feel queasy yourself.

He moves off, and the miners clearing the rail track gaze at him with hatred and work on in silence, muscles bulging, sweat trickling down their bare backs to their ribs, making white gashes on their blackened skins.

The pit is a black book, telling how the earth makes war on humans, and how here under the ground the boss makes war on his workers, forcing them to economise and speed up the work, while plundering the timber for his own use, snatching props and joists from dangerously overhanging ceilings. He looses danger from its chains and unties death's hands to gain an extra pfennig. He is a marauder looting his own army, sending it into battle with rotten weapons, into positions he himself has undermined, weakened and surrendered.

The Works Committee does everything possible to obstruct his business activities. My companion – I won't mention his name, and will let the peak of his miner's cap conveniently cover his coal-smeared features – swings his lamp to right and left to dispel the blackness closing in on all sides, and from time to time he slaps the walls and strokes the coal like a black horse with a dewy wet mane. 'See those iron brackets securing the steep ladders? They were our doing', he says with pride. 'Before, they stood free. A miner would risk his life using them. See that wooden hatch covering the manhole? Management wanted to leave it open, until a miner whose lamp had gone out fell through and was killed. See those steel bolts where the rail track breaks off at the edge of the shaft? We had to go on strike to get them. It was just a black hole before, and cost the lives of several of us. A pony would trot up with its tub to the lift for the coal to be loaded, and if it was late, tub, pony and driver would fall in. See all those nails sticking out of that new strut on the wall? I have the authority to rip them clean out and fine the overman for negligence, because in the event of the smallest landslide they could kill a man. Two or three years ago I couldn't have done that!'

Throughout the pit there is evidence of the Works Committee's small victories. Its defeats are in the miners' graves at the bottom of the deepest shafts, where all is crushed, disillusioned, filled with distrust and despair, and those who were buried alive raise their fists to the roofs of their earth coffins in impotent rage.

The night shift has started. From far off, the miners' movements at the first coalface look strange. Or do they just appear so through the dim lamplight? Are they just exhausted? If lunatics can go about their work without opening their eyes, they would undoubtedly move like these workers repairing the coal-chute. The coal shines like the snow of the hard winter they're all thinking about, lifting their heads longingly to a narrow crack in the ceiling, as if morning might dawn through the weight of the earth.

A group of three older workmates sit to one side on a pile of new boards. The oldest of them watches us approach with blank white wide open eyes. He is fast asleep. He can hear his name being called, and the light from our lamps strikes those pale shades, and slowly he wakes.

'What are you doing here? Your shift ended hours ago', my companion says.

'We can't leave, he didn't let us off', they say.

It turns out that the three of them live some fifty kilometres away, and the boss has always let them leave ten minutes early, in time to catch their train. Not out of the goodness of his heart, but because they're some of the best workers he has, and it's not worth losing them just for the sake of a few minutes. Tonight the new overman met them by the lift and sent them back to work, and when they reached the station their train had already left without them. They waited there two hours, but to go home by the next one in the middle of the night would have meant being late for the morning shift, and being late would mean the sack. So they came back, not knowing what else to do, and crept down to the mine again, humiliated, exhausted, perhaps already unemployed.

Two were in no party, the other was an old SPD man, who stood guard for us at the corner as we talked. 'But relieve me when you lot have had your say, I want to hear about Russia too'.

Three times night swung the heavy gong of its clock, but in the dark depths of the pit it couldn't be heard. Bringing their lamps closer, gleaming like their coal-ringed eyes, the miners talked, taking it in turns, passing the tale from one to the next, like one worker passing his pick to the next. None of them could remember the events of the 1918 revolution as a whole. For them it stretched back over a decade of strikes badly fought and lost. Each of them had lost faith in socialism from one specific betrayal, one single act of treachery. The old man poisoned by *Vorwärts'* toxic articles against Russia. The young miner crippled in a crushed strike. Another hit by the flying shrapnel of a speech by Social Democrat Noske. Stories of recent injuries in the mine, no more than a few days old.

The SPD worker who had been standing guard told how the union had broken their strike last year, three days before the Conciliation Commission delivered its verdict, against the wishes of the miners, and despite the fact that the strike had lasted twenty-five days and could have held out for as long again. How the union leaders had broken workers' solidarity, preventing the transport workers from coming to the aid of the striking coalminers, putting pressure on the metalworkers to betray their comrades, a betrayal that would never be forgotten. How they'd whipped up discord and disunity between the different branches of labour, rubbing salt in the wounds of the proletariat. 'I'm an old Social Democrat, and my two friends here are honest working men, but together we were strike-breakers!' he says. 'The union and the party told us to do the work of traitors. Oh yes, the unions talk to us like the Kaiser did – *"Kumpels, raus oder du kriegst eine!"* (Get out, mate, or you'll get one!) Where will it end? What will they do with a hundred thousand unemployed?' The old man laughs, his face like a piece of rain-soaked canvas. 'They'll put us in camps surrounded by machine guns, that's what they'll do! *Sie haben noch Mätzger genug! Darum kriegen wir Schlag wie junge Hunde!'* (They've enough butchers, we'll be flogged like puppies!)

Young comrade T., forgetting all caution, shouted at the top of his voice, his coal-matted beard sticking out from his face like a stake: 'The Saar was on strike but we worked! Didn't you see, hundreds of trains full of strike-breakers ready at the stations! They started moving as soon as the strike in England began! They accused us of striking for "English coal!"'

T. and his comrades had gone to see the old man at his home to offer him their worldview, unstained by Social Democracy's betrayal of the proletariat. But people are so distrustful and fearful now, they no longer believe anyone. Let's see if the communists can hit capitalism with a good rifle, break it up and take the good bits, and string together their own weapons from them. The *Kumpels* (pitmen), in their dark underground lairs, dream of a utopia built around Lenin's name, and the fragments of his teachings that have reached them down here. Lenin said the cell must be at the point of production – in one way or another he expounded this idea many many times. Why is it that communists are unafraid to reach out to workers in the mines and factories and visit them in their dirty homes, while the unions, which supposedly represent them, are allowed to hide from them and sit on high beyond reach, giving orders? They ought to come down here. It would be as easy to knock some sense into them here as to reach for your water bottle on the wall.

'*Kein Berlin, keine grossen Menschen. Hier, hier, mit uns!* (No Berlin, no big-shots. Here, with us here!) That's how our unions ought to be!' Not knowing how better to express his thoughts, comrade T. lifts his lamp to a new prop driven into the wall, swarming with blind grey subterranean butterflies. Wherever you have underground timbers there are these semi-translucent moths, living and rotting with them in the darkness.

'Goodbye comrades. Maybe we'll meet again in different circumstances'.

'No, pretty sure we won't live that long!'

I don't remember at which end of the underground labyrinth I met a burly old man, a Bavarian peasant, stretched out on a pony-driver's plank-bed in a hidden corner where the overman never went, where he could stretch out bliss-fully and rest his legs for half an hour, feeling the special chill from the earth, like its breath, rising through the cracks of the hard bed into his body. Behind him, like stooks of corn in a field, were all the years he had worked here. He hadn't counted them, and he hadn't looked back. He hadn't known about polit-ics, he'd hacked coal, clamped to the earth on his strong peasant's feet. He had twice been to war, but even then he hadn't woken up – a worker who all his life had thought like a farmhand. His grandfather and great-grandfather had been ploughmen, and he was a ploughman too, turning over and digging up the coal, throwing into the mine's black furrows the seeds of his youth. It was only a law passed recently by the Reichstag that made him lift his head. According to this law, sixty-year-old miners would have to work another five years before they received anything from the state. The old man had walked towards his pen-sion over mountains of coal, like an ox going home from the field dreaming of rest and a night's sleep. And suddenly, right at the gate where he could glimpse home, hear the dogs barking, see the lighted windows, he had to turn round in the night and go back down into the cold deep earth again. He stared at his big hands, lying on his knees like rakes, with which he'd raked so much coal in his life. They were too heavy, he wanted to take them off, lay them down on the coal by his pick and shovel, and rest.

'After work I'll have a glass of Schnapps in the pub', he said, and suddenly pain welled up in him. There was no money for that drink. How had it happened? Sixty years old, and he couldn't afford some Schnapps. '*Schuften und schuften auf meine alte Tag*'. (Slaving, slaving until my old age) He had sown and sown and nothing had grown, not a single grain, not one crop. Deep in the earth, confused thoughts about the sadness and injustice of life were breaking through his numbed brain, like a stream from under a rock. 'Wait till I pass away, then I can stick my hands in my pockets!'

It was only after these underground wanderings, listening to the voices coming from the dark keyholes of the earth, that you began to realise what connects the German worker in these years of defeat with Russia. There was no crevice, no lair in the pits, where even the gloomiest most defeated miners, who bear the whole burden of Germany's present stabilisation on their shoulders, weren't talking about the Land of the Soviets, like exiles talking of their distant homeland. And linked to their hopes for Russia is another hope they cherish in the deep darkness, each in his own way, and guard jealously from the victors. At present it's only a pale shoot, growing without sunlight by the weak light of their lamps – the idea of working-class unity.

At one face: 'Humans alone made war, why is peace and unity impossible in the world?'

At another: 'Why are the capitalists united and we're not?' '*Mensch, man hat a Spass daran, wenn die Hand gehen!*' (Man, it'll be good when we're all marching together!)

At a third, the deepest and blackest: 'Please give our thanks to Russian workers who sent us grain last year in the strike, in our time of need. The union gobbled up everything in our strike fund with big spoonfuls!'

www.ingramcontent.com/pod-product-compliance
Lightning Source LLC
Chambersburg PA
CBHW061554120626
46550CB00004B/1482